ROUSSEAU'S SOCRATIC
AEMILIAN MYTHS

ROUSSEAU'S SOCRATIC AEMILIAN MYTHS

A Literary Collation
of
EMILE
and the
SOCIAL CONTRACT

By Madeleine B. Ellis

Ohio State University Press : Columbus

Library of Congress Cataloging in Publication Data

Ellis, Madeleine B
    Rousseau's Socratic Aemilian myths.
    Includes index.
    1. Rousseau, Jean Jacques, 1712–1778. Emile
    2. Rousseau, Jean Jacques, 1712–1778. Contrat social.
    I. Title.
    LB518.E4   370.1   76-28197
    ISBN 0-8142-0223-3

TO MY MOTHER
LILIAN FITZMAURICE ELLIS
THE COMPANION OF MY LIFE AND OF MY WORK
THIS BOOK IS GRATEFULLY DEDICATED

CONTENTS

Foreword   ix

Acknowledgements   xiii

I   INTRODUCTION   3

II   FOUNDATION   37

III STYLOBATE   81

IV   THRESHOLD   145

V   TEMPLE STRONGHOLD   195

VI   INNER SANCTUM   305

VII CONCLUSION   383

Index   417

Foreword

Without going so far as agreeing with Diderot, who called the *Emile* "une espèce de galimatias," critics have generally had difficulty in appreciating this work fully, viewing many of its sections as digressions, paradoxes, or outright contradictions. The same can be said for parts of the *Contrat social*, which usually are dismissed as mere "padding." What is even more typical in modern Rousseau criticism—and an author such as he seems to provoke it— is the tendency to interpret these texts from a twentieth-century viewpoint, anachronistically ascribing to the author motives he could not even have conceived in his time, or pushing some of his statements to conclusions he never intended. Not that such studies are invalid: there are in the works of all great authors implications of which they themselves were not always aware. That is why, for example, Diderot could refute Voltaire's objections to the materialism in the *Lettre sur les aveugles* by reminding him that his own statements in the *Lettres philosophiques* substantiated the blind Saunderson's position. That is why both Voltaire and Rousseau were regarded as heroes in the French Revolution despite their comparative political conservatism. And a monumental work like Cassirer's *The Philosophy of the Enlightenment* does not lose its validity or utility because he imposes a systematic, Hegelian "synthesis" on an author like Diderot even though it does not correspond to the Encyclopedist's own temperament or methodology.

But there comes a time in the explication of any significant work when we must ask ourselves, What was the

author's intention when he wrote it? Has he given us any
clues as to what plan he followed or as to how we are to
interpret his writings? Not to do so is to risk misinterpret-
ing or overlooking passages that are essential to that plan
and to understanding their artistic and philosophical significance. It is to these questions that Professor Ellis
addresses herself. Rousseau more than once claimed that
his *Emile* and *Contrat social* were of one cloth and formed
an organic whole; but critics have either taken him at his
word or dismissed it as another Rousseauistic paradox. It
is not surprising that no one until now has fathomed that
unity and *proved* it. The task requires a painstaking collation of texts, a complete familiarity not only with Rousseau's
works but with those of the classical sources on which he
relied, and, finally, a dispassionate, scholarly will to
understand the author whether one agrees with him or not.
This last requirement is particularly difficult to achieve
when dealing with an author like Rousseau who somehow
brings out the polemicist in some critics and leads them to
write either hagiography or demonology. Not the least of
this book's merits is its calm, matter-of-fact approach that
is neither advocacy nor condemnation but explication in the
highest sense. One reads its "revelations"—for that is
what they are—with a sense of discovery that, because of
the tightly reasoned and convincing evidence, compels
assent.

Professor Ellis has found the key not only to *Emile* and
the *Contrat social* but to the central core of Rousseau's
writings. Through her lucid and entirely convincing dem-
onstration, she has come as close to the intentions, methodology, and meaning of these texts as anyone can hope to
do. She captures the Genevan's mythical (and mystical)
bent and clarifies many an obscure and heretofore baf-
fling allusion that can only be understood in the context of
the master plan he followed. In so doing, she gives us a
new insight into the artistry of this author who so person-
alized Socratic and biblical imagery that without Dr. Ellis's

quotations of chapter and verse we would not have recognized them as such. There will always be new and "contemporary" interpretations of Rousseau's works; but Dr. Ellis has brought us once and for all back to the intentions and sources of the author himself, without which knowledge much of what he wrote remained for us enigmatic and obscure. Her book was sorely needed! And it will necessitate the abandonment or reevaluation of many an ingenious but henceforth untenable interpretation that our profession had hitherto taken for granted.

Words like *masterful* or *brilliant* are so often used in contexts such as this that they tend to lose their meaning. Yet how else underline the importance of Dr. Ellis's impressive accomplishment, which represents years of thorough preparation? *Rousseau's Socratic Aemilian Myths* is not just another book on Rousseau. It is bound to become required reading for anyone wishing to understand him; for it is a touchstone for the comprehension of the Genevan's allegorical language and, thus, to a truer interpretation of what he himself regarded as the *summa* of his writings: *Emile*.

John Pappas
Fordham University

Acknowledgments

The author wishes to express her appreciation to the publishers of this book, especially the director of the Press, Mr. Weldon A. Kefauver, and the editor, Mr. Robert S. Demorest, for their thoughtful consideration and editorial advice. She is also profoundly grateful to friends and colleagues who helped handle many practical problems encountered in the work of publication. They are: Dr. Otis E. Fellows, professor at Columbia University; Dr. Wallace S. Lipton, professor at the City University of New York; and more especially, Dr. John N. Pappas, professor at Fordham University, who moreover generously offered to read the manuscript and kindly accepted the author's invitation to write a Foreword to the book.

She also takes pleasure in acknowledging her indebtedness to other friends and colleagues whose good offices facilitated the progress of research during the many years of work that culminated in the book. They are: Dr. Henri M. Peyre, professor emeritus of Yale University, who, at an earlier stage in the study, graciously consented to read the Introduction; the late Dr. Charles Z. Wahl, professor at the City University of New York and a lifelong friend, whose invaluable services, including bibliographical assistance, the loan of books, and occasional replacement of the author in various professional capacities during periods of intense research were terminated only by an untimely death in 1972; and finally the late Dr. J. S. Will, professor emeritus of the University of Toronto, whose illuminating conversations on literary method and the problem of form in the French novel never failed to open up vast perspectives in the spheres of aesthetic creativity and the nature of beauty, which are hardly alien to the theme of this inquiry.

In fine, she would record her deepest debt of gratitude to Lilian Fitzmaurice Ellis, whose lively interest in Plato, stimulating enthusiasm, and patient self-sacrifice, played a major role in the genesis of the work and without whose support it is certain that this book would never have been written.

The story of human nature is a fair romance. Am I to blame if it is to be found only in this book? It ought to be the story of mankind.—Rousseau, *Emile*.

Come then and let us pass a leisure hour in story-telling and our story shall be the education of our heroes.—Plato, *The Republic*

All these things spake Jesus unto the multitude in parables; and without a parable spake he not unto them.—Gospel of Saint Matthew

My treatise on the Social Contract... being cited several times and even summarized in the educational treatise must pass as a sort of appendix to it, and the two together make a complete whole.—Rousseau to Duchesne

Such is the good and true City or State and the good and true man is of the same pattern, and if this is right every other is wrong.... The same principles and habits... pass from the individual into the State.—Plato, *The Republic*

For behold the kingdom of God is within you.—Gospel of Saint Luke

I
Introduction

By neglecting the language of symbolic expression that speaks to the imagination we have lost the most energetic of languages.[1]—*"Emile"*

A CAUSE CÉLÈBRE

After two centuries of constant subjection to the tireless scrutiny and merciless probing of scholars, Jean-Jacques Rousseau, who discloses the intimacies of his life so freely, still hides the secret of his thought. For unlike most of his contemporaries he understood the value of mystery and of poetry, not only to express more effectively the intricacies of his own personal apprehension of truth, but also to allure the minds and souls of his readers. He hints that his reticence is intentional when he says: "I do not write for those who must be told everything." Again he adds significantly: "He who tells all tells little, for in the end no one is listening."[2] He consciously declines to lend himself to a neat positivistic interpretation that simplifies the critic's task.

Yet his purpose is clear enough, and it never varies. In all his works the same question is raised over and over again. "Where is wisdom? Where is happiness?" is the Sphinx-like riddle propounded by him from the beginning of his career when the *Discourse upon Arts and Sciences* won him fame in Paris and all Europe in his fortieth year. Precisely the same question provides the major theme of a decade of writing including other pieces written in the French capital, like his *Discourse upon Inequality* and the article on *Political Economy,* as well as famous books composed at Montmorency, such as the letter to d'Alembert on the theater, the novel *Julie,* and the political and peda-

[3]

gogical treatises of the *Social Contract* and *Emile* that were supposed to bring his literary career to a virtual close at the age of fifty.[3]

In each work in turn the author asks: Is it the lover of knowledge who possesses the secret of happiness? Is it the worshiper of Mammon, or the devotee of power and glory? Or is it the man committed to some indescribable pleasure of the body? By merely posing such problems, he unsettled people and cast doubt upon common assumptions that lie at the foundations of a materialistic society. As he pondered these assumptions in his mind, his own view of life slowly took shape as the very antithesis of current beliefs about the value of power, wealth, and self-indulgence for the attainment of felicity. His ideas are quite fully defined in *Julie*, which, as I have shown, synthesizes the content of all his previous publications.[4] But his philosophy is best expressed in the two works intended to be his last, especially *Emile*, to which the *Contract*, or treatise on citizenship (a summary of a projected work on *Political Institutions*) is by his own admission a sort of appendix. He wished the latter to precede the main volume in the bookshops, although it actually followed. His desire was that *Emile*, a production of the first magnitude, might appear as his definitive answer to the problem of happiness, to be succeeded only by memoirs reserved for retirement and posthumous publication.[5]

But *Emile* and the *Contract* shattered his dream of repose and brought in their train a host of other works that he felt obliged to write "to defend his honor and ideas." For he found to his dismay that to stir the conscience of the age is a dangerous undertaking, as many another imprudent idealist has also discovered from the time of Socrates or Christ down to our own day. In Rousseau's case persecution and exile immediately followed the publication of the two treatises. A Parisian decree of 9 May 1762, directed against the author of *Emile* and especially the unorthodox profession of religious faith contained therein, and an analogous Genevan decree directed a week later against the writer of both books made him into a religious and political martyr at once. Yet only a few months after the blow had fallen and while wounds were still fresh, he wrote to a correspondent thus: "It mattered little that a band of children should not act out their tawdry comedy, but it mattered greatly that what I have said should be said. Thank heaven, my task is done. I shall have no more anxiety on that score."[6] Here he alludes particularly to *Emile,* which touched off the disaster. Apparently his distress did not preclude a sense of relief since his book had gone abroad with its message to the world.

Rousseau pleads on his own behalf nowhere more fervently than in the hitherto neglected *Levite of Ephraim.*[7] Except for the ending, it was written in the coach as he took leave of his adopted land and fled to the Swiss countryside north of Geneva. It is important because of the light it sheds upon the author of *Emile*'s attitude toward his own work.

The brief prose-poem in four cantos is partly inspired by the concluding chapters of the Book of Judges in the Old Testament, but mainly by the circumstances of its composition. The writer turns the biblical narrative into a myth to adapt it to his true theme, which is the story of his own spiritual life, and tells how the culminating achievement of his career brought persecution and the threat of death upon him. Moved by these iniquities, he begins the poem by denouncing "crimes" that God's people must avenge and from which the enemies of inhumanity, however "debonair," may not avert their eyes without deserting the cause of justice. The biblical theme becomes Rousseauist.

Indeed, the Levite in the poem is Rousseau. The latter endues himself with the office and garb of a minister of the Lord who is dedicated to the service of a spiritual temple. Elsewhere too he is similarly arrayed. For example, in *Emile* he assumes the vestments of a Savoyard vicar.

[5]

Moreover, at the moment when he completed the poem, he donned the Armenian costume, popular a century earlier. It appears as a sort of pilgrim's cloak or philosophic pall, reminiscent of the robes of Socrates, or perhaps of Christ, or the medieval monk, as well as the Levite whose role he borrows in the poem.

Rousseau's Levite, like the one in Judges, belongs to the tribe of Ephraim. Now Ephraim is used in the Old Testament as a synonym for the twelve tribes of Israel, which in the poem typify Christendom. Like the ancient Levite, the modern one leaves the hillsides of his own country and finds a bride in Bethlehem-Judah. But she is not a "concubine" as in the sacred text. The reader who is on intimate terms with the writer already begins to see in her a reincarnation of the Rousseauist "Sophia," or wisdom, a new vision of divine wisdom born in the city of Christ two thousand years ago and comparable to the image of the Solomonic bride in the Book of Wisdom or the Socratic Lady Philosophy in Plato's *Republic*. At once the Levite's soul is knit with hers. But, since she is not of his tribe, he may not marry her according to God's law. This impediment in the poem has no equivalent in the biblical source, and Rousseau admits it in a footnote, as if he considered the innovation significant. The note reads: "I know that the children of Levi were free to marry in all tribes, but not in the case supposed here." He forbears to explain further, but his thought is not unintelligible. If the bride of the poem is indeed a concept of divine wisdom, no man may lay exclusive claim upon her. The mystic union is consummated nonetheless. The fruits of this union in Rousseau's life would presumably be his early discourses, which, together with *Emile,* he esteemed as his finest productions.[8] In the poem, as in the biblical verses, the Levite then conducts his lady to his mountain home, where he remains for four months. Similarly the writer of the second *Discourse,* after professing to woo wisdom in his work, journeyed to his native land, to which he dedicated

[6]

the piece, and there he remained for the same space of time.

But the Levite of the poem finds the soil of that country inhospitable to his bride. She sighs for Bethlehem-Juda, or the city on high that is her birthplace and proper abode. Unlike her biblical analogue—and henceforth I shall refer to the sacred text only in the case of deviations from it—she does not "play the whore against her lord." The bride in the new version tires of him who has allegedly renounced all else to follow her, and finally eludes him. Here the writer betrays disenchantment with his native Geneva and Calvinist faith and perhaps personal remorse as well. For after his return to France he became enamoured of a worldly "Sophia" in the person of Sophie d'Houdetot. At that moment in time he was faithless to the real one, like Socrates' errant philosopher who is led astray from his calling and abandons his lady.[9] Rousseau's return to the cult of wisdom is also indicated in the poem where the Levite returns to Bethlehem to be reconciled with his bride, whom he woos and wins once again.

In the second canto he sets out on his journey through life by her side, making his way "to the house of the Lord" and to his "mountain dwelling," where the writer of *Emile* professedly longed to withdraw. The Levite's lady newly recovered now appears as an image of that book where a definitive vision of Rousseauist wisdom is enshrined. On the road to his final resting-place the servant of the Lord tarries awhile, not in a city of infidels, says the poet, but among God's people, his own brethren. There a kindred soul, a fellow Ephraimite, befriends him. But as darkness falls, fiendish men, reminiscent of the wild-beast natures from whom the Socratic philosopher takes refuge, demand that the stranger be delivered into their power. For, we are told in another passage unparalleled in the sacred text, he is an uninvited guest in their country. So was Rousseau in France. To humanize them, he offers them the bride for whom he had dispossessed himself of all else.

[7]

In the same spirit the author professes to have given *Emile* to the world. But the offering is vain. The diabolical men of the poem, suggestive of the "unworthy persons" who dishonor the Socratic Lady Philosophy, "tear her away from each other like beasts." Rousseau's words here represent a new departure from the biblical verse that reads: "They knew her, and abused her all night." The modification lends further weight to my view of his theme, since evil men could hardly be said to "know" divine wisdom in any sense. According to the modern Levite, they cannot even dishonor her since her misfortunes only sanctify her. The writer said virtually the same thing of *Emile* in a defense of the work.[10] At last the priest in the poem finds his bride lying lifeless on his path. In rage and despair the "barbarous" man takes her back to his home in the mountains, mutilates the body, and sends the flesh far and wide to all God's people. Then he goes on his way to the "house of the Lord" and calls upon the justice of heaven. Again he appears as an image of the author pleading in favor of his crowning achievement.

In the third canto the chosen race gathers together before God, coming "from all the cantons," says the Swiss writer, again taking leave of the scriptural text. In the divine presence they swear to avenge innocent blood, whereupon the new Levite, unlike the biblical prototype, dies. He therefore does not share in the ensuing vengeance. The story of revenge adheres quite closely to the Old Testament version. But it is employed by Rousseau to show the futility and tragedy of all religious conflict, considered as a form of fratricide.

The last canto, written at Môtiers in the Swiss mountains, is less inspired by the Old Testament than the New, and bears witness to a mitigation of bitterness wrought by the passage of time. It contains an incident of his own invention. A fresh generation of Ephraimites—evangelical Christians, if we wish—makes new sacrifices comparable to the Levite's in an effort to redeem the brutish natures of their fellows. The poem ends on a note of pardon and Christian charity, contrasting with the outcry of despair and demand for justice that precede. The ending is reminiscent of the Sermon on the Mount, where the writer frequently found images and ideas: "Love your enemies, bless them that curse you, do good to them that hate you...."

Of course, he never did witness a union of Christendom in his defense like the scene imagined in the *Levite*. But he could hardly have been surprised, since in the greater part of the poem he envisages his fate in a dramatically tragic light and emphasizes the curious cleavage between his own view of his life and that of his detractors. He does the same elsewhere. For example, on the eve of exile he wrote to a friend that "the only man in France who believes in God is doomed to be the victim of the defenders of Christianity."[11] A fortnight later he wrote to a Swiss journalist: "Sooner or later... reasonable men, perhaps finally Christians... will see with surprise and indignation that a disciple of their divine master is treated among them like a scoundrel." Two months afterward when the archbishop of Paris condemned his book as the work of the Antichrist, he replied in the following vein: "The defender of the cause of God... (dishonored, exiled, driven from state to state without regard for his poverty or pity for his infirmity...) is forbidden fire and water in almost the whole of Europe." In fine, telling the story years later in the *Confessions,* he speaks of the "outcry of malediction raised against me with unexampled fury in every part of Europe.... I was impious, an atheist, a madman, a wild beast, a wolf." In all these contexts he underlines the discrepancy between public reaction to himself and to his work, and the character of both as he sees it.

During his exile the discrepancy grew as fresh attacks were made upon him. It is true that, after he renounced his Geneva citizenship on 12 May 1763,[12] his compatriots made formal representations on his behalf, but they were

[9]

easily silenced by the government of the city-state. In the autumn of 1763 the latter published a book entitled *Letters from the Country* to justify itself against him. A year later he replied in his *Letters from the Mount,* the very title of which recalls what he terms Christ's "greatest sermon."* In the letters he alludes to the evangelical saying that "a prophet hath no honor in his own country." He vindicates himself as the apologist of religion, and calls the Gospel "the rule of the master," and his own works "the commentaries of a scholar." Why, he asks, is the former "citizen of Geneva" now dubbed the destroyer of religion and of all governments? He contends that it is the rulers of the city itself who are overthrowing its constitution by their arbitrary decrees.[13] Inevitably public hostility overtook him at his country retreat. Again he who saw himself as a disciple of Christ was identified as Antichrist and used accordingly,[14] being driven from place to place until persecution mania robbed him of peace of mind for the rest of his days.

Throughout these vicissitudes Rousseau, posing as a spokesman of religious and moral order, presents himself personally and not merely ideologically as a follower of Christ in the conduct of life, and at the same time evokes memories of Socrates. As Malesherbes once observed, he made a point of cherishing poverty and suffering like the evangelical teacher. And again like the latter he proved, as he says, that a prophet goes unrecognized at home. On the other hand, his friends identified him with Socrates, who also honored poverty and simplicity of life. The death of the Greek sage, like that of the Son of man, occupied Rous-

---

*To be exact, one ought correctly to write "Jesus Christ," since Rousseau most frequently uses both names, as he does in the context to which I refer here. Indeed, out of thirty-three references to the founder of Christianity in *"Emile"* and related works in *O.C.,* Pléiade, vol. 4, the author writes "Jesus Christ" twenty-six times. However, for practical purposes I have decided to use the shorter form "Christ," since the meaning is always made clear by the context. Regarding the expression "Son of Man" occurring below, I have used the capital S, although Rousseau himself writes "son of man": see "Morceau allégorique," *O.C.,* 4:1053.

seau's thoughts from the moment he achieved fame, as though he half expected to meet a similar fate.[15] Five years before tragedy befell him, a young admirer of his compared the life of the new Socrates to that of the old. More than three years later, a friend warned him to prepare himself to drink the hemlock. When he was finally forced to do so figuratively speaking, the comparison was commonplace.[16] Indeed, we ourselves, as we contemplate the role he plays in the *Emile* case, are reminded of the Socratic philosopher described in a passage of the *Republic* where the "wisest of the Greeks," having deplored the grievous manner in which the best men are treated in their own states, enumerates those who, in spite of adverse circumstances, may yet become worthy disciples of philosophy.[17] By some strange coincidence Rousseau fits into every category: the exile, the invalid, the man born in a mean city whose politics he contemns and neglects, one who leaves the industrial and mechanical arts in favor of philosophy, or, finally, one who is possessed of the inner sign of a genuine vocation. Such a man, says the sage, "holds his peace and goes his own way." These very words recur at the end of the *Letters from the Mount* where Rousseau takes leave of Geneva for the last time. Whether or not, as he contends in *Emile,* he was not a man of his century—and he says the same of Socrates and Christ—his fate was not unlike that of the two figures in the past whose lives held most fascination for him. And it was brought upon him mainly by a work that, in his eyes apparently, was not unworthy of a professed disciple of both.

ENIGMAS AND CLUES

Emile has emerged as one of the milestones of Western culture. With more insight than authors usually have in the appraisal of their own compositions, Rousseau saw it from first to last as his "most useful, best," and "most important" work, the one "most worthy" of himself, by compar-

ison with which all his other works are mere pamphlets.[18]
He was hardly mistaken. In spite of the reservations of
many modern readers, it is recognized by our best critics
as his most complete book and one of the major productions of our civilization. Small wonder if he was at a loss
to explain public response to it.

He was all the more bewildered since, in his words, all
his works convey the same message, though they are vari-
ously interpreted. *Emile* and its "appendix," the *Contract*,
which is cited and abridged in the pedagogical treatise, form
according to his letters a complete whole. So do *Emile* and
the *Discourses*, which he calls "inseparable."[19] In the
Confessions he pleads further that everything daring in the
Contract was already said in the *Discourse upon Inequality*.
Thus he joins together in a single body of thought *Emile*,
the *Contract*, and the *Discourses*, as he also does *Emile*
and *Julie*. Yet he lived in comparative tranquillity in France
until his masterwork made its appearance to rock the foundations of Europe, whereas the *Contract* created hardly
more than a few slight tremors, except in Geneva.[20] Why?
If his ideas are dangerous, are they not just as dangerous
in one book as in another? Perhaps so in their quality as
ideas, provided we succeed in recognizing them as the same.
Nevertheless, there is a vast difference. *Emile* possesses
a power to which the reader responds in a way that sets it
apart from the *Contract* and from all Rousseau's previous
writings with the exception of *Julie*. That power lies less in
the ideological content than in the attractive form of the
work that gives potency to ideas. Although the subtitle of
Emile, Concerning Education, suggests a philosophical
study and is analogous to the title of the appendix, *Concerning the Social Contract,* yet the main title of the pedagogical treatise is that of a literary work wherein abstract
concepts are presented by way of myths or images. The
latter make it far more readable and hence more liable to
criticism than the companion volume and are far more provocative than the ones in *Julie*.

Emile, as opposed to the *Contract,* abounds in highly expressive visual imagery that serves a serious intellectual and spiritual purpose. I am not speaking of a few metaphors scattered here and there to illustrate a point in the story. I am referring to vast symbols and allegories that spring from the book itself and are an intrinsic part of it as they are of all great literature. They constitute an important aspect of the content of the work and not merely the form. But here let me explain my use of these terms that are by no means inflexible. The form may be conceived as the measure of the artist's craftsmanship, his patience, his command of his medium, his knowledge of technique, stylistics, and syntax. The content may be seen as the measure of his imagination and vision and may be said to consist of both body and soul, a material content and a spiritual one that correspond intimately to each other. The visionary and imaginative aspect of literature provides a fine clue to meaning in a book like *Emile* and hence is of primary concern here.

In the past the images therein have been accorded one of two varieties of treatment on the part of critics. Either they have been regarded as whimsical and childish, absurd and insipid, with the result that the writer often emerges as an incredibly stupid and boring pedant. Or else they have been altogether ignored in an attempt to go directly to the ideological core of the work. This method can foster the impression that the book is full of sophisms and contradictions and that, in spite of some valuable contributions to knowledge, it has serious flaws that make it hardly more than a document. Such attitudes are decried by monsieur Burgelin in his introduction to the Pléiade edition.

Fortunately, today some critics are beginning to suspect the presence of at least two or three weighty symbols in its pages, and their attitude toward it is therefore more sympathetic. Nevertheless, they still confine their investigations mainly to historical research or moral and philosophic speculation. Their work is extremely valuable, but it does not exclude the need for a thorough examination of the author's

[13]

use of imagery and its implications.

This is all the more true since the meaning of the most fundamental literary motifs of the book still remains strangely enigmatic. Rousseauist criticism includes serious studies of other literary problems, and even of this one in the case of works like *Julie* or the autobiographical writings. But it has not yet scratched the surface of the emblematic conveyance of ideas in *Emile,* as compared with the abstractions of the so-called appendix. My purpose here is simply to set out in this new direction with the conviction that it is a valid one. I shall do so by inquiring into the mythical expression of thought in *Emile* in the same way as critics have done, for instance, in the case of Plato. Without hoping to exhaust the theme, I shall attempt to come to grips with the writer's artistic imagery as well as his ideology and then face the double challenge of aesthetic appreciation and philosophic interpretation at once. Thus I shall consider *Emile* as the work of a thinker whose methods are essentially artistic rather than philosophical.

An exploration of the myths of *Emile* proves to be vastly rewarding aesthetically and ideologically too. When the images are penetrated and relieved of their spiritual content, the book turns out to be a concrete allegorical presentation of doctrines communicated in a more theoretical way in the *Contract* as well as in the sequels of both and in earlier works. The discovery of this fact makes it possible to shed fresh light upon the ideas of the two books in question. In order to accomplish this purpose while examining the myths of *Emile,* I have chosen to give to my study the form of a collation of the masterwork and its appendix. The collation testifies to the truth of Rousseau's own judgment about their essential identity and shows that they evolve according to one and the same plan. By virtue of a penetration of symbols, the relationship of texts rises to the surface quite naturally and easily.

This aspect of my work is also admittedly unconventional. Many commentators see a serious cleavage between

[14]

Emile and the *Contract*. They believe that the one sets forth the philosophy of individualism and the other that of collectivism, that the one represents solitary, isolated man whereas the other defines social man, integrated into an ideal community.[21] However, there are exceptions among critics, especially recently. Some writers now believe that the two works complement each other and that *Emile* describes an artifically produced "natural" man to match the city of the *Contract*. They recall that for Rousseau true pedagogy implies politics—etymologically, "citizen-ship"—just as, according to the *Confessions,* politics implies pedagogy. However, they visualize the political ideal as the theoretical and rather irrelevant culmination of education in *Emile* instead of its very essence from the beginning. They therefore conclude that the author temporarily isolates pedagogy and politics, especially since in his view society that ought ideally to perfect man's nature actually corrupts and destroys it. Yet it is conceivable that the mythical Emile does indeed abide in the imaginary city from the moment of his birth and that training in citizenship is the real theme of both books. This idea springs from a collation of the two, which in turn is made possible by a study of the allegorical forms of the pedagogical treatise actually reflected in the appendix.

However subtle he may be, Rousseau confesses in *Emile* that he is not overlooking the resources of art. He admits that, like *Julie,* the book is a novel, though a pedagogical one, and he is not speaking only of the so-called storybook ending. This is true whether or not he planned it as such in the beginning and whatever conclusions we may deduce from the first version extant in the so-called Favre manuscript. The definitive *Emile* is the story of human nature, the romance of the soul that, according to the author, ought to be the record of the race. He draws attention to the literary nature of his work by providing therein a thorough and methodical exposition of his literary profession of faith.[22] This aesthetic doctrine, supplemented

[15]

by reflections contained in the *Essay upon the Origin of Languages,* the *Dictionary of Music,* and books 9 and 11 of the *Confessions,* furnishes a key to the secrets of his art.

Although in the two books of the autobiography he is really speaking of *Julie,* he invites a comparison with *Emile,* and so his words may be taken as applying to both. Besides, he confesses elsewhere that *Emile* like the romance of *Julie* is full of his usual daydreams and is the final outgrowth of his country walks of which the first fruits were the love story.[23]

The memorialist's description of the creation of *Julie* is well known. The writer, surrounded by the splendors of nature in Montmorency wood, weaves for his fancy an enchanted world of perfect beings, descending from the empyrean, or rather, constructed from within the self. Such are the "daydreams" that reappear in his work from *Emile* to the *Dialogues,* which by his own admission took shape, like the *Discourses,* in a similar manner. Those dreams are the substance of what Formey called, with more truth than he perhaps intended, the mythical "world of Emiles."[24] And to borrow the autobiographer's words about *Julie,* the vision in *Emile* is the setting for a painstaking analysis of the human heart, intended to be comparable in psychological truth to great literature of the previous century, in spite of the "perfection" of his creatures. The characters are outwardly the same as in the love story, though fewer in number. Apart from the "divine Sophia," there is a tutor or governor and his disciple, both of whom like the corresponding characters in *Julie* mirror the author himself, at the same time as they represent sensitive, contemplative humanity in search of wisdom and happiness. Both works are therefore autobiographical novels used to convey ideas. The passages in the *Confessions* relating to the one are valid for the other.

Rousseau's aesthetics set forth in *Emile* and the other works already mentioned shed light upon the creative

[16]

process described in the memoirs. In the educational treatise he defends the use of imagery and formally declines to
communicate his thought by transporting us suddenly to
the sphere of pure intellect. He censures his famous contemporaries for relying too much upon cold reason "as if
we were all mind." He reproaches them for neglecting the
most energetic of languages, that of signs which address
themselves to the imagination and heart through the eyes.
This language is also described in the *Essay upon Languages*. It is the utterance of "genius" conceived in the
Dictionary of Music as rendering ideas through feelings,
to convince the mind and sway the soul at once. He illustrates the point in *Emile* by taking examples from biblical
and ancient Greek writers. He admires their skill in en-
duing reason with a body to make it felt. In his own words
he too has recourse in his book to "the language of symbolic expression," that is, to parables, allegories, legends,
and visible forms that are the hallmark of the artist.[25]

He goes still further to emphasize the importance of aesthetics and the value of taste to convey ideas. In the pedagogical novel and in the *Dictionary* too he defines taste
as "the power to judge what is pleasing to most men." In
Emile he recognizes that this power is indispensable to one
like himself who hoped to be of service to others. But although he associates the two issues, he does not confuse
them. He is careful to separate the agreeable, which is the
realm of taste, from the useful, which is for him the domain
of ethics, and takes pains to distinguish moral beauty from
physical. But he also hints at a link between them. For
instance, he says that taste opens the mind to all beauty
including moral ideas. But, as was ever his wont, instead
of theorizing about these affinities, he leaves us to discover them for ourselves in the figures and events of *Emile*.
By doing so we can see how he, whose professed desire
was to devote his life to spiritual truth, approaches his task
by appealing to our love of beauty. If the appeal was less
effective in *Emile* than it was in other books, it is because

[17]

of the gravity of the message entrusted to its myths.

The author has more to say about the matter of pleasing and about the form and content of beauty. All true models of taste, he warns, are to be found in nature and not in the whimsical imagination of extravagant artists. Nature is therefore the subject of the art he favors, as he says in the *Confessions* too. He adds that a knowledge of its ways and modifications is to be cultivated by the frequentation of refined society since social life develops an understanding of the heart and trains the thinking mind to make discriminating observations and judgments. This means that he appeals to reason and the intuitive imagination rather than to unbridled fancy as the appropriate faculty to explore the natural theme. It also confirms the fact that the nature he visualizes is that of man, to which his most ecstatic landscape pieces serve as a background, or whose moods they transcribe. In fine, his ideal is indeed the psychological truth of Boileau and the "classics,"[26] which incidentally provides a key to the riddle of wisdom and happiness.

The author of *Emile* is well aware that, by scrutinizing the intimacies of nature, he is walking in the footsteps not only of the great seventeenth-century French writers but of their immortal precursors of ancient Greece and Rome. The governor in the book chooses both Plutarch and La Fontaine to discover the secrets of men's hearts. But in general, like Boileau he favors the ancients as models in all genres. He mentions history, eloquence, and poetry both dramatic and lyric. To these we might add the "Socratic" variety, if we may so describe the prose dialogues of Plato, such as the *Symposium,* which is used for a study of aesthetics in the fourth part of *Emile* and is not indifferent for an understanding of the fifth.

Yet although Rousseau's aesthetic doctrine may be dubbed "classical," in actual practice he transcends Boileau and the ancient ideal of objective truth to favor the inward personal spirit of Christianity. In fact, medieval Christian tradition is the source of his so-called romantic tendencies

[18]

to introspection and lyricism, and he deliberately brings it to terms with Greek culture of twenty-five hundred years ago. For example, in the *Discourses* he emphasizes the bonds between Platonic or Socratic philosophy and Christianity. These bonds can be seen throughout his work from his denunciation of the theater, as closely linked with Tertullian and Bossuet as it is with Plato or Socrates, to the later autobiographical writings like the *Confessions*, with its echoes of Saint Augustine in what is substantially a "classical" analysis of the human heart. To illustrate further, the heroine of *Julie*, whose creator openly professes to be a disciple of Plato and Socrates, is compared by the author of the *Confessions* to the seventeenth-century *Princesse de Clèves*, which conforms to the Greek ideal. Yet she is also "the new Heloïsa" whose prototype belongs to the Middle Ages and whose lover, Saint-Preux, bears a name synonymous with the chivalry and passionate dedication of the medieval knights-errant, to whom, incidentally, Emile is also compared. In the pedagogical novel and its appendix, Plato, or rather that old master of Plato, is still Rousseau's. For in *Emile* he as usual repairs mainly to the literature of thought for his ancient models. But they never stand alone. The whole of *Emile*, as well as the *Contract*, which is synthesized in the conclusion of the main work, is dominated by two figures, namely, Socrates as introduced by Plato, and Christ, whose evangelical image is set in the context of all biblical literature. The association of the two is discernible in the *Levite of Ephraim*. Besides I have already cited a passage in the *Letters from the Mount* wherein the author calls Christ his "master." He does the same in the letter to the archbishop of Paris. He accords this distinction to none but Christ and Socrates, however much he is indebted to seventeenth- and eighteenth-century thinkers whose influence only underlines his own originality. His chosen models are the two whom he represents as the leaders of his spirit.[27]

[19]

Moreover, he achieves a certain success in reconciling them and in uniting Greco-Roman and Judeo-Christian tradition in general. This was no easy task since the kingdom of Christ, which as we are reminded in the *Contract* is not of this world, had become falsely alienated from the kingdom of nature and natural man. Rousseau was well qualified to assume the delicate task of compromise by favor of his sympathetic attachment to the evangelical and biblical writings as well as to some of the best works of pagan philosophy. Of course, the idea that Christ has long been regarded as mystically foreshadowed by the Socratic picture of the "just man" in the *Republic* furnishes him with an initial link between the two. But he is chiefly enabled to bring them together by his very personal vision of the "divine" master whose "divinity" consists for him in what might be termed his divine humanity. He overlooks the ascetic and militant image of Christ against which he openly rebels in the *Contract,* and throws into relief the deeply human qualities of the Son of man.[28] Thus he succeeds in accommodating the wisdom of Christ to humanistic and especially Socratic tradition.

The great virtue of such accommodation for the present purpose is that it furnishes valuable analogies to enhance our appreciation of *Emile* and the *Contract.* Both traditions are clearly visible in the imaginative and intellectual content of the pedagogical novel in particular. In fact, the author of the latter openly expresses his admiration for the Platonic dialogues, especially the *Republic,* which he regards as a pedagogical romance. There the chief speaker, who is Socrates, tells a "story" about "the education of heroes."[29] The writer of *Emile* who tells a similar story is steeped in the ancient one. He is also steeped in the Bible, to which he repeatedly alludes. Since both abound in figurative imagery, parables, myths, and allegories used to convey thought, it is not surprising that he too has recourse to the same visual devices to shadow forth his ideas. In exploring these devices, I shall attempt to disclose the verifiable

[20]

affinities of the two works under discussion with the Platonic dialogues and the Scriptures and to establish concrete correspondences between these great landmarks of our culture.

Indeed, the imagery of those ancient writings reflected in Rousseau provides a useful key to the relationship between his pedagogical novel and its political appendix. For example, in the *Republic*, to which he compares the two books, we have a "pedagogical" and "political" treatise together. Socrates' object therein is to portray the nature and duty of a good and honorable man, to describe the essence of justice and injustice and their effects upon the soul, and to determine the rule of human life so that men may know the way of happiness.[30] To achieve his purpose, he deals at one and the same time with the soul and the city. The two are fused into a single vision where the state is used as an external image of the inner man. With a view to seeing the nature of justice in the individual soul, he looks at it on a large scale in the city-state, which is his political ideal as it is Rousseau's and where, being magnified, that elusive virtue is more clearly seen. He makes no distinction between the two entities, finding the same principles in both: the will, reason, and gainful faculties in man correspond to guardians, rulers, and people in the state. "The good and true City or State, and the good and true man" are "of the same pattern," says he; for cities are made out of the human natures in them, and governments vary as men's dispositions vary. Conversely, "as the government is, so will the man be."[31] Thus Socrates continually reverts to the soul, beginning with it and concluding with it. The reason is, he explains, that it is better to be ruled by divine wisdom dwelling within ourselves rather than by an external authority. But if this cannot be, then we must submit to the latter so that we may be all, as far as possible, under the same government, "friends and equals." He observes that such is the intention of the law, as seen in the education of children, whom it refuses to set free "until we have established

[21]

in them a principle analogous to the constitution of the State, and . . . have set up in their hearts a guardian and ruler (Rousseau would say "sovereign and governor") like our own . . .," meaning like those of his imaginary city. Then they may go their way. In other words, we must establish a "city within" them to be their own, one that fulfills in its ordered beauty the true nature of the soul in her original purity. The Socratic man of understanding is "statesman and ruler" in that mysterious city whose pattern, we are told, exists nowhere upon earth but is "laid up in heaven." Yet he succeeds in fixing his eyes upon it with a view to setting in order his own house and his own city and living after the manner of the celestial model in private and in public life called "politics" and the "warfare" of the spirit.[32] In the opinion of the Greek sage true education must therefore reveal to us "the kingdom of God," which is not of this world but lies within us. Christ's teaching has no other object. The author of *Emile* and the *Contract* could hardly escape the effects of these doctrines whose themes and forms turn out to be his own.

Indeed, in both books he takes up the Socratic and Christian imagery of the soul and the city. We see this in many a passage of each where the nature and constitution of a city and a man are compared.[33] Occasionally, it is true, he is led by the mode of the day to draw a parallel between the state and the human body. However, he does so mainly in his early article upon political economy, but never in *Emile* and only in a rare passage of the *Contract* when it suits his purpose. This occurs when he wishes to emphasize the difference between them or where the theme is death and the spiritual metaphor is inappropriate for a man like himself who believes in a future life.[34] The distinction he makes between the body of a man and the state is that the former is the work of nature and the latter the work of art. He had shown this in 1756 in a fragment dealing with the state of war. There he also says that the body politic, unlike the human body, is not limited in size and strength. He says

[22]

the same thing of the mind and soul in *Emile*.[35] In the past most of us, in discussing his similitude of individual and state, have simply affirmed or denied that he accepts the validity of the "organic" parallel in the *Social Contract*,[36] but have failed to explain his special use of it. Nor have we discerned the Socratic and Christian spiritual metaphor that pervades both books throughout.

In the majority of cases this is the suitable one. In Pauline terms the city is a "mystical body" or, as Rousseau says, a rational, moral being. So is the soul. Of course both city and soul are based upon men's natural needs and relationships, as he never wearies of reminding us.[37] But just as a rightly ordered city, in spite of its natural basis, is a work of art and not of nature, a creation of reason and not of instinct, so is a rightly ordered soul. This explains why Rousseau employs quite as much artifice in its formation as he does in that of the city. They are as equally "artificial" as they are "natural," art being for him a means to fulfill nature's purposes in civilized life.[38] Like Socrates he poses as a sculptor, a painter of constitutions—in fine, an artist. His creative artistry is clearly visible in *Emile*, where we shall behold the human soul bearing an image of a celestial city or "order," to which she quite naturally responds and which is proposed as a pattern of life upon earth in any milieu, even the most disordered. He is also a creative artist, though to a lesser degree, in the *Contract*, which possesses the austere beauty of mathematics, closely related to the antique simplicity of *Emile*. The beautiful city is a counterpart of the beautiful soul.[39] It is magnified into a faithful likeness of its spiritual prototype who must remain true to herself reflected therein and avoid all innovations, according to both Rousseau and Socrates. My collation serves to bring out this imagery.

In the light of it, both books turn out to be treatises of education or, if we wish, legislation, since all laws are but "trifles ... of the one great thing, namely education and nurture." Moreover, both deal with "politics," or citizenship, as a Socratic symbol of moral life. And both face the problem of spiritual "warfare" created by opposing forces within the world of man and outside. These three themes, "military tactics, politics, and education" that are the "chiefest and noblest subjects" of the *Republic*,[40] are also those of Rousseau's two books. The "legislator's" aim in both is to discover a *reasonable* constitution of nature in the realm of the soul and of human affairs, and thus to bring man into harmony with himself and with the divine will manifest in him. As a result *Emile* turns out to contain all the laws of the Rousseauist city of the *Contract*. As the author explains in the former, the hero learns to rule himself without external laws and government, which will never exist in their "true" form in the objective world. To paraphrase a Pauline text favored by Rousseau, he replaces the written letter of ordinances carved upon stone by a spiritual rule engraved in the heart to release men from the external yoke of their "tutor the law."[41]

Indeed, he is well aware that he has no alternative but to spiritualize his city as his masters did their own. Its only hope of realization would be within the precincts of the heart through the action of the mind and will, or perhaps within the family through a process of outward diffusion. In both books he is therefore an explorer of the inner world and of human truth rather than a political or pedagogical theorist in the strict sense, whatever terminology he uses. That is why he places the *Contract* within the context of the soul in *Emile*. Moreover, even though his imaginary order will never materialize as a city in the usual meaning of the word, yet for him it still remains the pattern of both public and private life, "politics" and "warfare," the life of man and the citizen who is natural man in the social and civil state.[42] For the principles at work in the inner world and in external conduct must be identical if men are to be consistent with themselves. Thus even in an anti-society the hero of *Emile* will live after the manner of the Rousseauist city and no other.[43]

[24]

This view of Rousseau's two books is confirmed by a study of the preface to each. In what, to coin a word, I would call the Aemilian one, added at the last minute as prefaces usually are, the writer pledges himself to the art of forming men. This he calls the first of all public "utilities," using the word not in the usual pragmatic sense but in the Socratic one, with all its moral and spiritual overtones. In the preface of the *Contract* he professes to seek a lawful and safe rule of administration to govern men. The purpose thus defined in both is the same, since "formation," or education, is a kind of "government" or administration by law. The point of departure in each case is that of Socrates; but it is also that of Christ, who in Rousseau's eyes is the archetype of the legislator-educator. To proceed with the preface of *Emile,* the author promises to accomplish his purpose by studying the child and his growth to manhood and to adopt a method that follows the course of nature. In the preface to the appendix he proposes what amounts to the same thing, namely, to "take men as they are and the laws as they may be." The mode of procedure in both cases is Socratic. In the pedagogical preface he adds that, although his method is based upon the natural order of things, his readers will see in it nothing more than the dreams of a visionary. This idea recurs in *Emile* itself and in the *Letters from the Mount,* where it is also applied to the *Contract.* In the *Letters* he imagines the novel and its appendix relegated, together with the *Republic,* to the land of chimeras.[44] Socrates had no illusions either about the judgment of his contemporaries who saw in him a "star-gazer," a "dreamer," and a "visionary." And Christ too was so regarded by his own people. Thus in this aspect of the Aemilian preface, Rousseau joins company with his masters and faces the charges laid against them. He explains why he takes the risk. It is allegedly because he is dealing with principles that determine the happiness or misery of the human race. This phrase is repeated in the autobiography, where it refers however to the *Contract.*

But, he asks in the same preface—and Socrates raises the question too—is his system really impracticable? Of course so, he replies, if we try to combine it with existing evil and create thereby dangerous inner tensions in man. That is why he would, in the familiar evangelical phrase, sweep the threshing-floor clean. Socrates does so by clearing the tablet of the mind before he begins his task of education. Christ likewise warns against putting a patch on our old habitual life and evil ways, or pouring the new wine of his wisdom into "the old Adam."[45] The Rousseauist system is also chimerical if the will is weak, says the author of the preface to *Emile,* explaining that the will determines the feasibility and success of all spiritual effort. However, he adds, such practical applications of the pedagogical art are not his concern in the book, which sets forth an ideal rather than the actual conditions of life. The same is true of the *Contract,* which aims to define general principles. Since he is not a moralist as he is called,[46] he does not deal with practical problems and specific cases. But whether his system is called feasible or fanciful, he defends it as suited to "men as they are"—the criterion in both texts—and well adapted to the human heart. These latter words, which occur in the Aemilian preface, are used in reference to the *Contract* in the *Letters from the Mount* and *Considerations upon . . . Poland.*[47] The conclusion of the two prefaces is also similar, and again recalls Christ and Socrates. It runs thus. What he suggests in *Emile* is "best for men themselves and for others too," a constantly recurring preoccupation in the *Republic*[48] and also reminiscent of the Mosaical and Christian "Love thy neighbor as thyself." What he proposes in the *Contract* is the same: to ally what justice permits with what human interest prescribes. The two prefaces prove clearly that in both books Rousseau, like the masters of his choice, advocates a system or order of life designed to advance and enrich the nature of man and bring human beings into a truer communion with each other through the practice of justice. And like the same masters he is con-

[26]

vinced that there is only one form of city or soul and that is his own. All others are "false."

In fine, in both prefaces, as in both books, the author is asking the same questions that he had posed at the beginning of his career: "Where is wisdom? Where is happiness?" His reply, like Plato's, is essentially an artistic and intellectual scheme of man and of the world in its relations to human conduct and to the question of justice and inner truth. Although that reply has a literal relevancy to the problems of politics or pedagogy—an aspect that has been repeatedly examined—it also constitutes a whole philosophy of life, a "theory" of reality in the etymological sense of "vision." Some critics are beginning to realize that *Emile* at least is more than a pedagogical manual and that it is really a framework for philosophical research, although, of course, they confine their investigations to the development of human nature therein since their purpose is not to study allegorical figures or to trace the consistent parallelism between the novel and its appendix and their counterparts in antiquity. In truth, even though *Emile* was begun at the request of a mother, both it and the *Contract* are directed to the same audience as the *Republic*, which has the same theme and object as Rousseau's books and is the fruit of the same passion for wisdom[49] conceived as the knowledge of good and evil.

That the subject of *Emile* is indeed wisdom as opposed to knowledge in general explains not merely the author's delight in the conversation of Socrates and Christ or the teaching of Solomon[50] but also the anti-intellectual tone of numerous passages in the book. Here we are confronted with a treatise of education written by an autodidact who, like Socrates, professes to be neither a scholar nor a philosopher, although he pretends to be "a friend of truth."[51] Yet he boasts of teaching "the art of being ignorant," warns against "the perilous paths of vain knowledge," and seems bent upon convincing men that they know nothing at all. Moreover, he advises against answering a child's

[27]

questions and declines to discuss the teaching of reading or writing, for he is "ashamed to toy with such trifles in a treatise of education." He even declares that he hates books and brands them as "the scourge of childhood." Furthermore, he considers research in cosmography and physics as a form of "amusement," forbears to trace courses of study of any kind, and accuses speculative learning of preparing men for a "life of contemplation in a solitary cell." In fine, he regards only one book as indispensable, this being neither Plato nor the Bible but the "book of nature." Not that he excludes intellectual toil. But that is achieved, if at all, outside the philosophical framework. For him real education is not concerned with "such trivialities."[52] He intimates as much in his prefaces. Indeed, in all his work, from his first youthful essays upon education[53] and earliest *Discourse* onward, he is concerned exclusively with wisdom, the discernment of good and evil, as the only key to happiness. This concern underlies the intellectual humility he preaches, whether he practices it or not. He cites the example of Christ and especially of Socrates, the wisest of men who regarded himself as "a hesitating inquirer" in the search for wisdom.[54]

The litterateur approaching the text of *Emile* is puzzled by its strange proportions. The five component parts vary so greatly in length that it appears unbalanced, and especially by comparison with the author's other works. Without speaking of *Julie,* the six parts of which are symmetrical, consider the four parts of the *Contract,* the content of which corresponds to the first four of *Emile.* In the former Rousseau has even been suspected of inserting "irrelevant" material as a pretext for illustration but really to balance and "fill out" the treatise.[55] In fact, balance is quite as significant in a book as it is in a building, and the arrangement of the inside ought to be visible from without. What then does the apparent imbalance of *Emile* mean? There are five parts in the definitive version, the first three being relatively short, even the rather longer second one that originally included the first and was subsequently divided into two.[56] These three parts cover the period from birth to fifteen years. Then come two massive ones that begin again from birth, but this time it is birth into "life," as opposed to "existence." The writer even says that everything previously treated was merely a preparation for education—presumably what Socrates calls the preamble. Indeed, as we shall see, the themes of the first three parts are closely related to three great "waves" that the Greek sage must overcome before he can establish his city. This would suggest an ideological reason for the separation of the first two parts and the curious formation of the whole. But anyone concerned with literary problems as a key to thought must look further, especially in view of the very different shape of the *Contract*, which nevertheless has essentially the same content according to the promises of the preface.

As I have said, the two books contain an ideal image of the human soul that is the prototype of the Rousseauist city. In one the city has the austere shape of a fortress or citadel. In the other the kingdom within is conceived as a tabernacle or temple of the divinity and is therefore designed as such with a triple approach to the main structure. In Rousseau's words the soul, or rather, the heart, that mainspring of the human spirit, is the only true temple of the Godhead. The imagery is biblical, by analogy with the body considered as the temple of the soul and consequently of the spirit of God.[57] The scriptural figure makes the fabric of *Emile* intelligible. But although the temple of the book occasionally recalls the shrine of Solomon or of Justinian, it is basically of Greek design and resembles the sanctuary of Apollo at Delphi with its harmonious natural setting, or else the Parthenon in Athens, a vision of ordered beauty amid the disorder of an antisociety. The first three parts are like the three steps of the raised foundation of a Greek temple. In *Emile* this threefold foundation, to which the first three parts of the *Contract* will be seen to correspond, represents the main concepts suggested in the two prefaces: the nature of man, its lawful engagement, and the government of reason.

The temple proper of *Emile*, like that of Delphi or Athens, has Ionic elements inside but a Doric exterior, comparable in character to the citadel of the *Contract*. Indeed, in the Aemilian temple, as at the Delphic one, the Spartans that filled Rousseau with republican fervor at the age of six occupy a privileged place. At the threshold of both is inscribed the legend "Know thyself," although in *Emile* it is gradually transmuted into the Christian "Forget thyself." The main body of the book is also disposed like the Greek shrine. It is split into two unequal parts, the second rather smaller than the other. Passing through them, we make our way first into the ideal social order of the *Contract;* then into the equivalent civil order, which for Rousseau is a source of sanctifying grace and where all elements of the appendix are gathered together. Both parts, like those of the Greek temple, have three naves. And just as the main chamber of the ancient sanctuary contained an image of the godhead in its midst, and as Apollo the sun god of Delphi stands in the midst of the *Republic,* so the deity in whose likeness man is made occupies a similar place in *Emile,* in the profession of faith of the Savoyard vicar. Before it is a Rousseauist version of the Delphic sacrificial hearth where the eternal fire burned at the navel of the earth. In the pedagogical novel the sacrificial fire is the offering of the soul to the divinity by the purification of the passions. And as the Pythian oracle spoke from the innermost point of the Delphic shrine, so in *Emile* the oracular "celestial voice" of conscience or of law utters the dictates of wisdom in the secret places of the soul. Nearby rise two statues like those that once surrounded the figure of the god at Delphi. They are images of Socrates and Christ who dominate the world of the spirit, a world reflected in the city of the *Contract*.

Finally, in the Aemilian temple we are admitted into the inner sanctum of the small room beyond, which has no corresponding part in the citadel. It is filled with treasures and votive offerings consecrated in honor of Sophia, priestess of the soul, as the heroine appears in the book and as she was reportedly conceived in its projected sequel.[58] The Rousseauist tabernacle, like the Delphic shrine of the god of light and the Parthenon of Athena-Minerva, is dedicated to divine wisdom whose name Sophia bears. At this stage in the hero's progress, the force of the emotions transforms what seemed like a pagan temple into a Christian church dedicated to Saint Sophia. The Parthenon itself underwent a similar change in the early Middle Ages before it became a mosque. But like it the fabric of *Emile* remains basically Greek as the shape suggests.

There are so many points of contact between Rousseau's imagery and the Greek temple that there can be no doubt about the pattern of his work, which cannot be overlooked in a literary study. *Emile* heralds the neoclassical movement in art that was already under way when it appeared. The movement received impetus from the author's thought that impelled France to seek in antiquity a new ideology and a new aesthetics through a fresh study of ancient literature and art. *Emile* and its appendix are among the most significant creations of that trend.

In my collation I shall follow the writer step by step while he constructs the temple or stronghold of the soul or city. Thus we shall see that the spiritual shrine of the novel is governed from the first by the same principles as the visionary fortress-like city of the *Contract*. In the larger work these principles are expressed in concrete forms to illustrate their nature and interrelationships until they are finally merged into a vast synthesis in the fifth part that emphasizes the artistic and philosophical unity of the whole and accentuates its fundamental idealism. In that part the temple appears as a living reality, the dwelling-place of Sophia, through the ministry of one in whom we must recognize the Rousseauist Levite of Ephraim who finally withdraws in favor of the priestess herself. The same idealism is translated in the *Contract* into an austere architectural design.

1. "En négligeant la langue des signes qui parlent à l'imagination l'on a perdu le plus énergique des langages" (J.-J. Rousseau, "Emile," *Oeuvres complètes*, 4 [Paris: Plèiade, 1969]: 645). Hereinafter, all references to the Pléiade edition of Rousseau's complete works will be indicated by *O.C.;* moreover, unless otherwise indicated, all references to the "Contrat social" and "Emile" are to volumes 3 and 4 respectively of that edition, and will contain only the page reference. For the sake of a homogeneous text, all quotations including those from Rousseau, Plato, and the Bible, are given in English. In the case of Rousseau, major quotations are also given in French in the footnotes. Those among the epigraphs of this book read: "C'est un assés beau roman que celui de la nature humaine. S'il ne se trouve que dans cet écrit, est-ce ma faute? Ce devroit être l'histoire de mon espèce . . ." And again: "Cet ouvrage (le traitté du contrat social), étant cité plusieurs fois et même extrait dans le traité de l'education en doit passer pour une espèce d'appendice, et . . . les deux ensemble font un tout complet . . . ."

2. "Mais combien de fois . . . ai-je déclaré que je n'écrivois point pour les gens à qui il faloit tout dire." Cf.: " . . . Il ne faut pas toujours tout dire; celui qui dit tout dit peu de choses, car à la fin on ne l'écoute plus" (*O.C.*, 4:437 n. [a] and 541).

3. J.-J. Rousseau, "Lettre à Christophe de Beaumont," *O.C.*, 4:929. Cf. J.-J. Rousseau, *Correspondance complète*, vol. 7, ed. R.A. Leigh (Geneva: Institut et Musée Voltaire, 1965-), p. 332, letter to Vernet, 29 November 1760. Hereinafter, *C.C.* with volume and page number refers to this edition of the correspondence. Rousseau also told others that he had stopped writing and planned to retire: e.g., ibid., 7:244, letter to Lalive de Jully, October 1760; 9:311-12, letter to Moultou, 12 December 1761; 11:24, letter to Néaulme, 5 June 1762. Regarding this plan see also J.-J. Rousseau, "Confessions," *O.C.*, 1:560-61, 562, 572, 574.

4. *Julie or La Nouvelle Heloïse: A Synthesis of Rousseau's Thought (1749-1759)*. (Toronto: University of Toronto Press, 1949).

5. J.-J. Rousseau, "Lettres à m. de Malesherbes," *O.C.*, 1:1136-37, 1144. The four famous letters are also to be found in *C.C.*, vol. 10. The reference given here is to letters of 12 and 28 January 1762, where Rousseau implies that *Emile* and the *Contrat* are his last works. Cf. n. 3 above. He wanted the *Contrat* to appear first, as he tells the publisher, Rey: *C.C.*, 10:235, letter of 9 May 1762. Later he expressed pleasure at the proposal that the Parisian publisher, Duchesne, sell the two books together: ibid., p. 281, letter to Duchesne, 23 May 1762. For the *Contrat* as an "appendix," see ibid.

6. " . . . Il importoit peu que ce tas d'enfant ne jouât pas sa petite comédie, mais il importoit beaucoup que ce que j'ai dit fût dit: grâce au ciel, ma Tache est faite: je n'aurai plus de souci sur ce point" (*C.C.*, 14:168, letter to Malesherbes, 7 December 1762. He here refers to court intrigues behind the Paris decree.

7. "Confessions," loc. cit., pp. 586-87; and cf. "Projets de préface," *O.C.*, 2:1205-7. See also the first chapter of the *Essai sur l'origine des langues*. Mme

M.A. Simons remarks on the light treatment normally accorded to the poem, which she considers important for the evocation of a primitive society and of the origins of evil therein: *Amitié et passion: Rousseau et Sauttersheim* (Geneva: Droz, 1972), pp. 82-88.

8. "Lettres à m. de Malesherbes," loc. cit., p. 1136 and n.2.

9. Plato *The Republic* 6. 495. All references are to the Jowett translation.

10. "Lettre à C. de Beaumont," loc. cit., p. 1002. For the dishonoring of the Lady Philosophy, cf. the sequel to *Emile* and see Chapter 6, note 18, below.

11. "... Le seul homme en France qui croie en Dieu doit être la victime des défenseurs du christianisme" (*C.C.*, 11:36, letter to Moultou, 7 June 1762). For the other references in the paragraph, see ibid., p. 153, letter to Morancourt of Berne, 25 June 1762; "Lettre à C. de Beaumont," loc. cit., p. 931; "Confessions," loc. cit., p. 591. The French texts read as follows. To the journalist: "... Il [mon livre] sera lû tôt ou tard par des hommes raisonables, peut être enfin par des Chrétiens, qui verront avec surprise et sans doute avec indignation qu'un disciple de leur divin maitre soit traité parmi eux comme un Scélérat." To the bishop: "... Le défenseur de la cause de Dieu, flétri, proscrit, poursuivi d'Etat en Etat ... sans égard pour son indigence, sans pitié pour ses infirmités ... se voit interdire le feu et l'eau dans l'Europe presque entière ...." In the memoirs: "Ces deux Decrets furent le signal du cri de malediction qui s'éleva contre moi dans toute l'Europe avec une fureur qui n'eut jamais d'exemple .... J'étois un impie, un athée, un forcené, un enragé, une bête féroce, un loup."

12. *C.C.*, 16:164-68, letter to J. Favre, 12 May 1763 (rough draft and final version); cf. *Lettres écrites de la montagne*, 5, 8, and 9 (hereafter cited as *Lettres de la montagne*).

13. *Lettres de la montagne*, especially 4 through 9. For the above quotations see *O.C.*, 3:734, 768. Regarding the government's reaction, cf. "Confessions," loc. cit., p. 623. The *Lettres de la montagne* were burned at the Hague on 22 January 1765 and in Paris on 19 March 1765.

14. "Confessions," loc. cit., p. 634; cf. pp. 627-28; and J.-J. Rousseau, *Correspondance générale* (Paris: Colin, 1924-34), 14:85, letter to Du Peyrou, 8 August 1765. Hereinafter *"C.G."* with volume and page number refers to this edition of the correspondence, which must be used to supplement the other until the latter is complete. See also "Vision de Pierre de la Montagne," *O.C.*, 2:1233.

15. He refers to the death of Socrates in the first "Discours," *O.C.*, 3:15; in the "Dernière Réponse," ibid., p. 73 n, in the "Lettre à d'Alembert," *Oeuvres complètes* 1 (Paris: Hachette, 1885-98):260; in "Julie," *O.C.*, 2:224; and in "Emile," where he also speaks of the death of Christ: p. 626. Hereinafter *"O.C. Hachette,"* followed by volume and page numbers, refers to the aforementioned edition of Rousseau's works.

16. *C.C.*, 4:165, letter from Roustan, 5 March 1757; cf. p. 91 and 7:174, letters from Deleyre, 26 August 1756 and 7 July 1760. See also 8:178-79, letter of 26 February 1761; and 11:71, 83, 89; 12:175;13:245;15:82, 273; *C.G.*, 12:359; 19:275; 20:35. These references are to letters dated from June 1762 to January 1771, addressed to Rousseau by various correspondents. They are just a few striking examples of the many available. For a study of the comparison in question see R. Trousson, *Socrate devant Voltaire, Diderot, et Rousseau: la conscience en face du mythe* (Paris: Minard, 1967), pp. 67-103. If we identify Rousseau as the protagonist of the fragment "Morceau allégorique sur la révélation," as it is possible to do, he there associates himself with both Christ and Socrates: *O.C.*, 4:1044-54.

17. *The Republic* 6. 496.

18. For Rousseau's first judgment see *C.C.,* 9:311-12, letter to Moultou, 12 December 1761; cf. letter to journalist of n. 11 above; "Lettre à C. de Beaumont," loc. cit., p. 960; "Emile," p. 859; and "Confessions," loc. cit., pp. 409-10, 566-68. Burgelin calls it Rousseau's most complete work and one of the key works of our civilization: *O.C.,* 4:1xxxix.

19. "Lettre à C. de Beaumont," loc. cit., p. 928; *C.C.,* 10:281, letter to Duchesne, 23 May 1762; "Lettres à m. de Malesherbes," loc. cit., p. 1136 and n. 2; "Confessions," loc. cit., p. 407.

20. It was not condemned in Paris, Berne, Holland or Spain: *O.C.,* 3:810 n. 2.

21. See, for example, R. Derathé, "L'Homme selon Rousseau," in *Etudes sur le Contrat social de J.-J. Rousseau* (Paris: Les Belles Lettres, 1964), pp. 215-17; M. Einaudi, *The Early Rousseau* (Ithaca, N.Y.: Cornell University Press, 1967), pp. 17-18. Einaudi has doubts but sets them aside: p. 13 n. 26, and cf. pp. 241-42. However, O. Vossler sees that the place of the *Contrat* is in *Emile: Rousseaus Freiheitslehre* (Göttingen: Vandenhoeck and Ruprecht, ca. 1963), p. 208. J.H. Broome sees a relationship of the two in *Rousseau: A Study of His Thought* (London: Arnold, 1963), pp. 50 and 104. L.G. Crocker follows in *Rousseau's Social Contract: An Interpretive Essay* (Cleveland: Case Western Reserve University Press, 1968) pp. 43, 57, 75, 77, etc. J.S. Spink and P. Burgelin see the same relationship: *O.C.,* Pléiade, 4: xlii-lvii, especially liii, xciv-xcvi, cxlix-cl, 242 n. 2 and 838 n. 1.

22. "Emile," pp. 671 ff.; cf. pp. 397-99, 645-51, 717 ff.; cf. chapter 5 below. "Pygmalion" is also important for Rousseau's aesthetics, but I shall discuss it separately in chapter 6.

23. *C.C.,* 7:332, letter to J. Vernet, 29 Nov. 1760.

24. "Emile," p. 437 n. (a).

25. For Rousseau's views on the language of symbolic expression see "Emile," pp. 645-51. Cf. *Essai sur l'origine des langues,* chapter 1. For his definition of taste and its proper models discussed below, see "Emile," pp. 671-73; cf. pp. 397-99 and even 407 ff. See also "Dictionnaire de musique" under the term *goût.*

26. In "Emile" he pays tribute twice to Boileau: pp. 442, 537.

27. Whenever I quote Socrates or speak of him as Rousseau's master, I mean Socrates as presented by Plato. I have used the name of Socrates for artistic reasons, adhering to the imagery of "Emile." Burgelin in his critical edition of "Emile" mentions Plato or Socrates thirty-one times, but of course he does not pretend to deal with interrelationships on a large scale. C.W. Hendel draws attention to Rousseau's platonism, especially in the "Lettres morales": *Jean-Jacques Rousseau, Moralist* (London and New York: Oxford University Press, 1934), pp. 298-316. For the reference to the letter to the archbishop see loc. cit., p. 960, where Rousseau calls Christ his master. For his personal attachment to Socrates see note 16 above. Trousson, mentioned therein, sees him as transferring his allegiance gradually from Socrates to Christ especially in *Emile;* but, of course, this idea does not affect the evidence of Socratic influence combined in the book with Judeo-Christian from beginning to end.

28. "Emile," pp. 625-26; and "Lettres de la montagne," loc. cit., pp. 753-54.

29. *The Republic* 2. 376. We shall see that *Emile* and the *Contrat* contain a very complete and personal commentary of *The Republic,* and that *Emile* also contains Rousseau's view of *The Symposium.* Both books have allusions to other Platonic dialogues. In order not to confuse the issue, I have in general refrained from

giving references to the latter, which would also have had the effect of increasing the volume of the notes.

30. *The Republic* 1. 344, 351, 352; 2. 365, 367; 3. 403; 4. 427-28; 5. 450-51; 6. 484; 9. 578; 10. 608, 618. Cf. *The Symposium.* Cf. 1 Kings 3:9; Prov., passim; Wisdom, passim; Heb. 5:14.

31. *The Republic* 2. 368-69; 4. 434-35; 5. 449. Cf. 6. 498; 7. 540; 8. 544, 549-50, 553, 557, 562; 9. 577.

32. Ibid., 9. 590-92. Cf. 8. 550, 553, 560.

33. "Emile," pp. 519, 524, 530, 632 n; "Contrat social," pp. 355-56, 358, 361, 363, 369, 385, 386, 395-96, 408, 432. In the last case the comparison is only implied.

34. For the first case see ibid., pp. 361, 363, where Vaughan sees the "organic" comparison; for the second see pp. 421, 424. See J.-J. Rousseau, *Du Contrat social,* ed. C.E. Vaughan (Manchester: At the University Press; London and New York: Longmans, Green, 1918), p. xxviii; also J.-J. Rousseau, *The Political Writings,* ed. C.E. Vaughan (Cambridge: At the University Press, 1915), 1:70. For the article on political economy see *O.C.,* 3:244. It dates from 1754-55.

35. "Emile," p. 281. For the fragment see *O.C.,* 3:604-6; cf. "Contrat social," pp. 424 n. 2, 425. See Chapter 4 below regarding "Contrat social," pt. 3, chaps. 10, 11.

36. For example, Vaughan as in note 34 above; R. Derathé, *J.-J. Rousseau et la science politique de son temps* (Paris: Presses universitaires de France, 1950), pp. 410-13; Einaudi, op. cit., pp. 170-72.

37. For the role of nature in "Emile," see pp. 247-48, 466-67, and passim; for the "Contrat social," see pp. 378, 393, and "Emile," p. 837; cf. "Lettres de la montagne," loc. cit., p. 807; "Considérations sur le gouvernement de Pologne," *O.C.,* 3:973, 996, 1001, 1027, 1041 (hereafter cited as "Considérations").

38. For the role of art or artifice in the "Contrat social" see pp. 360, 424, 431; for "Emile" see pp. 311, 320-21, 325-26, 329-33, 437 ff. and n. (2) on 1420, 501 3, 663, 764-65, 773-78, 801-2. For the city as a set of moral relationships see *C.C.,* 19:190, letter to Col. Pictet, 1 March 1764.

39. "Julie," loc. cit., pp. 223-24. Cf. *The Republic* 2. 361; 4. 419-20; 5. 472; 6. 484, 500-501, 505; 7. 540.

40. *The Republic* 10. 599. For the quotation at the beginning of the paragraph see ibid., 4. 423.

41. 2 Cor. 3:3 ff.; cf. "Emile," p. 454. 2 Cor. 3:6 and 17; cf. "Emile," p. 471. See also Gal. 3:24; cf. 5:14, 17, 22-23; cf. Rom. 7:14; 1 Tim. 1:9. For the statement that true laws will never exist in the external world see "Lettre à C. de Beaumont," loc. cit., pp. 941 ff. All biblical references are to the King James version except in the case of the so-called apocryphal books, where I refer to the Ronald Knox translation.

42. "Emile," pp. 469, 483-84, 662, 669, 763-64.

43. Regarding the alleged opposition of man and citizen, humanitarianism and patriotism see, for example, S. Cotta, "La Position du problème de la politique chez Rousseau," in *Etudes sur le Contrat social de J.-J. Rousseau* (Paris: Les Belles Lettres, 1964), pp. 183-90. For the difficulty of reconciling the two see P. D. Jimack, *La Genèse et la rédaction de l'Emile de J.-J. Rousseau* (Geneva: Institut et musée Voltaire, 1960), pp. 123-25. Burgelin finds the dis-

tinction superficial: "Emile," p. 248 n. 4. However, he retains it: 251 n. 3 and 324 n. 1. See chapters 5 and 6 below.

44. "Emile," pp. 250, 350 n, 548-49; "Lettres de la montagne," loc. cit., p. 810; cf. "Considérations," loc. cit., p. 1041, which, however, refers only to the "Contrat social."

45. Matt. 3:12; Mark 2:21-22; Luke 5:36-38. Cf. *The Republic* 6. 501; 7. 540, and second "Discours," *O.C.,* 3:180.

46. See "Mon portrait," *O.C.,* 1:1120: "Je suis observateur et non moraliste."

47. "Lettres de la montagne," loc. cit., p. 807; "Considérations," loc. cit., p. 1041.

48. *The Republic* 3. 407-8; 4. 428; 6. 496; 10. 619. These passages contain phrases obviously echoed in the Rousseauist "best for themselves and for others too."

49. For the *Contract social* see C.G., 7:147, letter to Rey, 11 March 1762; for *Emile* see "Lettres de la montagne," loc. cit., p. 783. Cf. *O.C.,* 4:242 n. 2. Rousseau saw clearly that the object of law in the ideal city is eduction in this sense: second "Discours," loc. cit., pp. 187-88: cf. "Emile," p. 250.

50. For Solomon see 1 Kings, Prov., Eccles., and Wisdom.

51. "Emile," p. 348. The expression occurs in *The Republic* 6. 487. For Rousseau's so-called intellectual humility see *O.C.,* 4:348 n. 3 and cf. 483 n. 1.

52. For all these statements see "Emile," pp. 339 and n, 358, 370-71, 428, 436, 443, 446, 454, 487, 523, 536-37, 543, 619-20. 624-25, 676; cf. also first "Discours," loc. cit., p. 26; preface to "Narcisse," *O.C.,* 2:970-72; cf. "Lettre à C. de Beaumont," loc. cit., p. 945.

53. "Mémoire présenté à m. de Mably sur l'éducation de son fils" and "Projet pour l'éducation de M. de Sainte-Marie," *O.C.,* 4:3-32, 35-51. These date from 1740 and 1743.

54. See, for example, first "Discours," loc. cit., p. 13; "Dernière réponse," loc. cit., p. 94. Cf. *The Republic* 1. 336-37, 354; 2. 368; 5. 450-51; 6. 506; 7. 530.

55. *O.C.,* 3:384 n. 6 (relating to part 2, chapters 8, 9, and 10); 414 n. 1 (relating to part 3, chapter 8); 444 n. 1 (relating to part 4, chapters 4, 5, 6, and 7).

56. Jimack, op. cit., p. 171. Regarding the divisions of the Favre manuscript and subsequent modifications see also *O.C.,* 4:1xxxiv-lxxxvii, 298 n. 2 and 426 n. 1.

57. "Contrat social," pp. 384-85: the city is called an "edifice." It is also so called in "Emile," p. 849. Rousseau draws the same parallel in his criticism of the abbé de Saint-Pierre's "Polysynodie," *O.C.,* 3:641. For the comparison of the "heart" to a temple see "Emile," p. 632. Cf. Luke 6:48-49; especially John 2:21; 1 Cor. 3:9-10 and especially 16-17; 2 Cor. 6:16. Rousseau refers to the biblical image in "Emile," p. 744.

58. "Emile et Sophie" *O.C.,* 4:clxiii-clxiv.

II

Foundation

All the myths of *Emile* have their origin in the opening part that contains the exposition of the novel and the first foundation of the mythical sanctuary therein.[1] However, they are subtle and elusive since the writer's artistry always remains unostentatious and even deliberately concealed until it becomes the quiet handmaid of ideas. His images, being quite suited to the task assigned to them, fulfill it almost self-effacingly. Yet if we ignore them, the words are paradoxical and perplexing. To some extent they must be. This is true not only because a certain ambiguity or mystery resides in all genuine art, but also because the symbols in *Emile* lend themselves to more than one meaning. They retain their natural, apparently obvious values at the same time as they transcend them to burst the bounds of literal interpretation and evolve into vast metaphors and allegories of much larger significance. The writer provides many hints of their presence along the way. However, in the more mystifying passages we are required to make that "willing suspense of disbelief" for which the poet pleaded and defer judgment until all available evidence has been pieced together. The main advantage of such effort is that in the end it affords a deeper and broader understanding of *Emile,* its appendix, and the sequels to both than might otherwise be possible.

THE SOUL AND THE CITY

The first pages of the novel have no specific equivalent in the appendix. After a brief introduction the book opens, like the second *Discourse,* with a moving dedication to the only mother the author ever knew, the city of Geneva, which he always declared to be his model in the *Contract*. Although he had been disenchanted by his birthplace since 1754, nevertheless at least until 1762, when that city became for him the cruelest of stepmothers, she still remained in his mind a symbol of something far more than he had actually found there. And so *Emile* is dedicated to a new Geneva existing "in his heart," his own apprehension of a "wise order" of things that finally appears in the form of the eponymous hero's bride, Sophia.

In the past, of course, we have interpreted the dedication only literally, without regard to the litterateur's use of art forms. We have identified the mother in the dedication with another in the first phrase of the preface, the "good mother" for whom he began the pedagogical work as he says in that text and repeats in *Letters from the Mount* and whom he names in his memoirs as madame de Chenonceaux.[2] But apart from the fact that the mother in the preface is not necessarily the one in the dedication, in the first page of *Emile* she is expanded into a symbol extending far beyond the proportions of an individual.

There is plenty of evidence to support this contention. The dedication, incorporated into the substance of the book, is introduced by a famous battle cry directed against our social or unsocial if not anti-social institutions. It reads thus: "Everything is good as it emerges from the hands of the creator of things: everything degenerates in the hands of man." It is man, we are told, that disfigures nature's beauty, especially the soul, which, in the manner of Fénelon, Rousseau likens to a frail plant that must be lovingly tended. This image, dear to his "masters," recurs at intervals throughout the book.[3] The plant must be hedged about, says he at this point, by the devoted mother, whom false laws rob of the authority that is rightfully hers. Just when the puzzled reader is beginning to wonder what meaning he is attaching to the term *mother,* he promises to explain it later. The mystery is less recondite than it appears to be. He loves to identify the motherland or city-state of his dreams with a vigilant and affectionate mother and frequently does so in other works, particularly political pieces of the 1750s. So do his masters and their followers. Take the example of Socrates, who teaches his heroes that their country is "their mother and their nurse."[4] There is also the case of the Christian "Holy Mother Church" that in some respects is not unlike Rousseau's spiritual city. And so we may, if we choose, expand our view and see in the tender mother to whom *Emile* is addressed a new avatar of the Rousseauist city where the soul allegedly beholds herself as she really is and where the subjective and objective worlds meet in one. The book closes in a similar manner, with a sort of divinization of woman as the personification of the author's hopes for humanity visible in Sophia.

Before setting forth his aspirations, Rousseau sketches a curious image of the so-called zero degree of natural human ignorance, reminiscent of Condillac's statue of a man possessed only of disconnected sensations.[5] It evokes an imbecilic creature unacquainted with his own powers and their uses and distinguished from a newborn child only by size and brute strength. He is therefore not a newborn child, nor yet the primitive man of finely trained instincts seen in the second *Discourse*. He is untrained and unintegrated man, even though he lives surrounded by others. He is therefore the soul of modern man, stripped of his seductive trappings. This is the starting point of the spiritual ascent that is the theme of *Emile*.

Rousseau next visualizes the ascent itself and discovers the range of his lofty ambitions in the book. Anyone who desires to leave that uncivilized state and make his way to the heights has a threefold need. He requires strength of faculties and organs; the society of others to teach him to use those resources; and enough experience of the world to form a mature, discriminating judgment. Now, if he is to enjoy the singleness of purpose necessary to progress, he must perforce be guided by the first of these, since it is regulated by nature and lies beyond the scope of human power. He must be governed by the faculties of body and soul, which are latent in men at birth and which must grow and perform each one its proper function in relation to the others, according to the designs of nature herself. The author now describes her in the most engaging terms that strike an imposing contrast with the picture of the solitary brutish creature described above. It is she who bids us, untrammeled by false opinion or otherwise impeded, select among the objects round about us those that are agreeable in the first instance; then those that we deem suitable or meaningful for ourselves; and finally those that, in our considered judgment, promise us a happiness or perfection matching the idea of both furnished by reason. This view of nature unfolds before us a vast spiritual and aesthetic evolution leading from the lowest instincts to the highest intellectual ideals. The author's ultimate goal is to minister to the full flowering and fruition of all potential faculties. Such are the perspectives suggested to the mind by his triple-tiered view of nature's genuine tendencies that determine the whole course of Rousseauist education.

Having disclosed the infinite possibilities within man, he then hints in enigmatic terms that they can be fully realized only in his own idea of moral order, which corresponds to his own view of social and civil order since the one is born of the other. He does so by describing the perfect city or moral person of his fancy. But he sets it within the framework of contemporary society and immorality to provide an impressive contrast between them.

Thus he begins by denouncing our anti-society that molds a man not for himself but for "others" who are consequently opposed to himself and embody conflicting private interests prevailing in our midst. Like Socrates he despises such a society for shaping man to please the shifting tastes and tempers of the motley multitude, as he charged in the opening lines of the book. In his eyes a forced and false cleavage is thereby fostered between the soul and the semblance of a city, man and the so-called citizen, the world of man and the world of men.

By way of antithesis to this state of affairs, he proceeds to define his dream. This freeman of the new Geneva assumes the person of an ancient Roman or Spartan to expound the inner, moral discipline that his concept of social life entails, as opposed to our presumably anti-social ways. The ideal Rousseauist moral being is painstakingly shaped by the lawful claims of others that are identical with his own and alone can call his entire nature into play and bring it to full growth. But that "larger growth," as Socrates also says,[6] is possible only in "a State which is suitable to him" and in which he may find and recognize himself as he essentially is. This means that the city must be patterned after the human soul and become an integrated whole, as closely knit together as its spiritual prototype. In that case it excludes individualist eccentric instincts, considered by Rousseau as a perversion of nature but favored as a rule of life by many of his contemporaries. In his view, as we have seen, both city and soul are fashioned by the processes of art; and infinite skill, rather than spontaneous impulse, is necessary to preserve the true spirit and aspirations of natural man within the fabric of the social and civil order.

In a fresh antithesis with the ideal, Rousseau looks again at contemporary society. Warning anew that instinctive feelings cannot be trusted in a true civil order, he shows that if they are, as is the case in actuality, they are distorted into egoism and are at variance with the human will seen as an expression of nature's highest dispositions. The result is that the soul is a kingdom divided against itself, belying her own real nature and useless to the world as well. In his belief men can no longer be true to themselves and at the same time "citizens" of the earthly "cities" of their birth.

The conflict between an anti-society and our true nature that ought to find its plenitude in social life creates an abyss between domestic education, such for example as a youth might receive in his father's house in some distant province, and public education, which is that of public opinion in the modern "city." Rousseau deplores the contradiction between the two types of formation, which ought ideally to be one. To give an idea of public education as it should be, he cites Plato's *Republic,* paying tribute to it in a passage that corresponds harmoniously to another in the last part of the book. In what is much more than a "passing greeting," as it is still being called, he describes the great classic as the finest treatise of education ever written rather than a political work in the usual sense. True, he goes on to say that the type of education of which he speaks as exemplified therein is no longer possible. But this does not mean that he takes leave of the book or his masters. For Socrates says the same thing: until the famous republic comes to the birth in objective reality— an assumption that has as little political validity as it does in the case of the *Contract*—the system of formation prescribed by the sage must be confined to the inner world or "city of just souls." Public education, successful in Sparta centuries before the age of the Greek philosophers, who took that example for their model as Rousseau himself did, was as pernicious and fatal in their time as it was in his. Socrates says so, warning continually against the evil effects of contemporary opinion incompatible with the ideal order he proposes as a spiritual entity. The author of *Emile* heeds the warning. He explains that since, in the actual chaotic state of human affairs, there exists and can no longer exist in the world of actuality either city or citizen as he has just defined them, public education or the education of public opinion is out of the question.[7] He is therefore unable to have recourse to it to supplement that of the home as he does in the idyllic sphere of the *Letter to d'Alembert* or in his work on the government of Poland, where he is himself the chosen legislator. According to his correspondence, that was the kind of education by which he had profited personally in the city of Geneva, consisting of traditions and maxims handed down from generation to generation. He adds that ideally he would favor a form of education midway between the Greek-Spartan public kind and the monarchic domestic type, combining the education of public opinion with that of the family.[8] But in *Emile* he is obliged to reject prevailing opinion as false, and to resort to "domestic education" exclusively, which might turn out to be the kind of self-discipline to which Socrates has to resort in the end. In Rousseau's own words he proposes to form "natural man" for himself alone, that is, to fulfill and consummate his entire nature and thereby render him better prepared for life with others in their anti-social state than if he were fashioned according to their wayward hearts and fitful passions.[9]

The tribute to the *Republic* is only a harbinger of things to come. Indeed, there is a constant and consistent parallelism between Rousseau's two works and the Platonic dialogue of which he provides a complete personal interpretation. However, the parallelism emerges only from the second part onward where he deals with the formation of the self-conscious being. Yet the first part of both works contains many allusions to the *Republic,* which, together with the Bible, was clearly his *vademecum,.*

In undertaking to form natural man for life in our society, he describes his task in Socratic terms. He must, he says, emulate the pilot who casts anchor in order to hold firm and avoid being carried away by the high seas. The image conveys an idea of the overwhelming flood of popular opinion that he, like another Socrates, is compelled to resist. The symbol of the pilot is an ever recurring one in the novel and is linked with a famous allegory in the *Republic,* that of the "true pilot" or governor, reason, who rules over city and soul and who "must and will be the steerer whether other people like it or not."[10] Similarly Rousseau would stem the tide of prejudice in his book by means of reason. He adds the image of the anchor

[43]

to suggest further that he will do so by having recourse to the stability and permanence of basic principles.

This idea leads to the next. His "natural man" will, says he, be formed to endure the good and evil of the "human condition" from which none of us is dispensed, whatever our rank may be. He confesses that for him "natural man" is "abstract man" whose entire being must grow and mature in an ever more precise adjustment to reality in the pursuit of life's loftiest aims. In other words, he proposes to create, in the Socratic manner, an IDEA of man corresponding to the IDEA of the city in the *Contract* and sometimes called Socratically the "real" one. It is intended as an absolute prototype of which all individuals are mere counterparts and, by comparison, mere semblances of men, but which as an inextinguishable, unalterable essence survives in each one of them. For he believes with Montaigne that "each man bears within himself the whole form of the human condition." Thus he visualizes as the object of his work the human self as distinguished from a disordered one. His "man" is intended to be timeless and no more a man of his century than the portraitist who paints him.[11] In him we are expected to find a common denominator and a promise of fulfillment as we do in humanity or, better still, as the Spartan did in Sparta or the Roman did in Rome. Indeed, he is later compared to both. Even though he has been modernized and christianized, he is reminiscent of the generalized man of humanistic art who belongs to a race of beings finer than the ones we know, and who is visible in the noble archaic statues of Greece or the classical carvings of Phideias, the "canon" of Polykleitos or the gentle forms of Praxiteles to whom the author of the first *Discourse* pays tribute. Since Socrates compares his "heroes" to those serene beings, so unlike the passionate souls of Greek tragedy, it is not improbable that his disciple was thinking of the same sculptures as contrasted with Condillac's statue evoked above. *Emile* is his own

[44]

"canon." Like the ideal state of nature of the *Discourses* and the ideal city of the *Contract*, the ideal man of the novel portrays a hypothetical state that, even if it never existed and even if we can never attain it, is still proposed as a criterion for comparison and judgment.[12] This portrayal, based partly upon abstract reason and partly upon observation of our deformities, constitutes the main value of the book.

The author mentioned that he would fashion his model by means of domestic or natural education. Resorting to artistic methods, he next evolves the symbol of the home to express his views about the role of society in man's formation, its actual and ideal relationships to the human spirit. Significantly enough, it is precisely at this point that the *Contract* joins company with *Emile,* and the two books then proceed according to an identical pattern throughout the four parts, the fifth part of the novel being a synthesis or culmination of all that precedes.

The same fifth part, anticipated in the first, throws light upon the present context. There family society is ideally pictured as a "little city" or homeland, a reflection of the political order of the Rousseauist city-state symbolized in the mother whose sanctuary is the home and who is therefore the link between the miniature city and its larger counterpart.[13] This symbol was present in the dedication. Family affection, he explains in the end, must be the natural ground and motive of all conventional bonds and love of state, and that first of all societies is the basis of the other, on condition that it is held together as it should be, not merely by natural instinct but also by just such conventional bonds. That being the case, the city of his desires will materialize only if the family is first akin to the soul, and results from the happy self-expansion of human nature fully consummated by art. He did not think so in his earlier years when, under the influence of Socrates, he excluded the family as an educational institution. But now he passes beyond his Greek masters and the

[45]

whole classical world, including his revered Spartans, through the profound influence of a Christian ideal of the home and family life, conceived as securing and enhancing the ancient model of ideal human formation. For in the mythical fifth part he allows himself to fancy that the "little city" of the family may, if dreams come true as they do therein, not merely exteriorize an inner life of exquisite order but also expand beyond its natural bounds through some unlikely communion of men of good will until the blessed "city" enshrined in the hearts of its freemen is born. Then that city would be, as it were, an expansion of the home and of all the sentiments of home, its intimacy, dignity, and security translated into unity, freedom, and equality. The vision of the last part is anticipated at the juncture we have now reached in the first where contemporary actuality is juxtaposed with the ideal and belies it.

There is an abyss between them. The author, contemplating what he regards as the shaky foundations of our weary world slowly sinking into the mire of human error and vanity, suddenly bursts forth in a famous outcry: "Civilized man is born, lives and dies in slavery: at his birth he is bound in swaddling clothes; at his death he is nailed down in a coffin; all his life long he is imprisoned by our institutions." These words have a matching pendant in the vigorous beginning of the *Contract* where the subject is defined: "Man is born free and everywhere he is in fetters."[14] What, asks the writer, could possibly justify such a scandalous mutilation of human nature on the part of brute force? Yet in the same text he adds that in his system there is no question of resorting to force to oppose force. On the contrary, says he, he intends to show how submission to constraints may be lawful and indeed the only way to social order—an orderly life in society— that is men's "sacred right" and consummates nature's best intentions by means of social conventions. He does so in both books.

[46]

In actual society, however, submission always appears as a form of slavery. It is betokened in the novel by a vivid literary image, that of swaddling clothes which allegedly impede physical and spiritual growth. Rousseau knows full well that this is not the logical place to deal with the question, to which he reverts later to treat it in its proper sequence. In the present passage he uses the "barbarous" custom of swaddling an infant as a concrete portrayal of social duress, in a manner somewhat similar to Locke, who, however, approves of such constraint as protecting rather than increasing the child's weakness.[15] Rousseau is also familiar with an impressive allegory in the *Republic* of a comparable nature. There Socrates, who is as I have said the chief speaker, sees men who are ignorant and require to be educated as prisoners in a den where they are confined from their childhood and have their legs and necks chained so that they are unable to move or turn their heads toward the light. The metaphor in *Emile,* though more familiar and domestic, is quite as effective as the ancient one. It serves to project artistically the wretched state of those who are victims of both ignorance and social oppression. This symbolic interpretation finds support in Rousseau's article on political economy where he deplores the condition of men whose life and liberty are reportedly at the discretion of powerful overlords with the result that they cannot even use their own strength to defend themselves. In the same context he protests that the members of a state should be treated with the same honor as the limbs of a man's body. Here domestic images illustrate political views exactly as in *Emile.*[16]

In the latter he pursues further the allegory of the miniature city in its present state of decline. Reflecting upon the modern family where the mother is replaced by hirelings, he constantly alludes to the larger counterpart of the home in the great society. The child's bands, he observes, are a contrivance of paid nurses whose sole interest is mercenary and who seek only to spare their own pains and live in peace. He says the same of modern laws and rulers whose object is the peace that safeguards property instead of virtue that is the aegis of the soul.[17] He adds that nurses resort to the expedient of bands on the pretext that an unfettered child may in some way injure itself. In a similar vein, in the *Letters from the Mount*, he accuses the despotic Genevan government of fettering the nation under the same pretext. The juxtaposition of texts gives to *Emile* a new breadth of meaning hitherto unsuspected.

The symbolism becomes more conspicuous as the writer proceeds. A true mother, he asserts, does not engage hirelings. She nurses her own children, not merely to provide them with material sustenance, but to give them the tender care to which their hearts cannot fail to respond throughout life. In the article on political economy and in various political fragments, he applies the same idea to the mother city, "the common mother of her citizens," who wins their love by watching over their constitution and keeping it intact. She rules their hearts, he says, not by indulging their whims for material goods that fix men's attachments on inanimate objects, but by devoting herself to their entire happiness, which does not come from bread alone though they may not live without it.[18] Again, scenes of private life are used to express a political philosophy as in *Emile*.

In the novel he carries forward the theme of maternal neglect in phrases with the same political overtones that shed further light upon the allegorical scope of the work. For example, he says that although mothers have the power to transform our world, they never will. Just as he said earlier that there no longer exists nor can ever again exist city or citizens, so now he mournfully prophesies that women will nevermore be mothers and that there can be no more children either in the true sense of the term, with its connotation of filial devotion present too

[48]

in his concept of the citizen. He also bewails the opposite excess that makes no less havoc of human life, maternal overindulgence that forbears to temper the soul by
plunging it metaphorically in the waters of Styx to make
it invulnerable. Sparta, of course, was in his view guilty
of neither of these excesses. Their effect upon the child
is said to be either tyranny or slavery, both of which grow
into inhuman passions to starve and stifle the rich resources
of his nature.

To make matters worse, says the writer, the woeful results of the mother's transgressions are intensified by those
of the father, who, prompted by her example, fails to fulfill his office as true teacher. She alone, we are told, possesses the power to restore him to his duty as educator
and legislator, or the embodiment of law that begets men
and citizens. Rousseau warns of the remorse in store for
the man who fails in his responsibility to train his children
to be both.[19] In fine, he declares that a new order can
emerge only if both parents watch over the child from birth
to manhood. Otherwise, in his belief, lawlessness steals
into all hearts to make its way gradually into conduct
and undermine at last the foundations of our world.

This dismal picture of the home is reportedly drawn
from life and is the antithesis of the myth of the fifth part
which is reminiscent of the *Letter to d'Alembert* and *Julie*.
It is also the antithesis of a delightful evocation of the
homeland in the first few chapters of the *Considerations
upon the Government of Poland,* a work in which Rousseau displays considerable empirical skill in applying the
principles of the *Contract* to a hypothetical constitution
of Poland. This new tableau, by reflecting every trait of the
somber one in reverse, underlines the symbolism of the
home in *Emile* as an image of the city, both being an en-
largement of the soul. In the text of the *Considerations* in
question, he urges that order in human affairs can be secured against brutish passions only if it reigns supreme
within the hearts of men who are their own most vigilant

[49]

watchmen. And it will reign in their hearts most effectively, he says, if it prevails in their homeland and if they find in her a good mother who dispenses the simple joys of life that can be shared with others. The order and harmony he extols would emanate from institutions like those of Moses, the Spartan Lycurgus, and the venerable Numa, whose laws trained men—as does the ideal father in *Emile*—by creating bonds between them and the homeland. Such bonds included traditions and burdensome formalities that were an inextricable part of the fiber and fabric of their lives. Those ancient symbolic usages were sanctified by religious associations, by reciprocal devotion and the charm of exclusiveness that set men apart and instilled in them a pious concern for the land of home as a prime motive in human behavior. That land, says the writer, christianizing the ideal with lyrical feeling, is like a good and true mother who watches over her children at work and at play and never leaves their side from birth to death, nursing them as a mother should and winning their love for herself and each other. This text with its constant but discreet allusions to *Emile* adds fresh justification to the broader interpretation of that book openly suggested by Rousseau himself in the fifth part.

The imagery of parental authority in *Emile* is also Socratic, even though the Greek sage excludes the image of the family. Speaking of his heroes, the citizens of the republic, he refers quite freely throughout the book to their country as their "nurse and mother," as I have said. He refers just as freely to "their father the law."[20] The difference between the two thinkers is that Rousseau is swayed by his emotions and likes to imagine both country and laws as a material possibility—however unlikely—in his precarious dream of idyllic family life.

The parallel of the home or family and the homeland or city is also developed in the second chapter of the *Contract*, "Concerning the First Societies." The author reflects upon the family as the most ancient of all societies

[50]

and also the most natural in the sense that it is bound together by the natural authority of the father, at least during the minority of children. But even within the miniature city here as in *Emile,* he sees a father's sway restricted to the child's "preservation," which for him is that of the human constitution both physical and spiritual, and the advancement of what he called in the first chapter men's inalienable right to a well-ordered life in society. Moreover, he says clearly what he illustrates later in the novel, namely, that at the age of reason children are free, by the very nature of man, to pursue that goal for their own best advantage and that if they remain subject to the father, they do so voluntarily by some solemn though tacit agreement designed for the same purpose. The implication is that the father is morally bound by some such engagement from the first. The author then draws the obvious analogy: "The family is therefore ... the first pattern of political societies: the ruler is the image of the father and the nation is the image of the children, and all born free and equal alienate their freedom only for their own good."[21]

Rousseau's view of paternal authority prevents him from assimilating it to arbitrary monarchic power as many monarchists have done.[22] He opposes them in the same chapter of the *Contract.* His conception of a father's rule here as in *Emile* is closer to Socrates' thought and exemplifies the divine right of "natural and political law," which is that of man's entire constitution and lies at the basis of the philosophy of *Emile* and the *Contract,* supposedly ensuring human freedom. Paternal rule as he sees it has nothing in common with absolutism.

In a half-facetious, half-ironic passage at the end of the chapter he makes light of the pretensions of kings and monarchists. Since he is himself, so he says, a descendant of king Adam and of the emperor Noah, whose sons divided the universe among them, he has as much right as anyone to claim to be the legitimate monarch of the human race. We may infer that every descendant of our common sire is sovereign and king like his father before him. But the writer adds that Adam was king of the world, as Robinson Crusoe was king of his island, as long as he was the only inhabitant. In that case, since he was king not of the race he was later to father but of the "world" where there was no other inhabitant but himself, he could hardly have exercised his kingship beyond the kingdom that lies within. We are supposed to conclude that his descendants, if they would preserve their birthright, must be rulers of self and make as few claims as possible upon others. If they fail to observe this discretion and self-discipline, the results are presumably such as we have seen in the home: disorders that breed tyranny and slavery first in the soul, then in the miniature city, and finally in the larger one.

According to Rousseau tyranny and slavery in public and private life thwart the best aspirations of nature as visualized in the perfect human pattern of us all. This is the theme of the next two chapters of the *Contract,* "Concerning the Law of the Strongest" and "Concerning Slavery."

The first one, like the whole treatise as he said at the outset, is directed against the so-called law of the strongest, the law that might is right, which he calls the "established one." In the second *Discourse* too he contends that it is the law of our society. He now warns that it is no law at all because it frustrates "lawful powers" or faculties that a man is morally bound to respect by the very nature of his being. To discredit it is also the object of *Emile,* where he rebels against violence masquerading as "justice" and "subordination" and denounces laws devised for the sake of the strong. Socrates' purpose as presented in the *Republic* is the same. The entire book grows out of his protest that a truly just man cannot harm others and that justice cannot be defined as obedience to laws made in the interests of the stronger. This thesis carries him through to the end where he shows that such "laws" are nothing but lawlessness, and make desire "lord of the

[52]

soul" so that individual men are robbed and oppressed and the best elements in them are enslaved to the worst.[23]

Rousseau's chapter on slavery complements the other and betrays the same spiritual preoccupations. He begins by saying that all lawful authority (excluding none, not even a father's) is established through agreements or moral engagements. In that case no such authority can be founded upon slavery—the basis of the anti-society in the second *Discourse*—since a man of sound mind could hardly consent to renounce everything in exchange for nothing and live in slavery that divests him even of the moral rights and duties belonging to humanity. A state of slavery is incompatible with his nature that endows him with the freedom of will necessary to morality, thereby enabling him to follow his preferences and judgments, make moral decisions, and assume responsibility for his acts. Rousseau denies that slavery can be lawfully established by war as his adversaries said.[24] For him a state of war cannot exist among persons either in a hypothetical primitive condition where there is supposedly no reason for enmity or in a true social and moral order where law reigns. War, says he, can exist only among "states" or ideological entities. And in time of war a "just prince" does not rob "individuals" of physical existence or moral life, which depends upon freedom, unless they are caught, arms in hand, intent on robbing others of the same rights. Again he has taken leave of our familiar world where, in his opinion, men live in a perpetual state of war. His thought is akin to that of Socrates, for whom external "warfare" is a symbol of inner conflict. For the Greek sage the real problem is that man is at war with himself, the selfish desires of individuals within us being at strife with spirit and reason called the "guardian" and "just prince" of the soul. All faculties are personified. And his treatment of "individuals" is similar to that prescribed in the *Contract*. He distinguishes between lawful and lawless ones. The former, limited to necessary desires, must be not enslaved or plundered but tamed by reason, and only the latter may be constrained by force and dealt with as "barbarians." Rousseau's concept of order is similar to the Socratic one and proceeds, like the master's, from some solemn commitment that can motivate men to cultivate their superior faculties and control the others, bringing all into a single harmony through the most attentive self-direction. The commitment can be no different from the one to which the father is morally bound in *Emile* as educator of "men and citizens."

A COVENANT OF FRIENDSHIP

Such an engagement is, in the author's belief, the only hope for those who would find happiness amid the vicissitudes of life as it is. He proposes the same solution in both *Emile* and the *Contract*.

The exposition of the novel leads very gradually to that solution. He finally introduces the characters, a governor and his disciple. They are not father and son in the biological sense in spite of those impassioned words about the vocation of a father as the child's true teacher. The governor is an ideal creation whose person the author assumes, calling himself Jean-Jacques. In this office he rises above himself, like one of the Socratic kings come to life at last. Possessed of their sublime virtues, he appears as the reason that is friendly to human nature and ministers to its needs. Like the same heroes who forgo all gold and silver for the sake of the diviner metal within, he takes no fee in return for his service. In this respect he also resembles the writer's two masters. Socrates despised contemporary philosophers for exchanging their wares for money, and the evangelical Good Shepherd would not be confused with the hireling. Yet the Rousseauist governor later seems well enough endowed with this world's goods. Small wonder if we are disposed to believe, as we are informed, that he is "more than a man."

[54]

We are further told that not only must he be formed especially for the disciple but so must the whole setting of the story. Thus the author combines the action of the milieu with that of reason to foster and serve human nature. In the sphere of "domestic" education, he is characteristically as preoccupied with the power of environment as Socrates is. The idea that society can make or mar the individual, lead him astray or redeem him, always appears in his work as a Socratic version of eighteenth-century determinism. It is presumably to save men from the fatal influence of contemporary life that Jean-Jacques descends from the famous republic, or Sparta or Rome or the new Geneva, to bring them a safe rule of life and restore them to themselves. But he assumes his task as reluctantly as the Socratic kings,[25] for, like them and unlike the monarchs of this world, he is aware that kingship is a form of ministry to others.

His mission is defined in terms that suggest the conditions of success. He will "conduct" a creature of the writer's fancy from birth to manhood when, at the end of the book, "the law" sets the hero free. The child, who remains anonymous in the first version until the third part, is now in the definitive version called Emile or Aemilius, a name hardly conferred upon him at random, for Rousseau was convinced with Plato that the name of a thing expresses its nature and may not be arbitrarily chosen. In this case it casts light upon the governor's intentions. "Emile" means "industrious," but for the author it has other associations too. He elsewhere conveys his veneration for the "tomb of Cato and the ashes of Aemilius," the latter being identified as the son of the wise legislator of Rome, Numa Pompilius, from whom the family of the Aemilians, illustrious Roman patriots, was descended. Emile is to be one of them. The governor's purpose is, we are told, best assured if he is as close as possible in age to his pupil. Moreover, the latter must be his only one and is yet to be born when the book opens. This fact assures Jean-Jacques of making a fresh start, to

[55]

build life anew and avoid the pitfalls of the preface in accordance with the teachings of Rousseau's masters. The Greek sage erases the past and begins with a clean surface by taking only those of ten years of age or younger and training them in the habits and laws of his city.[26] His professed disciple takes even less risk by seeing that Emile is trained from birth in the habits and laws of the Rousseauist order of things.

In fact, Jean-Jacques, like the author's masters, aims, we are told, to teach nothing but the duties of man, and these include those of the citizen as he sees them, even in the midst of a chaotic world. This aim is closely allied to that of Socrates, who vows, according to the Platonic dialogue, to "leave every other kind of knowledge and seek and follow one thing only . . . to learn and discern between good and evil." The Greek thinker ponders the effect of all worldly goods and natural and acquired gifts upon the soul, and selects or excludes them according to their bearing upon justice and virtue. Passages of that kind are akin to Rousseau's text. So are similar ones from the Sermon on the Mount where the speaker urges his listeners thus: "Seek ye first the kingdom of God, and his righteousness; and all these things shall be added unto you." The latter phrase explains why, in spite of Rousseau's exclusive preoccupation with moral rectitude, Emile is in the end culturally enriched beyond the average, although that is not the present theme.[27] Since Jean-Jacques is, so to speak, the leader of his spirit, he is called his "governor," and as such he conducts him without instructing him, in accordance with Socratic principles. The term *governor* is the one applied to Socrates' noblest heroes, called philosopher-kings in the *Republic* because they embody man's highest faculties.[28] This fact adds weight to the suspicion that the Rousseauist ruler is one of them. The term has the added literary advantage of carrying forward the image of the pilot. This is the helmsman (*gouverneur*) who manages the helm (*gouvernail*) and steers the vessel of the soul on

[56]

its course toward wisdom and happiness. Again he calls to mind the true steersman in Socrates' allegory of the ship of the soul in the guise of the ship of state, who is guided by "the stars" and has the same goal as he has.

The presentation of Emile follows that of the governor. He is natural, abstract man of whom we spoke before, existing within Jean-Jacques, the author himself, and supposedly in all of us. He is said to possess a "common mind" and to be a very ordinary human being, at least at first, though not as he grows older and his differing education takes effect. Nevertheless, his nature is the well-favored, felicitous nature of man, instinct with all the infinite possibilities of growth glimpsed earlier.[29] The habitation chosen for the child contributes to the symbolism of the figure. This inhabitant of the earth lives in a temperate zone, preferably in France, which Rousseau twice called "the native land of the human race."[30] Less understandable perhaps than the choice of an abode is the information that Emile is rich and highborn. But of course he is a king, a descendant of king Adam and, as such, shares in the sovereignty and kingship of the soul, though perhaps not in the other sovereignty that rightfully belongs to the common man, according to the author's persuasions.[31] If "man is king of the earth," as he is later called, he has been divested of that kingship. He has also been defrauded of his inheritance of which he nevertheless retains moral possession in the book, even though that may not save him from starvation. If he also has an inheritance in the land of his fathers, as the author says of Emile, it would conceivably be that land itself to which, however, he may not lay claim. If we interpret the hero's endowments otherwise, Rousseau seems determined to bestow upon him all the privileges that both his masters deemed perilous for the conduct of human life. In that case he is resolved to make the exercise of spiritual kingship as difficult as possible. For such is the destiny to which Rousseauist man is called, as we have already seen.

[57]

At this juncture the nature of the curious society of characters is disclosed. Emile is called an "orphan" to indicate his rather detached relations to his parents according to the flesh, for we soon discover that they are alive.[32] Whether or not he is an orphan in the literal sense is immaterial because he must obey only Jean-Jacques, who is gravely invested with all the rights and duties of the sire and his spouse. We are informed that this is the governor's only "condition." But for a man with Rousseau's ideas on slavery, it necessarily implies volition. This implication is confirmed by the "essential clause" of their association specifying that they must never be separated except with their own consent. Obedience and consent are correlatives. But in the author's conception Jean-Jacques and Emile regard themselves as so indivisible as to consider their happiness in life together as an object common to them both, providing them with a powerful motive for mutual affection and fidelity. The "essential clause" is therefore the one and only "clause" of the "treaty" that unites them in lifelong friendship.

The "treaty," as it is specifically termed, gives rise to a number of problems. First, what is the real clue to the riddle of Emile's orphanhood? Why is Jean-Jacques not his father in every sense rather than only spiritually as minister of the law? The truth is that the author means to accentuate artificial or conventional, social or moral rather than "natural" ties between them, and to portray in a mythical manner his idea of lawful authority, which originates in a spiritual commitment and not in nature even if it fulfills nature's loftiest designs on man's behalf. Some recent critics have seen this, but then they explain that the governor is thereby freer than the father would be.[33] But this hardly accords with Rousseau's view of paternal authority. For him that authority, if it is "lawful," is no different from any other. From his standpoint Jean-Jacques might well have been the natural father and still served the author's purpose. But this would have caused ambi-

[58]

guity, for many thinkers of the time, failing to understand the true nature of paternal authority, regarded it as the origin and image of monarchic absolutism, as we saw above. Consequently he decided in favor of a conventional relationship. However, Emile, like Socrates' citizens, comes to see himself as bearing a filial kinship to the Rousseauist city and its laws visible in the principles and powers under whose parental authority he is brought up. That is why he and his governor often address one another as "father" and "son."[34] As for the orphan's "parents," they are probably the "semblance of order" and "false laws" of his birthplace, in accordance with the same Socratic image.

The "treaty" or "contract" upon which the governor's authority is based is that upon which the mythical temple of *Emile*, like any other structure, is to be built. This covenant takes the form of friendship that becomes an important leitmotiv in the book to symbolize the contractual quality of the union of the two characters.[35] Indeed, their friendship is called "the most sacred of contracts" and is the foundation of the child's religious faith and the source of all grace in his life.[36] The contract of friendship is also the one that unites Socrates' citizens, for whom "friends have all things in common" and whom he binds together under the guardian and ruler by giving the "wealth or power or persons of the one to the others" to create a "wise order" in "the greatest of states," however small.[37] The Rousseauist covenant of friendship is the same, although the two have never before been compared. It may also be likened to that of the chosen people in the Old Testament. For example, Abraham, we are told, became God's friend by favor of a "covenant of promise" which is the law. The same covenant unites the members of the "mystical body" of Christ or society of the church.[38] The engagement upon which Rousseau's whole novel is based is not unlike the sacred promises of Socratic and Judeo-Christian tradition and envisages an analogous simple, patriarchal, or evangelical life, comparable to that of his imaginary city.

The comparison is far from inappropriate. There is a certain mysticism or religiosity in the Rousseauist or Aemilian covenant. Jean-Jacques does not contract with Emile as another person, or with Emile's "parents" as some of us have supposed in the past.[39] There is no evidence at all to that effect. He enters the agreement at the moment of his ward's birth. This is a figurative or literary way of saying that the child is literally born of the covenant and is tacitly committed by his very nature to the law of reason that endows him with moral life and is indeed the Socratic father that begets him. Likewise the author in the person of the governor is morally born of the same vow made years before on the way to Vincennes and effective at Montmorency. By this vow he means to break away from a disordered past. The self that is "more than a man," or reasonable will, enters a bond of friendship and agrees to minister to the "Emile" or ideal human prototype within himself and presumably within us all.[40] The fact that, as we were told, the two must be as close in age as is feasible means that this must occur as early as possible. Rousseau contracts with himself under two different forms that appeal to the imagination so that the characters are essentially though not artistically one. At the same time he identifies himself with all mankind and presents the story of his own supposed redemption as an ideal story of the race, since in his eyes the friendship of reason for human nature is the society into which we all are born without exception. Thus he proposes to provide for that self-culture which is the one truly effective force in the cultivation of the species, pledging his faith to a humanistic ideal whose obligations are mythically illustrated and fulfilled in Emile's education. In doing so, he enters into a spiritual communion with what he considers to be the best leaders of the human conscience, among whom he chose Socrates and Christ to be his own. At the

[60]

same time he intends to "hand down to posterity a Rousseauist way of life," as Socrates would phrase it;[41] for in following the teaching of his masters, he fully appropriates it to himself.

At the end of *Emile*, Jean-Jacques describes his pledge to the hero: "My young friend, when at your birth I took you in my arms and called upon the Supreme Being to bear witness to the engagement that I dared to contract, and vowed to devote my life to your happiness, did I myself know what engagement I was assuming? No: I only knew that in rendering you happy, I was ensuring my own felicity. By making this useful inquiry for your sake, I made it common to us both."[42] The results of the said inquiry are incorporated not merely into a summary of the *Contract*, which this very passage serves to introduce, but especially into the whole of *Emile* itself, as the wording clearly implies.

In fact, Jean-Jacques' oath in *Emile* is that of the *Social Contract*, with which it has previously been compared but never identified.[43] The purpose of the pledge is stated in the fifth chapter of the *Contract*, entitled "That It Is Always Necessary to Go Back to a First [or fundamental] Covenant." There the author says that a true association of men is born of a common unifying interest to which they adhere freely by an act of total, unanimous commitment.[44] This is exemplified by Emile's governor, who voluntarily takes as the law of his life what he believes to be the interests of human nature, which he regards as identical with his own. He thereby works diligently to win the conscious consent of Emile until the disciple enters the covenant as freely as himself and the two appear as a perfectly integrated whole. With the same idea in mind Socrates defines his object as the common happiness, before formulating the terms of the covenant of friendship.[45]

The covenant is the theme of the sixth chapter of the *Contract*, "Concerning the Social Pact." Rousseau begins by observing once again that men who live according to instinct find themselves in a state of warfare and that this "primitive state can no longer last," for the race would perish if it did not change its ways. Many political theorists see in his words an evocation of some chaotic prehistoric past. They protest that a contract can be effected only in civil society and that to use it as an explanation of society is to bring forward the effect as an explanation of its cause. This is, of course, true. In spite of his imagery, the author is not speaking of the past, and that is why he uses the present tense. He is referring to what he regards as the primitive ways of present-day anti-society and the prevailing state of civil war in which men actually live, and suggests a mode of deliverance. This interpretation emerges clearly in the light of literary symbols and a collation with *Emile,* which contrasts external anarchy with what is meant to be the inner harmony of a well-ordered life.

According to the chapter on the pact, men can "preserve themselves" or ensure the integrity of the human constitution by uniting together in peace and friendship and combining their strength to protect the person and property of everyone; but in so doing, each associate must "obey only himself" and remain as free as before. This latter stipulation poses a problem. It implies that there is a hierarchy within the self—that there is a self made to rule and another made to obey, and that their reciprocal action ensures freedom and must not be impeded by the proposed union of powers. The solution advocated by Rousseau is the social contract. Before defining its clauses, he says that they have "perhaps" never been enunciated, though of course they have, by Socrates and biblical writers. Nevertheless, in actuality they have in his view been replaced by the spurious historical contract of slavery regarded in the *Discourses* as the origin of existing political aggregations. If the lawful one exists, we see no trace of it. It is as much a myth as Socrates' "royal lie" designed to teach men that their country is their mother and their nurse, and that they are all brothers.

[62]

This famous ancient lie or "audacious fiction"—to which I alluded in discussing the symbolism of the family—immediately leads the sage to define his object as the common happiness and to formulate the covenant, and is the first of three "waves" that he must overcome to found his city. The author of the *Contract,* like that of *Emile,* having approached the pact in the manner of his master, formulates it after the same example. It demands, he says, the total commitment of every "associate" with all his rights, his person, and his power to the supreme direction of the sovereign will in an august communion of the just wherein each one consecrates himself to all as an indivisible part of the whole. The tempting idea that this is a doctrine of "extreme collectivism"[46] simply vanishes in a psychological interpretation of the book, which its affinity with the novel and the *Republic* requires. It is the doctrine of humanism whereby a man obeys only his own reasonable will or human self instead of his senses and passions or those of other people. The act of association or Socratic friendship in the *Contract,* like the one in *Emile,* gives birth, says the writer, to a "moral, collective [or composite] body" and endows it with "unity, a sense of self, a life and a will of its own." The complex social person, visible in *Emile* in the friendhip of its heroes, is here called a "city" or "republic" and "state" or "sovereign power." According to Rousseau, the moral person, or active thinking being, can alone make men into "citizens" and restore them to their rightful "sovereignty," provided they "subject" themselves to its laws. Thus in the novel Jean-Jacques as citizen of this mythical society shares in its supreme power to whose will he subjects his relationship with Emile in order to play the role of a Socratic king and to secure man's original constitution by serving the true aspirations of nature[47] with respect to the human person as well as property.

The seventh chapter of the *Contract,* "Concerning Sovereignty," contains more abstract reflections that also find

[63]

an outward equivalent in the society of friends in *Emile*. The author of the chapter shows that the act of association or friendship is a reciprocal pledge of the public or moral person with private individuals who do not contract with one another but with themselves, as members of the sovereign toward individuals, and as subjects toward the sovereign. If the sovereign is the enlightened will serving nature's ends, like the Socratic guardian and ruler, then individuals would correspond to individualist desires as they do in the *Republic*. This confirms again the spirituality of Jean-Jacques' engagement in the novel whereby the various elements within him are integrated under the rule of the best. The idea is entirely Socratic.

The author of the *Contract* says further that, although the covenant, including deliberation resulting therefrom, is binding upon individuals in their relations to the sovereign, it cannot bind the latter to himself and could therefore—at least theoretically—be dissolved by him. Consequently, in the novel Jean-Jacques, entering the friendship that unites him with Emile, acknowledges the freedom to dissolve it and thereby makes his act of commitment a truly moral one. But the possibility of dissolution is remote since he has totally identified his own happiness with Emile's, and pursues it as the object of the bond of friendship that he uses to vindicate the purposes of human nature as already defined. As long as he participates in sovereignty, he cannot do otherwise, according to the doctrine of the chapter of the *Contract* under discussion. There we are told that since members of the moral body cannot be hurt without injury to the whole, the sovereign who by definition seeks the latter's advantage can have no interest contrary to theirs. Consequently he need give no guarantee of his engagements toward "subjects." It is said to be impossible that a body would want to harm its own members. We may be tempted to question the logic here[48] and imagine that the sovereign will may indeed choose to harm itself, since in the next part of the book we are told that "if it pleases a nation to hurt itself, who has the right to prevent it?" But in

[64]

fact, there is no contradiction between the two texts since a nation's "pleasure" is not the sovereign will but the slavish caprice of individuals who stray from the pledge to Socratic "divine wisdom" in man and jeopardize the welfare of the entire moral person and human creature. In the novel such caprice is represented as alien to the idealized Jean-Jacques, who remains true to his role as minister or servant of the enlightened will of the society of friends.

The conclusion of the chapter in the *Contract* is consistent with his demand for obedience in the novel, a demand that is logical enough if indeed, in the words of Socrates, "the pilot must steer whether other people like it or not." The writer declares that since the "private wills" of "individuals"—vagrant desires for gain or power—may conflict with a man's own will as member of a moral person, whoever refuses to obey the latter will be "forced to be free." This applies, of course, only to those who choose to honor the humanistic commitment. Thus Emile is constrained, by the persuasive power of friendship that favors his happiness, to obey the reasonable will, born of the promise as he, by his nature and destiny, also is. By learning to obey, he learns to reign in the future kingdom within.[49] In both texts Rousseau teaches not the divine right of the people, as one might think, but the divine right of man, for in theory at least he is a genuine humanist.

The covenant of friendship in *Emile* presupposes, says Jean-Jacques, a "robust constitution." Since he enters the engagement before the disciple's birth, the constitution must be that of man, the potential powers of nature that are activated and fostered by the moral force of friendship, as the strength of the city made in man's image is generated and intensified by a union of men. The stipulation of strength leads to a violent diatribe, comparable with others in the *Discourses,* against the art of medicine as practiced in contemporary society by charlatanical physicians. The outburst is inspired as critics are agreed, by Socrates in the *Republic*. The point we have hitherto over-

[65]

looked, however, is that Rousseau's text implies the same
distinction between the good and bad physician as the ancient one, and is quite as symbolic as the other where the
two are an image of the true and false statesman.[50] Physicians, warns Jean-Jacques, who doctor disease, and are
therefore imposters, make a man "useless to himself and
to others," since excessive care of the body makes its
demands tyrannical, and inimical to the cultivation of the
soul. Like the Greek sage he would avoid doctors who allegedly turn men into cowards and remove them from society and their duties. He will permit no such people—
or philosophers or priests either—"to spoil his work,"
says he, adding that the quest for truth is as fatal as the
art of medicine. A man who heeds these warnings will, he
affirms, "live more for himself and for others," a familiar phrase used by Socrates to define his object in the
Republic, as I have observed. The luminous language of
this famous passage of *Emile* betrays the underlying symbolism of the book. The protest against physicians, philosophers, and priests "meddling in his work" shows that
Jean-Jacques, like both the author's masters, represents
all three in another, "truer" form, and means to minister
not to disease but to health of body and soul in the manner
of the Socratic physician or statesman. His disciple will
not go abroad for his law or physic, to cite the sage whose
imagery Rousseau adopts not only here but in the *Contract* too. In his opinion the true statesman is like a true
physician and uses the most fundamental ordinance of all,
that of the covenant, to preserve the human constitution,
physical and spiritual, implanted in man at his birth and to
prevent disorders from occurring to overthrow the delicate
balance of powers. His thought is closely akin to that of
Socrates in a passage following the oft-quoted diatribe
and accentuating its symbolic value.[51] The sage declares
that it is only charlatans who go about making and mend-
ing peoples' laws and lives, doctoring and complicating
disorders; whereas the true physician and statesman makes

[66]

men sound in body and mind through discipline and austerity of life, and guards against excesses that are the root of all evil in soul or city. In *Emile* Jean-Jacques, like the Greek master, undertakes to anticipate maladies of body and soul and ensure the robust constitution of faculties that is his primary concern.

With this in mind he transports the child to a country retreat at Montmorency village that was the author's own refuge from the world and whose simplicity and rusticity of character are comparable to those of his ideal city. Emile and his governor live there for a dozen years or more. Indeed, the setting of the whole work is rural life, except for the second half of the third part and the end of the fourth. The two friends reside in the cottage of a nurse who is intended to typify the blessings of that life still possible today. She is described as healthy in body and heart, a countrywoman of country-grown habits. At her side the "tender plant" springs up in a not unfavorable soil. True, we are still in actual society; but its flaws are less visible and more readily concealed by the governor, who constantly provides against the spectacle of coarseness and vulgarity.

The choice of a rustic scene represents a compromise for Rousseau, who is unwilling to withdraw the child altogether from our familiar world, as many of us in the past have thought that he did.[52] To paraphrase his preface, the good he proposes is here allied, not with existing evil, but with whatever traces of beauty and goodness he is able to discover in the world about him. His reverence for the country and naïve faith in its felicitous moral effects are, of course, characteristic of the modern spirit. These qualities, which also link him with the pastoral poets of antiquity, distinguish him from his Greek master. Socrates had no illusions at all about the country. On the contrary, he sends all persons over ten years of age into that uncivilized place which matches their fierce natures, and then educates the remainder in his city. Jean-Jacques takes

[67]

the opposite course with Emile, for whom the country is the setting of an image of the Rousseauist city visible in the society of the hero and his governor.

In that simple bucolic scene the hero's life unfolds, much as the author's spiritual life unfolded in the same place, or so he says. In the book the governor, who has already professed to teach only the duties of man and citizen and nothing else, is solicitous for both physical strength and personal cleanliness, for he sees a moral and spiritual advantage in bodily health. Accordingly Rousseau protests once more, though in a less sweeping symbol, against swaddling clothes that trammel both body and soul. He would allow the organs and faculties to expand to the fullness of their powers as he enacted in the beginning, in order that nature's highest purposes may be fulfilled in the disposition of human and social life.

Broaching the story of Emile's evolution, he again visualizes the spiritual ascent that is the subject of the book as it is that of the *Contract*, and he does so in words that are echoed at this point in the latter. His object in the two cases is to describe the advantages of the covenant, and both texts are evocative of Socratic and Judeo-Christian tradition.

In *Emile* he proceeds from the aforementioned starting point, the monstrous image of unintegrated man, in order to trace in his own experience and allegorically in the hero's the natural genesis of humanity gradually emerging from a "primitive state of ignorance and stupidity" toward a future full of unlimited possibilities for the liberation and expansion of human powers. In the *Contract* he contemplates the same spiritual ascent at the beginning of the penultimate chapter of the first part, "Concerning the Civil State." He will show, he says, how a "stupid and ignorant animal" may be transformed into an intelligent being, a man, and he uses the language of the novel to describe the transition from instinct to morality and justice. He imagines how the impulses and appetites of an

[68]

unintegrated creature are gradually replaced by the voice of rights and duties through the counsel of reason guiding the inclinations, with the result that human faculties are exercised and developed, ideas are expanded, and feelings ennobled.[53] This is also the theme of the *Republic* where Socrates' heroes are "compelled" to emerge from darkness and imprisonment (that is, ignorance and slavery) in an underground den, "reluctantly dragged up a steep and rugged ascent," and "forced into the presence of the sun himself" in "the upper world." The same theme is also biblical, suggestive of the chosen people led from the "house of bondage" toward the promised land under the guidance of great lawgivers and educators like Moses and Christ, whom Rousseau admired as such.

The idea that integration into a perfect moral and social framework can alone save the human constitution is entirely in accordance with the spirit of Rousseau. It is to be found even in the second *Discourse,* which contains the famous but enigmatic picture of the serene savage. In that work the life of hypothetical natural man in an indigenous state is called simply "amoral" and "not unhappy." This is in conformity with the Socratic idea that moral powers, pictured in the *Republic* as "soldiers" and "rulers," are called into action only to purge an unhealthy state, but not at the origins of society. Rousseau has the same idea in the *Discourse.* It must be admitted, of course, that in that work man's "amoral" and "not unhappy" condition appears idyllic by comparison with the author's tableau of modern anti-social and uncivil life wherein people are perpetually embroiled in a state of civil war. But in the dedication of that work as in *Emile* and the *Contract,* we are supposed to see how vastly superior to both is the life of natural man in the Rousseauist order of wisdom and happiness.

In the last two chapters of this part of the *Contract,* where the benefits of the covenant are more specifically set forth, the author acknowledges the difficulties of the projected ascent. In the penultimate one, which I broached above, he warns that progress from the prevailing instinctive state to his ideal order that pretends to preserve intact the spirit of natural man in society is possible only if the two advantages implied in the covenant itself are in fact assured. They are freedom and property, and are intended to safeguard physical and moral life, which is the whole purpose of the pact. He explains that natural freedom, which is necessarily limited by an individual's strength, must give place to civil liberty exercised under the direction of the sovereign will. He adds that the unlimited right to all a man covets and can get by force and first occupancy must be replaced by the ownership of what a man really possesses. The question of liberty is handled in this chapter, and property in the next.

In discussing the value of civil liberty, he observes that the civil state also affords moral freedom and that this alone makes one really "master of himself," a phrase that occurs in the same context of *Emile,* as we shall see in a moment. Moral freedom, he says, is that of one "who obeys the law he has prescribed for himself," meaning one in whom desire obeys the enlightened will. He calls this the "philosophical" or, as we say, psychological meaning of the word. But it is really a definition of civil freedom in his own city, where a man obeys only himself. In other words, the difference between civil and moral liberty is that the former would exist in the external world in an imaginary and impossible ideal order, whereas the latter would obtain exclusively in a just soul or communion of just souls and would be the only course open to men in our chaotic society. And so he says that moral freedom is not his subject in the *Contract,* where the city is figuratively or allegorically exteriorized. But in the same text he implies without any irony whatsoever that such freedom may compensate less fortunate men than the freemen of his city for the loss of both natural and civil liberty too, since in actuality, as he sees it, both forms of freedom are replaced by civil servitude. His real preoccupation is the moral or spiritual liberation of all potential faculties that enables men to perform their natural functions, overcome external obstacles, and reach the "rational idea of perfection and happiness" proposed at the outset.

In accordance with these principles, the training of Emile's will begins at birth with sensorial education. The experience he undergoes is reminiscent of that of Socrates' prisoners as they first appear in the lowest sphere of the underground den. The Rousseauist governor regulates the child's sensations of pleasure and pain with a view to preventing him from being fettered by habit or enslaved to new and false needs. He thereby follows the recommendations of the author's projected work on *Sensitive Morality,* described in the ninth book of the *Confessions.* He applies these rules to teach Emile to reign as "master of himself" and "to do his will as soon as he has one," fostering in his soul vague notions of the freedom and equality of the Aemilian city. Numerous and varied sense impressions of objects and animals too are used to make him intrepid in the presence of the unknown. The same sensations presented in a suitable, logical order also serve to cultivate his perceptive powers. For the early education of the senses anticipates, however remotely, not only the action of will but the exercise of reason too, long before either one has begun to wake from the drowsy sleep of childhood.

This education of the receptive and perceptive powers is accompanied by an awakening of the child's capacities for expression that grow in proportion as his needs increase. The delicate question of need brings us to the second advantage of the covenant without which the spiritual ascent of both books would be threatened. This is the one that safeguards physical life, substituting property, regulated by the sovereign will, for the lawlessness of desire. Property is the theme of the last chapter of the first part of the *Contract,* which can be best understood if it is read in the context of *Emile.*

[71]

The chapter on property is entitled "Concerning the Real Domain [or Property]," as opposed to the personal domain of freedom. It has shocked many of us. The same writer who fiercely vilifies private property in the second *Discourse* here gravely discusses it as a right, protected by the sovereignty. However, in all fairness we must admit that in the *Discourse* of 1754 he is attacking not the institution itself but what he considers to be a scandalous abuse of it. On the other hand, in the *Contract* he presents it in a fair and noble form, such as might exist in a perfect world of perfect beings or in the kingdom within some exalted spirit of well-ordered life. But even if we failed to understand the mythical character of his city, we should hardly be justified in concluding that he subjects property rights to the sovereign or enlightened will for the purpose of favoring a tyrannical form of collectivism. The very idea is contrary to the spirit of Rousseau and the *Contract*.

The property rights he defends are not, as some of us might think, based upon the "right" of first occupant authorized by work and cultivation.[54] They are based upon the needs of life. Indeed, he shows the fallacy of the so-called right defined above when he says that the sovereign, in relation to other states, has no other claim over the territory it occupies except that of the first occupant. He intimates that this is no claim at all. He explains that it becomes one only through the establishment of property in its natural form based primarily upon need, a fundamental condition illustrated in *Emile* from the first and supplemented later by other conditions, especially work. A key passage in the *Contract* reads: "Every man has a natural right to what is necessary to him." Contrary to what we have long believed, property is indeed for Rousseau a natural right if the indispensable qualification is met. He adds that the positive act or law that makes a man the proprietor of such goods as he needs to live excludes him from all the rest. This, he says, is why the right of first occupant is honored in *civilized* society. The reason is that in such an

[72]

ideal society it is restricted to need. He adds: "The right of first occupant cannot be extended beyond need and work." In his view the claims of labor without need do not suffice. As he says in the second *Discourse,* why should a man appropriate the fruits of his efforts if he exceeds his needs at the expense of other people's? In that case the human race goes wanting, and men like Emile in the end are robbed of a dwelling place on earth and the blessings of the soil that nature bestows upon all. In his own city, on the other hand, property, based upon a natural right to the necessities of life, is subordinate to the sovereign will, which ensures the fidelity of subjects to their promises by confirming that right as lawful. To make his meaning doubly clear, he adds that, if men are in the process of forming a union (as in the case of the Aemilian city or that of the *Contract*), then they have a right to occupy only the amount of land sufficient to provide for the needs of all. He explains that property in this form replaces natural inequality of strength and intelligence by moral and lawful equality. But he admits in a footnote that the cities of the earth are otherwise. His meaning is further accentuated when he concludes by saying that the social state is advantageous to men only as long as all of them have something and no one has too much.[55] Thus if property provides all men with the necessities of life, he regards it as a lawful institution endorsed by the enlightened will. So does Socrates, whose heroes are confined to need from the first and whose "man of understanding" finally regulates his own property to provide against disorder in the city within him, such as might arise either from superfluity or from want.[56] But no nation will ever do likewise, and Rousseau knows it. His city is an allegorical one meant as a pattern of a harmonious life. Consequently in the *Contract* there is no question at all of distributive action on the part of an autocratic state, as one might imagine, but only of self-control in a few rare souls. In fine, in the matter of property he holds out no hope for the poor

[73]

and the oppressed, as he does in the case of liberty. Moral freedom is possible even under a despotism. So is moral equality, which does not, however, prevent a man from starving to death. To say this is to anticipate the conclusion of Emile where the hero, faced with a choice between freedom of spirit and the needs for which our society allegedly makes no provision, chooses liberty as the better part and is ready to die for it if he must.

The principles of the *Contract* providing for freedom and the necessities of life, or Rousseauist property, are those of Emile's governor in responding to the child's needs. The latter are expressed by cries and gestures, or tears if needs go unfulfilled. The author sees tears rather than cries of joy as "the first link in the long chain" of the social order since it is to the former that men respond most readily through pity or sympathy. If that order corresponds to the one illustrated in the relations of governor and child in the book, then the "chain" is regarded as a bond of friendship. Emile is gradually being enmeshed in it and prepared for the author's idea of a happily constituted life that later takes shape as a shrine of the soul or fortress of the city. That life is foreshadowed here. When the infant feels some need and pleads for help, the governor satisfies the need if possible; but if not, he forbears to brutalize the child and offend its inborn sense of justice or even to act at all, since in his opinion such is the way of nature and of order. Moreover, in providing for needs, he never exceeds the bounds of physical necessity or yields to unreasonable desires that would violate the same concept of order even before his ward is aware that it exists. He limits himself further by ministering only to needs with which the child cannot cope alone. The latter is left free to do so, in order that his physical strength may be as far as is possible the extent of his desires, and his claims upon others reduced to a minimum. These rules are elementary applications of what is meant by liberty and equality in the two chapters of the *Contract* just discussed.

The governor adheres dispassionately to them even when Emile develops facility of speech. Far from being solicitous, he attends only to words perfectly articulated and corresponding to the restricted realities of a young life. In doing so, he continues to confine his action to necessity that gave birth to the Aemilian city and that of the *Contract*. It is likewise the mother of Socrates' "invention," as the great sage himself says.

The reader is by now aware of the value of the *Republic* for an understanding of the interrelationship of Rousseau's two books. The first part of both contains elements scattered throughout the great classic from the beginning almost to the end. The author's description of the ideal city in the opening pages of *Emile* and his tribute to the Platonic dialogue were priceless clues. But even more revealing was the imagery: the image of the educator as husbandman and pilot come to the aid of men hampered in their growth and frustrated by currents contrary to their nature; and the image of the bands from which he frees them to place them under the parental care of their mother who is the city and their father who is the law. For like Socrates, Rousseau in both books is stirred to action by "false" laws, made in the interests of the stronger and creating tyranny and slavery, and is thereby motivated to go in search of the true law of justice. Like the master he finds it in the covenant of friendship that frees its participants from charlatanical statesmen, portrayed as sham physicians and philosophers, and that allows men to live for themselves and for others as well. And again like the sage he envisages a spiritual ascent made possible by that law which bids a man obey his highest faculties and confine the desires to bare necessities.

We are now prepared to move upward to the second part of the temple foundation or understructure of the city. As

[75]

Socrates' prisoners rise from the lowest to the highest of four spheres of human knowledge, so do the friends of the Aemilian city or freemen of the *Contract*. And just as *Emile* and its appendix are linked and interlocked in the first phase, so they are in the second and its sequels. Both works are expressive of the same idealism in personal or social life. This parallelism is Rousseau's most powerful and eloquent plea against the alleged actual cleavage between man's inner disposition of himself and the conduct of his affairs in social and civil life. The same parallelism also brings out the distinguishing mark of *Emile* where an intellectual formula is translated into mythical terms through attractive situations and characters that make a powerful appeal to the mind through the medium of the imagination.

1. Although Rousseau calls the divisions of *Emile* and the *Contrat social* "books," I have found it easier to refer to them as "parts" in order to avoid ambiguity in my own text. Moreover, since the collation follows the order of Rousseau's text, page references to the two works are given only if passages are cited out of context.

2. "Lettres de la montagne," *O.C.*, 3:783. Cf. "Confessions," *O.C.*, 1:409. For the dedication to Geneva see "Lettres de la montagne," loc. cit., p. 809.

3. "Emile," *O.C.*, pp. 245-46, 331 ff., 643. Cf. Fénelon, *Les Aventures de Télémaque* (Liège: Grandmont-Donders, 1865), p. 47. Ulysses, speaking of his son, says: "Qu'il soit comme un jeune arbrisseau encore tendre, qu'on plie pour le redresser." Cf. *The Republic* 6. 491-92. Cf. Matt. 13:3 ff.; Luke 6:43-44. The opening sentence of *Emile* quoted above reads: "Tout est bien, sortant des mains de l'auteur des choses: tout dégénère entre les mains de l'homme."

4. *The Republic* 3. 414; 5. 470; 8. 549. Cf. Rousseau's "Discours sur l'économie politique," *O.C.*, 3:258; the fragment "De la patrie," ibid., p. 534 and 536, where he calls the motherland "a tender mother"; and "Considérations," ibid., p. 962.

5. Rousseau alludes to it in "Lettres morales," *O.C.*, *4:1096*.

6. *The Republic* 6. 496-97.

7. Yet in his opinion a man must be a citizen: "Emile," pp. 262, 469, 655, 667, 669, and throughout the fifth part. For the "passing greeting," mentioned above, see J.S. Spink in *O.C.*, 4:1xxxiii.

8. *C.C.*, 5:241-42, letter to Tronchin, 26 November 1758 (reply to Tronchin's letter of 13 November, ibid., pp. 219-21). Cf. *O.C.*, 4:xlii-lxxviii, 248 n. 4. In "Considérations" he says that public education is possible only for free men. He means that in an ideal city, where laws would prevail instead of indi-

viduals, the education of public opinion could be combined with formation within the family since in such a case opinion would be true. But in his view this is not so in our society, whose public educational institutions he deplores. R. Grimsley suggests that he does so because he was deprived of "regular studies": *J.-J. Rousseau: A Study in Self-awareness* (Cardiff: University of Wales Press, 1961), p. 39.

9. He promised in the preface to do what is best for men themselves and others too.

10. *The Republic* 6. 488. Cf. "Emile," pp. 251, 440, 489-90, 567, 652. Broome is the only critic to remark upon the extent of the image: *Rousseau: A Study of his Thought* (London: Arnold, 1963), pp. 91, 202.

11. "Emile," pp. 378-79, 459, 550, 762, 860. Rousseau differentiates between the natural object (the human constitution as it is organized) and the natural means (instinct that cannot be trusted in social life). He distinguishes between the instinctive individualist who must be disciplined and the human self which is his whole object and which, in the Socratic manner, he calls "divine" or "the divine in man."

12. Cf. d'Alembert's comments on Rousseau in his "Jugement sur la Nouvelle Heloïse" and "Jugement sur Emile," *Oeuvres posthumes* (Paris, 1799), 1:121, 123, 125, 128, 133-34. Cf. Einaudi, *The Early Rousseau* (Ithaca, N.Y. Cornell University Press, 1967), p. 99. See also the preface to the second "Discours." Regarding the Greek sculptors mentioned above, Rousseau names two of them (Praxiteles and Pheidias) in the first "Discours," *O.C.*, 3:22.

13. "Emile," pp. 699-700. Cf. dedication of the second "Discours" and the text itself in *O.C.*, 3:119-20, 168. For the influence of Christianity on Rousseau's view of the family, see "Emile," p. 739. Burgelin sees that the family is a little city founded upon a contract and having its own laws and moral code but without viewing it as an artistic image of its larger counterpart: *O.C.*, 4:cl..

14. "L'homme est né libre, et par-tout il est dans les fers." Cf. *Emile:* "L'homme civil nait, vit et meurt dans l'esclavage: à sa naissance on le coud dans un maillot; à sa mort on le cloue dans une biére: tant qu'il garde la figure humaine il est enchaîné par nos institutions." Broome and Burgelin connect the two outbursts: J.H. Broome, op. cit., p. 81; Burgelin, *O.C.*, 4:253 n.3. The latter also sees that swaddling clothes are a symbol of human destiny, but he expounds the whole passage literally rather than figuratively.

15. *O.C.*, 3:352 n. 3. (erroneously marked n.2).

16. Loc. cit., pp. 255-56. For the Socratic allegory see *The Republic* 7.514.

17. "Emile," p. 245 n.

18. "De la patrie," loc. cit., pp. 534-36; "Discours sur l'économie politique," loc. cit., p. 258.

19. "Emile," pp. 262-63; cf. "Confessions," loc. cit., pp. 357, 415-16, 594-95. Cf. *C.C.*, 2, letter to mme de Francueil, 20 April 1751; 9:67-68, 89, 92, letters between Rousseau and mme de Luxembourg, 20 July, 7 and 10 August, 1761.

20. *The Republic* 7.520; 8. 548, 569; 9.575.

21. "La famille est donc... le premier modèle des sociétés politiques; le chef est l'image du père, le peuple est l'image des enfans, et tous étant nés égaux et libres n'aliénent leur liberté que pour leur utilité."

22. "Emile," p. 838; cf. second "Discours," loc. cit., p. 182; cf. "Discours

sur l'économie politique," loc. cit., pp. 242-43; first version of the "Contrat social," pt. 1 chap. 5, pp. 297 ff.; cf. also the definitive version, p. 352 and nn.4 and 5 (erroneously marked nn.3 and 4). Rousseau's adversaries here are, in his view, Grotius, Hobbes, and Aristotle. Burgelin sees that for Rousseau the father is bound by a convention from the first: *O.C.*, 4:310 n.3 and 838 n.2.

23. See books 1 and 9 in particular. Cf. "Emile," pp. 524-25.

24. For example, Grotius, Hobbes, Pufendorf. For Socrates' ideas on "warfare" described below, see *The Republic* 5.469-71. Cf. 8.554; 9.571-72, 575.

25. Cf. Fénelon, op. cit., 6, 99 and especially 21, 377.

26. See chapter 1 above and *The Republic* 3. 405-8; 4. 426; 6. 501; 7. 540. For the reference to Aemilius, see "De la patrie," loc. cit., p. 535. For Rousseau's interest in names and their meaning see "Essai sur l'origine des langues," especially the end of chapter 4. There he refers to Plato's views on the subject in the dialogue, the *Cratylus*. For explanations of the hero's name see L.P. Shanks, "A Possible Source for Rousseau's name 'Emile,'" *Modern Language Notes* 17 (April 1927): 243-44; P.D. Jimack, *La Genèse et la rédaction de l'Emile de J.-J. Rousseau* (Geneva: Institut et musée Voltaire), p. 191; and Burgelin in *O.C.*, 4:265 n. 1. Sources suggested are La Bruyère and Plutarch.

27. The theme is defined in "Emile," pp. 262, 266, 311, 469, 483-84, 550-51, 654-55, 662, 667, 669, 764.

28. *The Republic* 4. 445; 7. 520, 540. The Pléiade editor, who also compares Jean-Jacques with the Socartic philosophers, sees him as the embodiment of wisdom, of the impersonality of law and reason (4:263 n. 3) or the reasonable will (p. 319 n. 2); cf. p. 343 n. 1; see also pp. 362 n. 2, 539 n. 1, 639 n. 1, 652 n. 1, 661 n. 1, 789 n. 1,866 n. 1. Cf. pp. cxii-cix, cxxvii, cxxx-cxxxi. However, he does not distinguish between the governor and the lawgiver as do Plato and Rousseau. Cf. Broome, op. cit., p. 95; and Crocker, *Rousseau's Social Contract: An Interpretive Essay* (Cleveland: Case Western Reserve University Press, 1968), p. 26.

29. Cf. "Emile," pp. 465, 502-3, 536-37, 665, 794, 832. He is an average man, not a genius, though "well born."

30. "Lettre à m. Philopolis" (1755), *O.C.*, 3:235; and "Les Prisonniers de guerre" (1743), *O.C.*, 2:870.

31. Regarding the kingship of Emile or of man, see "Emile," pp. 423, 458, 469, 471, 582, 583, 665. For his wealth, p. 691.

32. See pp. 325-26, 358, 379, 434, 470, 505.

33. See, for example, *O.C.*, 4:cxxx, 268 n. 1.

34. See pp. 649, 765, 820, 857, 867; cf. 884, 917 (in "Emile et Sophie"). Cf Fénelon, op. cit., pp. 71-72.

35. "Emile," pp. 522, 539, 639, 648-49, 653, 660-61.

36. Ibid., p. 520 n. Cf. "Contrat social," pp. 363, 468, where the author speaks of the sacredness of the social contract.

37. *The Republic* 2. 375-76; 3. 402; 4. 423. There Socrates conceives the contract exactly as Rousseau does.

38. Eph. 2 and 4. For the "covenant of peace" or of "promise" in the Old Testament, see Ezek. 34:25; 37:26; Ecclus. 39:11. Cf. Heb. 8:10; 10:16.

39. See, for example, *O.C.*, 4:1xxxvi-lxxxvii.

40. Rousseau insists that this agreement—the basis of self-education— occur as early as possible.

[78]

41. *The Republic* 10. 600. For the identification of Jean-Jacques, Emile, and the author, see "Emile," pp. 633-34, 772, 820, 858. The book contains many traces of the author's own experiences and anticipates the "Confessions" in pages inspired by his life at Bossey and Turin; his pedestrian expeditions; his joy and disillusionment at Annecy and Chambéry; the idyll of the Charmettes, however chastened; his tutorships at Lyons and Paris; the Venetian interlude; the tragic events of his sojourn in the French capital; and his retreat to Montmorency.

42. "Mon jeune ami, quand à ta naissance je te pris dans mes bras, et qu'attestant l'Etre suprême de l'engagement que j'osai contracter, je voüai mes jours au bonheur des tiens, savois-je moi-même à quoi je m'engageois? Non, je savois seulement qu'en te rendant heureux j'étois sûr de l'être. En faisant pour toi cette utile recherche je la rendois commune à tous deux" ("Emile," pp. 814-15).

43. See, for example, *O.C.*, 4:649 n. 1.

44. Rousseau insists upon unanimous commitment, and a unanimous, harmonious soul or city. Cf. "Contrat social," pt. 4, chap. 2, and "Considérations" loc. cit., pp. 440, 996. Cf. "Emile," pp. 839-40. Cf. *The Republic* 4. 422-23; 8. 554, where Socrates does the same.

45. "Emile," pp. 424, 539, 639, 649, 660. Cf. *The Republic* 4. 419-21. For the governor's action on Emile's will, see "Emile," pp. 320-21, 362-63, 651-52, 661, and cf. 765.

46. See Vaughan's edition of the *Contrat social*, p. 128, and of the political writings, 1:61 ff. Cf. S. Cotta, "La Position du problème de la politique chez Rousseau," in *Etudes sur le Contrat social de J.-J. Rousseau* (Paris: Les Belles Lettres, 1964), pp. 177-90; Crocker, op. cit., pp. 90-91 and passim. Rousseau's "royal lie" has posed a problem for many of us in the past. Incidentally, studies on the origin of Rousseau's contract never go back to *The Republic*. Some go back to the Bible however.

47. It does not and may not violate nature. See "Lettres de la montagne," loc. cit., p. 807, and R. Derathé's note 3 on p. 1444. Cf. "Contrat social," p. 393. Cf. "Emile," p. 837. The fact that Rousseau really envisages the sovereignty of the soul is, of course, visible throughout "Emile," sometimes conspicuously. See, for example, pp. 476, 544 and note.

48. See, for example, Vaughan's edition of the political writings, 1:70 n. 2. Cf. "Contrat social," p. 394, and cf. p. 369; also p. 363 n. 2; and "Emile," pp. 586, 841. Cf. Crocker, op. cit., pp. 63 ff. One should note that *vouloir* is used in pt. 1, chap. 7, and *plaire* in pt. 2, chap. 12.

49. See "Contrat social," pt. 3, chap. 6, p. 411. Cf. Fénelon, op. cit., pp. 25, 89.

50. *O.C.*, 4:269 n. 3. For the parallel between Rousseau's attack on doctors and Plato's, see, for example, ibid., n. 2. The image of the physician-statesman recurs in "Contrat social," pt. 1, chap. 3 at end.

51. *The Republic* 4. 425-26, and cf. 7. 536; 8. 564, 567.

52. See, for example, *O.C.*, Pléiade, 4:xciv-xcvi, cv-cvi, cix-cxi, 550 n. 1.

53. Cf. the language of "Contrat social," pt. 1, chap. 8, p. 364, and "Emile," pp. 280 ff. For the evolution of the "intelligent being," see the second "Discours." Cf. political fragments, *O.C.*, 3:504-5; "Emile," pp. 548-49; "Lettre à C. de Beaumont," *O.C.*, 4:936-37.

54. This has been suggested on the basis of the garden scene in "Emile," pt. 2. See *O.C.*, 4:330 n. 1, and cf. 331 n. 1 and 688 n. 2. But the symbols

seem to indicate that there the child comes into brutal contact with the disorders of actuality, contrasted with the order and justice of the Aemilian city taking shape within the soul. See chapter 2 below.

55. Cf. the second "Discours," loc. cit., pp. 176-80

56. Regarding "private" property, Socrates removes possession from the rule of desire and places it under that of the highest powers.

III
Stylobate

In *Emile* and the *Social Contract* the same meticulous preparations are made before the temple or citadel begins to take shape. Just as the genesis of both structures can be traced to a single commitment, so the foundations of both are laid in an identical rigorously disciplined formation, subject to the same canons or laws for the ultimate fulfilment of that engagement. The evolutionary character of the *Contract,* hitherto unrecognized, is heavily emphasized in the second part. One of the advantages of a collation with *Emile* is to accentuate this.[1] The term *stylobate* is suited to convey the idea of an evolutionary process, and in fact might well be applied to the first three parts of both works. It is properly used of the triple-tiered foundation from which the pillars of the Greek temple arise. Since it comes from two Greek words meaning "pillar" and "to walk," it is suggestive of the stability of eternal principles and the progressive dynamic movement of life toward their fulfillment.

The second part of both books is devoted to the relationship of happiness to wisdom and law. We have not previously seen that such is the theme of this part of *Emile,* but a collation of this kind leaves no room for doubt on the subject. It shows that there the novel has two main divisions and it reveals clearly the real nature of each. It proves that the first division sets forth the basic principles of Rousseauist education, the virtues to be fostered in the soul and the laws needed to ensure them, and it discloses thereby that this section of the book contains the substance of the entire second part of the *Contract* and for that reason is necessarily the most theoretical. It

[81]

proves further that the second division of the same part of the novel depicts a type of education governed by the laws of the first and calculated to produce the virtues defined therein. Indeed, the great value of a collation here is that it leads to an understanding of the plan and purpose of the pedagogical work at this critical point and a realization that the second part of both treatises, and not merely the *Contract,* is in fact the book of the law.

IN SEARCH OF SOPHIA OR THE LAWS OF WISDOM

This part of *Emile* traces the child's development from the moment he becomes conscious of his own identity until he reaches the age of ten or twelve years. When it opens, he has just learned to speak and walk, at the cost of a few bruises and as many tears that provide lessons in courage. As soon as a sense of self awakens, the child becomes a moral being capable of happiness or unhappiness, whereupon Jean-Jacques phrases the familiar questions raised repeatedly throughout the book: "What then is human wisdom? Where is the path of true happiness?"[2] Here as in all his work Rousseau links the pursuit of wisdom and felicity. The "wisdom" he professes to "love"—these two words being English equivalents of "philos sophos"— can alone bestow that bounty in his eyes. This means that the governor is already in search of "Sophia," or wisdom, who is to become the bride of Emile and to whom the temple of the soul is dedicated.

The bliss promised in *Emile* and the *Contract* is a state, both present and permanent. In the author's opinion, as expressed in the novel, to sacrifice the here and now to some receding future is as much a travesty of wisdom as to jeopardize the future for the sake of some fleeting pleasure of the moment. Hence Emile's governor protests against contemporary teachers of youth who fix their eyes always on the morrow, crushing boyish spirits with an intolerable yoke of tasks and duties that cast a shadow over the lighthearted world of childhood and may turn out to be either useless or harmful. He denounces the "false wisdom" of men who ignore the present for the sake of what may never be in the event of changing circumstances or premature death. On the other hand, he makes it clear that the happiness for which he pleads precludes a licentious and spoiled child. Obviously in *Emile,* as in the appendix, he envisages the greatest possible felicity that the present moment holds in store for the future.

In his view the nature of happiness depends upon the nature of the being destined to enjoy it, which is the "Emile" within us or human self more or less intensely felt in the hearts of all men. He explains: "Let us not forget what suits our human condition. Humanity has its place in the order of things; childhood has its place in the order of human life; the man must be treated as a man and the child as a child. Give to each one his place and keep him there. Control human passions according to man's constitution. That is all we can do for his happiness."[3] In other words, the natural organization of the human constitution and faculties must be respected and taken as the boundary of a man's life at each phase in his growth. More precisely, the writer exhorts men to restrain desires that exceed their real faculties, and are therefore "imaginary" or unreasonable, and to maintain a balance between the two.[4] The object of this rule of conduct is to activate the will that matches human powers and is therefore reasonable, and to give it mastery over the soul so that the latter may be "rightly ordered" and "at peace" with itself. For such is the author's concept of the normal hierarchy existing within us. Rousseauist happiness is consequently achieved by establishing well-balanced moral relationships among the component parts of a man's nature as he evolves in the process of formation, thereby bringing him into ever closer conformity with the perfect human prototype of us all. As we were told in the beginning that felicity demands the fulfillment of the natural constitution, taking account of the gradual expansion of forces called into play in three

[83]

successive stages marked respectively by the need for what pleases, suits, and perfects us. It connotes a general completeness of life—what Socrates calls "the fullness of all that life needs"[5]—regarded as the aim of all true education and legislation.

Yet the author defines happiness here and throughout the book with Stoic or Spartan austerity as health, strength, and a good conscience, all of which are to be found within the self. Fortunately he explains what these ingredients entail for one who, in his search for felicity, refuses to separate it from wisdom and professes to be concerned only with the duties of man. Strength is for him the ability to exercise our resources in order to provide for true needs without being tormented by useless cravings that ultimately lead us far beyond our reach. Health is not simply physical well-being as "false wisdom" teaches, but moral and spiritual well-being as well, including the ability to accept pain and death with equanimity by making good use of our faculties in dealing with the here and now. In Socratic terms it is the institution of a natural order and government in the various parts of both body and soul[6] to ensure a well-ordered life in the present that is also a promise for the future. As for conscience, he sets the matter aside for the moment. But the definition of health and strength already encompasses man's total being that is necessarily the rampart and rule of his life.

Using Stoical language, Rousseau calls his rule the "harsh law of necessity," as he did in *Julie;* but, since obedience and consent are correlatives, it inevitably leads him into a discussion of freedom implied in the definition of happiness. For harsh though it is, it liberates the human will and reason and all human powers necessary for the preservation of life both physical and moral. This perpetual liberation of the faculties that enables them to do what is considered to be their own natural work and act harmoniously in constant adjustment to each other unimpeded by slavish desire is precisely what he means by

[84]

freedom. The man who does his will, says he, is the one who can do it without making claims upon others and thereby enjoys freedom, the first of all life's goods without which happiness as already defined is impossible. Consequently the author formulates his fundamental principle of education, or, if we wish, legislation, in these terms: "The really free man wills only what he can do and does what he pleases." This maxim anticipates the law of freedom that is a correlative of the law of necessity. He adds that all other rules flow from it. Of course this must be so, since like the other it is the law of the human constitution, which for him is that of happiness. It reappears in similar words in a defense of the *Contract* contained in the *Letters from the Mount,* where it is adapted to the city-state, "the sovereign nation that wills of its own accord and of its own accord performs its will."[7] The implication is that such a nation is happy. Here as in *Emile* felicity consists in the exercise of freedom of spirit, the free interplay of human endowments however confined, employed according to their natural hierarchy under the rule of the enlightened will, or rather, under the law of necessity.

Rousseau's obsession with the disciplined human will as the secret of wisdom and happiness in the novel is, of course, matched in the *Social Contract.* The importance attributed to the development of that faculty in the child so that he can ultimately participate in moral life is reflected in the first three chapters of the analogous part of the handbook on citizenship, where the Socratic similitude of city and soul becomes increasingly visible. The first chapter contends "that sovereignty is inalienable." Since the general will alone, as opposed to wayward desire, can direct the strength of the state toward a common happiness, sovereignty, says the author, resides only in the exercise of the will thus defined and can never be alienated; and the sovereign, who is a composite moral being, can be represented only by himself. Power can be transferred but not will. He explains why. A "private"

[85]

will, or that of an individual, naturally has exclusive preferences; but the general will always tends to equality, since by definition it seeks the happiness of the entire moral person in which all parts share alike, according to their nature. That happiness is threatened by tendencies to partiality that indulge one part at the expense of another. In Rousseau's view such tendencies are fostered by the modern political idea of representatives and contemporary theories of monarchy that he regards as immoral because they deprive the composite person of freedom of will and self-mastery. A nation, he concludes, that promises unconditional obedience loses its moral life and ceases to be a nation. In that case it is like the soul of a man who, by surrendering his moral freedom, divests himself of inner life. For as we have seen, within the composite creation of the soul the enlightened will must continually guard against individualist desires that would enslave it. The chapter on the inalienability of sovereignty is full of spiritual implications. So is the next one, which is closely related to it and is entitled "That the Sovereignty Is Indivisible." Again alluding to kings and representatives, he explains that sovereignty cannot be divided into individual rights and powers, whether they are vested in a single person or body, or in several. The reason given is that all powers are subordinate to the one they serve to consummate. And since that is a moral one, it may not be divided any more than it may be alienated, although it may, of course, be shared.

It might be useful to show briefly how these ideas are applied in *Emile*. There sovereignty belongs to the moral being formed by the two characters. It is visible in the friendship of reason for human nature, which is nothing else but the enlightened will. Until Emile's formation is complete, the governor enforces that will which favors the human constitution and he opposes the private and personal interests of one or another part that wars against it. But the power assigned to him as governor is not for that reason a portion of sovereignty, even though its bearer also shares in the supreme authority. It is a ruling power used to nurture the sovereign faculty in the disciple and bind him to an ideal communion of men who know what sovereignty is and how to wield it.

Rousseau reaffirms his faith in human nature when he discusses the object of the will in the next chapter of the *Contract,* entitled "Whether the General Will Can Err." He begins by asserting that it is "always right" and always aspires to the common happiness, although his ultimate intention is to show that unfortunately the deliberations of men do not necessarily possess the same rectitude. "We always will our good," says he alluding to the supreme faculty, "but we do not always see it." In defending man's essential integrity, he is not thinking exclusively of distinguished spirits consciously pledged to his own city or to the pursuit of perfection, an ideal present in mankind in varying degrees of intensity. He believes that all men without exception naturally will their "good,"[8] which is, as he has said, what suits the orderly human constitution, its powers, their proper functions, and balanced relationships. Curiously enough the idea has been translated into the doctrine of the natural or spontaneous goodness of man, which has, by some strange twist of fate, become associated with the name of Rousseau. I say "strange" even though he obviously rejects the dogma of original sin, which, he says, does not explain the sin of Adam. But even so, he does not believe in spontaneous goodness. In his eyes, as we know, primitive man is amoral, and his modern counterpart is immoral and the cause of all evil. It was other eighteenth-century authors who imagined that men were spontaneously good and needed only to follow their instincts to live rightly even in our society.[9] Rousseau's idea of natural goodness is rather akin to that of Socrates and the Stoics, who also teach that moral goodness conforms with human nature in its pristine purity, although it would be impossible for modern men with their distorted

[87]

instincts to attain to the fulfillment of the human constitution without the strenuous and harmonious concurrence of all faculties both physical and spiritual and their careful and constant adjustment to each other and to the whole. That is why the author of *Emile* begins education by providing for the training of the will through the guidance of reason.

In the chapter of the *Contract* under consideration the threat of capricious desires and illusions is treated in the same manner as it is in the novel. According to the writer men who naturally will the good are led astray both by faulty judgement and the seductions of private affections. The result is that the general will may conceivably not be the will of all. But he is convinced that in the case of "citizens," the enlightened will emerges from a conflict of personal preferences and passions balanced against each other. However, he admits that this would not be so in the case of members of disordered states where partial interests are collective and can hardly be counterbalanced by individuals. Indeed, he warns that such tyrannical elements, particularly those that are akin to one another, if allowed to grow numerous and powerful, soon overthrow the moral person. The only solution he feels is to weaken their influence by preventing them from uniting with one another. In the eighth and ninth books of the *Republic* Socrates utters the same warning against the complicity of tyrannical elements in a disordered city or soul and proposes the same solution. Moreover, in the case of "citizens," he too recommends the ordering and harmonizing of irrational principles to release human powers. That is the educator's great problem in *Emile*.

The chapter just discussed has provoked the wrath of Rousseau's critics, and in a sense understandably so. They protest that his unanimous, harmonious being is a product of intolerance, and they suspect that his real purpose is to subdue opponents of majority rule and get rid of political parties. However, he does not say that he trusts the majority or even unanimity in any society indiscriminately, any more than he would trust good to prevail in any man. He made that clear at the beginning of the chapter. Of course, he would do so in a well-ordered city made up of "citizens" of well-ordered life as long as they remain true to themselves so that good and necessary feelings directed by reason prevail over all others. But in a disordered anti-society like ours made up mainly of disordered men, he says that the majority would inevitably overthrow the moral being, in which case he would be intolerant of the multitude and sympathize with the wise man who takes refuge from its madness. Moreover, he knows as well as anyone that if his own city were indeed a political entity, virtue would be, as Socrates says, a matter of habit or necessity, and this he neither expects nor desires. He is simply describing an ideal order to be taken as a rule of life, and the issues at stake are moral and spiritual rather than "political" in the sense in which his critics use the term. In the present instance he throws light upon the proper or normal organization of the human constitution as he sees it and illustrates the action of the supreme will for the good that is supposed to foster and cultivate simple moderate desires and prevent the others from growing. The will can perform this function in a well-ordered life, but in any other it can hardly tame the wildness of passion. In its action it may well be guilty of intolerance. But the intolerance favored is that of a man who insists upon allaying inferior elements within himself and mastering them in order that they may be ruled by the naturally superior ones. Any other interpretation would be contrary to the spirit of Rousseau's work.

To revert to the corresponding context of *Emile*, he there proceeds to wrestle with the problem of the passions and illustrates the value of his "fundamental maxim" of necessity and freedom to cope with the great plagues of tyranny and slavery engendered by them. Returning to the themes that inspired him in the beginning, he again denounces the so-called law of the strongest and the warfare

[89]

that enslaves, and describes each of these within the state and the family in accordance with the analogy already drawn between them. First, society in its present form robs us of our strength and resources by subjecting us not to true laws, acts of the sovereign will and our own, but to the arbitrary decrees of powerful factions in our midst. Likewise, in the little society of the family, parents subject to their own petty whims the limited capacities of a child who can hardly fend for himself. Second, the great society in its present form, instead of taming men's restless impulses, fosters and multiplies them, thereby weakening its victims still more, making them slaves of self as well as of others. Similarly, in family society, foolish and indulgent parents flatter the caprices of a child, making it as dependent as a slave and imperious as a tyrant, these being two faces of the same medallion, as we have seen. The remedy prescribed is simple enough. Society and family alike must ideally obey the fundamental rules of necessity and freedom, or the rule of the human constitution that nature herself imposes upon all and that alone can liberate the faculties. Both institutions must confine their services to a minimum, ministering exclusively to the real needs of man determined by his place in the order of things; and both must demand of him only what is really profitable by the same standard. No one, says Rousseau, not even the father, has a right to command a child to do what is useless to him.[10] These rules would make both the child and the man dependent only upon the nature of things and of human faculties and would thereby release the sovereign will to pursue its lawful end. In the author's view if this will were once enshrined in law, it would be armed with all the resources liberated with itself and would prevail in both family and state. Only under these conditions, says he, can the ordinances of men be made as inflexible as the laws of nature that are their proper pattern. Only thus can he visualize men enjoying the bounties of a hypothetical state of nature combined with those of social life

[90]

in the city. These blessings are freedom and morality as contrasted with tyranny and slavery, the evils of both states to which we are said to be presently exposed.[11] The passage in *Emile* shows how he would achieve the purpose of the chapter of the *Contract* just discussed, namely, the gratification of man's natural will for the good, by placing legislation and education beyond the reach of human or inhuman passions. He himself admits that such an enterprise is tantamount to "squaring a circle" and quite as realistic.[12] Nevertheless, since for him it is the only remedy for our woes, he prescribes it as the impossible object toward which all moral effort must be directed.

He makes the same double plea in favor of freedom and morality in the *Letters from the Mount* and in the *Considerations* as well as in the *Social Contract*.[13] In the *Letters* in question he pays tribute to a sublime concept of liberty and the creative exercise of will. Freedom, says he, consists of not being subject to the "will of others" that is not also our own and is therefore, by his standard, a form of lawlessness. Freedom consists further, says he, of forbearing to subject the will of others to our own that is not also theirs and is therefore, by the same token, equally lawless. From this two-edged definition, intended to outlaw tyranny and slavery, he reasons that there can be no liberty without justice to safeguard that of all men by subjecting them equally to the supreme rule of law. Accordingly freedom means obedience to the law and nothing but the law that imposes equal conditions upon all and so is burdensome or harmful to none. This is the Aemilian law of the nature of things or rather of the human constitution. The man who obeys it makes a virtue of necessity, although in the end the law of necessity is elevated into a law of love.

This dignified concept of freedom recurs in the *Considerations* on Poland. The author-legislator warns the Poles, most of whom lived in slavery, that the laws of freedom he enacts are more austere than the yoke of tyrants and are incompatible with slavish passions. Consequently, says he, the serfs cannot be freed until they have first been "educated," by which he means as usual that they must be taught to bear the yoke of true laws. The soul must be freed before the body, and then education or legislation will make every formal law superfluous. As in the case of Emile, the will must be trained before the fully formed man can be set free. In both books Doric or Stoic austerity—the rule of necessity entailing as it does that of liberty—makes possible the freedom that releases human powers and is the essence of happiness.

Rousseau's double plea on behalf of freedom and morality in the *Contract* occurs mainly in the fourth to the sixth chapters of the second part. These are key chapters in the book and the subject of most controversy. They are closely related to his protest against tyranny and slavery in *Emile*. Indeed, at this stage in the progress of his thought, the two texts are so conspicuously allied that the novelist himself directs the reader to the chapters in question, and so the parallelism here is generally recognized. The value of a collation appears nowhere more strikingly than in the case of critical issues like the integrity of the will and the measures proposed to anticipate abuses.

The object of the fourth chapter, "Concerning the Limits of the Sovereign Power," is to guard against the tyranny of arbitrary rule. Rousseau begins by reminding us that the city—and the same is true of the soul—is a moral person, or, if we wish, an active thinking being, whose life consists in the union of its members. Its first task is therefore, he explains, to preserve itself, its moral life, and hence its unity. In Christian terms, to draw a comparison, it must not be a kingdom divided against itself if it is to stand firm. Or in Socratic terms it must not be at war with itself, but must save its constitution by instituting a natural order and harmony in the use of all its parts. To fulfill this purpose, according to Rousseau, it must have absolute power over them, to move and dispose them in a manner suited to maintain the life and unity of the whole. This "will power," directed by the righteous law-giving element, bears the name of sovereignty, as he has said. His statements, which sound logical enough in the context of a collation that brings out the mythical character of his city, have surprised many of us in the past, leading us to wonder whether he is advocating some form of unruly popular absolutism or totalitarianism.[14] That would be true only in the case of an earthly city or if the idea of absolute power were applied to inferior elements producing a disordered state that is thereby reduced to slavery and is neither moral nor rational nor even a being in the strict sense, since it would lack unity, organization, and life.

The fact is that Rousseau's "absolute" power is far from arbitrary. It is circumscribed by the austere limits of the sovereign will and human resources, to secure men against the tyranny of passion. These limits are the very theme of the chapter. Each man, bound by the covenant, must of course obey the authority of the enlightened will. But in addition he possesses the natural rights of a private individual whose claims for freedom, gain, or honor may be vindicated on the condition that they do not violate the orderly disposition of the moral being but remain within the bounds of simple moderate desires that follow reason.[15] Such claims are ensured by sovereignty. For the latter—subsequently manifested in conscience—is restricted by its own object described as "common utility," the "common interest" or happiness of the whole moral entity, and already recommended in *Emile* as a safeguard against tyranny. Consequently it may impose upon its subjects no privations of strength, wealth, or freedom that are not absolutely necessary or useful for the welfare of the entire moral person, and are not demanded of all in common. This rule, which determines in practice what the demands may be, reduces them to a minimum. Moreover, in the ideal order herein envisaged, the same rule ensures that a man who acts on behalf of others acts also for himself, motivating him to seek

[93]

his happiness in that of the community conceived as a single moral entity, or, if we wish, in that of the ideal man in whose essence each one of us shares. This proves, at least to the author's satisfaction, that equality before the law, and the notion of justice produced thereby, derives from natural self-interest. In saying so, he has in mind the promises of the preface, to combine what law permits and what interest prescribes so that justice and utility are not divided. In his favorite Socratic phrase, he is training men "for themselves and for others." He achieves this purpose, according to the present chapter, through the equality that the covenant establishes among the powers who share in it. An act of sovereignty, says he, is an engagement of the moral person with all its members but with none in particular, so that by submitting they obey only their own will. But the sovereign power may not exceed the general agreements relating to the common object, which is by definition a moral one. There is no question of tyrannical rule, at least on the part of that power which represents superior faculties of soul and their natural or normal relationship, whether it is shared by a communion of men or embodied in a single man who is ruler of self. The message of the chapter is that the higher faculties, rather than individualist desires, must decide what is necessary or useful to the whole, since it is desires that give rise to tyranny by exceeding lawful claims.

The rights that individuals retain in Rousseau's city are defined as the advantages of the covenant and are formulated at the end of the chapter, as they were in the previous part. They are said to be freedom and the security of strength and life, or Rousseauist "property." In the world about him as he sees it, these two rights are violated, and each man enjoys "natural independence," which, under social conditions, entails the power to dispossess others of both of them.[16] That world is as alien to the city of the *Contract* as it is to the society of friends in *Emile* where the author takes the same precautions to maintain freedom and strength by confining his view to what is useful to the entire moral person and suited to his place in the order of things and of human life.

Not surprisingly, this chapter of the *Contract* has stirred up a "hornet's nest of words." The statement at the beginning about the absolute power of the will over the moral person that has brought forth charges of authoritarianism and despotism is balanced, in the writer's eyes, by the defense of individual rights that follows. But this only brings fresh charges of duplicity upon his head. It must be said that, if the text is interpreted positivistically, it is easy to create an artificial cleavage between a doctrinaire version of Rousseau and the true spirit of his work. But to do so, we should be obliged, among other things, to ignore the fact that the individual rights he means to protect in his mythical realm are indeed defined in the last paragraph, however inconsiderable they may seem to our way of thinking. If on our part we undertake to defend the existing order against his ideal city and champion individualism against humanism, we must reply to his charges in that paragraph and show that men do not in fact enjoy natural independence in our society, or possess the power to harm others in their persons or their property. But it is impossible to prove this since our world is imperfect actuality. On the other hand, he has removed to some Aemilian realm where the greatest human attribute is enthroned as sovereign ruler to sanction the lawful claims of individuals for freedom and security, freedom being the power to exercise each faculty according to its proper purpose and security promising only the necessities of life and nothing more. His one preoccupation is, as he said at the beginning of the chapter, to save the constitution of the moral person, and he is convinced that this is possible only if the enlightened will assumes command and imposes upon all individual parts one and the same obligation to contribute in their own way to that end.

Before passing from the question of tyranny to that of slavery, he discusses the risk of death facing participants in the oath of the covenant and tries to show that such risk

[95]

does not imply either of those evils. He does so in the fifth chapter, "Concerning the Right of Life and of Death." Its theme, like that of the previous one, forces him to begin by recalling the purpose of the engagement. Previously he said that the pact envisages the preservation of the moral person. Now he declares that it envisages that of participants. If we fail to connect the two statements, we might be tempted to infer from the second one that for him as for Hobbes[17] physical existence takes precedence over freedom, even though the latter is in his view the very condition of inner life. In point of fact, the sovereign will as guardian of the constitution or spiritual being of city and of soul is also guardian of all elements integrated into it, including subject desires that are, so to speak, its Socratic "maintainers."

In this chapter of the *Contract* Rousseau considers the possibility that men entering such a union may have to die for the values to which they are committed, either in warfare or as a punishment for crime. By warfare he does not mean that which enslaves, as in the previous part, but that which frees. He means the warfare of a life dedicated to the discipline of the spirit and the pursuit of an ideal communion of soul and of men, for there are supposedly no other wars in his city.[18] When he comes to deal with the death penalty inflicted upon criminals, he says that a malefactor who betrays the city and makes war upon it must be exiled or put to death, not as a "citizen" but as an enemy. That is the treatment accorded by Socrates to "barbarians," who typify immoral passions in a passage discussed in my previous chapter. If we bear in mind the similitude of city and soul, Rousseau's words may be taken as metaphorically as those of the Greek master. They may also be taken as figuratively as those of Christ about the right eye plucked out and the right hand cut off, that one member should perish and the entire body be saved. But the militant spirit of the divine master in the New Testament is tempered by a peaceful soul that left a deep and lasting

[96]

impression upon his modern disciple. Consequently, even in the present context the latter does not betray uncompromising rigor, as we have sometimes believed.[19] On the contrary, in his city there are no executioners at all since his government is presumed to make them superfluous. The writer of *Emile* goes even further: if in other cities maladministration forces men to do wrong in order to live, then it is the magistrate or governor who ought to be hanged.[20] But an evangelical spirit of mercy prevails in the end in the text of the *Contract:* "Let us leave these questions to the just man who has never faltered and who never stood in need of grace." The phrase echoes that of the master: "Let him who is without sin cast the first stone." In fine, whether he is speaking of the warfare of life within the soul or outside, his main concern is the threat of spiritual death posed by the slavery of passion.

In the next chapter of the *Contract,* "Concerning Law," he finally faces the problem of the liberation of the reasonable will from the midst of conflicting interests and dubious influences, and its ultimate emergence and consecration as law. This chapter is usually considered to be a repetition of the fourth,[21] but though interrelated the two are as different as the rules of necessity and freedom or the two cases contemplated in *Emile:* fathers may make no useless and tyrannical demands upon a child, nor yet foster slavish passion in its heart. Likewise in the *Contract,* after a chapter on the limitations of sovereignty comes one on the absolute rule of law as the only effective safeguard against slavery.

Law, says the writer, is an expression of the voluntary engagements of the moral being and is necessary for the conduct of its life, to give it movement and will power to translate its integrity into action. The implication is that the only alternative is spiritual death. Here as in *Emile* true law is said to conform with the nature of things,[22] which is that of the constitution or moral person functioning according to the Creator's intentions. Consequently Rousseau adds that justice comes from God and emanates from reason alone. In other words, it is derived by reason from the nature of the spiritual being and therefore from the divine prototype. But, he reflects, if we knew how to receive it from that transcendental source, we should require no laws at all or government either. Now, to teach the art of dispensing with external ones in the case of both, since in our world we shall never have either, is precisely his purpose in the handbook on citizenship, designed for the freemen of a city that will never be seen. It is also his purpose in *Emile,* as he says in the book itself as well as in his letter to the archbishop of Paris. In the end the hero needs neither external law nor government, which, we are told, are necessary only for children or childish men who have never been taught. But there as in the present chapter of the *Contract,* the author admits that anyone who obeys the laws of justice does so at his own expense, unless positive enactments, however unworthy they may be of grown men, provide a sanction to save him from the lawless passions of other people, and in the world of actuality that will never be. It is only in the spiritual Socratic and Rousseauist order that positive laws preserve the complex moral person within the natural mold, and they do so only for those who choose to enter therein and who are not thereby protected from the passions of others in an alien society. Unlike some of his contemporaries, Rousseau does not even imagine that he can control the anarchist. His "just man," Emile, lives in our world where justice is reputedly obedience to the law of the strongest, or lawlessness,[23] and where such a man faces the threat of martyrdom exactly as he does in the *Republic* or in the New Testament.

The main point of the chapter on law is that, although true laws are in the very nature of things and of man, yet there is a vast difference between natural law instinctively obeyed and moral law based upon a voluntary engagement and consciously embraced. The law of reason alone can provide against slavery by preserving the proper order and balance of the faculties within the fabric of society where instinct cannot be trusted. It proclaims the sovereignty of the enlightened will of human beings over the slavish desires of individuals. Consequently Rousseau says that law, like the will it expresses, proceeds from the entire moral person, upon whom it is equally imposed; for it is simply a general principle whose object is as universal as its motive. In biblical terms, with the law as with God there is no acceptance of persons. In Socratic thought law is the spokesman of the divine wisdom of the true philosopher that advises about the whole and all its parts and is contrasted with the false wisdom of imposters who abuse mankind and "make persons instead of things the theme of their conversation."[24] Rousseau has assimilated the lessons of his masters and made them his own. He believes that real laws are as impartial as the will of ideal man in the hearts of all men, and as impersonal as the mathematical abstractions of the *Contract*. He also believes that in a true city they alone rule over all, including the governor-prince, whose first task is to enforce them upon himself. Being acts of the human will, they ensure both justice and freedom of spirit, which are the conditions of physical and moral life, as we have seen. Indeed, the author's main object in proclaiming the absolute rule of law is to defend the rights and freedom of the human person within every one of us and to teach men the art of self-mastery as security against moral slavery.

In the chapter on law as in the earlier one on the pact, which is the first of all laws, the Aemilian city of the *Contract* is wistfully called a "republic," a word suggestive of Plato and Socrates, who apply it to the spiritual city or soul governed by law. In Rousseau's view, as we have seen, true politico-moral laws exist only in that visionary Socratic city, in the Bible, or in works like his own. For the city to materialize, the body of the nation would have to register the acts of its own will for the good, and thereby ensure its unity and moral life. But unfortunately individ-

[99]

ual judgments are obscured by "multitudinous desires"—the "blind multitude" of undisciplined elements in the soul that are like childish men in the city and foster tyranny and slavery. Consequently a system of legislation poses problems, which are, of course, those of education: "It is necessary to show people things such as they must appear, to discover for them the right path that they seek, to secure them against the seductions of private wills...." To accomplish this miracle, the author has recourse to a legislator or educator who finds in ancient traditions the remedy for the great plagues besetting mankind, and who is, of course, himself.

It is necessary to pause here and dwell upon the relationship of the *Contract* and *Emile* with the *Republic,* where Socrates, as the main speaker, plays the role of legislator-educator exactly as Rousseau does in both his books. From the part now under discussion to the end, a consistent parallelism emerges between Rousseau's works and the ten books of the Greek classic. Much of the first four of the latter is reflected in the present part of the former, although the order in which ideas are presented is not necessarily the same in each case. In the first book of the *Republic* Socrates too begins by raising the question "Where is wisdom? Where is happiness?"; and, convinced that both are to be found in justice, he refuses to separate them. He starts with a simple definition of happiness similar to Rousseau's, defining it as freedom from the passions and possession of the necessities of life. Then he too faces the problem of justice. Having said that the just man cannot harm anyone, he launches forth, like his latter-day disciple, on an attack upon contemporary laws of so-called justice that cater to the interests of the stronger and lead not to happiness but to misery. In the second book he embarks upon a search for the laws of true justice that, according to him, ensure virtue, strength, and happiness. When his listeners protest that in actual society such laws as those carry no sanction, with the result that the just man falls a prey to the wicked, he admits it but undertakes to disclose the advantages of justice in inner life, these being the fulfillment of all the deepest aspirations of the human soul. To clarify his meaning, he creates an ideal republic where the just man would be happy among his fellows. In doing so the master says clearly that his true purpose is to illustrate the aforesaid felicitous effects of justice within the soul by looking at that virtue on a large scale in the state where, being magnified, it is more easily detected. He broaches his sketch of that mythical order by saying that its origin is need; the real creator of the state is necessity. It is only when an interlocutor insists upon exceeding that rule and going beyond "the true and healthy constitution of the state" that the sage considers the problem of education or legislation in order to purge the luxurious one and restore it to health,[25] whereupon there appears a blessed city that no man has ever before beheld, except perhaps in its spiritual prototype or Spartan counterpart, if we set aside biblical literature. The sketch he makes is closely matched in Rousseau's books, and the education he proposes is identical with Emile's. He begins by training the "guardians" of his city who embody spirit, akin to Rousseauist will. The content and method of their formation—corresponding to Emile's at the end of the present part—is described in the second and third books of the *Republic*. The fourth book is that of the law, which is the term I used to designate the second part of Rousseau's works. There Socrates depicts the character of the moral being that he is shaping. In the first half of the book he formulates the laws that govern the city and its heroes, and are in fact the principles of their life and education. In the second half he outlines the virtues begotten in the city and the soul by such laws. Rousseau in both his books begins with the laws and the virtues they engender, and, although in handling the material he inverts Socrates' order, he is profoundly indebted to the master.

For the purpose of explaining the relationship more

[101]

clearly and Rousseau's use of the aforesaid books in the present case, I must recall that the second part of *Emile* is divided into two unmarked sections, and that the first of these contains all the material of the pendant part of the *Contract*. We are now in the midst of that section which is based mainly upon the fourth book of the *Republic,* although the author has begun by borrowing fundamental principles from the second and third books to which, as I have just said, he reverts a little later in *Emile.* Having begun in this way, he then defines the advantages of his principles, including the virtues of the moral person that are the ultimate goal, and in doing so adheres closely to the second half of Plato's fourth book. As we shall see, the virtues he preaches—all implied in the rule of the enlightened will—are Socratic. The rest of this section of *Emile* and the corresponding chapters of the *Contract* formulate more specifically the laws of education or legislation that are intended to beget his Socratic virtues in the soul and the city. And his laws turn out to be no different from those of Socrates set forth in the first half of the same Platonic book. In the second and last section of the present part of *Emile,* he turns to Plato's second and third books to deal with the content and method of the hero's education at this stage, designed to enforce the laws and nourish the virtues extolled. The education prescribed is exactly the same as that of Socrates' guardians in those books to which I shall be referring frequently in handling that theme. Such comparisons throw into relief the images that evolve in *Emile* once the principles have been clearly set forth in the first section now under study. Indeed, this is the most theoretical part of the book, as I have already warned.

I said above that in defining his principles and the virtues they foster as he has done up to this point in the second part of the masterwork and its appendix, Rousseau has at no time strayed from the Socratic teachings. I shall elaborate briefly before proceeding. In the second half of Plato's fourth book Socrates begins by posing again the familiar

[102]

questions raised in the opening pages of the *Republic:* "Where is wisdom? Where is happiness?" He finds both in a rightly ordered constitution of city or soul. Such a one, says he, possesses all the virtues. It is endowed with wisdom that advises not about any particular thing but about the whole, and considers how it can best deal with itself and with others. This knowledge is that of the guardians of the city or Socratic spirit that guards the soul: "And so by reason of the smallest part or class, and of the knowledge which resides in this presiding and ruling part of itself, the whole State [and soul], being thus constituted according to nature, will be wise . . . ." Moreover, it possesses courage, which is fear of nothing but a violation of the law and its commands implanted by education. It also has temperance, which is the virtue of a man or state that is "master of self," and wherein all parts of the moral being are agreed that the naturally superior and smaller principle will rule the greater mass of the naturally inferior, that the few with moderate desires under the guidance of reason will control the meaner and manifold desires of the many. Such a man or state also exercises justice whereby each class or faculty does one thing only, the thing to which each is adapted and assigned by nature. By favor of these virtues, says Socrates, the soul or the city is "rightly ordered" and "at peace" with itself—words quoted textually in *Emile.*[26] It is, he adds, free to act, to provide for its needs and the care of its person, and to perform its work in public or in private life. It is in a state of health and well-being. Rousseau is utterly imbued with these maxims in the work discussed in the foregoing pages. He now broaches the question of formally defining his laws and their implications in accordance with his fundamental principles, a problem which the sage handled first.

To return to the *Contract,* as I have said Rousseau is himself the lawgiver there as in *Emile.* The next chapter "Concerning the Legislator" brings this out. Admittedly he begins by saying that the lawgiver is quite outside the

[103]

constitution of the being he fashions, and shares neither in sovereignty nor in government, whereas in *Emile* he shares in both in the guise of Jean-Jacques. But as he frequently does in his writings, he plays more than one role in the novel, where, in his function as author, he is in truth legislator in his own city as he is in the *Contract,* quite as much as Socrates, who is not visible within the pale of the imaginary city of the *Republic,* is in fact its legislator as he himself says.[27] In undertaking this function in the *Contract,* the writer fancies that he is generously endowed. For the lawgiver of that book, like the educator-author of *Emile,* is theoretically a sage possessed of superior intelligence who knows men and their passions without being blinded thereby and who serves the happiness of others hoping to win for himself only the favor of generations to come. Indeed, he is "divine" since he provides a pattern for Emile's governor who, though a mere imitator, is himself "more than a man." This "divinity" proceeds from the wisdom that Socrates calls the divine in man and that Rousseau describes in this very chapter as belonging to "the gods" and "sublime." Later by implication he virtually admits having himself assumed the office of legislator, for he makes claims attributed to the wise lawgiver of the *Contract,* professing to have taught the duties of man for the happiness of others and asking in return only the honor he "has a right to expect from posterity."[28]

His task in the *Contract* is depicted like that of the educator in *Emile.* It is to beget a moral person by transforming the instinctive physical individual into a harmoniously organized and highly complex set of disciplined spiritual relationships implicate in the cultivated human soul or in the city. And the results are the same: a man whose faculties are thus liberated, expanded, and integrated into a larger entity or Socratic "single human creature"[29] gains in strength and perfection, even though the vaster being may not be visible to the eyes of flesh.

[104]

The lawgiver, in performing this task of education, has the same limitations as the governor who follows his direction. He may resort neither to authority nor to reason to induce people to accept his laws. Reason, we are told, is the end product of his work as it is of the educator's. According to Rousseau, that is why great lawgivers in the past, like Moses, Lycurgus, and Numa, have honored the"gods" with their own wisdom. If this is a lie, it is a Socratic "true lie," since the legislator has already been compared with "the gods" and his "divine being" is really man's. Through his "sublime reason" the laws of nations can allegedly be made as inflexible as those of nature, as the author of *Emile* enacted, so that people "may recognize the same power in the formation of man and the city." In the light of my collation this last phrase is highly suggestive. It implies again that the city is made in the image of the soul. As there is a hierarchy in the one, so there is in the other, a fact that has surprised some of us in the past.

In *Emile* the legislator-educator's laws or rather the author's are enforced by Jean-Jacques and are used to shape a moral being that answers to the Rousseauist city. Since those enactments are supposedly in the nature of things, which is the rule of life, the child's caprices simply encounter physical obstacles or unhappy effects that perform the function of law. The author, who is about to frame his Socratic ordinances, everywhere betrays the fact that he has the master in mind. For example, in recommending such stringent asceticism, he suddenly raises a question asked and answered by the Greek sage at exactly the same point in the argument, just before issuing his laws: Is he not defeating his own ends and losing the happiness he covets? He denies it, reasoning as follows. A child exposed to a few perils that are in the nature of his constitution can at least delight in his freedom. In any case, he could hardly find contentment outside his nature. Besides, if his weaknesses prove painful, they have the advantage of nurturing compassion in the heart. Moreover, they do not cause misery

[105]

unless they are accompanied by insatiate and insensate desires that also alienate others. These statements contain the substance of Socrates' reply to the same question: the happiness contemplated is not the gratification of one or another of the faculties but the welfare of the entire human creature or composite being. The author of *Emile* agrees that this is attainable only under the laws of its constitution, whose rule serves to control the disorders of children and parents, too, to save young persons from slavery and tyranny in themselves or in others, and to postpone for them the yoke of existing civil bondage. His discussion about the disciple's happiness is equivalent to that of Socrates at the same stage.[30]

So is another such discussion in a chapter of the *Contract* where he reverts to the question of happiness but which I must examine a little later. It is preceded by three others wherein he defines his laws. Now, since their content belongs to a train of thought that runs through the following pages of *Emile,* I shall proceed with the latter. The theme is the nature of the laws, which is, of course, the nature of the being who is led toward wisdom and happiness by their persuasive power.

As we know, Rousseau's only motive in the novel is to teach the laws that are intended to mold the soul and mythical city, or, as he said at the outset, to teach the duties of man and citizen. His laws, like those of Socrates, are really all one and the same, that being the law of the natural constitution. He begins by showing how the law of necessity, already formulated, takes the place of the laws of reason, which the child cannot know.[31] But these laws that constitute the whole of education and that Emile consciously embraces much later are really no different from the other since, in the author's opinion, true laws spring from necessity or need. However, at this stage he advises against reasoning about them since in his Socratic view the training of will takes precedence over that of a supposedly dormant reason. Consequently, his entire discussion of law in the novel assumes the form of a protest against the use of reason to teach duties. Until the age of reason the child in the book, thanks to the governor's precautions, knows only necessity, impossibility, and constraint. In other words, he is made aware only of the physical world, and his virtue is a matter of necessity. In this context as well as in the *Contract,* Rousseau agrees with Socrates, that if children or nations either understood the language of reason, they would need neither education nor legislation to rule their lives. In *Emile* he also concludes with the master that to know good and evil, to feel the reason for a man's duties, is the study of a sage, not of a child of ten.[32] A governor who is imprudent enough to reason with the latter must, we are told, resort in the end to threats or bribes that only encourage deceit. "The laws," says the author significantly, "use the same constraint with grown men." But he explains that such men are "children spoiled by education," for "the sage needs no laws." The child who is to become that sage is simply kept in the place to which his weakness and ignorance assign him. He submits happily to necessity, to the force of things as they are, which is the rule of law in the *Contract* being "engraved on the heart" and mind.[33]

Rousseau's second law—called "the greatest, most important and most useful rule"—is that of so-called negative education, which is really that of freedom and implies the doctrine of natural goodness.[34] Expounding that doctrine, he sees men endowed with a single natural feeling, self-love, that is good and useful in its original form. However, since in his view vicious habits and prejudices easily take root in what he calls the most dangerous interval of human life, from birth to the age of twelve, he has recourse to the principle of "negative education" that replaces instruction on the governor's part by strong negative action designed to secure the heart and mind against taint or flaw from without. But this principle has a positive value since it provides at the same time for the exercise of freedom, for the

[107]

natural growth of the future ministrants of reason, the body, organs, senses, and strength, while the action of the governor's reason keeps the feelings in check. The law of negative education is indeed that of freedom and has results as positive as the governor's ministry, which, however, is invisible to the child.

This law leads to the enactment of a third. Education must be adapted to the child's particular character or cast of mind, which must therefore be studied before any attempt is made to train it. Here Rousseau is mindful of Socrates' advice about the importance of finding out "the natural bent."[35] The author of *Emile* professes to emulate the wise physician, who probes his patient's temperament before prescribing treatment. Again the image of the true physician, dear to both his masters, recurs.[36] In that guise Jean-Jacques appears in the novel as the custodian of the laws of wisdom.

These deliberations of *Emile* are reflected in the aforesaid chapters of the *Contract,* all three bearing the same title: "Concerning the Nation." They are the eighth, ninth, and tenth chapters of the second part that contain a definition of the laws determined by the nature of the nation to be governed by them. Hence their title. These chapters have in the past been judged irrelevant.[37] Yet their enormous value rises to the surface in a collation with *Emile* and comparison with the *Republic*. To dispense with them is to dispense with the author's laws, which are the same as they are in the novel although the order is reversed.

In framing the laws of the *Contract,* he actually invites an analogy with *Emile* by drawing parallels between a man about to be educated and a nation about to receive a system of legislation. For instance, in the first of the three chapters he says that nations like men are docile to law only when they are young, before evil customs and prejudices become so deep-rooted that people cannot bear the physician to treat their afflictions. Again the favored image recurs and in the same context as in *Emile*. The writer of the *Contract* adds that a nation must possess the vigor and health of youth if its laws are to obtain any hold upon the heart. And yet he warns that the wise lawgiver or physician must not be in haste, as he said of the educator. Like the latter the legislator too must take time to prepare the ground first and examine the character or natural aptitudes of the nation that is to be disciplined, for "there is for nations as for men a time of maturity that one must await before giving laws." By this he means positive ones as opposed to negative, since natural aptitude is itself a law and can be observed through the period of waiting and watching or negative formation that is also a law in both books and not merely in *Emile*. The author of the *Contract* himself suggests the comparison with the law of negative education in the novel when he adds that a ruler who fails to exercise the restraint recommended is "like a French tutor who trains his pupil to shine a moment in childhood and then to be nothing at all forever afterward."

In the next chapter Rousseau carries on the analogy of a nation and a man, for both of whom the best constitution or finest formation is not that of nature's vagaries, like giants or dwarfs, but rather the natural canon or standard. Weighing the comparative disadvantages of gigantic nations and small cities, he still favors the city-state in the belief that it can develop resources to maintain itself against attacks from without by fostering a healthy and robust natural constitution that is well-governed, one with itself and united. In other words, it enjoys freedom. That is the very purpose of the negative formation prescribed.

The third in the sequence of chapters is just as clearly patterned after his view of the laws in *Emile*. In it he is concerned with finding a suitable proportion between the wealth of a city, its property so to speak, and the number of its inhabitants. The land must suffice to support them, and they must be as numerous as it can sustain, for the city must be neither rich nor poor, but one and self-sufficing. Here we recognize not only the author's views on

[109]

private property but especially the law of necessity, which protects the integrity of nature against inordinate desires. We must therefore face the fact that the laws of the city, formulated in the chapters just analyzed, are those of Rousseauist education. In the *Contract* the author concludes the discussion by echoing the very words of the novel, when he adds that the period of a nation's "institution" is the most critical in its life since the constitution is likely to be overthrown by threats from without and ruinous repercussions within. These potential disorders parallel those in the domain of inner life at a comparable stage.

The next chapter of the treatise on citizenship is entitled "Concerning Various Systems of Legislation." Its main theme is the common happiness, which, as I remarked above, is defined as it is in *Emile* and in the fourth book of the *Republic*. As usual the author reduces it essentially to freedom and equality. He does not dwell here upon the former since he has already said what he means by it. It proceeds from the law of negative formation that favors the orderly growth of natural resources and faculties. Reverting to the question of equality, he reconsiders the two aspects of power and wealth. Power must be exercised by virtue of rank and the laws, by which he presumably means that rank and power depend upon the law of natural aptitude, which is that of the constitution with its hierarchy of faculties. As for wealth, no one must be rich enough to buy another man or poor enough to have to sell himself. This is an effect of the law of necessity. In fine, he urges moderation of property and prestige in the great and of greed and covetousness in the others. Again the hierarchy in the city reflects the one in the soul. As Socrates says in the same context in a passage paraphrased earlier, the few superior powers with moderate desires led by reason must control the covetousness of the rest. Any truly moral person imposes appropriate restraints upon himself and avoids anything that threatens to disorder his life. In *Emile* the governor inconspicuously imposes them upon the child for the sake of a happiness that depends upon just such measures of austerity. In the *Contract* as in the novel the educator-legislator finally secures that object by modifying his system according to natural and local conditions, or rather, "the nature of things." It is logical that throughout this chapter where the author discusses happiness, he continually alludes to the laws designed to guarantee it. Unless we see this, we can hardly understand the chapter heading.

As I have said, he frames his ordinances exactly as Socrates does in the first half of Plato's fourth book. The Greek master, whose first law is, of course, that of the covenant, also legislates against wealth and poverty, which divide a city or soul into two or more separate entities always at variance with each other. In addition he makes a law regulating the size of the city, which must, like Rousseau's, neither expand nor contract, being neither large nor small but one and self-sufficing. Another of his laws governs rank or function, which is determined by natural aptitude. According to this law every member of the city, or faculty in the soul, is put to the use intended by nature, each to one work, so that the moral person is never at issue with self, reason ruling, with spirit as guardian and the covetous principles subject to the others.[38] These ordinances minister, of course, to all Rousseau's aspirations expressed in the law of necessity, which controls desires; that of negative education or freedom, which governs the growth of faculties; and the rule about following the natural bent to ensure that one does one's own proper work. In the same context Socrates adds that all his regulations are really just trifles of one great thing, education and nurture, whose main principle is that "friends have all things in common," this being the law of the contract, which is that of the constitution. To effect this principle is the second gigantic "wave" to be overcome in the founding of his city, so that the moral being may be one with all its parts, whether its kingdom lies within or outside. He conceives the educational process as conducive to that end only if it safeguards and perfects the natural constitution, fulfills the latter by means of art, and keeps watch against lawlessness, which steals in first in the form of amusement, then penetrates into manners and customs, contracts, laws, and constitutions, to overthrow all rights in the end. In his view an effective educational process like this necessitates few laws, as Rousseau agrees. For example, in the present context the sage declines to legislate about other things that men, disciplined by laws like his, need not be told at all but that are the sole object of all our enactments. Among these he mentions markets, insults, lawsuits, taxes, police, and harbors.[39] Statutes about matters of that kind simply try to patch up a constitution as disordered as that of intemperate invalids, and this the Greek teacher—and Christ too—refused to do.

It is worth observing again that Rousseau's laws favor the same virtues as Socrates': wisdom, fortitude, temperance, and justice. Yet in the case of *Emile* the child is as unaware of the virtues as he is of the laws. The law of necessity breeds courage by teaching him to fear nothing but its infraction; that of negative education or freedom imparts temperance by protecting him from vice and error through the sway of superior powers; and that of the natural bent teaches justice by inducing him to do his own proper work in life and use his faculties according to their normal functions. At the same time he unconsciously learns to submit to the law of reason, which cultivates wisdom in the Socratic sense and promises a happiness suited to the constitution of the entire moral being. He is thereby being educated for the practice of virtue, the virtue of one who is his own law and needs no other. But he knows nothing of all this. It is his governor who anticipates lawlessness, and he does so in the manner described by Socrates: by nurturing the constitution, guarding against lawless amusements, and fostering "the habit of good order" by way of manners and customs that replace laws.

[112]

We witness this in the second section of this part of the book.

The last chapter of the same part of the *Contract,* called "Division of the Laws," illustrates the importance of the Socratic method of education just described and provides a good transition to a study of Emile's formation at this stage. In that chapter the author begins by saying that the true theme of the treatise is the fundamental political laws derived from the "natural" constitution, these being rules of citizenship applicable anywhere rather than particular civil or criminal laws, since he makes no practical application of his general principles within a private society in the usual sense. That is also true of *Emile* in the first four parts. But in the same chapter of the appendix he confesses that his precepts really depend for their effectiveness upon other laws, those of custom and opinion that fix the constitution for all time. These laws are used to reinforce the rest, particularly those of necessity and freedom or negative education that govern Emile's training here and throughout the book.

THE FORMATION OF A SOCRATIC GUARDIAN

The child's education as a conscious being begins at this point where Rousseau, having defined his principles and laws, sets out to depict the moral person and sketch his "city within," visualizing it externally as a society of friends to emphasize the importance of oneness. The education proposed is that of a Socratic guardian, to be followed later by that of a philosopher-king. Rousseau's debt to Socrates is so great in this section that he stops in the very midst to acknowledge it. Consequently I shall begin with an exposition of the plan of the model and then compare it to Rousseau's at this stage before embarking upon my rather unconventional interpretation of the Aemilian text, in order to prepare the reader for what follows. The source in this case is, as I have said, the second and third books of the *Republic.* There Socrates, in order to purge

[113]

an unhealthy state and form his own city, trains men to be skilled in "warfare," choosing natures fitted to guard the constitution, and hence called "guardians." I referred to them earlier as corresponding to "spirit," comparable to Rousseauist will, in the soul. Their training consists of "music," designed specifically for the discipline of the soul, and "gymnastic," designed apparently for that of the body but really for both. The great sage commences with music. In the Greek sense music means all the arts over which the Muses preside and which produce harmony in the soul by bringing its various elements into reciprocal accord. In the education of the Socratic heroes it includes stories in addition to melody and rhythm. For the moment I shall confine myself to stories and defer my discussion of melody and rhythm as well as gymnastic until I come to speak of Rousseau's treatment of them. My present purpose is simply to show that the general plan in both cases is the same.

In the second book of the *Republic* Socrates observes that the young must be trained by means of both true and false stories or myths, and he begins with false or fictitious ones. But he objects to harmful ones, casual tales devised by casual persons, even those of great storytellers like Homer and Hesiod. Indeed, he censors such writers. He charges them with giving an erroneous representation of the nature of heroes whom the young are supposed to emulate, with the result that the latter are led astray, especially since they cannot judge for themselves what is allegorical and what is literal. He alone, as founder and legislator of the new state, will dictate the form in which tales should be cast and the limits that must be observed. For example, he will not have poets telling his guardians that heroes hurt anyone, violate oaths and treaties, or indulge in lies and deception. This three-pronged attack upon harmful false myths and the three lessons implied therein continue to the end of the second book. In the third he passes on to what he calls true myths, melody, rhythm, taste and gymnastic.

Emile's education as a Socratic guardian is similarly struc-
tured. As I have said, it is governed by the Rousseauist and
Socratic laws of necessity and freedom or negative education—which Socrates calls "the strain of necessity and the
strain of freedom," though the Greek word for "strain"
also means "law"—and finally by the law of natural
aptitude. The education of the Rousseauist guardian is also
divided into music and gymnastic, and for him too music
comes first. It includes what I shall call "parables in
action," harmony and song. The parables are the Socratic
stories and myths that fashion Emile's mind. But they are
not recounted. They are played out in life. And, as in the
case of the model, there are both false, though not harmful,
ones and true ones. Rousseau, like the sage, begins with the
former and uses them to illustrate his law of necessity.
There are three of them and they are not devised by casual
persons but by the governor himself or rather by the
educator-legislator who, by the way, transmutes the substance of Socrates' thought into his own. For example, the
three false myths teach the same three lessons for heroes
formulated negatively by the master and summarized
above, and in exactly the same order, although, as we shall
see, the images are more familiar. Before passing on to true
myths to exemplify the law of freedom or negative education, the author makes a direct frontal attack upon "positive education" at this level, particularly our concept of the
training of reason, and casts aside all studies and stories
relating to an alien world such as the three R's, geometry,
languages, geography, history and fables. Again like the
sage he refuses to have his "guardian" indoctrinated with
erroneous conceptions of heroes and heroism. In such
manner he handles the substance of Socratic education up
to the end of the second book of the *Republic*. Next he
turns to the third book, which is the source of inspiration
for the rest of his hero's formation at this stage. After
covering gymnastic quite briefly, he dwells at length upon

[115]

true myths or parables, and then concludes with harmony, song, and taste, following the master step by step in every detail to the end of the present part. This general outline will serve to initiate the reader into the real spirit of Rousseau's text.

He begins his task in a Socratic manner by recognizing that Emile and his governor live in an unhealthy society even though they inhabit a peasant's hut in Montmorency village. He admits that it is difficult to raise a child like an insensitive being, far from the sight of human passions. Nevertheless, he clings to his idealism since he is providing us with a pattern of perfection that may well lie beyond our grasp, as the great sage says, but still remains the goal. In an effort to reach it, the governor begins by transfiguring the surroundings, however superficially. He does so by having recourse to patriarchal and Christian charity, whose influence modifies that of the Greek model. He has a compassionate attitude not only toward Emile, or spirits akin to his own as do Socrates' heroes, but also toward "spiritual valetudinarians" and "fierce natures" from which the academic philosopher takes cover "like a man who has fallen among wild beasts."[40] In fine, suffering humanity finds in him a father as it does in the missionary of the Gospel or in the person of Job, whose words are almost quoted in the text. He thereby wins the love and esteem of the villagers in order to become master of Emile's surroundings as well as of the boy himself. He also implants in the little spectator of his actions lessons in morality that bear fruit years later when the temple of the soul is visibly transformed by clemency into a Judeo-Christian shrine. But he forbears as long as possible to speak of such things, for, says he, he will not play the tempter by letting the innocent taste the fruit of the tree that brings a knowledge of good and of evil. If the child chances to witness some vice, he is told that it is a disease, though he is ignorant of diseases of the spirit. But the word contributes to the image of Jean-Jacques as the good physician going about with the boy beside him like the divine master with his disciples or Socrates with his, to heal the sick in an unhealthy world. That world is in the end the greatest bond of necessity to which the hero must submit since it can never be changed, but the providential governor never leaves his side lest lawlessness gain a footing within the invisible pale of a well-ordered life.

Under his direction the aforementioned myths are enacted. The first three, the fictitious or false ones relating to a false order of things, belong to "the strain of necessity," as I have said.

They begin with a Rousseauist parable of the sower presented in the form of a dramatic dialogue.[41] It is designed to give the child some idea of morality before the age of twelve, but only in case of necessity to prevent him from harming others[42] by instructing him in so-called justice and the origins of property in our anti-society. It is logical to begin with this since our laws are concerned primarily with property rather than propriety of life. The scene is set in a garden that is an earthly paradise until the child tastes of the fruit, which changes it into an image of the world as we know it. There he and his governor work together tilling the soil of which Emile finally takes possession by planting a bean, a possession more sacred and respectable, we are told, than that of explorers like Balboa, named here and in the *Contract* too. It is more sacred because this son of man rightfully possesses the earth that is indispensable to his livelihood. To till it is his natural and necessary vocation. The new Aemilius, like his Roman forebears, is born to be not only a patriot but a husbandman too, as he ideally is at the end of the book, and true to the name of "industrious." As the beans spring up, the governor explains: "That belongs to you." He is referring not to the earth but to its fruits, which are simple, necessary ones and upon which Emile has lavished his time, his labor, and his person. But soon the gardener Robert ploughs up the "wretched" beans, for he has already sown the earth

[117]

with Maltese melons, an exquisite delicacy. This, we are informed, is the child's first experience of injustice.[43] In spite of some ambiguity about the victim and villain of the piece and in spite of Jean-Jacques' principles, which ought logically to favor lowly beans instead of Maltese melons, he nevertheless makes his apologies to Robert and admits that he ought properly to have inquired, before tilling the soil, whether it had already been ploughed by others. When Robert replies that there is no need to make such inquiries since the whole earth is already covered with "mine" and "thine,"[44] Emile complains that he has no garden. The answer comes back: "What has that to do with me?" The implication is that the son of man has been defrauded of his birthright by greedy husbandmen who have cast out the heir and robbed him of the means of life. The drama is resolved when the kindly Robert, whose counterpart in the great world beyond may be less cordial, agrees to allow the friends to cultivate "a corner of his garden." They offer him half the harvest in return to give the child an idea of property rights and the principle of exchange as they prevail in our disorderly state of life.

This myth shows clearly enough that the moral being shaped by the author exists only within the society of friends and not outside. For him Robert's claims based exclusively upon work and first occupancy cannot, as we know, take precedence over need, as they do in actual society. His "moral being," like that of Socrates,[45] is subject to the law of necessity, which, in the alien world of the myth, is ignored, and so is the common happiness that is Emile's. This is so in spite of the contrivance of exchange, effective enough to feed the poor, perhaps, but more so to fatten the rich, who, in Rousseau's view, should possess only the ground that they need and that they can and do till by their own unaided efforts. Otherwise, humanity goes wanting. It is represented here in the person of the dispossessed Emile, who looks in vain for a "corner of the garden" of the world to be his own. At the end of

[118]

the book, where the little phrase thrice recurs, he has not yet found it and never will.[46] The writer uses the same phrase in the second *Discourse* in his vigorous denunciation of property in its present form wherein the usurpations of the rich have been consolidated by a historical contract disastrous to the majority of mankind. That pact is the antithesis of his. It turns most men into orphans like Emile, bereft of their Socratic nurse and mother. Soon, says the author of the *Discourse,* looking back through ages past, "it was no longer possible to find a single corner of the universe where one could be free of the yoke." We see this in the parable of the sower in *Emile* that subtly foreshadows the dénouement of the story, accentuates the artistic balance of the book, and gives relief to its meaning.

The point of the myth was to teach the child the first Socratic lesson and prevent him from harming others. In the view of modern men he has done an injury to Robert and suffers the consequences. But if his pathetic protest seems to justify him, then he has learned that the just man is doomed to become the victim of our "laws," as Socrates' disciples protest and the sage admits. He has also discovered, like the Greek heroes, that he can possess and cultivate nothing except himself. For if he is to be a husbandman at all in our midst, it is a Socratic and Christian allegorical husbandman of the soul rather than of the soil, whose real vocation in life is not to earn bread.[47] And so he will not covet his neighbor's ill-gotten goods but will render unto Caesar the things that are Caesar's, even if they are not rightfully his at all. In fine, he will bow to the law of necessity, including even an arbitrary yoke imposed upon him by others. And he will do so willingly, not resentfully. For he is also being taught that, regardless of adverse circumstances, the virtues born of his own law—the Socratic law of Jean-Jacques' city of the *Contract*—are by their very nature the greatest good of the soul, to whose essence they are intimately suited. The freedom he enjoys in the exercise of his faculties supposedly compensates him for material privation. The author has devised the myth in such a way as to convey the main thesis of his work.

In the following myth, also fictitious, he creates other imageries to teach the sage's second lesson, that good men do not violate oaths and treaties. Here the child—surely a vulgar Emile belonging to a "false" order of things—breaks the windows of his chamber more than once, is then left to suffer the ill effects of cold, and is finally confined to some "windowless place" until it occurs to him to make an agreement with his governor whereby he may recover his freedom on condition that he respect the window panes. Indeed, he is forced to do so by the law of necessity, here presented in a fairer form than in the first myth. The governor accepts the proposal on the grounds that it offers advantages for everyone. His object is, of course, to encourage the child to keep faith with his engagements. This apparently trivial sequence of very ordinary events is employed to dramatize all the elements of a true covenant and to portray property in an equitable form in accordance with the principles of that covenant which lies at the basis of all moral engagements in the book. For example, the suggestion of a pact originates with the child, who is the weaker party, whereas in the historical order as depicted by Rousseau in the second *Discourse* the idea of a pact originates with the powerful rich. The child in *Emile* implicitly consents to renounce his natural independence, limited strength, and the power to harm others, for the sake of freedom from the nameless place; for his own safety, now obvious even to him; and for the protection of property in a just and reasonable form based upon need and the common welfare, including his own.[48] The benefits of such an engagement are as conspicuously present here, even to the mind of a child, as they were absent in the parable of the sower. In fine, the agreement conforms with natural dispositions even if we are in the midst of a world that is the antithesis of Emile's.

[120]

This story too is full of symbolism. The author hints at the presence of symbolic elements in a concluding remark referring back to the previous tale: the little gardener, making a hole to plant his bean, did not dream that he was digging a dungeon where his knowledge would soon encompass him. The "windowless place" or dungeon in the present instance is therefore mythical. It could hardly be taken literally since a little later in this same part of *Emile* Rousseau beseeches us never to confine a child to a dungeon. It is as symbolic as the underground den in the *Republic* and has the same meaning. According to Socrates himself his prison house represents the lowest and darkest sphere in the world of sight, a world that typifies intellectual vision. In that sphere men are imprisoned in darkness and chains, which are an image of ignorance and slavery. This image is reflected in the story in *Emile* where the conscious being suddenly becomes aware of his plight and discovers a remedy. The windows therein are also symbolic and suggest light or the opposite of intellectual darkness. In the *Moral Letters* (1757-58) the writer says that the windows of the house of human understanding are the senses, the basis of elementary reason.[19] In *Emile* they would represent for the child the most rudimentary reason that bids us, blind as we are, respect the windows of our friends so invaluable to ourselves. But for the governor they are the eyes of the soul, its wisdom and that of the law which belong to him against whom the child's rebellion is directed. The little window-breaker is an image of the lawbreaker whose revolt is that of our "false" society against the precepts of justice and the first of all laws, which is the covenant.

Rousseau carries the myth further to teach the sage's third precept, that good men do not lie. If the little vandal fails to respond to the trust reposed in him and violates the promise volunteered by himself for his own immediate advantage, then he suffers the unhappy consequences of lying as a natural sequel, under the inflexible law of nec-

[121]

essity. For example, he is unjustly accused, or distrusted when he speaks the truth. But according to the text, he is not the real Emile. The latter is supposedly not tempted to lie since he is made to feel that it is in the interests of his happiness to be sure that those who supply his needs and whose friendship he enjoys see things as they really are, for fear they may err at his expense. And unlike the little lawbreaker, he has no occasion to break promises since he has none to make: having no reason to alienate others, he is not obliged to make terms with them. To harm no one, concludes the writer as he began, is the most important of all moral precepts. It is by no coincidence that, as we have observed, this is the precept that stands at the very beginning of the *Republic*.

After the three "false myths" with their Socratic messages meant as a safeguard against the evil ways of the false states of this world and before illustrating the law of freedom in an ideal world, Rousseau stops to acknowledge his debt to Plato as well as to the ancestors of Aemilius. Like the young Romans the disciple is astir and on foot from morning till night, and his childhood, like that of the Greek heroes in the *Republic* here actually named, is all festive games and music that replace schoolroom and books. This is confirmed hereafter. In the author's view, governors of small children ought to make a delight out of objects of instruction, for he is persuaded with Socrates that, at this early age, education should be an amusement suited to the blithe and sprightly nature of the child. He follows the master to the letter, as he himself implies, and does so with the most felicitious results.[50]

Before proceeding with this happy formation by way of true myths and music, he launches his attack upon the disastrous moral effects of modern "positive" education that appeals to a child's reason. For he is always inspired by the same preoccupation with the duties of man in the Aemilian city. Like another Socrates protesting against the injustice of a disordered society and its abuse of the means of education to shape men in its image, he outlaws the studies normally prescribed at the present stage such as the three R's, geometry, languages, geography, history and fables. He contends that, although they may prove valuable later, they are not only useless to a child under twelve but also, if taught at that age, may ultimately prove unfavorable to the acquisition of wisdom and happiness since they create in his mind a false impression that he knows something. Rousseau is convinced that he does not, that childhood is the sleep of reason, that children retain only sensations, images, and sounds rather than ideas, and consequently only seem to possess knowledge. Moreover, in his opinion most of the lessons assigned to them are better suited to adults. Young people conclude that study is reserved for childhood, as indeed it usually is, whereas the writer believes with Socrates that the pursuit of wisdom and knowledge should be the main business of grown men. For the time being, it is the occupation of the governor rather than Emile. Even later when the hero is initiated into traditional studies, he is simply given a taste for them, "for he has all his life long to learn."

To prove his point, Rousseau comments upon the studies in question. For example, he denies that children can cope with the abstractions of geometry, or rather with what, in accord with Socrates, he calls "imaginative hypotheses."[51] However, as we shall see in a moment, Emile is early encouraged to observe and compare geometrical figures, as part of the training of a childish reason of sense. As for languages, at his age they allegedly serve to teach only useless words void of the subtle modifications of ideas that belong to the spirit of a race. As for geography and history, it is too soon in the author's belief to transport the child to faraway places, which to a very young mind are mere names, or to carry him back into ages past even if he belongs there. History is not a catalogue of names, deeds, and dates, but an inquiry into moral issues and the human heart in every century and country. Knowl-

[123]

edge of that kind is considered perilous at present because the spectacle it offers is hardly more charming than the Rousseauist vision of the past in the second *Discourse*. It reflects our anti-society with its unseemliness magnified a thousandfold and reveals, so to speak, the skeleton in the closet of mankind. As Socrates would say, it teaches us that heroes do harm, violate oaths, and tell lies.[52] In Emile's case its ugliness is to be replaced by "fair sights and sounds" that are the acts and words of those about him, designed to turn his mind into "a goodly treasure-house" for the benefit of his conduct at all times.

The same happy experiences also replace La Fontaine's fables, which contain images of moral deformity as noxious as those recorded in history. Rousseau attacks them as violently as Socrates condemns Homer and Hesiod. Like the master he will not have some poet or storyteller of dubious intentions interfering with his work. Yet he seriously doubts whether children really understand the fables since, like the Greek sage and in the same context, he says that young persons cannot judge what is allegorical and what is literal.[53] But if they can, then the apologues are considered quite as baneful as history since they give the same false account of heroes and heroism. They reflect a disordered world where the Rousseauist covenant and laws are eluded and the common happiness is ignored. The examples he chooses include the following: "The Fox and the Crow," in whom he sees cunning knaves and simple fools; "The Cricket and the Ant," who symbolize for him the greedy rich and suffering poor; "The Wolf and the Dog," who in his eyes portray lawless independence making a mockery of moderation and docility, which, though exploited and abused, he considers preferable to a life of open warfare. He also cites fables showing powerful tryants like the lion devouring the substance of the weak; and others representing satirists in the form of stinging gnats as powerful as the shafts of ridicule against which virtue itself is not secure. It is far too early for such lessons as these at the present stage of Emile's formation. And so Jean-Jacques excludes them for the moment. But as I suggested above, he does not do so definitively in the way that Socrates banishes Hesiod, Homer, and the tragedians; for unlike the academic philosopher the Rousseauist hero is not to withdraw from our midst altogether. Rather, he is to be a tower or temple of strength therein as we are told later.

In that case he must get wisdom, and the author is convinced that he will never do so at this age by way of books. At twelve Emile hardly knows what a book is, though, like the young Poles in the *Considerations,* he early learns to read and write for his real and present pleasure and advantage. But Rousseau declines to discuss such "nonsense" as the three R's since his theme is education, and so far they have little to do with it. The governor's purpose is not to impress people with the boy's brightness, like the foolish tutor in the *Contract,* but to find the way of happiness for them both and for mankind. That is the whole scope of wisdom's laws, which would now be imperiled by lessons in history, fables, geography, or languages. Those studies belong to another world that Emile must first be prepared to resist by a very different kind of discipline.

This discipline is governed by the law of negative education, the Socratic "strain of peace and freedom," as opposed to the "warlike strain of necessity" that relates to an anti-society. As the legislator enacted, it is primarily directed to the expansion and refinement of the powers of reception, the skilled cultivation of human faculties and the early formation of sages through the negative element of purity from vice or error recommended to act as a positive influence. It was foreshadowed in the concluding pages of the first part. The body, organs, and senses grow and flower in an exquisite environment of natural charm and comely manners through the "music" and gymnastic prescribed by Socrates for his guardians in the third book of the *Republic.* There, as I have said, the sage deals

[125]

with true myths, melody, rhythm, and taste, accompanied by an austere form of gymnastic suited to train the spirit. Likewise in *Emile,* as I have also said, gymnastic is accompanied by more parables in action—true myths this time—as well as training in harmony and song. By exercising and perfecting his physical powers, the child learns to direct them independently and acquires skill in adjusting himself to all things about him in their relationships to him, while at the same time he develops enough reason to discover those relationships and discern what suits the nature of his being. Throughout this phase he therefore combines the operations of body and mind, the functions of athlete and sage, and in so doing he becomes as much of a Spartan as the Socratic guardians are.

But it is the governor's duty to see that the boy uses his strength and reason without caprice or vanity. He performs this duty self-effacingly by ensuring that his ward remains subject to the law of the human constitution. Consequently he is the real master, though the boy thinks he is. As such, we are told, he captures the other's will and maintains it at one with his own. The latter is, of course, the enlightened will of the society of friends represented by himself and his masters, a society into which Emile is being integrated. Within a necessarily limited scope the young hero is unconsciously formed physically, intellectually, and morally, simply by pursuing the object of the will in the simple elementary form of his own real present and concrete advantage and happiness. That is because the governor takes his proper place as "helmsman" or pilot, the helm being the law. He is also a seer possessed of intuitive vision that reveals to him the secrets of the heart. According to that vision, he continues to select all the circumstances of the boy's life as he has done from the first, "paying attention to the year and seasons and sky and stars and wind," like Socrates' pilot of city or of soul. In this way he uses reason to serve the will and safeguard its integrity. It is idle to protest that the child is being "indoctrinated" since he is merely an image of the morally committed man over whom the power of the reasonable will would have to exercise the same insight and vigilance if the ideal order were ever to become a reality.

To depict the governor's vocation, Rousseau tells a famous story inspired by personal experience. It is a parable of the finest order and is told in two parts to show Jean-Jacques' double action in negative education as both seer and steersman. In the first a spoiled child, who is, of course, not Emile, thrice startles his newly appointed governor from his couch at midnight for the sole purpose of forcing him to light a candle. The governor, unused to capricious behavior, confines his ward to a dark closet for the remainder of the night. The same child is as capricious by day as he is by night and insists upon being escorted on walks whenever he feels inclined. When the governor, still unsubdued, refuses to comply, the rebel wanders off alone but is secretly followed by one of his mentor's accomplices, who sees that the event is attended with much unpleasantness but no great danger.

The parable is transparent enough to be interpreted with a fair degree of certainty. In the first part a helpless child who lives and moves in a world of intellectual shadow, drenched though it is in material sunshine, would control the light that belongs to the seer and force him to be led by the blind. For the candle, like the windows earlier, represents the light of the mind, as Rousseau indicates later in another context and as he did in the case of the windows.[54] Socrates uses the same image when he bids his disciples "light a candle" and search about for justice. And we may observe parenthetically that it is he who does the bidding and not they. In the Rousseauist text the darkness of the closet, like the windowless place in the former myth, symbolizes the opposite of intellectual light, the state to which the child's ignorance relegates him. In the last phase of the story he who meanders aimlessly abroad

[127]

in the world, a prey to his own vagaries, would neverthe-less have the true "helmsman" follow him, instead of the reverse. He is like Socrates' mutinous sailors in the afore-mentioned parable of the ship of the soul or city who in-sist upon steering though they are not steerers at all. The symbolism in Rousseau's myth is simpler, and has the un-obtrusiveness that we usually associate with the term *clas-sical,* while at the same time it affords a powerful projection of his message.

Broaching the problems of negative education in the ideal Aemilian world, he begins with physical training corresponding to the Greek sage's simple or military gym-nastic in the third book of the *Republic.* This training en-visages primarily the improvement of the soul, as the two philosophers phrase it, and is characterized by Stoicism and asceticism. All year long Emile goes clad in light gaily colored robes and walks unshod and bareheaded. Like the Socratic heroes he grows used to various changes of water, and like them is trained to abstain from excess in sleep and every sort of intemperance, and to avoid enslavement to all habit except that of order; for according to the ancients and Rousseau, too, habit soon becomes a second nature. Like the same Socratic heroes of the Greek classic, he is hardened to pain and death and, in the midst of his pleas-ures, is no more aware than they of the fasting, fatigue, and hardships he endures. He learns to swim the Helles-pont "in his father's canal" and to rejoice in all the ele-ments, again like those young Greek athletes, called by Socrates wakeful, lean, and wiry dogs. By such means as these his soul is tempered and made invulnerable.[55] For the object is to develop, not robust muscular strength, but a taste for fortitude and temperance, without ever calling them by their names. It is these two virtues combined that make him into a sage and athlete too by strengthening not only the will but the reason as well and nurturing them together to bring them into natural accord or friendship with each other. Gymnastic, by helping to foster them both

[128]

in the soul, plays no small part in the preparation of the Socratic and Rousseauist guardian. The author of *Emile* follows the master so closely here that to treat the latter's ideas on the subject separately would be far too obviously repetitious.

In the last pages of this part of the novel Rousseau turns back again from gymnastic to music as already defined. True, he calls this phase the education of the senses, and in the past we have simply accepted it as such. On the surface he appears to present it in that form. But he does so in order to adhere at least externally to the fashion of the day and pay his respects to the sensationalist doctrines of his contemporaries. Nevertheless, his purpose is both broader and deeper than theirs. We can close our eyes to this if we choose, and confine ourselves to a literal reading of the text since it always lends itself to a double interpretation. But if we overlook the possibility of a literary reading too, then we ignore the fact that Rousseau is an artist as well as a thinker. As is usual with him, it is his art that betrays his real thought here, although the former remains as "classically" unostentatious as ever. That is one reason why his motives have previously eluded us. For example, in the so-called education of the senses, he follows a significant symbolic order, but always with the utmost discretion. While training the senses in the sequence in which they naturally take their place in human life, he uses that sequence to typify the gradual raising of the mind to moral truth by the cultivation of reason and will, for which this training like simple bodily exercise is really devised. To revert to the Socratic image of the ascent of the soul from the underground den or lowest sphere in the world of sight, Emile is gradually turned away from intellectual and spiritual darkness toward a childish wisdom that prefigures Sophia.[56] The process is accomplished by true myths, harmony and song that are conveyed in the form of lighthearted games in the fairest of settings. It is true that the hero thereby learns to use his senses ju-

[129]

diciously but he is also oriented toward the virtues, however unwittingly, for Jean Jacques never averts his eyes from the goal. However, it is only a penetration and elucidation of myths that can tell us so.

The first of the true ones is that of nighttime games. The pretext for these games is the training of touch to teach the child to walk in darkness like the blind, to see at night, and to have no fear. This idea implies that the governor is concerned not merely with the cultivation of touch but with that of reason and spirit too. The rest of the myth confirms our suspicions. Many people, says the author—and he was no exception[57]—fear the dark, "even philosophers and soldiers" possessed of reason and courage, and Emile must be both. He explains that this fear is caused by ignorance of our surroundings, and he thereby suggests that the darkness of which he speaks is essentially that of the mind. To dispel both weaknesses, the governor imagines sprightly games at bedtime. It is in this context that we are warned never to confine a child to a dungeon, a word that inevitably suggests the symbolism of previous myths. To illustrate his meaning, Rousseau narrates a scene from his own childhood, one that has resonances in the profession of faith of the Savoyard vicar further on, but is not included in the *Confessions.* In the scene in question he appears as a boy of ten sent alone upon an errand at night to fetch a Bible from the pulpit of the unlighted temple of Bossey and stimulated to find his way and banish fear by the reassuring proximity of others. Engulfed in the darkness of that "vast place," he at last reaches the holy book that contains, says the vicar later, not one revelation but two. The priest makes this remark to his disciple, a young exile who appears groping through the obscurities of revelation and is comforted by his mentor's words: "The God whom I adore is not a God of darkness." These are signs enough that the exile is foreshadowed by the blind boy of Bossey striving to overcome his blindness. Emile is mystically present in that boy, as he allegedly is in

[130]

all of us; but the real one knows nothing of churches or revelation either, although he already possesses religion without professing it, like Socrates' heroes whose early theology is a rudimentary sketch of the virtues. For although he plays in intellectual darkness, since such is the lot of childhood, in doing so he acquires not merely balanced bodily movement but a trace of the Socratic virtues as well, especially courage and a groping reason of sense.

Obviously darkness here is as symbolic as it is in the story of the little lawbreaker or that other child of midnight fantasies of whom I spoke before. Rousseau habitually used it to typify mental and spiritual obscurity in both *Emile* and the *Contract*.[58] His divine master does the same, for example, in the Sermon on the Mount, where the light of the body is the eye corresponding to spiritual vision, and darkness is the reverse. And, as we know, so does Socrates, who often advises that his guardians must have eyes and not be blind or feel their way about, like men in the dark. His allegorical den where men grope about through "shadows of images of objects" is the real setting of the Aemilian myth. Even when the Greek heroes go forth from the den into the world of light as philosopher-kings and are sent back later to perform some duty among the blind, they must again get the habit of seeing in the dark, where most of us are content to pass our lives.[59] In Rousseau's view Emile must possess the same skill as the Socratic models if he is to fare well in the world as we know it since it is there that he must live.

The next of the true myths shows children running races for cakes in miniature Olympics, which appears as a violation of the author's principles about the ill effects of competition only if we are unaware of the imagery, as we have hitherto been. The theme of the great games is a favorite motif in *Emile* as it is in the *Republic* where, in the very book of that dialogue echoed here, the Greek sage says that his guardians are in training to win a more glorious

[131]

victory than the Olympic conquerors. Rousseau, like the master, treats the games as a symbol of life, and it assumes immense proportions in the book. It recurs in several contexts where the only element that varies is the prize: first cakes, then honor, then the Pauline "crown that never fades," and in the fifth "act," wisdom herself in the person of Sophia.[60]

The pretext for the childish races is the training of the eye to take a firm hold upon things and guard against illusions. The boy learns to measure and compare the varying distances of several courses, one for each competitor, all leading like the radii of a misshapen circle to a single goal in the form of a cake. In time he learns to choose the shortest and most direct way to the goal, by making spontaneous estimates at a glance. Thus while he is thinking only of innocent pleasures and cakes, all his resources of mind and will are being called into play. But the will takes precedence over the reason. Jean-Jacques provides a hint of this in his reply to the child, who complains about the varying lengths of the courses: "In a gift I give of my own free will, am I not master of the conditions?" These words are reminiscent of the evangelical parable of the laborers in the vineyard where men, toiling for a material reward, are meant to portray souls in quest of the meed of virtue. The master who engages them claims the freedom to reward them as he sees fit and to do what he will with his own.[61] The situation in Emile is comparable, including the master's reply, since the cake, like the reward of the biblical laborers, is a result of the effort of will and mind and body necessary to obtain it. This story suggests a view of life that is realistic enough for a child. It projects a rudimentary form of justice and wisdom, and at this stage a cake is a suitable incentive. The implication of the book is however that our world is full of grown men running for cakes and that Emile is not to be one of them.

The writer also comments upon the discipline of reason in the mythical races. The child soon acquires a "visual

[132]

compass" to evaluate the courses, which are like so many roads leading through life, and to choose the shortest and simplest one to the goal. The compass that the governor "puts in his eyes," as Rousseau phrases it later, represents childish reason based upon sense perception. For, says the writer, sight is the sense least separable from the judgments of the mind, and so later he uses it to represent the vast capacity of the systematic genius.[62] Socrates does likewise, and so does Christ in various ways. In the Aemilian myth Jean-Jacques is therefore cultivating the judgment since he does not assume, as others do, that it already exists in the child. He forms the latter's reason instead of reasoning with him. And he does so with a view to the moral function of reason as a spiritual director to serve the will and lead the boy to the practice of a childish image of virtue beyond which many men never advance. But for him the tiny drama of these boyish races is but "the mimic preliminary exercise for a larger contest," the race for Sophia, that is the governor's sole object, unseen by the child but visible enough to an attentive spectator. Jean-Jacques is gradually leading Emile from the mental and spiritual darkness of the Socratic den into the world of light.

Like Socrates, Rousseau passes next from stories and myths to harmony, rhythm, and taste. In approaching these, one must realize that the whole of musical education including what has preceded is intended to ensure a harmonious nature and the agreement of all faculties for the practice of virtue.

Still under the pretext of cultivating the sense of sight, Jean-Jacques gives lessons in drawing and painting, taking nature as a model to train the child to observe objects and their appearances and to see the real truth and beauty of things. He also provides instruction in the proportions and relationships of geometrical figures.[63] But he uses these studies to prepare the eye, the reason, and spirit for the discernment and pursuit of order in human life and

[133]

to impart rhythm and harmony to the soul through a knowledge and appreciation of the rhythm and harmony of nature. And so the writer's enthusiasm for these occupations reflects his personal taste for the arts far less than it does his delight in the setting of his stories and its presumably felicitous moral effects upon the child.[64] This motive that suffuses his text is accentuated in the light of the Platonic one he follows. There Socrates says that harmony and rhythm "depend on... the true simplicity of a rightly and nobly ordered mind and character." By this he means one in which there is a rhythmical interplay of faculties working in unison, with leaders leading and followers following. To foster such dispositions in his heroes, he too resorts to the painter's art and the study of beauty, convinced that grace and harmony are "the twin sisters of goodness and virtue." He ordains that artists "express the image of the good in their work" and avoid images of evil. In the Rousseauist text Jean-Jacques is supposed to be just such an artist, and his "work" is Emile, as he frequently says. To accomplish his purpose, he continues to follow the master, who insists that the young Greeks dwell not in some "noxious pasture" but "in a land of health, amid fair sights and sounds," including the words and deeds they witness. This rule applies to Emile, as we know. So do the rest of the sage's comments in the same context. Adapted to the Rousseauist hero, they show that beauty, "the effluence of fair works," diffuses about him powerful influences to conform him to themselves and prepare him for the beauty that is spiritual. Emile therefore exemplifies Socrates' conclusion that rhythm and harmony of environment impart grace to inner life and teach the disciple to "perceive omissions or faults in art and nature" and make him love the good and hate the bad "even before he is able to know the reason why." Rousseau is utterly imbued with these maxims.

To complete his treatment of rhythm and harmony, he has recourse to the teaching of musical instruments, under

[134]

the pretext of refining the senses and training the ear, but obviously for the purpose of disciplining the spirit, as Socrates does by the same means. The boy is taught to hear well, especially at night since, like the Socratic guardians, he still dwells in partial darkness and must be as alert as they are. But as in their case the passive organ, the ear, is perfected by the active one, the voice, which is trained in speech and in song. The author's recommendations about these matters reflect the convictions of the master regarding melody and song, the various modes of music and their effects upon the soul, contained in the very context of the *Republic* that is the model here. In melody and song the Socratic and Rousseauist "strain of necessity and strain of freedom" favor either the grave Dorian mode of the Greeks intended to bring the soul of the sage into harmony with the order of the universe, or the warlike Phrygian mode, becoming to the athlete. The same laws in both texts banish the relaxed Ionian manner and the sad pathos of the Lydian as being unsuited to a boy. Rousseau concludes by citing the very words of the *Republic*, that "all this must be simply an amusement" and nothing more, at least for the child.[65] But for Jean-Jacques it is a serious business since the writer is obsessed by the Socratic affinity of beauty and moral order.

Next he turns his attention to taste, or appetite, treating it not merely literally but also in an allegorical manner to prefigure aesthetic judgment, which is already being prepared by the education of music and is, as we have seen, mystically linked with spiritual life. Indeed, there is a section on aesthetic taste and an essay summarizing its conclusions at the end of the fourth part that matches the passage on the present theme at the end of the second. The literary parallelism between physical and artistic taste is subtle and significant. For example, the writer says of the child's appetites that the rule in the selection of food is what pleases the palate, while his definition of good taste in aesthetics is what pleases most men. Moreover, in both

[135]

cases he is at pains to explain that he is not speaking of what pleases because it is useful—in the matter of food "healthful"—but simply of what is pleasing in itself. And so the guide in the choice of Emile's food is nature or natural taste, which is his own. It favors the most simple and universal tastes that are also regarded as best in the realm of aesthetics, where the guide is the same. In both areas Rousseau admits however that modifications occur through the influence of climate, manners, way of life, age, sex, character, and environment.[66] There is another point not to be overlooked. Not only does he give us here a fore-taste of his later reflections, but the essay that follows and synthesizes them itself combines the themes of aesthetic and physical taste, with moral overtones that are also present here.

In fact, there are definite proofs that the passage on appetite has figurative and spiritual implications in addition to the obvious literal meaning. For example, the author does not insert it in the part on gymnastic where he spoke of the drinking of water. He introduces it at the end of what Socrates calls musical education. The sage does likewise, using appetite as a transition from music to gymnastic since his order is the reverse of Rousseau's. There Socrates treats the subject allegorically in the context of the views on aesthetic taste and spiritual beauty that I summarized above, and associates the sense of taste with both aesthetics and spirituality. In doing so, he warns that he will not have his guardians nourished with images of moral deformity, nor will he have them "browse in some noxious pasture, feeding upon many a baneful herb and flower day by day" and "gathering a festering mass of corruption in the soul." Here as in *Emile* physical taste is an image of aesthetic taste regarded as the bulwark of the austerely disciplined city or soul. The passage in the *Republic* leads to a discussion of food and drink that opens the Socratic treatment of gymnastic. In the great classic, as I have said, gymnastic follows music since, in the speak-

[136]

er's view, "to the mind when adequately trained we shall be right in handing over the more particular care of the body,"[67] an idea confirming that his main preoccupation is always the formation of the soul. The same idea pervades the corresponding pages of *Emile* on appetite, where, moreover, Rousseau's Spartan prescriptions about physical taste echo the master's, since they are dictated by the same motives. For example, in the midst of them he refers us back to the mimic Olympics and to the cake that the boy earns by his own efforts of body and spirit and the practice of an elementary justice meant to foreshadow true wisdom. Strangely enough, in the same context of the *Republic,* in a passage to which I alluded in speaking of the races, Socrates too, recommending simplicity and temperance of appetite in his heroes, emphasizes the fact that the men are in training for a contest greater than the Olympic games, which is the pursuit of wisdom. This thought brings him to denounce "sweet sauces" and "unnecessary pleasures," which, as he reminds his listeners, corrupted the original healthy state of men and made education indispensable to purge away luxury. And so appetite is not morally inconsequential for him, any more than aesthetic taste is. A sophisticated appetite represents symbolically a harmful way of life that must be purged. But he will do the purging, not physicians, who are thereupon denounced in the famous passage to which I referred earlier. He concludes again that gymnastic, including the training of appetite, envisages chiefly the improvement of the soul. Rousseau obviously agrees.

The moral issues in the passage on physical taste in *Emile* emerge further into view when the author says that the child must be nourished, not by the flesh of animals, but by the fruits of the earth, which is "our nurse and mother." He is simply quoting Plutarch. But how curious that he contrives to bring to a close this interval in Emile's education exactly as Socrates concludes that of his guardians by telling them that "the earth is their mother and their nurse'' to whom they are forever bound! The object of the Greek philosopher's so-called royal lie is to make them care more for the city and for one another. This intention is implicit in *Emile* where the author expresses the belief that a flesh diet leads men to live like wild beasts, fosters cruelty, and stifles pity in the soul. He is still concerned with the duties of man in the city of the *Contract,* even though in actuality its freemen are robbed of the fruits of the earth to which they are entitled.

The Socratic idea of purging away luxury is also present in Rousseau's text when he affects to deal with the sense of smell. For example, having admitted that it is weak in a child, he says that he would not arbitrarily reduce the number of agreeable sensations in life by using pleasant aromatics to hide a dose of physic whose bitterness makes a child forever insensitive to their sweetness. The bitterness that purifies body and soul is as much a part of Emile's training as it is of the training of Socrates' guardians. Rousseau's views on the "education of the senses," which create the impression that he is adhering to the mode of the day, contain teachings at least 2,500 years older than contemporary sensationalist doctrines.

This part of the book ends with a portrait of the child as the embodiment of all principles set forth so far. His friend brings him forward into an assembly of scholars and invites them to question him, though he has only a childish sort of reason, formed as a basis for common sense. The scene is reminiscent of Christ at the same age sitting in the temple amid doctors of the law and astonishing them with his understanding and answers as he goes about the Father's business.[68] In Emile's case the "father" is the law, visible as a friendly presence by his side. They depend not upon each other but upon the society of their friendship, for, we are told, they are always in agreement and find their greatest happiness together. In that society we have an image of the mythical city within whose bounds the hero's portrait unfolds. He remains as subject to the law of necessity and of freedom as Jean-Jacques does to that of reason, these being one and the same law of justice. But the child observes moral rules, without having any knowledge of them, through the action of his governor and by virtue of the laws of custom and true opinion that prevail round about him and are the lawgiver's main concern. What few moral ideas he has relate to the covenant, property, and freedom. His reason has been taught not to gather useless data but to rule his person, direct his strength, and execute his will. Moreover, although he does not know it, he is born to govern others too by his superior talents and experience and may do so through the force of his example, regarded as more persuasive than "all our discourses." Only such men as this bear rule in the Rousseauist city, for, like his Greek master, the author does not favor equality of equals and unequals alike, whether they be men or faculties of soul. Equality of that kind would not lead to the felicity he seeks within the nature and limits of the human constitution.

The portrait of the child with Jean-Jacques recalls Socrates' conclusion to the education of his guardians or spirit. For example, the best Socratic heroes—who alone are chosen to become "rulers"—possess the power of command or self-mastery and a love of the city or brotherhood, such as Jean-Jacques has been nurturing in Emile. These qualities are bred in them by their education that humanizes them in their relations to each other, which are those of the Socratic and Rousseauist order of friendship. They too obey the laws of necessity and freedom. They possess nothing that may impair their virtue as guardians and men of temperance and courage. For example, they have no property of their own beyond what is absolutely necessary, but live together like soldiers in a camp, as do Emile and Jean-Jacques in their empty, austere rustic room. They are ruled not by desire but by the highest human faculties and forgo all riches for the sake of the diviner metal within, as do their modern counterparts. For the Aemilian governor

[139]

or philosopher-king is himself presented as a good guardian of self and of others, of the reasonable will or law, and of the constitution of soul or of city that is its principle materialized in Emile. It is to loyalties like these that the covenant of friendship has committed him.

Emile is therefore drawn into the image and likeness of an ancient order of things exemplified in the friendly companionship of ideal beings that results from the covenant and executes its laws. That order is also the one in the *Contract* that springs from the same principles. The happiness it bestows is exemplified in Emile at the end of this part. Confined to the necessities of life, he enjoys freedom, the harmonious and voluntary direction of all his faculties in accordance with the aspirations of human nature and the proper exercise of human powers. Even though the hero is aware only of the rudimentary ideas of this philosophy, the author has already completely confided in his readers. The more we contemplate the two books together, the more they interlock and fuse into one.

1. A collation makes it clear that Rousseau is "laying the foundations" in the first three parts of the *Contrat* as well as *Emile* and that the moral being does not emerge until the fourth part in both cases. In the past most of us have thought of the city or moral person as being already formed in the first part of the appendix, whereas the oath proposed there is effective only in the fourth part.

2. See, for example, "Emile," pp. 304, 692, 814-20.

3. "... N'oublions pas ce qui convient à nôtre condition. L'humanité a sa place dans l'ordre des choses; l'enfance a la sienne dans l'ordre de la vie humaine; il faut considérer l'homme dans l'homme, et l'enfant dans l'enfant. Assigner à chacun sa place et l'y fixer, ordoner les passions humaines selon la constitution de l'homme est tout ce que nous pouvons faire pour son bien-être."

4. For the importance of the balance of powers to keep one's place, see *O.C.*, 4:303 n. 1 and 304 n. 1; cf. also P. Burgelin, "L'Idée de place dans l'*Emile*," *Revue de littérature comparée* (Paris) 35 (1961): 529-37. Regarding Rousseau's distrust of imagination in this process, that faculty was, of course, a source of happiness for him personally, but there is a difference between imaginary desire for material things and imaginative insight that transports one beyond their sphere: see M. Raymond, *J.-J. Rousseau: la quête de soi et la rêverie* (Paris: Corti, 1962), pp. 81-83.

5. *The Republic* 5. 465.

6. Ibid., 4. 444. Rousseau's definition of happiness does not change through-

out "Emile": pp. 455, 512-16, 536, 678, 691. It always includes health, the necessities of life, and freedom to use the faculties. Cf. the profession of faith in chapter 5 below.

7. "Le Peuple Souverain veut par lui-même, et par lui-même il fait ce qu'il veut": "Lettres de la montagne." *O.C.*, 3:815. Cf. *Emile*: "L'homme vraiment libre ne veut que ce qu'il peut et fait ce qu'il lui plaît." Burgelin compares the free man and free city but declines to identify them on the grounds that the meaning in *Emile* is anthropological and not juridical: *O.C.*, 4:309 n. 2. However, a collation forces one to identify them. Besides, Rousseauist law is based upon Rousseauist anthropology. Freedom as it is defined is enjoyed by Emile in slavery: "Emile et Sophie," *O.C.*, 4:916-17.

8. " ... On veut toujours son bien, mais on ne le voit pas toujours." Cf. "Emile," pp. 245, 248, 322, 586, 595, 600-604, 653-54, Cf. "Contrat social," pt. 4, chap. 1; "Julie," *O.C.*, 2:571; "Lettre à C. de Beaumont," *O.C.*, 4: 935 ff.; and "Dialogues," *O.C.*, 1:668, 670. Such references could easily be multiplied.

9. Rousseau's harsh realism as opposed to the permissiveness of his contemporaries has aroused a great deal of criticism: e.g., Crocker, *Rousseau's Social Contract: An Interpretive Essay* (Cleveland: Case Western Reserve University Press, 1968), pp. 50, 72, 80-89, 91, etc. Seillière is much closer to Rousseau than he imagines when he writes, "Je pense, moi aussi que la mystique naturiste—si elle est à temps ramenée vers la tradition stoïque et chrétienne en morale—pourra laisser quelque jour la condition humaine améliorée de façon durable" (E. Seillière, "Alain contre Emile," *Journal des débats*, 40th year, no. 2029 (13 January 1933), pp. 73-76.

10. Burgelin sees that even in the child's minority the father commands lawfully only for the good of his offspring: *O.C.*, 4:310 n. 3.

11. Cf. second "Discours," *O.C.*, 3:176-80; "Emile," p. 848, and cf. p. 311.

12. "Emile," p. 263 n. 3; "Considérations" *O.C.*, 3:955; *C.G.*, 17:157, letter to the Marquis de Mirabeau, 26 July, 1767.

13. "Lettres de la montagne," loc. cit., pp. 841-42, 891. "Considérations," loc. cit., pp. 953-55, 972-74. For the *Contrat social* see below.

14. For example, C.E. Vaughan, S. Cotta, L.G. Crocker, J.I. McAdam. Cf. chap. 2 above, n. 45. For Crocker see his aforesaid study of the *Contrat social*: pp. 44, 46, 57-58, 61, 62-63, 73, 74, etc. For McAdam see "Rousseau and the Friends of Despotism," *Ethics* 74 (1963): 34-43. J.-D. Candaux is inclined to support Vaughan's views: *O.C.*, 3:812 n. 5. On the other hand, Derathé is conscious of the discipline implied in the idea of sovereignty: ibid., p. 372 n. 3. Cf. R. Derathé, J.-J. *Rousseau et la science politique de son temps*. (Paris: Presses universitaires de France, 1950), p. 117. A. Cobban also sees Rousseau's concern for human rights, e.g., "New Light on the Political Thought of Rousseau," *Political Science Quarterly* 66 (1951): 272-84. So does Broome in *Rousseau: A Study of His Thought* (London: Arnold, 1963), pp. 64-66.

15. Cf. *The Republic* 9. 591-92. The sage takes heed that no disorder occur in the city within, such as might arise from superfluity or want, or from private or public honors. The same may be said of Rousseau's perfect man or human self as opposed to the disordered individual.

16. He is clearly referring to the state of affairs in actual society. See "Lettre à C. de Beaumont," *O.C.*, 4:937 ff., where, explaining the ideas of *Emile*, he depicts the third state in the evolution of humanity and refers to the second "Discours"; see loc. cit., pp. 173-76. He is opposing those of his contemporaries

who favored luxury, materialism, and benevolent despotism. Cf. Einaudi, *The Early Rousseau* (Ithaca, N.Y.: Cornell University Press, 1967), pp. 26 ff.

17. *De Cive*, chap. 8 ("Du Droict des Maistres sur leurs Esclaves").

18. Emile is prepared for the supreme sacrifice: pp. 743, 745, 823.

19. See. for example, *O.C.*, 3:376 n. 1. In any case, criminal law is not Rousseau's theme: ibid., pt. 2, chap. 12, p. 394.

20. "Emile," pp. 468, 473.

21. See, for example *O.C.*, 3:378 n. 1.

22. "Emile," pp. 522-23, 837; "Contrat social," p. 393. Cf. Chap. 2 above, n. 47.

23. "Emile," pp. 524-25. Cf. *The Republic* 1. 343-44. In Rousseau's view the anarchist, nihilist, or immoralist can be controlled only by himself and no one else, except in the case of children.

24. *The Republic* 6. 500. For Rousseau's use of the term *prince* mentioned below, see chapter 4 of this study.

25. *The Republic* 3. 399.

26. Cf. ibid., 4. 443, and "Emile," p. 304.

27. *The Republic* 6. 497. In the case of Rousseau some critics have recognized him as the lawgiver, but then they do not distinguish between the lawgiver or educator on the one hand and, on the other, the governor, whom they call "tutor" in *Emile*.

28. "Lettres à m. de Malesherbes," *O.C.*, 1:1145.

29. *The Republic* 9. 588.

30. Cf. "Emile," pp. 313-16, and *The Republic* 4. 419-21; 5. 465-66; cf. also "Emile," pp. 512-17, and *The Republic* 7. 519-20.

31. Cf. "Emile," p. 458: "Au lieu des loix sociales qu'il ne peut connoitre nous l'avons lié des chaines de la nécessité." Cf. p. 311. Burgelin hints at the link between the bond of necessity and reasonable law: *O.C.*, 4:319 n. 2; cf. p. 317 n. 1.

32. Of course, Emile's virtue later becomes an effect of love and discernment: pp. 339-40; cf. p. 481; cf. *The Republic* books 1 and 2. Regarding the lack of reason in children see "Emile," p. 319; cf. *The Republic* 4. 441. Both Rousseau and Socrates warn against the abuse of dialectic on the part of children: "Emile," p. 319; cf. *The Republic* 7. 537-39. The sage concludes that "philosophy" is not the study of a child, but he defines it as "the practice of virtue in the highest sense," that is, through the autonomous use of the faculties: *The Republic* 3. 407. Cf. 6. 499.

33. "Emile," pp. 334 n; 454; 857; cf. "Contrat social," pt. 2, chap. 12; cf. "Considérations," loc. cit., p. 1001; cf. 2 Cor. 3:3; Heb. 10:16.

34. See, for example, "Emile," pp. 322-23; cf. "Contrat social," pt. 2, chap.8.

35. *The Republic* 7. 537. Socrates insists upon this throughout: 2. 370, 374; 3. 394-97; 4. 419-23. The doctrine of natural goodness is, of course, Socratic. See ibid., 4. 444 (justice is as natural to the soul as health to the body); 6. 505-6 (every soul of man pursues the good); 9. 586-87 (what is best for each man is also most natural). Moreover, the sage avers that his wisdom, which takes this into account, is the only true one: ibid., 5. 449; 8. 544. Rousseau says the same: "Emile," Préface; and "Lettre à C. de Beaumont," loc. cit., p. 945.

36. *The Republic* 3. 405-8; 4. 425-26. Cf. Matt. 9:12.

37. See, for example, R. Derathé, *O.C.*, 3:384 n. 6; cf. J.-J. Rousseau, *The Poilitical Writings*, ed. C.E. Vaughan (Cambridge: At the University Press, 1915), 1:31-33, 71-82.

38. *The Republic* 2. 374; 3. 394, 397; 4. 419-23, 430-34, 441-43. Rousseau exacts that rulers be superior in personal merit: second "Discours" and "Considérations," loc. cit., pp. 189 and 963.

39. *The Republic* 4. 425. Cf. Rousseau's "Considérations," loc. cit., pp. 1000-1003, where as usual he insists that very few laws are necessary in a well-ordered city. Regarding the law of education see *The Republic* 4. 423. In the second "Discours," loc. cit., p. 187, Rousseau recalls that in Sparta the law provided mainly for education. Fénelon adopts the idea in *Les Adventures de Télémaque* (Liège: Grandmont-Donders, 1865), book 14, pp. 246-48.

40. For the importance of mercy in the practice of justice, see "Emile," pp. 511-12. For the "valetudinarians" see *The Republic* 3. 405-6; 4. 425-26. For the idea that disordered souls are sick, see "Emile," pp. 327-28. Rousseau's text recommending charity and beneficence is very close to Job 29:12-17.

41. It was one of Rousseau's favorites: "Emile," pp. 331 ff., 461, 818, 834-35; *C.C.*, 9:125, letter to Usteri, 13 September 1761.

42. This is a Socratic and Judeo-Christian precept. See, for example, Rom. 13:10. Cf. *The Republic* 1. 335. Cf. Rousseau's second "Discours," loc. cit., p. 156; "Emile," p. 594; *C.C.*, 9:125 and 14:100, letters to Usteri and Moultou, 13 September 1761 and 25 November 1762; "Confessions," *O.C.*, 1:356-57, 455.

43. Cf. "Confessions," loc. cit., pp. 20-21.

44. "Emile," p. 467; cf. second "Discours," loc. cit., pp. 164 ff.

45. *Contrat social*, pt. 1, chap. 9. Cf *The Republic* 4. 443; 9. 571 ff., 581-82, 591. Again the sage limits gain and honor to necessity lest disorder occur in the soul. For the idea of property founded upon work, see chapter 2 above and note 54.

46. "Emile," pp. 834, 835, 856. Cf. the denunciation of property in the second "Discours," loc. cit., pp. 164 and especially 178: "... Bientôt il ne fut plus possible de trouver un seul coin dans l'univers où l'on pût s'affranchir du joug... "

47. *The Republic* 9. 589 (the "good husbandman"). Cf. "Emile," pp. 342 (after the garden scene Rousseau writes: "... Il n'y a point de propriété pour cet age en aucun genre..."); 467 and 469-70 (on the need to earn a living); 833 (the main business of life is not to earn bread); 856 (Emile can own nothing).

48. Cf. "Contrat social," p. 375.

49. "Lettres morales," *O.C.*, 4:1092. Cf. Jean Starobinski, *J.-J. Rousseau: la transparence et l'obstacle* (Paris: Plon, 1957), p. 30.

50. Regarding education as an amusement: "Emile," pp. 344, 403, 407; cf. p. 351. Cf. "Considérations," chaps. 1-4. Cf. *The Republic* 4.424; (6.498, where the idea is merely implied); 7.537; 8.558.

51. *The Republic* 6. 510; 7. 526-27. Cf. 533, 536-37 (where Socrates recommends geometry for children providing that "early education be a sort of amusement"). His complaint, mentioned above, about confining study to childhood is in 6. 498.

52. *The Republic* 2. 379 ff. Cf. 5. 450-51.

53. See above and cf. *The Republic* 2. 378. Burgelin sees Plato's influence

here: *O.C.,* 4:352 n. 1. Rousseau's apostrophe to La Fontaine is comparable to that of Socrates to Homer. He writes: "Monsieur de Lafontaine... pour mon élève, permettez que je ne lui en laisse pas étudier une seule (de vos fables), jusqu'à ce que vous m'ayez prouvé qu'il est bon pour lui d'apprendre des choses dont il ne comprendra pas le quart, que dans celles qu'il pourra comprendre il ne prendra jamais le change... " Cf. *The Republic* 10. 599: "Friend Homer... if you are able to discern what pursuits make men better or worse, tell us what State was ever better governed by your help... or if you were privately a guide or teacher of any... "

54. "Emile," p. 381. Cf. *The Republic* 4. 427. Cf. note 49 above.

55. For the value of gymnastic to train the soul: "Emile," pp. 359, 370-71. Cf. *The Republic* 3. 403 ff. (especially 403, 410, 412). Socrates warns against habit that becomes second nature in 3. 395. Cf. 404. Cf. "Emile," pp. 407-8. For the expression "habit of order" see *The Republic* 4. 425. For Socrates' comparison of athletes to dogs: ibid., 2. 375 ff.; 3. 404; 4. 422, 440.

56. It is more profitable here to refer to Socrates than to Locke, Condillac, or Diderot.

57. "Confessions," loc. cit., p. 566; "Rêveries," *O.C.,* 1:1007.

58. For the symbolic use of darkness see "Emile," p. 323, and cf. p. 344; and "Contrat social," p. 456 n.

59. *The Republic* 2. 375; 3. 404; 6. 484, 488, 506, 507-8; 7. 514 ff.

60. "Emile," pp. 393 ff., 525, 589, 806-7. Cf. *The Republic* 3. 403. Cf. 5. 465-66; 10. 613, 621. Cf. 1 Cor. 9:24-27.

61. Matt. 20:15: "Is it not lawful for me to do what I will with mine own?" Cf. "Dans un don que je veux bien faire, ne suis-je pas maître de mes conditions?"

62. "Lettres morales," loc. cit., p. 1093.

63. For Rousseau's personal taste for arithmetic and geometry, see "Confessions," loc. cit., pp. 179-80, 238. Regarding the notebooks in which he copied an elementary course in geometry, see *O.C.,* 4:399 n. 1.

64. Cf. Rousseau's work on "La Morale sensitive" as described in "Confessions," loc. cit. p. 409 and n. 1. Gilson in *Les Idées et les letters* (Paris: Vrin, 1932), pp. 275-98, like Faguet and Mornet before him, sees fragments of this work in *Emile, Julie,* and the *Contrat social.*

65. See notes 50 and 51 above.

66. "Emile," pp. 407-9; cf. reflections on taste on pp. 671-73. The essay is on pp. 678-91. See chapter 5 below. Regarding taste and morals see chapter 15 of the *Essai sur l'origine des langues.*

67. For this quotation and the one below regarding the great contest: *The Republic* 3. 403.

68. Rousseau mentions Jesus at the age of twelve in "Lettre à m. de Franquières," *O.C.,* 4:1146.

IV

Threshold

The symmetry of *Emile* and the *Contract* in the third part of each is as transparent and enlightening as it is in the two previous parts. As before, many an obstinate problem of the treatise on citizenship finds in a collation with the novel a simple, lucid solution. The confrontation and correlation of parallel currents of thought in both works and their transfer in the Socratic manner from the sphere of the one into that of the other have the effect that might be produced by fitting some hitherto half-understood abstract into its proper context.[1]

PREPARATIONS FOR KINGSHIP

In *Emile* the author begins by considering the boy's strength and the use to which it is to be directed. At the age of twelve to fifteen years—the period covered in this part—he has, we are told, for the one and only stage in life a surplus of physical and mental energy in excess of the amount required to provide for his limited needs. As a man he "is," or rather "would be," very weak but as a child he is relatively strong. Rousseau changes "is" to "would be." The fact that he at first used the simple present indicates that he is thinking of a man too. Emile's energy, bred of his friendship with Jean-Jacques largely through the restriction of needs to narrow natural bounds, is invested in work, instruction, and study. The author almost quotes from the Sermon on the Mount when he explains that the disciple will use his strength to lay up treasure for himself, not in coffers where thieves break through and steal, nor in barns like men who forget that life is more than meat, but in his person and mind, which are

[145]

most truly himself.

To what studies are his energies directed? This is tantamount to asking again: "Where is wisdom? Where is happiness?" For, in Rousseau's view, the only pursuits worthy of a child and the sage he is to become are those that convey a knowledge of what is really useful for human happiness and his own, that knowledge being wisdom. Childish reason must therefore be changed into common sense and adult reason, which order and adjust all faculties of soul in accordance with the constitution of the whole being and all its parts, and its place in the order of things. The governor will reduce Emile's inquiries to what is useful for this purpose and accessible at his age, namely, natural knowledge about things, their existence, and essential relations to himself. With this in mind Jean-Jacques prepares to dispel "the darkness of human understanding" by drawing aside the veil from the face of nature. In other words, the disciple is now to be led further away from the "darkness" of the Socratic den into the light by means of work and study, "the steep and rugged ascent" to which I alluded in my second chapter when I spoke of the evolutionary process that is the theme of Rousseau's two books.

First the governor measures Emile's intelligence according to his progress in geometry, with which, after the fashion of Socrates at the same stage, this part of the novel begins and ends. The moment the boy can discern what is "useful" and what is not, he is artfully led to speculative studies and induced, for example, to find a "mean proportional" between two lines, or so we are told. Indeed, the author uses the term twice to convince us that the child can be impelled by some strange need to discover the solution. Then, after proposing the curious mathematical problem, he exclaims mysteriously: "See how we are gradually approaching moral ideas that discern good from evil!" He adds that until now we have known no law but necessity, whereas at present we are consid-

[146]

ering what is "useful." Here the notion of the "useful" appears to be obscured by the terminology, which is at first sight dismaying. It is elucidated by the initial chapter of the matching part of the *Contract* where he twice describes government as "a mean proportional" between subjects and sovereign. If, authorized by that text, we replace the geometrical terms in *Emile* by the idea of government or kingship whose proper role in moral life they symbolize, we may infer that the useful knowledge the boy is about to acquire relates to the governing function of reason, the art of kings and sages, or philosopher-kings. He is to be initiated into the vocation of Jean-Jacques, who professes to confine his teaching to what leads to wisdom and happiness. Such is the real theme of the third part as revealed by this collation and confirmed by the context of the passage on geometry in the novel.

With a view to instruction in good government the governor stimulates natural human curiosity to train the boy's reason to embrace all that contributes to his own well-being or felicity. Such curiosity is, we are told, the kind that might move a philosopher, if relegated alone to a desert island for life, to visit his earthly habitation. This image that dominates the whole third part of *Emile* is interpreted by Rousseau himself. The island of the human race is the earth. In that case the solitary philosopher or "lover of Sophia" is an image of the race itself or abstract man, Emile, in search of what is useful for his happiness. Indeed, the lad is about to be transformed into a new avatar of Robinson Crusoe, and at his time of life he judges all things by the usefulness they might have for that hero of childhood whose happiness is as simple as his own.

Of course, the child's concept of the "useful" will fall far short of the governor's. Yet there is no discrepancy between them. Emile, limited to what is of "real utility," has a childish, Robinsonian idea of it since he is confined to the narrowest sphere in material life, but that is the very condition of the greatest possible spiritual expansion.

[147]

The harsh discipline that subjects him to necessity from the first still prevails under the law of expediency and liberates the spirit to prepare him for his destined place as sage and ruler in the world within. Hence the governor employs what is useful in the boy's eyes to train him for an understanding of what is useful to achieve wisdom and happiness through self-government, a process that depends for its success upon that narrow view of expediency in physical life.

The writer is here inspired not only by the Sermon on the Mount but also by the teachings of Socrates. For example, Jean-Jacques calls the useful "noble" and "sacred." So does the Greek master, who explains that all things become useful only by their use of the idea of good. For him what is useful is wisdom turned toward moral truth or, as he says, whatever draws the soul toward true being or the good. This is the very sense in which Emile's governor uses the term when he proposes as his object the felicity of the sage and defines the useful as whatever is conducive to that end. In fact, the useful studies ultimately recommended in this part match the Socratic ones, which, as the master admits, are commonly called "useless" but which in his eyes are "useful" if sought after with a view to the beautiful and the good; but if pursued in any other spirit (for example, that of the shopkeeper), they are quite useless. The same beliefs determine Emile's studies at this stage and the use to which his reason is put. If, in the words of the Greek thinker, "the excellence or beauty or truth of every structure... and of every action of man is relative to the use for which nature or the artist has intended them," then the excellence of reason is relative to its use for purposes of government and the enforcement of law for which nature has designed it, rather than for shopkeeping.[2] And so Emile is initiated into its real use.

The idea that the sum of physical and spiritual strength fostered in soul or city by the society of friends must be governed and directed to whatever is useful for the happiness of the moral being enunciated in the laws is the theme of the third part of the *Contract*. Like the matching third part of *Emile* it contains a study of government. The first chapter deals with the subject in general. It begins significantly with a comparison between the relationship of body and soul in a man and the operations of government and sovereignty in a city. "Every free act," says the writer, "has two causes ... one moral: the will that determines the act; the other physical: the strength that executes it." In like manner the "moral person" of the city possesses both strength and will. These are the legislative power belonging to the sovereign people, whose acts are general principles providing for common utility, and the executive power, consisting of specific deeds delegated to an agent. The agent performs the function of the brain or reason in the soul by moving all forces to do the bidding of the will so that desires may not exceed strength and body and spirit may be brought into unison. That is precisely the role of Jean-Jacques' reason in the novel, and it is also the art he teaches. In the *Contract* the agent of the sovereign, its minister so to speak, is termed "government," considered from the point of view of its function as the lawful exercise of executive power. The body in which it is vested is called the "prince," and its members bear the name of "magistrates," "kings," or "governors." The language and the mentality are both biblical and Socratic. The idea that reason must rule or, as the Greek sage phrases it, that philosophers must be kings, is the third great "wave" that he must overcome before he can found his city. His rulers, like Rousseau's, are called "kings," "ministers of justice," "governors," or "magistrates."[3] As in *Emile* and the *Contract,* they guide the resources born of the city toward the happiness that is its object, implying at once the narrowest material limits and the largest spiritual growth.

In the same chapter of the *Contract,* on government in general, this agent of the supreme power, who is as it were

[149]

a bond between body and soul, is accordingly defined as intermediary between subjects and sovereign, or, if we wish, between desires and will combined in the same persons. Since the latter are subject only to the law of their own highest faculty, the government of reason is subject to the same law and rules in obedience to it to maintain freedom. For Rousseau as for Socrates, Christ,[4] and the biblical writers too, true kingship or government is in the nature of a service, a ministry to others and sacrifice of self. He therefore rejects the idea accepted by his contemporaries that its institution is a covenant like that which establishes the sovereign power. This idea is all the more preposterous in his eyes since the ruling faculty is prone to be seduced by the blandishments of wayward desires. And so he considers it as subordinate to the constant will that remains an infallible guide to judge the use or abuse of reason in the executive power. To represent the latter as he sees it, he twice calls it by the mathematical term used as often in *Emile,* a "mean proportional" between sovereign and state, since it receives from the former both the directions it gives to the people and the force of which it disposes and which it may not exceed. This is in accordance with his Socratic vision of a well-ordered and harmonious constitution wherein all parts do their own work without interfering with others, the will being in high command, the governing power of reason ruling in obedience "in the form of a servant," and the subject desires or gainful faculties taking their natural place in submission.

It is to accentuate the value of objectivity in acts of government that Rousseau, like Socrates, has recourse to the language of mathematics in both books. But the Greek philosopher uses it to measure the happiness of the true governor or king, who is king of self, and to compare that sum of felicity with the misery of the tyrant. To describe the interrelationships of spiritual forces, he favors musical terminology, likening the three powers in soul or city— reason, spirit, and desire—to the higher, lower, and middle notes of the scale and the intermediate intervals, which must be harmonized into one. This idea is akin to that of the "mean proportional."[5] But Rousseau prefers the mathematical term and shows how appropriate it is to express his meaning. For example, in a city the ratio or relationship of subjects or desires to the sovereign will, a ratio that determines the strength and integrity of the governing faculty, depends upon many factors, including the size of the city or "moral person." In a large one, where the temptations of prestige and wealth are numerous and persuasive and the individual shares less in sovereignty, there is need for a stronger governing power, which in turn must be controlled by greater "will power." Since the process is endless, the author disapproves of large cities. Analogously in *Emile* he counsels all men not to extend their being through space and time in pursuit of power and wealth until their lives are at the discretion of events essentially foreign to themselves and causing disorder within them. In that case "imaginary" desires increase and multiply to deceive and enslave the proper agent of the sovereign will.

To conclude his general chapter on government, Rousseau declares that this new "moral person," as he calls the governing power, who is active as participant in sovereignty and passive as subject to the laws it enforces, has only a borrowed and subordinate life. It is an artificial body that is the work of another artificial body, the sovereign. Of course, for reason is a product of art necessary to consummate the disciplined human will in the complex civilized soul. The author suggests that to prevent its abuse in morals or citizenship is practically impossible. But he also says that, apart from its "subordinate life," it it must have a vitality of its own in order to perform its lawful functions, combine its resources, take counsel, deliberate, make resolutions, and enjoy the rights and privileges necessary to save the constitution. These are precisely the prerogatives of reason exemplified in Jean-Jacques' concept of government in *Emile,* where the neophyte is gradually initiated into its mysteries.

Since the Rousseauist governor approaches his task in the manner of Socrates, I might profitably explain the author's use of the *Republic* at this juncture. Whereas Emile's early discipline as a Socratic guardian was the theme of the second part, his training as a philosopher-king is the theme of the rest of the book. The third part contains the preparation for the education of a king; the fourth is an exposition of the formation required; and the fifth offers a spectacle of the inner realm of the ruler. Socrates, who has a fancy for musical terms since his purpose is to create and maintain harmony in the soul, calls the present stage "the prelude to the chief strain," coming after "the strain of necessity" and "the strain of freedom," and leading to the chief strain of kingship. For Rousseau too this is the prelude to his own chief strain, which is the next part and especially the Song of Orpheus, as he calls his profession of faith therein. His prelude is inspired by the sage's contained in the seventh book of Plato's dialogue, upon which he draws heavily. In doing so, he takes the opposite course to the one he followed in the previous part. There he began by describing the principles and virtues of the moral being and the laws devised to shape it, and then depicted the discipline required, inverting the order of the first four books of the *Republic.* Here he begins with the process of education, or rather the content and method of the basic or preliminary training prescribed, and then in the fourth part proceeds to describe the nature and formation of the philosopher-king. But since in the case of kings Socrates follows a sequence that is the reverse of the previous one, Rousseau still inverts the order. I emphasize this because it is probably one reason why we have not previously recognized that *Emile* and the *Contract* are essentially a Rousseauist version of the *Republic.*

[152]

For greater clarity let me show briefly how Socrates handles the education of kings from the fifth to the seventh books. In the fifth, having discussed the role of women, which is the apparent theme of the Aemilian finale, he deals with the problem of evil and the value of sympathy to solve it, and finally discloses his ideal, which is to ensure that philosophers are kings, ideas that recur throughout the next part of *Emile*. The sixth book deals with the philosophic nature and its vocation and is also an important guide in the next part of Rousseau's novel. The same sixth book culminates with a similitude of the sun that is matched by an analogous one in the midst of the corresponding Aemilian text in the profession of faith. In the seventh book the sage finally broaches his "prelude" and leads his prisoners away from the den into the light, but first redefines the happiness of kings and sages that he visualizes, exactly as Rousseau does in the present part. Socrates' "prelude" consists of studies "useful" to that end, to prepare the reason for its proper role as ruler, not shopkeeper. It also specifies the qualities and age of student kings. The reader will see for himself how closely the author of *Emile* follows his pattern.

The Aemilian prelude is heralded by a little similitude of the sun foreshadowing the real one, and both reflect the Socratic imagery. The writer here sees the sunrise as an immense fire in the firmament scattering "the veil of darkness" and of night. The same veil covers what he called earlier the dark recesses of the mind, where he feared to light the torch of reason too soon. Like the Greek sage he thinks of the sun as linking sight and visibility, and in this respect it is the Socratic "author of sight," which he has already called "the sense least separable from the judgments of the mind." Hence we have his sanction to see in the sunrise a dramatization of the dawn of manly reason. The child now beholds the earth in the light of reason—a light that proceeds from truth, which is bound to

[153]

turn out to be moral truth as is usual with Rousseau.

In the child's case, we are told, the light lacks warmth of feeling, since his heart is not yet stirred by the harmony of the universe. Besides, he contemplates the works of creation without seeing the "workman," whose absence is, however, rather obtrusive. In the next part when the great "artist" is at last revealed, Jean-Jacques exclaims how simple it is to rise from the study of nature to the search for its author, thereby confessing the reason for his present explorations of the "island" of the world. When Rousseau finally broaches the sublime theme and returns to the symbol of the sun, he uses it with very different effect in a new and fuller similitude in the profession of faith, where reason is by then perfected by feeling.

We come now to the "steep and rugged ascent" of the future Aemilian and Socratic king. It is designed to give him a taste for intellectual toil until his vision, still perplexed and weak, becomes accustomed to the brightness of reality, and he is able to rise to the upper levels of the higher intellect.

Among the "useful" studies of the spiritual ascent, geometry is employed both first and last to illustrate the proper and objective use of the speculative faculty in its role as ruler. But the boy's main study, which ultimately leads to the source and pattern of all kingship and sovereignty, is the exploration of the earth and the examination of the products of nature and of art in their relationships to himself. He thereby acquires a few elements of the Socratic natural sciences and of the industrial and mechanical arts. In recommending the arts and the sciences, he has not forgotten that he is the author of a *Discourse* contending that their restoration has helped "to corrupt morals," in the words of Fénelon.[6] But in his view morals are corrupted not by the proper use of the arts and the sciences but by their abuse in our society. For Emile the arts and the sciences are the preamble of the great revelations of the next part.

[154]

He begins with astronomy, combined with a rather unconventional kind of geography, for the purpose of learning how to orient himself in the world of things. His
governor's laconic, or rather Socratic, questions stimulate him to solve problems relating to the heavens and the
earth and the laws that govern them.[7] These researches
are complemented by a study of local topography and by
the making of maps of the immediate surroundings. Since
few of us at Emile's age have ever felt the "usefulness" of such knowledge to find our way about, it is logical to suspect the presence of symbolism here.

It resides in the concept of "orientation." Here the word
means the ascertainment of the compass-bearings of the
soul on its journey toward the good represented by the
sun, whose light, as I have hinted, is that of moral truth.
The idea is Socratic, as we know. Rousseau himself suggests the allegorical meaning. He does so by reminding us
in this very context that Emile already has "a compass in
his eyes" and then by teaching him soon after that the
mathematical instrument does not suffice and that he needs
a helmsman's compass, too, not in his eyes or in his hands
but in his soul. We shall come to that lesson in a moment.
Meanwhile we may observe that the author connects the
two compasses and intends a continuity of imagery, although he uses a different word in each case. The magnet-
ized needle turning upon a pivot suggests to the mind a
relationship with the geometrical instrument. Both are used
in the novel as images of reason trained in the helmsman's
art, and the helm, as we know, is the law. The boy learns
to use his reason to "orient" his life toward the proper
object of the will. Meanwhile he is unwittingly guided by
his *gouverneur*. The allegory of the pilot that necessarily
runs throughout the book becomes almost obtrusive in this
part on government. That is as it should be.

The Socratic heroes undergo the same discipline. After
beginning with mathematics, considered "useful to draw
the soul toward being" or moral truth, they approach as-

tronomy as another theme "useful" for the same purpose. As they do so, one of the sage's youthful listeners, momentarily losing sight of the goal, remarks that this subject would be "useful" to a general, a farmer and a sailor (though he is not thinking of the "true pilot") since it would help them orient themselves in a literal sense. The master in his reply expresses amusement at his young friend's "fear of the world" and desire to "guard against the appearance of insisting upon useless studies" that "purify and re-illumine the eye of the soul" to reveal moral truth. The object of such studies is the spiritual orientation envisaged by Rousseau. The latter takes to heart the sage's advice to the youth to face the fact that some persons will see "no sort of profit which is to be obtained" from his words, since the kind of profit desired has nothing to do with shopkeeping and lies beyond childish minds. Emile, though a child, is not one of them since Jean-Jacques uses his first lowly steps in the intellectual ascent to raise him at last to a loftier concept of what is useful for his happiness. That is because the governor follows Socrates' advice to the letter. For example, he uses "the spangled heavens" as a pattern with a view to higher knowledge, for which he prepares his pupil by problems to exercise his reason and teach him to reflect, deliberate and resolve, and ultimately to govern and orient the soul toward what is regarded as its proper end, namely, the good. So does Socrates.[8] Both quite obviously have in mind the great similitude of the sun to follow later.

Rousseau, like his model, is therefore mainly concerned here with the art of reasoning and of examining the truth of things. At this juncture, after the example of the master, he dwells upon the importance of that art. He warns that the child can acquire it only by using his reason independently. Accordingly, Jean-Jacques secretly induces him to learn alone, to discover his own mistakes and gather clear ideas instead of facts. Moreover, he refuses to be a slave to the boy's questions, and answers them only enough to

stimulate curiosity but not enough to satiate it. In exactly
the same context of the "prelude" Socrates too demands
that his prospective rulers develop great skill in asking
and answering questions, and advises against encouraging
them to interrogate and argue for the sole purpose of refuting other people. Jean-Jacques also resembles the master—
again in the same context—when he further arouses curiosity by connecting knowledge in a manner suited to a
child, one object naturally suggesting another to the mind.[9]

To ensure, however, that the young scholar understands
the difference between the use of reason and its abuse,
the Rousseauist governor devises a new parable that is,
appropriately enough, a tribute to Socrates but has hitherto
been ignored as such. In tracing meridians to make maps
to find their way about, the friends are led to the study of
the magnet and ultimately to the helmsman's compass.
One day they go to a fair where they watch a juggler using
bread with a magnet hidden inside it to attract a wax duck
floating upon water. On their arrival home they imitate
him. The same evening again at the fair they confound
the performer in the eyes of his audience and take pride in
displaying their prowess at his expense. The following
day they return to the scene of their triumph, only to be
mortified in their turn by one failure after another, while
the conjuror enthralls the spectators with his "miracles."
The moral so far is that reason has been put to the wrong
use, resulting in vanity, error, and disgrace.[10]

But there is more to the parable than that. The juggler,
secretly prompted by Jean-Jacques, as we are told in a note
testifying to the symbolism here, pays a visit to the friends
and complains that they had tried to rob an honest man of
his livelihood, the only talent he has to earn his bread.
Thereupon he discloses the secret of his exploits. When
they offer him a gift, he refuses it: he takes no money in
return for his teaching. Here he resembles not only the
author, who earned his living copying music, not writing
books, but also the two great masters, who took no fee

[157]

for their lessons. He also resembles Jean-Jacques. Before taking his leave, he reproaches the latter for failing to counsel the child in his ignorance. The older man's experience, says he, is the authority that must guide the other. At once the governor promises Emile to protect his interests in future by telling him of his mistakes beforehand. The reader is then informed that their relationship is about to change: Jean-Jacques is to be no longer an apparently complacent companion but a severe master. The change is anticipated by "our conjuror Socrates." For so he is called in this simple humble tribute to the teacher who uses the art of conjuring in the *Republic* to illustrate the illusions of the mind and the need for reason to combat them.[11] The scene closes with the words: "All this to make a compass to take the place of meridians"[12] for purposes of orientation.

This part of the story requires commentary. The hero is being initiated into the notion of work as a means of earning bread, an idea vaguely present in the races for cakes or mimic Olympics. For Rousseau this notion implies a rudimentary form of justice in the Socratic sense, demanding, as we said above, that each class or faculty do its own work and refrain from meddling with others.[13] The sage himself, that great magician, is brought into the story to teach a basic lesson in the specific virtue that was the whole object of his quest in life. Emile has just meddled with others, committing a real injustice and not an imaginary one as in the parable of the sower. Hence he is in need of positive government and the guidance of greater age and experience to teach him to practice true justice and prevent him from harming others and bringing misfortune upon himself, until he knows enough about the proper use of reason for these purposes. The conjuror performs a real miracle by preparing him to recognize the need for direction in due course, and in addition arms him against serious illusions and false miracles later on.[14]

The compass that, according to the conclusion of the

parable, Emile has obtained must therefore be the one Jean-Jacques promises him therein, the ministry of his governor's reason. Of course he possesses it already, but he is unaware of that until later when the myth of the magician takes effect. At no time does he have any other compass but a symbolic one. That is why the governor, having said that they now have a compass to replace meridians, proceeds to give his pupil a lesson in orienting himself by means of the sun. It is also why Emile later possesses no compass literally speaking when, lost in a wood, he stands urgently in need of one. Then it is the helmsman's reason that becomes "that trembling vassal of the Pole, the feeling compass, nagivation's soul." The pole would be divine wisdom, Sophia, toward which the pilot-governor's course is oriented.[15]

It is important to know what form of government Jean-Jacques embodies and teaches in *Emile*. The answer is abundantly clear in the novel and is reflected in several chapters of the corresponding part of the *Contract* dealing with different kinds of government. "The principle that constitutes various forms of government," in the wording of the title of the second chapter, is the number of governors to whom the executive power is entrusted. Rousseau begins by establishing that the more governors there are, the less active the government is, even though it may be more righteous. He then considers two forms both of which he rejects. The first is the intensely active rule of one, who consolidates within himself the force of the entire association but uses it to serve his own private interests or desires. The second is the government of the whole moral being in which the legislative authority reposes, whose will is righteous but whose governing power lacks energy, since its preocupation with general principles and abstract concepts makes it unable to cope with specific issues efficiently and expeditiously. The alternatives given only lead to an impasse and hardly correspond to the ideal situation in the novel.

[159]

In the third chapter, "Division of Governments," the author distinguishes three forms and emphasizes the role of the supreme command of will in their establishment: the democratic, suited to a small city, wherein the sovereign entrusts the administration to all or most of the people; the aristocratic, befitting a city of moderate size, wherein the sovereign confides it to less than half of them; and finally, the monarchy or rule of one man, expedient only for vast states. In all cases the difficulty of the subordination of powers accentuates the mythical nature of his city. And so he adds significantly that government is susceptible of as many forms as the state has citizens, suggesting that the only true one is self-government. This is the message of *Emile* too. Of course, one of the three forms or a modification of it must then be adapted to the direction of inner life.

The next (fourth) chapter of the *Contract,* "Concerning Democracy," deals with a form that Rousseau positively rejects as impossible. Yet many scholars today, like his contemporaries, see in the book a theory of democracy since he makes the king a mere governor to execute the sovereign will of the people. But a constitution of that kind would, in his Socratic terminology, be called not a democracy but a republic or ideal city.[16] He has already said that for him a democracy is a city wherein the administration is assigned to the whole nation and that the latter cannot cope with practical problems posed by the intrigues of private passions in particular acts, a truth that is also illustrated in the *Republic*. According to the present chapter, a city that would never face such problems would not need to be governed at all since it would be a minute epitome of the simplicity, equality, ascetism, and virtue of men so perfectly one that the execution of the laws would immediately follow from the sovereign will. He concludes that this form of government would be suited only to a nation of gods. He means, as we are told later in *Emile,* that the divine intelligence acts intuitively without reasoning and the divine will takes effect without means.[17] Men are otherwise, alas! And so the Rousseauist city is not democratic in the sense defined by the author, who in any case has long since rejected dwarf cities as he did giant ones in favor of those of moderate size.

Even if we confuse democracy with self-government, his ideal could hardly be called democratic in the Rousseauist view, since the term "self-government" suggests that there is a self to govern and another to be governed. But Rousseau does not confuse his terms. If, as democracy implies for him in any moral being whether city or soul, the resolutions of the will always remain the measure of the impulses of desire without the deliberations and guidance of reason, then as he has said the governing function, bestowed upon reason by nature herself, would not need to act at all to maintain a balance of powers and desires, and even self-government would be unnecessary. But that is impossible, even for Emile. He is being governed now as he is to be all his life long. Only he is not ruled democratically.

In the novel, as we know, Jean-Jacques' rule represents that of a distinguished minority like that which governs the inner world of the soul where there is a hierarchy among the faculties. In him the power of reason follows its natural vocation and rules in the service of the sovereign will. The compass, the tiniest part of the soul obeying the human spirit's deepest aspiration, rules the large part consisting of the great obscure and formless mass of multitudinous desires. Judgment and decision belong to the elite, for nature herself ordains it. The governor is at present teaching Emile that very lesson, and when the boy finally governs himself, he does so in the manner of Jean-Jacques.

In the *Contract* too Rousseau favors aristocratic rule. He does so in the fifth chapter, "Concerning Aristocracy." But he begins by stipulating that governors, like Socratic kings, be servants of the nation, or rather, of the righteous will. He distinguishes three forms of aristocracy. The first is natural, based upon age and "the authority of experience," says he, quoting the conjuror's words in *Emile*. This kind of government befits a child or, if we wish, humanity in its childhood. Then there is the elective aristocracy seen in the next part of the novel where the hero, having learned the art of self-government, appoints Jean-Jacques to be his "minister of education," or "governor," until he can safely serve and rule himself aristocratically, as he must do in the inevitable absence of the ideal social order. Finally there is the hereditary aristocracy, dismissed by the author as the worst of all.

He prefers the elective by reason of its visible benefits. They include the separation of the supreme will and governing faculty, and also the advantage of being able to choose as governors, not people who embody the desire for wealth and power as has supposedly been done in the historical past, but distinguished men of integrity, enlightenment, and experience. The rulers of his own city are, as we know, men who have proven their superiority. And so in this chapter he favors "sage rulers" or "philosopher kings," providing they rule for the profit of all instead of their own private benefit, and begin by ruling themselves. It is useless to reproach him for controlling "individuals"—or individualist desires—by means of a small select leadership since that is admittedly what he intends to do. He concludes by saying that under such an administration rigorous equality is not necessary, since governors must of course have the means to exercise their function. He said the same in the penultimate chapter of the previous part. This is not a violation of the principle that property must be based upon need before it can become a legitimate right in any city, however governed. It simply means that the governing power in city or soul is supported by gainful faculties and is reduced to the necessities of its station in life, as are those faculties themselves. This is the case in *Emile,* where all the conditions of good government are translated into the domain of private life.

The nature of good government is further elucidated in the novel by another parable, that of Montmorency forest. Before dealing with it, I must explain the context in which it occurs. Like the myth of the conjuror, this one too is connected with the study of the so-called natural sciences. The acquisition of the "compass" leads the friends into the vast domain of systematic physics. They create their own instruments to perform experiments in the world of nature in such a manner that the reason is slowly enlightened by clear, well-related ideas. Rousseau comments that among the many fine shortcuts to knowledge, we sorely need someone to teach us the art of learning with difficulty. Here he is still inspired by Socrates, who in the same context describes the attributes necessary to profit by his teaching and demands that his future kings be able to endure the severity of study, that they be sound in body and mind and lovers of the labor of both. Emile's "laborious researches" are dictated by the same considerations. They allegedly combine the gymnastic of the athlete with the intellectual discipline of the sage and raise him at last "from the amusements of philosophy . . . . to the true function of a man." Now a man's true function, still unknown to the boy, *is* philosophy, but not in the sense understood by the writer's contemporaries who discredited the term in his eyes, nor even in the sense of the study of science as some of us have recently supposed, but in the Socratic sense of the practice of wisdom for the sake of felicity. In order that the hero may practice it without compulsion as the Greek sage advises, he is taught that wisdom suits his nature and is useful for his happiness. For example, we are told that he is learning to exercise enough reason and foresight to see the value of work and submit to the law of necessity with a view to providing for the modest needs and simple happiness of natural man, in accordance with the Socratic law of justice herewith presented in a form slightly

[163]

more refined than before. But Emile is not yet a moral being since his virtues are practiced unconsciously and are still only "images of virtue." Jean-Jacques is preparing him for that higher vocation and training his reason for its proper role therein, simply by confining him to activities conforming with his childish notion of present utility. "What is the use of that?" becomes a phrase as "sacred" for Rousseau as it is for his Greek master, since it signifies what is useful to the boy in the present to pave the way for the happiness of the sage, as we were informed earlier. With that phrase the governor quells his ward's inquiries and teaches him "to interrogate like Socrates," says the writer, referring openly to the very context of the *Republic* by which he is here inspired. If Emile in his turn responds to his governor's rare queries in like manner, Jean-Jacques in his reply never loses sight of the double meaning of what is useful for his pupil's happiness, implying both limited material bounds and unlimited spiritual scope. This brings us to the parable of Montmorency forest.

In the midst of conversations about orienting oneself by the sun and observations about the position of the forest north of the village, Emile suddenly asks: "What is the use of that?" Jean-Jacques simply abandons the subject. But next morning he contrives to see that they go astray in those very woods, though, of course, he himself is far from lost. The boy sheds tears of despair though "the real Emile" never weeps. He is famished, and, to make matters worse, it is noon and dinnertime. After a while Jean-Jacques like another Socrates suddenly recalls the previous day's discussion. At midday they can find the north judging by the direction of the shadows. To make their way toward the village, they need only take the opposite course from the darkness toward the light. For the first time in his life the happy Emile addresses his governor as his "good friend" while they follow the path leading out of the woods. The new Robinson Crusoe at last discovers "the footprints in the sand," an awareness of others that will conduct him to the desired goal.

This parable, presented as a dramatic dialogue like that of the sower, clothes the author's ideas in visible imagery essential to the literary art. Here Emile appears as an image of natural man who is already unconsciously prepared for integration, since he sees that if he does not find his way out of the forest, he will starve. He is to become aware of the necessity for entering society in order to provide for the needs of life, the first and greatest of which is food, the very condition of existence.[18] He must go forth to procure what is "useful" for his well-being as simply as he conceives it. In fact, he is about to be transplanted from his country garden to the city of Paris in the second part of this phase of his training.

But other elements of symbolism in the myth show that the idea of usefulness extends much further than the boy can see. He not only moves from the woods to the social order to provide for his needs, but at the same time emerges from the shadows into the light, from the semidarkness of mental dawn toward the radiance of "truth." Now, as we have observed, that truth, born in society, is less intellectual than moral. Here it implies the idea of work as a form of Socratic justice for which the boy is being prepared. The parable contributes to lead him thither by way of spiritual "orientation"—the pilot's art—again suggested by the problems of astronomy with their allegorical overtones. Accordingly, almost immediately after the miniature drama, the writer again refers to the ultimate goal of Rousseauist and Socratic reason, unknown, of course, to the child: "the happiness of the sage and the glory of paradise." The author has this in mind, therefore, in the parable itself. He virtually says so in an allusion to it in the sequel to *Emile*—also inspired by *The Republic*—where it is interpreted symbolically. In an ethical situation in that fragmentary work, Emile says: "I took the direction contrary to the object that I was morally obliged to avoid, in the same way that I followed the opposite of the shadow

[165]

years ago in Montmorency forest."[19] In a sense the whole allegory is a new appeal to men to find their way out of the woods and their amoral or immoral plight, and to orient their lives toward justice and spiritual values already roughly sketched in the apologue of the conjuror Socrates.

Of course, the hero is not led from the woods by his own reason. He is guided by the light of the sun and the compass that he discovered as a result of his encounter with the conjuror, namely, reason in the *gouverneur* and the truth that lights its way. What is important here is that he feels this personally to the point of calling Jean-Jacques his "good friend." The phrase is suggestive of a Socratic utterance in Plato's third book where the sage, forming his guardians, anticipates the training of kings in words that resound throughout *Emile,* as we shall see: "When reason comes, he [the pupil] will recognize and salute the friend with whom his education has made him long familiar."[20] The reason that is friendly to nature must finally appear to him as such. But until it does and he has a "compass" of his own, he is brought to feel more and more deeply the need for Jean-Jacques' rule and is even led to implore it as a grace.

There is an allegory in the fourth book of the *Republic* that combines most of the elements of the myth of Montmorency forest and casts light upon the moral function of reason therein. Socrates and his friends appear as huntsmen in a forest in search of game, reminiscent of Emile's dinner. But the Greek master, like Jean-Jacques, has something else in mind, and the real object of his search is justice. His young friends, like Emile, "have just eyes enough to see what the master shows them." And although Socrates remarks, "Here is no path and the wood is dark and perplexing," yet we have the feeling that he is no more lost than the Rousseauist governor, for he suddenly finds the quarry as close by as the village in *Emile.* Rousseau is fascinated with the story. He returns to it in the fourth part where the lad goes hunting just before he discovers

[166]

true justice, and again in the fifth where the two friends lose their way thrice in the woods in their search for Sophia, who turns out to be close by. And so the Socratic symbolism of the hunt for wisdom employed in the third part is rich in potential reverberations and becomes, as it were, a recurrent motif or musical phrase sustained throughout the harmonious temple of the soul.

IMAGES OF JUSTICE

Emile is at last transplanted to the French capital to study the arts after exploring the sciences. To represent the spiritual isolation of natural man in a strange setting before he becomes active as social or moral man, to prepare him for that vocation, and to initiate him into society, the author has recourse to the allegory of Robinson Crusoe to which he alluded at the beginning of this part. The narrative becomes very personal here, for, in his autobiography and *Dialogues,* he is himself the "new Robinson Crusoe."[21] So is Emile. This is another confession that in the novel Rousseau is really telling the tale of his own spiritual aspirations. The allegory opens with a violent diatribe against "bookish learning," which has nothing to do with them. The fact is that Emile does not confine himself to reading the story of Robinson but acts it out in real life as in the case of previous myths. Indeed, this is the first one not invented by Jean-Jacques, although all are at least partially inspired by outside sources, especially the *Republic* and later La Fontaine's fables. The eponymous hero, like another Robinson Crusoe, learns to provide alone for the needs of natural man, which are those of his own life and happiness, beginning with the need for bread glimpsed in the conjuror's complaints and personally felt in the forest. He does so by means of the natural arts that a man may practice by himself and that afford no other felicity but freedom of spirit and the bare necessities of life. However, by favor of those very assets, he is soon to become an active moral being, "king of himself" as Robinson was

[167]

king of his island and Adam king of his. Indeed, Jean-Jacques uses the myth of the great hero of childhood to make his ward into a Socratic king or governor like himself by teaching him to use his own reason to serve his needs and those of others too, while making as few claims as possible upon his fellows.

Emile's kingship, anticipated here, raises problems posed in the *Contract,* particularly in the sixth chapter, "Concerning Monarchy." It is inspired by this part of the novel but deals largely with the world of actuality, which is contrasted with the ideal. Rousseau, moved by the spectacle of eighteenth-century despotism, has already shown the disadvantages of royal government in its contemporary form, and he does so again in the present context. This does not alter the fact that his own governors are called "kings," that Jean-Jacques is one of them and Emile destined to become one. The author never loses sight of the Socratic or evangelical kingdom within. His aristocratic governors and sages of the previous chapter are kings like those of Socrates, who makes no distinction at all between the royal and aristocratic forms of government and calls his rulers both "aristocratical men" and "philosopher-kings." When Rousseau comes to speak of royal government in the *Contract,* he simply reverses his own idea of kingship and shows the latter in practice as opposed to what it essentially is in his view. The whole chapter is a paradox. The kings evoked therein are imposters whose passions enslave them to the lowest elements and tyrannize the highest in themselves and in all those upon whom they depend. In its illuminating conclusion the writer actually refers back to the beginning of the *Contract* where he defends the kingship of man in Adam, "sovereign king of the world as Robinson was of his island." The heir of both is Emile, whose entire education is conceived to preserve his lofty birthright even when he is no longer alone.

According to the chapter in question, the kings of this world do not pursue the common felicity that is a powerful incentive for the "sages" of the previous chapter and the heroes of the novel. On the contrary, they flatter their own desire for gain and prestige as individuals, at the expense of human aspirations and the strength of the kingdom that is their birthright. They thereby sacrifice the true king's interest to tyrannical and slavish passions. In the author's opinion no government is so ruinous to freedom and the needs of the constitution.

It is not by accident that the rest of the chapter is devoted to the education of true kings. To "beget" them, we are told, we should have to do the antithesis of what we now do. Rarely, says the writer, do men "born to govern" or "steer" take the "helm" in a monarchy. Observe how the Aemilian myth recurs. He implies that those who presume to steer are not kings at all, but travesties of kings whose faculties are no more suited to the task than their training is.[22] For, unlike his own "kings," they are taught to rule other people instead of themselves. That produces tyrants, not kings who know how to submit to the law of reason for the sake of wisdom, the discernment of good and evil. The idea is as old as King Solomon and a good deal older. As I have just said, Rousseau ends the chapter by referring back to the beginning of the book where, in addition to establishing the kingship of humanity in the person of Adam or Robinson Crusoe, he declares that a city suffering from serious disorders at the hands of charlatans has a right to have recourse to the services of a true physician, meaning a real statesman, governor, or king.[23] The tyrants portrayed in the *Contract* as slaves are just such charlatans, and are the reverse of Socratic and Rousseauist kingship visualized in the sages of the previous chapter and in the heroes of *Emile*. The collation with the novel gives to the chapter on the monarchy a new breadth of meaning hitherto unsuspected, at least for some of us.

In the next (seventh) chapter of the appendix, "Concerning Mixed Governments," the author emphasizes the value of mixed forms, subdivided into parts handled differently, for the purpose of maintaining the equilibrium of the rational "artificial body" as an intermediary faculty or "mean proportional" between sovereign will and subject desires. He regards such inner adjustments as effective to preserve the ideal relations between the highest and lowest principles of soul or city.[24] In his eyes, if the balance were upset, the covetous and concupiscent elements in the guise of powerful private interests would soon seduce the reason to tyrannize and overthrow the moral being.

The author of the *Contract* next turns his attention to factors determining the wealth of a city and affecting its form of government. These are also the topics of the following pages of *Emile,* which begin with a discussion of the industrial arts and to which it is logical to revert before considering the appendix. As usual I shall confine myself to what is necessary to illustrate the interlocking of texts.

While practising the natural arts, the "new Robinson Crusoe" takes a step beyond them. Suddenly he is initiated into the mechanical and industrial arts that are born of society and make it necessary through the sharing and distribution of work and the resulting production of surplus goods. He learns that those arts make men useful to one another and mutually dependent, but does not yet suspect that they entail moral or immoral relationships. The governor traces the arts to their origins as he did in the case of property because the evolution of the moral being—the theme of *Emile,* the *Contract,* and the *Republic*—is that of human institutions.[25]

As is well known, Rousseau is here inspired by the beginning of the *Republic* where Socrates pictures the birth of our "luxurious" society and the conditions that necessitated the formation of his own austere one. In this instance the author of *Emile* violates the order of his model, since he uses the arts, as he did property, to bring the hero

[170]

into active contact with that luxurious state of which the Greek sage takes leave at the outset.

However, in dealing with the arts, he continues to shape the moral being or ideal order in the inner world or society of friends at the same time as he sketches it within an alien setting whose potential noxious effects, though hidden from the child, are visible to the reader. For example, under his governor's guidance Emile esteems the arts according to standards other than our own. He judges them not with an eye to opulence but by their use to Robinson Crusoe. If this rule seems to belong to "an imaginary order," as the writer admits, that order is the Rousseauist and Socratic one, reduced in the material sphere to necessity. The governor explains that his pupil, who is to be a sage, must know the truth of things before he knows men and their prejudices; for, he observes, "you do not lead a nation when you are like it." Here he hints at the kingly vocation for which Emile's judgment is being nurtured. Hence the boy knows nothing of our absurdities. Indeed, "he knows no other human being but himself," and he still has much to learn in that respect. He simply knows his own place in the order of things, being confined to it by the bonds of necessity or the law of his constitution instead of the laws of reason, which he does not yet recognize as such. He is therefore hardly more than a physical being. And so he esteems the arts by their usefulness to the simple happiness of a creature like himself or Robinson, and also by their independence of other crafts, which makes them easier to practice. For example, he values agriculture, metallurgy, and carpentry in that sequence, which is also the historical order of their development as traced in the second *Discourse*.

These studies serve as a preamble to lessons in political economy and considerations of wealth and its effects upon government. Emile cannot help but see that the surplus productions of the industrial arts lead men to exchange with one another for the purpose of supplying their

[171]

own needs. Indeed, he glimpsed something of the device of exchange in the parable of the sower, where, however, it was obvious that men had gone beyond the principle of need. He now proceeds to investigate the interplay of trade and commerce, studying the products of each country, the arts and sciences of navigation, and finally transportation problems arising through distance and the position of waterways. He learns that trade of every kind, including all social intercourse, depends upon conventional equality, which is therefore the first law of society. He also learns that, in the world of men, this law necessitates positive enactments and government, and that the same law, in the world of things, necessitates the invention of money to compare the value of goods of different kinds. These lessons, inspired by the Socratic text mentioned in the penultimate paragraph above, are limited to a consideration of economic relationships and exclude an explanation of their moral effects and abuses.

At this perilous juncture in Emile's formation where he is brought into contact with an alien world, Rousseau faces the risks involved in the work of government. In doing so, he has recourse to a critical point in the same Socratic text, although this is not generally known. It is the point to which I referred earlier where the Greek master, in his sketch of society at its origins, is reproached by his listeners for failing to give his citizens "a relish to their meal," whereupon he complies and then proceeds to purge away luxury with education and legislation. In Socratic phraseology, Emile is now to behold the unhealthy state of men who recline upon sofas and have sauces and sweets in the modern manner.[26] Jean-Jacques escorts him to a sumptuous banquet but artfully contrives to turn it into a mimic symposium. Together they imagine the enormous resources called into play to supply the luxury surrounding them, reminiscent of the Parisian feasts of the baron d'Holbach. But soon afterward, to offset any false impressions that may have been created in the child's mind, the

[172]

governor regales him with a simple rustic repast, seasoned with Socratic "necessary appetite," freedom of spirit, and delight in the society of good folk who are surely worthy of the Greek sage's "true and healthy state." Emile, like the writer whose rural repasts in life are transformed into veritable idylls in the *Confessions,* finds more real pleasure in the country feast and is thus preserved from the seductions of luxury by good government.

The symbolism is as clear here as it was in the discussion of appetite hitherto. The banquet of life, suggestive of the Gospels as well as of the *Republic* and *Symposium,* is represented by two meals, each reflecting an entirely different mode of existence. The simple one is Jean-Jacques' well-governed Socratic or evangelical "imaginary order." The luxurious one is our own ill-governed intemperate society where Emile passes unscathed. He is saved by some "sublime power" vested in his governor that enables him to stand firm against false opinion and the prejudices of wealth and power.

Shielded by that "superhuman" presence, he is soon to be taught to earn his bread in an alien setting. But first he is trained in many different arts and crafts to inspire him with respect for other people's work as well as his own. The double purpose here defined evokes the two aspects of Socratic justice, which are to do one's own work, and not to meddle with others. Emile is to practise that virtue within the society of friends, but in a land foreign to himself and his own city.

These pages of the book are the source of a much debated chapter of the *Contract* (the eighth in this part) about the connections between wealth and government, to which I alluded above. It is entitled "That Every Form of Government Is Not Suited to Every Country." In the past we have supposed that it was added simply to fill out the book.[27] But juxtaposition with the foregoing development of *Emile* disproves that. The author begins by saying that freedom is not the fruit of all climates. Hence it is vital to know "in what corner of the world" a moral being might be free to exercise his faculties according to their proper functions and find happiness therein. In dealing with this question that is hardly beside the point, Rousseau continues to confine himself to general principles. In a city, he observes, the government is supplied with necessities from the surplus produced by subjects; in the soul, of course, the governing power is supported by desires or gainful faculties. That is why Socrates calls the latter "maintainers and foster-fathers": they keep body and soul together, while reason brings the two into unison. The amount of the surplus, as the author of the *Contract* remarks and as Emile now knows, depends upon three factors: fertility of climate, determining the kind of work and number of workers required to till the soil; the nature of the earth's productions; and the needs of men. This passage adheres closely to the order of Emile's lessons in political economy. So does the following. The factors influencing wealth, says the writer, in turn affect the form of government since some kinds of rule are costlier than others and even rob people of their contributions and make them miserable. He alludes to contemporary monarchs, meaning tyrants and despots. Free states, like a democracy or aristocracy, require moderate resources that are wholly used for the common happiness.

In the rest of the chapter he reflects further upon the three factors determining wealth. Fertile southern climes, says he, where the soil requires little work and fewer workers to yield succulent fruits, produce the luxury that fosters despotism, whereas temperate zones of moderate wealth are hospitable to good polity and suited to free men. This may be one reason why in the beginning of *Emile* he chose a temperate zone for the hero's life. Yet in doing so, he implied that the climate of the child's birth is as symbolic as his wealth (although both may also be taken literally) and that northerners dwelling on an ungrateful soil are simply an "image" of the poor, whereas southerners living in a fertile land symbolize the rich. The same symbolism may be present in the text of the *Contract,* for there he discreetly admits that even if historically the reverse of his theory about southern and temperate zones were true, he would nevertheless adhere to it. In other words, if the ideal Greco-Roman city was born in the south that supposedly fosters despotism. it could be reborn anywhere on earth as it is in Emile, who though strong and free in a moderate clime lives in the midst of despotism. That is because what really determines wealth and freedom too is the third of the three factors mentioned in the *Contract,* the needs of men, to which the author reverts. He observes that if the south fosters wealth, it is also because southerners live on hardly more than air, with the result that a Spaniard could live for a week on a German's dinner, and "in Italy they regale you with sweets and with flowers." Austerity—the law of necessity—is the key to the author's ideal, which may easily come into being wherever the needs of men are few.[28] The whole passage indirectly evokes Emile's two repasts, symbolic of two different societies in any geographical area. It condemns all luxury that breeds tyranny and slavery. The latter occur, says the author concluding the chapter, in any country that has fewer inhabitants than it can sustain and whose wealth therefore exceeds and increases its needs. He thereby exalts the Socratic Aemilian city, whose needs and resources are evenly balanced and whose life is secure from the disorders of passion.

To revert to the novel, the new Robinson, having explored his surroundings, comes back at last to himself and his own "habitation." Thereupon the governor exclaims on an evangelical note: "Happy are we if, returning home, we do not find it in possession of the enemy who is lying in wait to enter and dwell therein." He refers to the advisability of anticipating the "unclean spirit" of the Gospel. Such illuminating phrases and imagery associated with Christ or Socrates are designed to carry us beyond the

[175]

child's point of view that is confined to material needs and reveal the vaster perspectives of the philosopher-king that depend upon the former for their realization.

The hero, all absorbed in arts and crafts and Robinson Crusoe, sees at length that he himself like other men will have to resort to an exchange of work and goods in order to live, and that society is therefore necessary to human life and in that sense natural. Since he is able to grasp the material side of social relationships before he can really become actively engaged, his governor's first task is to teach him to preserve life and to provide for his needs by means of those relationships. But again there are signs that the physical world of the child prefigures the moral one and that Jean-Jacques' real preoccupation is spiritual kingship, the training of reason to rule the gainful faculties and serve the sovereign soul of man. For example, the boy is compared to various kings in history who have "risen to man's estate" by learning to earn their daily bread. The son of man who is born a king must do the same. For "social man and the citizen," whose vocation is Emile's, must regard work as a debt to society that has to be repaid according to the law of justice. In Socratic terms there must be no drones in the hive of the city or the soul.[29] The drones are "spendthrifts" full of "unnecessary or useless desires" bred in idleness, and are the governor's great foe in his work as guardian of the constitution. They are foreign to the hero, whose name is synonymous with industry and who will "do his own work," or, in other words, practice justice. The industrious man who works to supply the needs of life is an image of the just man. The author's thought transcends any literal interpretation as much as the governor's transcends Emile's.

The theme of this phase of education is that of the ninth chapter in the third part of the *Contract,* where the key idea is also the preservation of life including moral life that depends upon the free exercise of the faculties. It is entitled "Concerning the Signs of Good Government," and is complementary to the previous one as freedom is a correlative of necessity. If the surplus wealth of gainful elements supports the governing power, the latter in its turn ensures the preservation and prosperity of those it governs. Rousseau begins the chapter by describing the blessings enjoyed by "citizens" as opposed to "subjects," meaning slaves. He mentions the freedom and security of the human person from crimes at home and wars abroad, and the circulation of bread instead of gold. These bounties are all that is necessary for the preservation and prosperity of men, which can be judged, says the author, by their number and population. It would be a mistake to conclude from this that he intends to ensure preservation at the cost of freedom, which is included in the bounties described. Obviously he is saying as clearly as he has done hitherto, that freedom is essential to life. He says so again in a note at the end of the chapter, declaring that the welfare of nations and the prosperity of the species depend upon liberty.[30] Moreover, in *Emile* the governor's concept of necessity and freedom is regarded as salutary for the life of both body and soul since it provides for the needs of the entire human creature.

The next two chapters of the *Contract* (the tenth and eleventh) are a corollary of the previous one and confirm the importance of freedom to life. They show that if the governing authority fails to safeguard liberty, the result is death. The first of the two is entitled "Concerning the Abuse of Government and Its Inclination to Decline." Rousseau warns therein that if the governing power of reason is seduced by passions intense enough to resist and oppress the sovereign will and break the covenant, then the collective body dies like that of a man. He pursues the idea in the next chapter, "Concerning the Death of the Body Politic." There he prophesies that issue as inevitable since no state lasts forever. As Socrates phrases it: "Even a constitution such as ours will not last till the end of time."[31] This means that even if it could materialize as a physical

[177]

entity in the objective world of actuality, it would not last as such. But Rousseau maintains that we possess the skill to make it last longer than most. Again drawing a comparison between the collective body and the body of a man, he explains that the human constitution is the work of nature and that our power over our life span is limited, but that the constitution of the state is a work of art whose life lies largely in our hands. But for Rousseau the human constitution includes not merely the physical life of the body but especially the sovereign powers of the moral person of soul or of city whose strength and growth depend as much upon art as does the state. But there is a difference. Although the passive being of a state dies like that of a man when its bonds with the sovereign or legislative power are severed, Rousseau could not say the same thing of sovereignty itself or the active being any more than he could say it of the human spirit, which is no different, for he professed to believe that it is indestructible and survives the body, as we shall see.[32] That is why, to describe the life of the city, he uses the Socratic similitude of city and soul; but to describe the death of the state, he adopts the contemporary analogy of the collective and human body. The life of the passive being may be prolonged, says he—and incidentally this applies in a limited way to the human body—by strengthening the active being or sovereign will, wherein the principle of life resides and whose austere laws invigorate the body and the heart. In this context the sovereign power, identified with will in the soul, is linked with the heart, presumably as the seat of fortitude, while, as we know, the executive power answers to the brain. It is only when the heart dies that "the animal" expires, says the author in carefully chosen words, to avoid suggesting that sovereignty might be destroyed. In a well-constituted state, he adds, the latter manifests itself in respect for the most ancient laws, by which he means his own that are over 2,500 years old.

In the novel Jean-Jacques, like the sage governors of the

[178]

Contract, ensures the preservation and prosperity of the society of friends and therefore of Emile by fortifying the hero's powers and anticipating the decline of the friendship of reason for nature. He does so, as we have seen, by teaching the boy the art of self-government or ministry of justice, the art of mastering the gainful faculties with a view to the pursuit of wisdom and lasting happiness.

These deeper intentions are further acentuated when the author speaks of a choice of work suitable for Emile. He prescribes manual labor on grounds that suggest his real purpose: the artisan is more independent of the caprices of fortune and of men, and hence more self-reliant than the husbandman. But at the same time he admits that husbandry is man's first vocation and Emile's, and he calls it, in the manner of the Greek master, "most useful and noble."[33] In recommending that it be supplemented by a trade, he hints that his words have spiritual implications, for he cites the evangelical saying that "the letter killeth, but the spirit giveth life," and explains that the object is less to teach a trade than to rise above the prejudices of men. He further suggests a moral motive by adding that the laborer, unlike the professional man, is exempt from dancing attendance upon scoundrels, courtesans, and the rich, and may therefore be a man of honor and justice. The governor's goal always remains a moral one. Emile is to do "useful," honorable work that is also compatible with humanitarian feeling. Nevertheless, he makes his own choice by following his personal idea of utility, selecting a trade of real value to the new Robinson Crusoe and adapted to his age, sex, and character. He chooses that of carpentry, and Jean-Jacques, who shares his entire life, serves an apprenticeship with him.

There is both internal and external evidence that the carpenter here is a mythical image of a man doing a man's proper work by repaying his dept to society and thereby practicing justice, and that his object is not to pursue gain but to serve an apprenticeship in manhood. For example,

[179]

the friends spend only one or two days a week in the master's workshop, and Emile never becomes a master carpenter. Moreover, the hero does not really earn his bread until he is twenty-five years of age, and then he would not ideally do so by carpentering. In the *Confessions* the writer, recounting the story of apprenticeships served by himself at the same age of twelve or thirteen, says he could not tolerate the idea of heaping up money by a mean employment, for, he adds, money never tempted him greatly.[34] In the *Considerations* he utters biblical-like warnings against the worship of Mammon. In a word, he has a Socratic contempt for the money-making arts and earthly dross current among men, "the source of many unholy deeds." Like his Greek master he associates the gainful faculties with illiberality and baseness, for they are concerned with desires "that maim and disfigure the soul with their meannesses." In his view such faculties must remain subject to the higher ones that make a man sovereign ruler of self. That supreme ruler and his work of ruling are foreshadowed by the Rousseauist carpenter, who is therefore the "maker of an image of justice" in Socratic terminology. He is as much a myth as the husbandman, who represents man's true vocation as a Socratic and Christian cultivator of the soul. Thus Jean-Jacques uses the arts and crafts to take another step upward in the ascent of the soul toward wisdom.

In fact, the myth of the carpenter is evocative of both Christ and Socrates. The latter's contempt for the money-making arts or faculties does not prevent him from bestowing upon the carpenter a distinguished place at the beginning and end of the *Republic*. In the third book, in the midst of the denunciation of physicians who remove men from society and their duties, the carpenter appears in the likeness of a man who refuses to "nurse disease" to the neglect of his customary employment, since then there would be no profit in his life. But his employment is not simply carpentering. It is what Socrates and Rousseau,

[180]

too, conceive to be every man's real work, which is the practice of virtue or true statesmanship.[35] At the end of the *Republic* the sage, having spoken of God as "the maker of the works of all other workmen," visualizes the carpenter, the maker of tables and beds, as a "creator" made in the divine image. The carpenter is closer to truth and reality than the poet who depicts the carpenter's work and is consequently only an imitator, says Socrates, ignoring the meaning of "poet" as the Greek equivalent of "maker." After what we have already witnessed of Rousseau's affinities with the master, it is difficult not to suspect that Emile is meant to be a reflexion of that Socratic carpenter. Having beheld all the works of creation, he is now being prepared for a vision of the Socratic "great artist" or Pauline "Master-Builder"[36] who is shadowed forth in his workmanship. The reason why the hero is not a master craftsman is probably that for Rousseau, as for Socrates, there is only one, and that is he in whose image man is formed. But the whole context suggests that a man molded in that divine likeness does not merely make tables or beds. Observe the moment chosen by Rousseau for the emergence of Emile as the carpenter-builder. We are precisely at that point in the book where the foundations of the temple are complete and the shrine itself about to be built. One is reminded of the carpenter of Galilee, the writer's divine master, who boasted that if the "temple" were destroyed he would build it up again in three days, meaning "the temple made without hands." Emile is a carpenter apprentice who, by making beds and tables, learns to practice justice and hence to build the temple of the soul or fortress of the city, guided by his governor and following the pattern provided by the master-craftsman, whom the Rousseauist legislator and educator professes to know. The Socratic and Christian imagery throws the meaning into relief.

We may observe that in the myth of the carpenter the author simply amplifies all the principles set forth so far.

[181]

By practicing justice in this new form, the boy does not merely render unto Caesar the things that are Caesar's, as in the parable of the sower. He renders unto God the things that are God's, although he does not know it. He performs this office by applying his strength to do his will, or rather, the general will for the common good implied in the idea of exchange, which the industrial arts entail. To the same end he is learning to acquiesce in the author's three Socratic laws by remaining within the bounds of necessity, by being ever one with himself and self-sufficing, and by doing the work to which he is naturally disposed, all within the precincts of a society of friends.

But although he is being prepared in this way for his duties as sovereign ruler, he is unaware of it. In fact, he is still ignorant of the identity of his governor. This becomes obvious when, having cultivated a taste for reflection, he feels impelled to inquire about social inequalities and asks how Jean-Jacques, who is rich, earns his bread. Of course, we know that the prince or governor is supported by the people, that the ruling power is supported by gainful ones.[37] But Emile's mentor forbears to explain this at present. He simply promises to reply later. What is noteworthy here is that he conceals his identity as long as possible. But he can hardly do so much longer since, as we are told, Emile's relations with others are soon to expand beyond the purely physical sphere. This "active, thinking being," as he is called, is approaching the age when reason is perfected by feeling to make him into a real philosopher or lover of Sophia. Only then can he recognize his governor as such and finally take his own place as sovereign ruler.

The real duties of man's estate, shown in his apprenticeship under the mysterious master and consisting of the practice of justice and acquiescence in ancient laws rather than the amassing of gold, are set forth in the related chapters of the *Contract*. There are three (twelve, thirteen,

[182]

and fourteen) that bear a single title: "How the Sovereign Authority Is Maintained."

In these chapters the author wrestles with the problem of securing the legislative power against the aberrations of the governing faculty, to preserve the life of the politico-moral body. He boldly asserts that the people must personally assemble to approve the constitution, sanction their own laws, and do their own work as they did 3,000 years ago. In contending that this is not impossible, he betrays his concern for spiritual values: "The limits of the possible in moral matters are less narrow than we think: it is our weaknesses, vices, and prejudices that contract them." He betrays the same concern when, after citing the example of the ancient Greeks and Romans to prove that his ideas are not the fanciful dreams of a visionary, he concludes: "What exists is therefore possible." The deft return to the present tense—"what exists"— shows that he is thinking mainly of the inner world. He adds that people must also assemble to govern themselves or else to provide for government by others in order that they may rule in obedience. For he still insists that the essence of the moral person consists of the harmonious correlation of obedience or necessity and freedom, subjects and sovereign being perfectly united in the citizen who binds himself to the law of his will and submits to be governed thereby. This ideal of the sovereignty and kingship of man being exercised in popular assemblies is possible in small rural societies protected from alien peril by federation with others akin to themselves, says the author, allowing his imagination to roam beyond the dim possibility of even one such city coming to the birth. In the less improbable case of the free soul, such protective federation would consist of bonds of friendship established with great spirits of the past and present. But since even well-trained governors are wont to impede the action of the sovereign power, he insists upon the regular manifestation and perpetual activity of the "constant will"

(later identified with conscience) as the aegis of the politico-moral body. The latter may be preserved and prosper
only if citizens avoid greed, cowardice, and idleness to
activate and cultivate their noblest faculties. In that case
they will do their own work like Aemilius, whose austerity of life, courage, and industry or justice are molding
him to inherit the high office and ministry of his forbears.

The next chapter in the *Contract* (the fifteenth) deals
with "Deputies or Representatives," of whom the author
has already expressed disapproval in the beginning of the
previous part. The chapter begins and ends with an evocation of men who shamefully pay others to do their work
for them, unlike the apprentice builder of the novel. Indeed, its relevance to the masterwork is confirmed in the
fifth part of the latter where Emile the carpenter refuses
to pay anyone to do his carpentering in his place. There
the novelist emphasizes the very point of the present chapter of the *Contract*. In the latter we are shown how modern
men pay others to wage "war" in their stead and wield
sovereignty on their behalf, or rather to enthrall and betray them. In the Socratic view they enslave themselves
to the greed for gain and the money-making arts. "The
word *finance,*" says Rousseau in this chapter, "is a slave's
word; it is unknown in the city."[38] In other words, the
free man or city practices in person the wisdom that contributes most to the well-being of the whole and all its
parts. An advantage of this course of action, according to
the *Contract,* is that the various parts are not obliged to
resort to particular remedies or "domestic cares" to patch
up disorders or gratify humors. That is what the carpenter
in the *Republic* declines to do, like the true statesman in
the same context or Jean-Jacques in *Emile*. The author of
the *Contract* adds that in the well-constituted entity
therein envisaged, no part is indifferent to its life and happiness or dares to say: "What has that to do with me?"
These are the words of men like Robert in the novel who
dwell in "false" states and are heedless of the common

[184]

happiness. That world is alien to Emile, who is learning that the well-ordered polity of the soul is his main concern on earth.

On the grounds of the foregoing considerations Rousseau rejects once again the modern political idea that the sovereign will can be "alienated" and its activity assigned to deputies. True, he adapts the concept to modern cities in his *Considerations*.[39] But he declines to make any such concession in the *Contract,* where he depicts a mythical city made in the likeness of the Rousseauist soul. In the chapter under discussion he honors the ideal order in a new tribute to ancient Greece and Rome. The Greeks, he says, did their own work because they preferred freedom, the free use of their highest faculties for the exercise of justice, rather than enslavement to the greed for gain. If we protest that slaves performed their menial tasks for them, a point raised by the author himself and used against him by his critics, he at once withdraws into the world of the spirit and admits that freedom is maintained only with the support of slavery or submission. Obviously this must be so if obedience and liberty are correlatives. He adds: "All that is not in nature has its disadvantages, and civil society more than anything else." Of course, since a true civil society implies morality and that freedom of spirit and ministry of reason which depend for their action upon the subjection of covetous desires. Modern men, concludes the writer, who cater to such desires do not have slaves, but they pay tyrannical masters to enslave them. As Socrates says: "The people who would escape the smoke which is the slavery of freemen has fallen into the fire which is the tyranny of slaves."[40] In the Platonic text this is the fire of passion that threatens the souls of men who neglect their own proper work. Rousseau is saying the same thing in both the *Contract* and *Emile.*

The end of the third part of *Emile,* inspired mainly by the Socratic "prelude," is devoted to the further education of the ruler. The hero's ability to use his reason to compare sensations and form ideas is perfected. Only the savage or solitary sage may be indifferent to the objects of our judgments and ask: "What has that to do with me?" So the author says in this context of the novel, in a passage reminiscent of another in the matching part of the *Contract* that refers to individuals who live exclusively for themselves alone. Emile the carpenter-builder, who is natural man living in the social and civil state,[41] is to be otherwise and must perforce exercise judgment. He must therefore avoid error by verifying sensations.

Among common errors of judgment caused by contradictory impressions of the senses, Rousseau mentions two in particular to which he alludes more than once and which he takes the trouble to solve. The first is the case of a ball rolled between two crossed fingers that produces an impression of two objects instead of one. The second is the example of a stick submerged in water that appears broken.[42] Jean-Jacques and Emile perform experiments to rectify the errors and generate in the boy a force of reason not easily led astray by the authority of others. There are three other alleged advantages of this method. First, he advances in proportion to his physical and mental strength, which, as we know, is born of the friendship of reason and is the sphere of its action. Second, he discovers the limits of human knowledge, especially his own. Third, he is taught how to learn, and will do so all his life long for love of the truth, or so the author says.

As usual, by "truth" Rousseau, like Socrates, means moral truth as he sees it, although Emile does not know it as such. The governor reveals his real motives when, after dealing with the correction of erroneous judgments, he describes the disciple's present formation in terms that have distinct moral overtones. Admittedly we are told that Emile possesses only natural physical knowledge and is ignorant of moral values or related matters. But this simply means that he does not know the name of the virtues he practices. Besides, the abstractions of geometry and al-

gebra, which he continues to study at this stage, are preparing him for the generalizations of the profession of faith
in the next. Moreover, the Socratic "images of virtues" he
displays, such as patience, industry, temperance, and courage, are preparing him for the social virtues of a man. To
possess the latter in their truth, the new Robinson Crusoe
has only to become aware of his moral relationships and
sensitive to them.

As I remarked above, Rousseau is still inspired by Socrates' prelude to the education of kings. The sage, too, has
recourse to the mathematical sciences to perfect reason
and lead it to moral truth. But to reach his goal, he ultimately renounces the senses, which his modern disciple
refuses to do; and there lies an important rift between
them. Nevertheless, in dealing with errors the sage cites
the same two examples as are given in *Emile*, the first one
in the context of the prelude and the second at the end of
the book. He is therefore a more likely source of inspiration than Descartes, who deals with one of the two cases,
or the *Logic* of Port-Royal, which deals with the other.[43]
When, says he in the prelude, the sense furnishes contradictory impressions, he summons to his aid calculation and the arts of measuring and numbering—while
Rousseau reverts to the senses themselves—to see whether
the several objects "announced to the soul" are one or
two. In Plato's last book he does likewise if the same objects appear straight when looked at out of water and
crooked in it. Such errors, he says, are due to "that weakness of the human mind upon which the art of conjuring
and . . . other ingenious devices imposes, having an effect
upon us like magic." This phrase probably suggested to
Rousseau the figure of the "conjuror Socrates" as well.
In addition to all these remarkable coincidences, the master's precautions against false impressions at the end of
the *Republic* immediately follow the idealization of the
carpenter exactly as in the case of the modern pedagogical
novel. In fine, the Greek thinker's presence can hardly be

[187]

doubted in the concluding tableau of Emile's qualities, which foreshadow those of a Socratic king.

The last pages of this part of *Emile* relating to the establishment of reason as the governing power in man, and proposing precautions against its vagaries, are reflected in the last three chapters of the same part of the *Contract*. These chapters are intended to show the way in which that power is set up within the moral constitution and also the need for the sovereign will to control its abuses. Two of them (sixteen and seventeen) are in a sense one, since both treat of the establishment of government, the one negatively and the other affirmatively. They are entitled "That the Institution of Government Is Not a Contract" and "Concerning the Institution of Government."

Rousseau begins by reaffirming his belief that only after the lawful power of the will has been firmly secured can the executive power of the ruler be instituted in its turn. This is, of course, the Socratic sequence followed in *Emile*. It serves, says he in the *Contract,* to keep the two principles as separate as they naturally are, the one dealing with general concepts and the other with specific cases. The special right of the governing faculty or governor, he explains, is to ask that another do what he himself does not do. In the novel Jean-Jacques, instead of appropriating that privilege to himself, has personally shared in all Emile's activities and thereby trained the guardian will and ruling power in his ward to confer the right upon him. This motive explains his reticence about his identity. It also explains why the will has precedence over the reason in the formation of city or soul: in Rousseau's thought it is the "will power" that commits authority to the governor. But he denies again, as he did in the beginning of this part, that government is instituted through a contract of the people with their chosen leaders whereby the one pledges himself to command and the other to obey. There is only one covenent in the city, and it is that of the original association. In *Emile* the demand for obedience is made by a servant of the sovereign and is conditional upon the consent of the will dedicated to the happiness of the moral person.

In that case how is the governing power set up? This is explained in the *Contract* and illustrated in *Emile*. According to the former, the law-giving element (visible in the society of friends in the novel) ordains that a ruling body be formed and then transform itself, by an act of the will, into a "democratic" governing power to consummate that ordinance and establish the government prescribed. For in the improbable world of the book, the entire city or moral person including sovereign and subjects must first learn the necessity and art of self-rule before it can execute an act of government by appointing others to do its will and then question their demands in the performance of that office. Accordingly, in the novel Emile is first initiated into the art of kings and then later induced to entrust himself in time of crisis to Jean-Jacques, whom he finally recognizes as skilled in that art. Indeed, the process described in the *Contract* is dramatically presented in the next part of the pedagogical work where the eponymous hero shares in the complex act of providing for government by voluntarily confiding the authority of governor to his "good friend" at a moment already prepared in this part of the book.

Rousseau's conclusions on the subject of rulers are to be found in the last chapter of the third part of the *Contract,* entitled "Manner of Preventing the Usurpations of Government." The statements contained therein led to the burning of the book in Geneva, for they had a much more revolutionary ring in the ears of his contemporaries than they do in ours. Governing powers, he says, are merely officers of the sovereign, whom they must obey as a matter of duty. If they fail to do so and if their rule is incompatible with the welfare of the whole, then they must be dismissed and replaced. Again, the idea is as old as Christ, who says that the "chiefest of all shall be the servant of all," or Socrates, who says that his philosopher-kings, though unpaid, must rule for the public good, not as though they were performing some heroic act, but simply as a matter of duty.[44] Otherwise, says he, they will bring about the ruin of the city. Rousseau means to avert this disaster by subjecting them to the constant vigilance of the lawful will, solemnly and formally summoned to act. In a similar manner the acts and intentions of a rational soul are scrutinized by the human conscience, which decides whether or not it is pleased with its present form of government. If not, it must be replaced by another.

The two books, in company with one another, have led us to the same point. In the *Contract* Rousseau describes a gradually evolving process quite as much as he does in *Emile*, even though in the past the abstract, mathematical form of the work has made it seem static in our eyes. One of the advantages of a collation of the two is to show the value of the work as a complete philosophy of life slowly taking shape as it does in the novel, whether or not we agree personally with the author's ideas. Another advantage is that the mythology of the pedagogical romance emerges more clearly by comparison with the appendix. Once the imagery is recognized as such it releases its meaning, as the body of a man expresses the soul. When it does, that mysterious essence proves to be no different from that of the companion volume, and in both cases the *Republic* is the model. These facts are even more strikingly visible henceforward. For the temple of *Emile*, like the fortress of the *Contrct*, is only now about to rise from the foundations laid down in the first three parts of both works. From the "stylobate," or threefold basement, the stately pillars of each one rise toward the empyrean where they belong like the "pattern" of the Socratic republic.[45]

1. I say this without forgetting that, according to the author, the *Contrat* is not only an appendix to *Emile* but also an epitome of a proposed work entitled

"Institutions politiques," fragments of which he destroyed. The latter statement does not alter the former or affect the indisputable proof of its veracity furnished by a collation of texts.

2. For all Socratic references in this paragraph see *The Republic* 5. 457, 458; 6. 505; 7. 523, 527, 531; 9. 589; 10. 601; cf. 621

3. Ibid., 1. 345-46; 5. 473; 7. 540. Cf. Matt. 2:2 and 6.

4. See, for example, Mark 10:43-44.

5. For the analogy of the scale: *The Republic* 4. 443. In 9. 587 Socrates shows that the true king is 729 times happier than the tyrant. Even studies on Rousseau's mathematical language do not draw an analogy with Socrates. See, for example, M. Françon, "Le Langage mathématique de J.-J. Rousseau," in "Notes rousseauistes," *Annales de la Société J.-J. Rousseau* 33 (1953-55): 243-46.

6. *Les Aventures de Télémaque* (Liège: Grandmont-Donders, 1865), p. 340. Erechtheus, whom Télémaque sees in the Champs-Elysées, says: "Je prévois ... qu'elle (la monnaie) ... entretiendra une infinité d'arts pernicieux qui ne vont qu'a amollir et à corrompre les moeurs ... " F. Bouchardy does not mention Fénelon in connection with the theme of the first "Discours": *O.C.,* 3:5 n. 2. See "Confessions," *O.C.,* 1:351, where Rousseau defines the theme thus: "Si le progrès des sciences et des arts a contribué à corrompre ou à épurer les moeurs."

7. Rousseau speaks as if the sun moved around the earth: "Emile," p. 433. Burgelin explains that he is probably interpreting the child's view: p. 431 n. 1.

8. All references in this paragraph are to *The Republic* 7.526-27.

9. Regarding questions and the abuse of dialectic, cf. "Emile," p. 339 n, 436, and *The Republic* 7. 534, 537-39. For the connection of knowledge cf. the same text of Plato and *O.C.,* 4:436 n. 3. See also "Confessions," loc. cit., p. 234. Of course, this was the whole idea of the *Encyclopédie:* See Diderot's article under that heading and d'Alembert's "Discourse préliminaire."

10. Rousseau discusses this incident in *C.C.,* 9:125, letter to L. Usteri, 13 September 1761.

11. *The Republic* 10. 602.

12. Burgelin poses the question of the connection between the story of the fair and the tracing of meridians for maps, and finds the sequence of ideas "bizarre": *O.C.,* 4:441 n. 2.

13. *The Republic* 4. 433-34, 442-43.

14. See "Lettres de la montagne," *O.C.,* 3:739, and cf. p. 744 where, in a discussion of miracles, the author warns that the marvels of chemistry and physics are not miracles. Burgelin connects this text with the conjuror scene in "Emile": p. 437 n. 2.

15. For the pilot see chapter 2 above and n. 10. The quotation is from the end of Byron's poem "The Island."

16. This is so in spite of his rather loose use of the term "democracy" in the "Lettre à d'Alembert," *O.C.,* Hachette, 1:256.

17. "Emile," p. 593.

18. *The Republic* 2. 369.

19. "Pour moi, je suivois la direction contraire à l'objet que j'avois à fuir, comme autrefois j'avois suivi l'opposé de l'ombre dans la forest de Montmorenci": "Emile et Sophie," *O.C.,* 4:912. For this work see chapter 6, note 18, below.

20. *The Republic* 3. 402.

21. "Emile," pp. 429, 455, 457-60, 474. Cf. "Confessions," loc. cit., pp. 296, 644; "Dialogues," *O.C.*, 1:812, 826; cf. *C.C.*, 19:71, 228, correspondence between Rey and Rousseau, 20 January 1764 and 17 March 1764. See the study by G. Pire, "J.-J. Rousseau et Robinson Crusoé," *Revue de littérature comparée* 30 (October-December 1956): 479-96, and cf. P. Nourrisson, *J.-J. Rousseau et Robinson Crusoé* (Paris: Spes, 1931), particularly chapter 1.

22. Cf. "Emile," p. 315, and second "Discours," *O.C.*, 3:194.

23. He says the same in part 1, chapter 3, at the end, apropos of the "law" of the stronger. The "true physician" would be the Rousseauist legislator who would "sweep the threshing-floor clean": second "Discours," loc. cit., p. 180 Cf. *The Republic* 3. 407 (the physician is called a statesman); 4. 425-26 (the statesman is likened to a physician). The image of the physician recurs throughout the dialogue.

24. Political theorists explain Rousseau's brevity on the subject by the distinction he makes between government and sovereign, which in their opinion reduces the importance of mixed forms. But on the other hand, the problem of balance is all the more complex by reason of this distinction. Burgelin considers this to be one of the most important problems in "Emile," as indeed it is: *O.C.*, p. 304 n. 1. He is speaking of equilibrium of soul, but that is the essential problem in the "Contrat" too.

25. It is a great mistake to fancy that Rousseu's sketch of the city begins here: *O.C.*, 4:466 n. 2; cf. p. 467 n. 2, which refers to *The Republic* 2. 369. In a sense, as I have said, the child's active initiation into society does, but even that has long since been foreshadowed.

26. *The Republic, 2. 372.*

27. For example, Derathé feels that the chapter is out of place: *O.C.*, 3:414 n. 1.

28. Cf. "Emile," p. 267. Beaulavon denies the possibility that a northern state could ever be as wealthy as a southern one since he takes the whole text exclusively literally: J.-J. Rousseau, *Du Contrat social,* ed. Georges Beaulavon, (Paris: Rieder, 1914), p. 249 n. 1. In fact, in the case of texts like the present one a collation with "Emile" is imperative. The novel is full of passages like the following:" . . . La misére ne consiste pas dans la privation des choses, mais dans le besoin qui s'en fait sentir": p. 304.

29. *The Republic* 7. 520; 8. 552, 554, 564; 9. 573.

30. Regarding preservation as an object, see chapter 3 above and cf. *O.C.*, 3:420 n. 1. For the importance of freedom see "Contrat social," pp. 419, 420 n. Cf. *C.C.*, 10:94, letter to Rey, 18 (11?) February 1762, where the author shows concern that the note at the end of the chapter be correctly printed.

31. *The Republic* 8. 546.

32. When he speaks of slavery as a form of moral death in the midst of life, that must be taken as a figure of speech, since the will that frees is "indestructible," and so a man may be released from slavery and restored to life.

33. *The Republic* 5. 457 (the useful is the noble). For the biblical reference that follows: John 6:63; cf. 2 Cor. 3:6. Burgelin, like Rousseau's contemporary Tronchin, and Montesquieu, too, see in technical training a departure from ancient education. But Rousseau, in the mythical figure of Emile the carpenter, is following Socrates and Plato to the letter.

34. "Confessions," loc. cit., pp. 30-31. Cf. "Considérations" *O.C.*, 3:1005. For Socrates' contempt for the money-making arts or faculties, which are forever abused, see *The Republic* 3.396, 405, 415-16; 5. 456, 466; 6.495-96, 7. 533; 9. 590.

35. For the carpenter see *The Republic* 3. 406; 10. 597.

36. Heb. 3:4.

37. "Emile," p. 480; "Contrat social," pt. 3, chap. 8.

38. See note 34 above. Cf. "Projet . . . pour la Corse," *O.C.,* 3:904 ff.

39. Loc. cit., p. 979. He provides against corruption by frequent changes of deputies and by subjecting them to imperative mandates.

40. *The Republic* 8. 569. Socrates' citizens are taught to fear slavery more than death: ibid., 3. 387.

41. "Emile," pp. 483-84, 550-51, 662, 764.

42. For the ball cf. "Emile," pp. 482, 486, and *The Republic* 7. 524. For the "broken" stick cf. "Emile," pp. 482, 484-85, and *The Republic* 10. 602.

43. The example of the ball is proposed by Descartes, and that of the "broken" stick is in the *Logique* of Port-Royal (3:20); but neither gives both examples, as Plato does: *O.C.,* p. lxvii (refers to Descartes) and 486 n. 1 (refers to the *Logique*).

44. *The Republic* 7. 540. Cf. Luke 17:10: "So likewise ye, when ye shall have done all those things which are commanded you, say. We are unprofitable servants: we have done that which was our duty to do."

45. *The Republic,* passim. See especially 9. 592.

V

Temple-Stronghold

In the fourth part of the novel and its appendix, Emile and his counterpart in the *Contract* are finally impelled to assume the social obligations that constitute the very fabric of the work in both cases. The moral person then comes to the birth, and the temple of the soul and citadel of the city become an identical reality.[1]

This part of the novel has a tripartite form. The shape and proportions recall the main enclosure or cella of the Greek temple where the cult image stood. In the ancient prototype the great rectangular chamber was divided by colonnades into three naves, the central one being the broadest and containing the likeness of the Godhead. Rousseau adheres strictly to that pattern in his spiritual shrine—where the creed stands in the midst of the mythical cella—but not, of course, in the fortress of the *Contract,* where, however, the themes are the same. In both cases they parallel those of the second part.

SAVING POWERS

In *Emile* the hero's progress is traced between the ages of fifteen and twenty. At the outset the moral being's forthcoming birth into life stands in counterpoise to the child's birth into consciousness in the earlier analogous part. Both events are the occasion for similar reflections upon the brevity of existence.[2] In the present case the passive sensitiveness of the child is replaced by the active moral or social sensitiveness of the youth that radiates beyond the individual. The passions, against which the governor's precautions were hitherto effective, inevitably wax strong at the advent of adolescence, says the writer, thereby underlining

[195]

himself the symmetry of the two parts. The approaching crisis is indicated by a storm-tossed agitated spirit compared to a ship at the mercy of the waves. The Socratic allegory of the ship of the soul or ship of state, artistically used from the beginning, recurs again. The governor, we are told, dares not leave the helm or all is lost. He appears in the shape of the wise Ulysses, whose name befits Jean-Jacques since he is the spiritual father of Emile, the "new Telemachus" of an imaginary city in the fifth part, as Ulysses was the father of the old. But before the youth can play his proper role, he too must, of course, become a helmsman and skilled in the art of steering his course through the passions.[3] At this point where most educations end, Emile's positive education begins since Rousseau intends, as he says, to consider the whole of life.[4]

The feelings play a much more important part in the Aemilian shrine than they do in a Greek temple in the pure Dorian style. The author discriminates between good feelings and bad in the same way that Socrates discriminates between good or necessary desires and evil or unnecessary ones. In Rousseau's reasoning the passions in their primal form are the work of God, whose name appears for the first time here at the very entrance to the sanctuary. They are considered to be the ministrants of our freedom and preservation. Their origin and principle is identified as the natural feeling of self-love, or love of the true self in its original purity. This self, or "real Emile," is distinguished from another one that, according to the writer, is born in our society and wars against the true one to enslave and destroy it by the perversion of self-love into selfishness. Self-love is said to be good on the grounds that it provides for our safety, leads us to love those who are well disposed in our favor and is content with the bare necessities of life. But selfishness is said to breed discontent, dissension, and enmity by leading us to compare ourselves with others in a conflict of interests with them and to expect to be preferred at their expense. Consequently, at the birth of moral and social consciousness in the disciple, the Rousseauist governor's great task is to prevent the vitiation of self-love and anticipate the cleavage between the true man and the false. And so, at the portal of the Aemilian temple, we may fancy that we read a Rousseauist and emotional version of the inscription of the Delphic shrine, whose legend "know thyself" is combined with the precept "love thyself." Since the writer regards knowledge as essentially an awareness of relationships, he is convinced that to know and love one's true self is to know and feel one's real relationships. Emile is therefore now to study his moral being by studying his spiritual affinities with others for the purpose of perceptively practicing self-love in its original form in order to contribute actively and effectively to moral and social order.

At this juncture the author reflects upon the earliest of these conscious and emotional affinities in human life that largely determine its direction. He contends that they do not naturally take the form of passionate love. He denies that a child, emerging from the solitude of Robinson Crusoe, begins by experiencing either moral love, which springs from intuitive knowledge foreign to him, or the less noble counterpart of that sentiment. In his view the senses are not naturally stirred until much later than is the case with precocious children today, whose curiosity about procreation is prematurely aroused. But he feels that, even under the most adverse circumstances, education can retard the first explosions of the most combustible temperament. Now since he is persuaded that delay increases vigor of body, of heart, and of soul, and in addition gives nature time to order and regulate the slowly evolving passions, he greatly favors it, as he did when he recommended the negative approach in the second part. It permits the child to feel what are considered to be his real affinities with others and enables the governor to direct the affections accordingly.

Seeking to define the nature and origin of these affinities, Rousseau rivets his attention on the moment when the

[197]

pupil, who has been placed in carefully chosen circumstances, begins to show signs of expanding sensitiveness and betrays feelings enlightened enough to tell good from evil. He observes that the youth's first feeling is an incipient sense of friendship. This was anticipated, of course, in the parable of Montmorency forest, in the hero's childish exclamation "My good friend!" It is friendship, we are told, that brings him into conscious contact with his fellow creatures and sows in his heart the seeds of humanitarian feeling by cultivating natural compassion, mercy, and generosity.

For in Rousseau's view sympathy is the source of friendship and is the fountainhead and archetype of all love. This sentiment represents to his mind the deeper motives that bring men to unite with one another in society. He sees them moved by pity for common frailties and sufferings that identify them with each other through the action of the imagination. Indeed, he considers pity to be as natural as self-love and he does so both in the present context and in his evocation of the primitive state of the second *Discourse* where, moreover, it replaces laws, morals, and all virtue. Consequently, in his opinion a child must be induced at this stage in his progress to behold our poor humanity as it intrinsically is, and to feel that he is a part of others so that he might be disposed by self-pity to tenderness on their behalf. Accordingly Emile is made to see suffering mankind in his parents "or ailing governor," for whom he feels the pang of compassion. This, we are now told, is "the first relative sentiment to touch the human heart in the order of nature." It transports him beyond himself and brings him at last into real communion with men, channeling the currents of sensibility into a broad sea of "goodness, humanitarian feeling, mercy and benevolence." Nevertheless, it is first generated in him in the form of a friendship that symbolizes an ideal social bond and as such is henceforth developed into a vast allegory in the book.

[198]

The author further reveals the value of his appeal to pity and its politico-moral implications by imagining a possible exception to the rule that we are touched by the grief of others rather than their bliss. For example, he admits that we are moved by the spectacle of a quiet scene of pastoral life, but explains the reason: it is because nothing prevents us from condescending to enjoy the same peace and innocence that are a man's proper resources and true wealth. That is precisely the way of life promised by the order of friendship in the book and its appendix. On the other hand, he argues, if we disclose to a youth the sad fate of most men whose lives are disordered, then he will see at once that he must blaze a path to happiness where no one's footsteps lead. That is the path wherein Emile is now being guided. He is to be induced to follow it by being made to pity those who do not and to fear their fate and the loss of his own austere happiness. To this end he learns ultimately to identify himself not merely with his governor but with the common people as well, and to love and pity all mankind as he does himself.

In accordance with these precepts Jean-Jacques as "observer and philosopher" or rather, psychologist, probes and guides the boy's heart and stirs natural emotions to nerve and sustain the will, directing it toward a felicity compatible with that of other men and consistent with human sympathy. In discussing the value of insight into pain as a principle of moral excellence, Rousseau reflects upon the differences in men's capacity for sorrow, which depends upon the degree of spiritual or intuitive perfection they have attained. He doubts whether insensitive souls who lack mercy, generosity, and pity can ever possess righteousness.[5] Compassion is therefore indispensable to the whole purpose of education and legislation in both books.

At this point in the argument he asks again, as he did in the second part, whether these precautions against pas-

[199]

sion are not jeopardizing Emile's happiness. The negative reply is the same as it is there, and the artistic parallelism with "the book of the law" intensifies the politico-moral overtones of the present part. For example, to show real unhappiness he imagines a youth of fifteen who scales "Mount Olympus" all at once to enter the brilliant society of the gods of this world and is doomed to disenchantment like the child victim of indulgence in the former part. Moreover, the same three proofs, advanced there to show that Emile was happy in his ascetic life, reappear here. For instance, although he now shares the pangs of others, such participation is, we are assured, voluntary and sweet. This view was foreshadowed in the second part where we were told that under natural conditions happiness includes pain, disposing us to pity. Besides, the youth allegedly enjoys not things but himself, like the child who, even while enduring pain, found delight in the free play of his faculties that made him, at least in his own eyes, master of himself. Moreover, the signs of his contentment in the present case, says the author, are the serenity of his countenance and also his enjoyment of the esteem and confidence of others. That observation calls to mind the earlier part where indulgence was depicted as leading to the alienation of others and a life of misery. Throughout this discussion of happiness Rousseau is therefore mindful of "the book of the law." The literary device of symmetry is intended to express artistically the idea that fulfillment belongs only to those who walk in its decrees.[6] To ensure that Emile does so at this turning-point in his life and that his happiness incurs no risks, he is restored to his country garden.

These arguments in defense of the hero's felicity are, like the ones in the pendant part, reminiscent of Socrates.[7] So great is the latter's influence here that I must stop and explain it. As I said in the previous chapter, this part of the novel is closely related to Plato's fifth and sixth books, in that order. There Socrates anticipates the formation of kings, whose preamble is contained in the seventh. For the moment I am concerned with the fifth book, where he is forced by his listeners to speak of the family life of his citizens—"how they will bring children into the world"— and what their relations with women will be. The sage then agrees to "begin again at the very foundations," exactly like his modern disciple, for he too considers "the whole of life." He recognizes that this is a critical moment in the formation of his city and threatens its very existence. Thus he is induced to discuss the education of women and the problems of love and marriage, which Rousseau insists upon deferring until later,[8] as the sage would fain have done. In this context he broaches the problem of evil, and he does so in the same manner as the writer of *Emile* and the *Contract*. For him too evil arises from a perversion of desire that causes dualism and discord within a man or a city. On the other hand, his chief aim as legislator is to secure the bond of unity, which he conceives as the greatest good of the moral being. This is, of course, Rousseau's aim in the pages on sympathy. The sage solves the problem of unity of feeling and discord in three ways, and here lies a difference between the two thinkers. First, unlike the author of *Emile* as we shall see, he educates women in the same way as men on the grounds that they have the same moral duties. Next he executes a law, much favored later by his disciple, whereby marriages are arranged between men and women of like nature. Finally he removes the family as he did property from the control of private interest or desire, whereas Rousseau, though likewise subjecting it to higher powers, still clings to an emotional image of it.[9] But Socrates' intention is akin to Rousseau's: to foster sympathy among his citizens or, as he says, to produce "common pleasures and pains," common feelings rather than exclusive private ones, and to remove disagreement about the use of the terms *mine* and *not mine*. The best-ordered state, says he, "most nearly approaches to the condition of the individual; as in the body, when but a finger of one of us is hurt, the whole frame, drawn toward the soul as a center and forming one kingdom under the ruling power therein, feels the hurt and sympathizes all together with the part affected."[10] This may also be said of moral afflictions in a well-ordered soul that has the same common feeling and is not at variance with itself so that, as the sage says, all powers speak "the language of harmony and concord." He thereby achieves peace in the moral being, which is further protected by two guardians "shame and fear" that reappear later in *Emile*. After speaking of the value of sympathy, Socrates next considers its effects upon felicity and again raises the question of happiness in the same way as he did earlier and as Rousseau does in identical contexts in each case. And his answer is the same: the felicity sought is that of the entire moral being as it is naturally constituted rather than that of any particular class or part at the expense of the rest. He also recalls what he said earlier about the happiness of his guardians, which is, he says, greater than that of the Olympic victors. It is surely significant that at the corresponding point in *Emile* the author shows the hero sharing the pains of others and yet happier by far than the child who scales Olympus. The relationship of the two texts is undeniable.

Rousseau takes up the Socratic image of sympathy, although he ultimately uses it in a much broader way as we have seen. However, he begins by following the master, fostering pity as the basis of ideal friendship and thereby deepening the latter with a view to leading Emile from the law of necessity and utility to the law of love. The well-ordered relations of the two protagonists become a pattern to enlighten the youth about all aspects of Rousseauist moral or social bonds and the "rights of humanity" that they are intended to secure.[11]

A literary interpretation brings this out. Jean-Jacques, we are told, uses the fire of adolescence as an instrument of education by acquiring for himself first of all a hold over his pupil's affections. This hold, says the writer, is all the more powerful to curb him since it is natural that the first bonds uniting him to mankind should embrace humanity in those nearby, particularly his governor, who shares with himself "common thoughts and feelings, common pleasures and pains." The very words of the Greek sage resound in the Aemilian text. As Emile becomes capable of affection, he allegedly grows sensitive to that of Jean-Jacques, which is akin to his own. Since their friendship, far from becoming exclusive, always remains an image of the ideal order and human rights, Rousseau now calls it "the most sacred of covenants," adding that it will not go unrequited. We know, of course, that the covenant so described is that of a man with his own sovereign will, and that friendship in the book expresses the same moral commitment. But Emile has yet to learn that. When the youth becomes aware of reciprocity, the governor, we are told, acquires a fresh hold upon him, "having long since bound his heart with bands." These bands of the law that bind the heart instead of the body take effect quite naturally as he reflects how richly endowed his life has been. But, in the writer's opinion, such will be the case only on condition that the governor does not claim obedience in return for his pains; for then the disciple, taken by surprise, would feel that he has been "bound by a contract without his consent." Again the terminology of the appendix recurs, and the symbolism of the covenant of friendship rises to the surface.

Jean-Jacques woos the youth's consent by speaking to him only of his duties to himself. Emile is thereby moved spontaneously to acknowledge a debt of gratitude to friendship and respond to it. For, says the author: "There is nothing that carries so much weight with the human heart as the voice of friendship recognized as such, since we know that it speaks to us only on behalf of our own interest." This phrase is obviously a Rousseauist version of a favorite Socratic one that anticipates the education of kings and to which I alluded in discussing the myth of Montmorency forest where it was also echoed in Emile's expression of gratitude to his friend. In the *Republic* the master, having said that the most potent education of all is that which makes a man love the good and hate the bad even before he knows the reason why, concludes: "When reason comes, he will recognize and salute the friend with whom his education has made him long familiar."[12] In the case of *Emile* this recognition, says the author, introduces the hero into the true moral and social order where justice and goodness are not abstract words or pure moral beings formed by the understanding but real affections of the soul enlightened by reason. Here he hints that he is translating the Socratic abstractions into more human terms. But to do so, he uses the sage's own images and ideas. Emile's grateful "recognition" of his friend conveys in an artistic form the first flutter of conscience, an acknowledgment of the duties or debts of social man, who is bidden by the precept of justice to render unto each what belongs to each so that, as Socrates says, everyone may have and do what is his own. The Aemilian hero now has an intuitive glimpse of that law which he already unconsciously obeys.

In his broader use of sympathy Rousseau takes leave of Socrates, and, as we shall see, there is evidence that he does so deliberately. Having begun like the Greek thinker by arousing sympathy between kindred souls like Jean-Jacques and his ward, he thenceforth transcends the master in his appeal to that feeling by carrying out his intention of extending it to all mankind including men of evil life, much as he enlarged justice to include mercy in "the book of the law." Socrates opposes the idea of pitying the wicked in many contexts, including Plato's fifth book where, after the passage on procreation and sympathy, he makes children "spectators of war" in real life and shows them how heroes fight against their "enemies"—which typify evil passions in themselves and in others—lest they become "prisoners" of "barbarians."[13] Emile emulates

[204]

those heroes later on when the same enemies threaten him personally. But meanwhile, he learns to pity all men without exception. Here the author is inspired by his divine master, whose precept of love is expanded to include both "friends" and "enemies," according to the Sermon on the Mount.

But thus far Emile, in pitying suffering humanity indiscriminately, is blind to distinctions between men and does not even recognize the wicked as such. His next step is to do so. The author explains why. Since the youth's social contacts are about to expand and he will be comparing himself with others in his search for a place among them and run the risk of being victimized by them, he must be prepared in advance for that experience by the sight of natural and civil inequalities and the social evils that we call "order." He must study society in men and men in society, combining politics and ethics as Rousseau himself does. The writer uses Socratic terms to describe our anarchic world whose "false" notions of justice moved him to write both *Emile* and the *Contract* as they moved Plato to write the *Republic*. In all three the point of departure, now redefined in *Emile,* is to discredit such notions and the "law of the stronger" that favor private interests at the expense of the public good, and to honor true justice that consummates human aspirations and fulfills the promises of "the book of the law." The Rousseauist hero is about to look upon the fierce opposition of good and evil in the world about him without yet feeling it in himself, and to see it as the cause of suffering in most men without withdrawing his sympathy from any.

To achieve this double purpose, Jean-Jacques would have him read the human heart and see that it is naturally good, that men are perverted by the prejudices of our society, unhappy in their iniquities and therefore worthy of his compassion. But lest the lad be led astray by them or fall a prey to them himself and hate instead of pity them, the governor briefly abandons his experimental method

[205]

and makes him a mere "spectator" of men's doings, like the Socratic children. The drama he beholds is compared to the pageantry of the Olympic games. In this chaotic contest, says the writer, men athirst for glory seek a perishable crown of bay; others engage in shopkeeping for the sake of gold; but the wisest of all are content to observe. The miniature Olympics of the second part come to mind to bring the artistic symmetry to the surface again and throw into new perspective the author's intentions. The implication is that in childhood Emile ran for cakes but in so doing acquired judgment enough to disdain to contend for foolish prizes. His object now is to acquire a sympathetic understanding of human nature and its weaknesses.

However, to avoid too close a proximity to the vices of men, he does not observe them in real life, like the Socratic children. Jean-Jacques finally has recourse to literary education, to history and later to fables rejected before but now considered morally invaluable[14] to show the youth the human heart, its folly and its misery, not in the present moment but in other times and places so that he might see the stage without ever taking part in the play. In a series of historical dramas that replace the parables in action, he is, as it were, led through the realms of the dead and thereby gazes upon the living and the unborn future too, "which are necessarily of like nature with the past." In fine, by observing the heart of men in this way he becomes, in Socratic speech, "a spectator of all time and all existence," like the Greek heroes described at the beginning of the sixth book of the *Republic,* in spite of certain differences of approach.

Emile's governor uses discrimination in the selection of his histories and renounces those that portray evil exclusively or that fail to tell the truth, since the matter at stake is the discernment of good and evil. He finds his ideal in biography on the grounds that by knowing the inclinations of individuals, one can see their combined effects in society, and he thereby executes the author's intention of deal-

[206]

ing with both together. He favors the faithful biographies of antiquity, particularly those of the Greek writer Plutarch, who lays bare the human heart without regard for the empty rules of neoclassical decorum. In those lifelike portraits Aemilius, an ancient Roman reborn in the world today but a stranger to it, is enlightened by a Greek artist of 2,000 years ago who testifies to the state of the human heart in our society and whose testimony is true. Rousseau could hardly pay a more impressive tribute to one to whom he is as indebted as Emile is. The hero is especially sensitive, not to models of virtue like himself that made the writer into an imaginary Aemilius at the age of six, but to the so-called slaves of passion that, thanks to the biographer's art, appear in the same truth as the martyrs of pain in life.

The experience is narrated in dramatic terms. The youth, looking through the eyes of Plutarch as "the curtain rises" upon "the stage of the world," contemplates the spectacle of vice and suffering there presented to public view. He takes his place in "the wings of the theater," or rather, behind the "scenes," and "watches the actors don and doff their costumes," observing "the play of cords and pulleys" that deceives "spectators" unlike himself. He derives from this spectacle the initial impression that he has fallen among "wild beasts" with whom he has no kinship. Yet the governor knows better for, we are told, Plutrch offers a whole "course of practical philosophy"— meaning psychology—and teaches a man "to know himself and grow wise at the expense of the dead." And so, although Emile hardly recognizes himself or his place in the "mad" multitude of an alien world since for him happiness is as simple and nearby as health, freedom and the necessities of life, yet he has reflected enough upon human errors to pity all the tortured hearts of men, even his enemies, who are enemies of the good and whose malice only betrays their misery. Or so the author would have us believe.

[207]

In these pages upon Plutarch he is fully aware of straying from the advice of his Greek master by bringing Emile to pity men of evil life whose pleasures and pains are not his own, but with whom he is somehow identified in sorrow. Rousseau reveals this awareness by his use of terms borrowed from the stage. For the sage's protest against appeals to pity for disordered souls is contained not merely in his discussion of "warfare" in Plato's fifth book but elsewhere, too, and especially at the end, in his renewed indictment of the theater and the tragic poets who portray lawless tyrannical feelings, "the creations of men themselves," not of God, and who are therefore "thrice removed from truth." By so doing, they cater, says he, to false opinion and to passions that impair the reason and pose a threat to virtue and happiness. He warns his disciples against them and their works, convinced that "from the evil of other men something of evil is communicated to themselves."[15] Rousseau, of course, knew these passages well. His essay upon theatrical imitation, written while he was working on *Emile,* is partly taken from them and, to some degree at least, so is the *Letter to d'Alembert.* His allusions to the theater in the section on Plutarch in the novel show that he has in mind the same Socratic text and that he is wilfully violating its precepts by favoring compassion for evil men.

But the Aemilian text also suggests that Socrates' objections to sympathy for the wicked are not valid in the present case. For example, we are told that Emile beholds not illusion, "thrice removed from truth," but truth itself. Moreover, the hero's impressions of the "madness of the multitude" and the image of "wild beasts"—the beastlike nature in man that needs taming—are conveyed in phrases borrowed from the *Republic,*[16] indicating the writer's sympathy for the Greek philosopher's viewpoint at the very moment when he disregards his admonitions. There can be no doubt at all that he has Socrates in mind since, in order to convince us that Emile, in pitying the

[208]

wicked, will not be tempted to imitate them, he takes the trouble to say that the youth will not imitate anyone, "not even Socrates or Cato . . . for a man who is alienated from himself soon forgets himself altogether." All this evidence combines to support the contention that Rousseau's thought on the educational value of pity on behalf of vicious men takes account of the sage's protests.

That he has the sage in mind is further indicated in the next development of the novel where he deals in his own way with Socratic warfare. There Jean-Jacques reverts to the experimental method to teach Emile the art of "war," not to combat passions still foreign to himself, but to guard against the errors of pride and false opinion that supposedly generate them. For example, in order to persuade him that if he is happier than others it is by virtue of the governor's reason and not his own, for he is a man and subject to weaknesses and errors like the rest of us, Jean-Jacques, who is "more than a man," provides him with experience of the world and purposely exposes him to humiliating accidents, as he did in the myth of the conjuror Socrates. However, he avoids perilous situations and at the same time imposes two other rules upon himself: he guards against assuming airs of false dignity and remains always at the youth's side, whatever happens. He is compared to a Roman captain, not of a ship but of a warrior who is Aemilius and whom he leads as a captain does his soldiers, even in retreat. In this role he strengthens the youth's earlier sentimental "recognition" of his friend, based upon self-love and sympathy, and wins new confidence based upon the authority of reason and superiority of knowledge, which belong to the "leader" (conducteur) whose wisdom serves the interests of human happiness. He achieves this by warning Emile beforehand against the perils with which he himself has secretly contrived to surround him in the war of life, but without yet giving him "orders." If his ward persists in running a risk, he "follows" him "gaily"[17] to share in silence the inevitable mortifications as in the con-

[209]

juror story, or else to lead him away to escape possible disaster if the risk becomes too great. As a veteran captain he will know in advance which expeditions are safe and which are hazardous, and the youth will in the end recognize this knowledge.

Once more Rousseau's symbols betray him. By resorting to images with military overtones, he again calls to mind Socrates, to whom he alludes in this context and whose advice about warfare is everywhere implicit in his words. As I have said, that advice is to be found mainly in Plato's fifth book, although throughout the dialogue life is described in military terms. In the fifth book, as we know, Socrates makes young persons view the war of human passions, not on the stage or in books that naturally arouse pity for the victims, but in real life, which is less likely to flatter that sentiment. But he takes certain precautions that have left their mark upon Rousseau. For example, the children are "taken to see the battle" as "spectators," are placed "under the command of experienced veterans . . . their leaders and teachers," are mounted on horseback and, if there is no danger, are "brought close up"; but if there is, "they have only to follow their elder leaders," who know how to anticipate peril and conduct them away to escape in time of need. In this way they witness the merciless and pitiless treatment dealt out to "enemies." The Socratic text proves how closely the author of *Emile* follows the master to show his hero confronted by a misguided world with which he must, however, sympathize.

In combatting errors, the Aemilian governor has recourse to the enactment of more parables, in this case inspired by La Fontaine's fables. Prompted by the latter, he secretly contrives appropriate situations, and later has the unsuspecting Emile read apologues to generalize his experiences. The author hints that much art and subterfuge are employed in these myths, but advises us that he does not intend to tell us everything, for, in that event, we should stop listening. If we were to accuse him of deception, he would probably reply with Socrates that "lies in words" are not "true lies" and are useful "in dealing with enemies," or as "a sort of medicine or preventive" to save our friends, and are also valuable "in the tales of mythology."[18] In fact, all three functions are combined in the present instance. Thus the hero learns the danger of flattery and pride from myths like "The Fox and the Crow" or "The Frog and the Ox," and acquires a gradually dawning recognition of reason as a friend to man and a bulwark against error.

Pages like those reminiscent of Socratic "warfare" might lead us to question Rousseau's originality, especially after the provocative statement that Emile does not imitate anyone, not even Socrates. Emile may not but the author surely does, although he does so in an original manner. Otherwise we should long since have discovered the close affinities of *Emile* and the *Contract* with the *Republic*. Like many great writers, including La Fontaine, he is deeply indebted to his classical and Christian inheritance, but skillfully changes the substance of his models into his own. For example, in the present instance it assumes an almost commonplace cast that is typical of him. If I point out resemblances, it is simply to throw new light on his work and thought, rather than to discredit or extol them.

The foregoing phase of the novel, where the governor anticipates passions and errors by having recourse to history and real-life fables, is closely allied to the first two chapters of the fourth part of the *Contract*. These chapters also deal with the problems of passions and errors and the value of bonds of friendship to solve them, although, of course, Emile's pity for the wicked, necessary for one who lives in a disordered world, is invisible in an exteriorized image of the perfect city. Indeed, the writer of the novel almost refers us to the matching phase of the appendix. For example, his above-mentioned observations about the connection of politics and morals, and about the character of a society

[211]

being visible in the men composing it, link the whole context clearly with the said chapters where the Socratic author shows how passions that oppress the will and errors that deceive it are as much a threat to the birth of the moral person or city outside as they are to that of the one within.[19] He also shows how those impediments of heart or mind from which Emile is saved through Plutarch and the fables may be overcome to make the moral person a reality. He is moving toward that goal at the same pace in both books. Again we become keenly sensitive to the evolutionary character of the *Contract*.

It is further underlined by a comparison of the present context with the second part. For by virtue of the same literary symmetry observable in the pendant parts of *Emile,* the fourth part of the appendix refers back to "the book of the law." It begins with chapters on the indestructible will and its manifestations, corresponding to the earlier opening chapters on the inalienable, indivisible, and unerring will. But whereas in the earlier ones the writer was concerned with proving that the sovereign faculty can and must be fostered to function autonomously in the moral being, and that it can and must be brought to emerge through all the conflict therein, here he shifts the emphasis to prove that no passion can destroy it or error delude it in a well-ordered life.

In the first chapter, entitled "That the General Will Is Indestructible," Rousseau begins by exemplifying that power in men like the Swiss peasants of the rural cantons, united together in a single body and animated by a common spirit to preserve and prosper the ideal community. The prosperity sought is not overshadowed by conflicting interests and is defined quite simply as "peace, union, and equality," to show that in such a society few laws are necessary, in fact, only those whose necessity is *felt* by all. At this point, like Socrates in Plato's sixth book, the author faces the incredulity of his hearers, who refuse to believe his words because they have never witnessed the truth of them. That

[212]

truth is illustrated in the novel, of course, by the friendship of Jean-Jacques and Emile, who are soon to settle their affairs in the manner described in the *Contract*. As we have seen, they too are linked together by feelings shared in common and by singleness of purpose to preserve and prosper the reasonable constitution of man's entire nature supposedly seen in their relationship. And their laws are the "peace, union, and equality" mentioned above. The law of equality forbids both wealth and poverty; the law of union enacts that the city be one and self-sufficing; and the law of peace bids each one do and have what is his own and refrain from meddling with others. These laws, which correspond respectively to those of necessity, freedom and natural aptitude, suffice to achieve the main purpose of the covenant or law of friendship and therefore of man's sovereign will.

The author of the *Contract* next contrasts his ideal with a "false" society wherein exclusive private interests such as the greed for gain and power conspire against the moral being or human creature to destroy its unanimity and divide its kingdom into incompatible shreds by subjugating the will, as he warned in "the book of the law." If they prevail, "the social [and moral] bond is broken in all hearts." As we were told in *Emile* and are told again here, the public good is then sacrificed to shameful passions that muffle the will and dethrone it to sit in its place, fabricating their own unjust decrees, which are, of course, those of the strongest. This is the chaos that was disclosed to Aemilius by Plutarch and that Socrates describes in a similar vein. As in the *Republic*, every word here is as relevant to the inner man as it is to the condition of social affairs outside.

Regarding the anti-society Rousseau concludes Socratically that the sovereign will though mute therein is not destroyed but remains "constant, unalterable and pure," like conscience, whose voice is its own voice, as we are later told. According to him and his master, senseless covetous and concupiscent desires, as distinguished from necessary ones that are the Socratic "maintainers" of life,[20] cannot quench the longing for good that somehow survives in men's hearts, however they may try to elude it. To achieve an ideal order, it is therefore essential to elicit their will as citizens, says he, by which he means men of integrity, and to take account of the right to "opine, propose, divide and discuss" that the governing agency of reason always takes care to reserve for itself.

Some of us have in the past inferred from the text here summarized that Rousseau means to divest the sovereign will of the right to propose new laws and intends to reserve that privilege for the governing faculty or government. The eighth and ninth of the *Letters from the Mount* are usually cited to support this contention. But they fail to do so. In the eighth he is speaking of the status quo in Geneva and suggesting a change. In the ninth he merely says that the legislative power in a city may not be activated by any one of those composing it, which seems fair enough. But in the seventh[21] he openly complains that the sovereign people have been deprived of the right to initiate legislation in his native city or to control the government that does. Even in the passage of the *Contract* under discussion, he obviously means to complain that the governing power "always takes care" to reserve such rights for itself. On the other hand, he demands that the will or "inner feeling" of conscience be elicited, as well as common sense, in the proposal and discussion of laws. Emile is trained to find necessary ones for himself, and with him, as with the Swiss peasants mentioned above, their necessity is always felt as well as seen.

The main idea of the chapter, namely that man's will for the good is indestructible, is also Socratic, as we know. For instance, Socrates sees the soul of the tyrant as unhappy, for, being a victim of passion, "she is least capable of doing what she desires," and the good self is tryrannized by the bad. But the good self and its aspirations remain intact. Consequently he speaks of the good "which every soul of man pursues and makes the end of all his actions," even though

[214]

we may not know its nature or true scope.[22]

The question of knowledge of the good and errors in judgment about the will's intent, posed in *Emile* through the enactment of fables is treated in the next chapter of the *Contract,* "Concerning Suffrage." Rousseau begins by reminding us once again that "will power" in a city is manifested by a healthful unanimous and harmonious agreement of all the various parts, resulting in a consensus of opinion in popular assemblies, unless, of course, men are unanimously dehumanized. But he admits that the actual falls short of the ideal, for the true self is led astray by the false. Hence he asks what degree of assent is required for the sovereign will to obtain in the moral person. That depends, he says, upon the seriousness of the matter at issue. The law of the covenant is the only one requiring total commitment in soul or city. We saw this in the case of Emile, who must himself consent to the covenant of friendship. In the city of the *Contract* dissenters who refuse to adjust themselves to the supposed reasonable constitution of nature and the ideal commonwealth and who reject the covenant are called "strangers." Socrates in the passage on "warfare" calls them "barbarians." They are excluded, or rather, they alienate themselves from the state that promises happiness. In less august matters in the Rousseauist city of the covenant, the opinion of the majority of its inhabitants suffices for the "constant will" of all "citizens"—including the dissenting minority—to prevail.[23] The writer maintains that in the case of committed men those who opine otherwise err; and that if they were to follow their own false opinions, they would violate their true will and be at issue with themselves quite as much as the victims of passion in an anti-society. Dissent, discord, and error inevitably exist within the self, however committed. But if the general will does not prevail in the majority, says Rousseau—and of course it would not do so in a disordered society like ours— then there is no more freedom. This applies not only to a state but to elements within the soul since moral and civil

liberty are equally impossible when superior powers are enslaved by inferior ones. His thought here echoes the later
books of the *Republic* where the soul or city is betrayed
into slavery by the sophisms of tyrannical desires. But he is
persuaded that in his own city such abuses can be prevented:
just as passions can be tamed by the human spirit, so errors
can be rectified by common sense. Witness the case of
Emile. The fables in action that served to correct him were
designed to teach him the proper role of reason as faithful
ministrant and friend to his own indestructible will for lasting happiness.

A few critics[24] feel that there is a certain ambiguity about
Rousseau's "retreat" to majority vote after the demand
for unanimity. The matter was raised in the third chapter
above. Some people realize that the so-called retreat is an
attempt to translate the will into practical terms. But even
so, the author does not say here any more than in the second
part that the general will prevails in the majority or even in
unanimity. On the contrary, he says that it may not. It would
do so only among moral beings who make the positive act
of commitment to it, and only as long as they are mindful
of their vows. Otherwise, sophisms carry the day.

That is what Emile's governor has sought to prevent.
Henceforward, from the part on "warfare" to the creed,
he carries forward his task of stimulating the reasonable will
and making the youth into a "lover of wisdom." That is also
Socrates' object as seen at the end of Plato's fifth book and
pursued throughout the sixth. The latter now becomes
Rousseau's main inspiration to such an extent that I must
deal with the two texts together. In the ancient one the
speaker describes the philosophic nature, deplores its fate
in our society, and examines the form of government
adapted to it or education of philosopher-kings.

Of course, the Socratic concept of the philosophic nature
with which Plato's sixth book opens has already served for
the presentation of Jean-Jacques, since only a philosopher-
king can "beget" one.[25] For instance, he who was able to

distinguish between the true man and the false must presumably possess his model's perfect vision of the reasonable and divine pattern of human life and like the model know how to order and preserve the laws of beauty, goodness, and justice in accordance with that vision. His friendship with Emile is supposed to exemplify this. And when in the present crisis he rescues the youth from the enemies surrounding him, he again resembles the Socratic "friend of truth and all the virtues" whose enemies are the ones kept at bay in *Emile* and the *Contract:* the passions of mutinous men who try to prevent the "true steersman" from steering; and the sophisms of the great throng who fashion people to their taste in assemblies, courts of law, theaters, and camps, and whose prejudices and passions are called "justice" and "injustice," "good" and "evil." Rousseau almost quotes the master's words in *Emile*. In the face of such enemies the saving power of the Rousseauist ruler is that of the Socratic one in the same context, the "divine power" of reason that the hero has just recognized as a friend to man. And so, as both thinkers phrase it, he may safely descend into the den of human affairs to fight in courts of justice and public places, and partake of labors, lessons, and dangers therein.[26] He now does precisely that.

Rousseau defines the object and method of this descent. The object is to perfect his knowledge of mankind and himself and teach him to deal with men and calculate the effect of private interests in civic affairs. As for the method employed, he makes his way into society by practicing beneficence under the guidance of a sage. In dispensing his lessons, Jean-Jacques imitates the Socratic kings in the corresponding Greek text and makes his disciple into a "living authority" to perpetuate the idea of the constitution that guided the legislator in laying down his laws. For, after their example, he draws the youth to share in the same social virtues of charity and humanitarianism that he himself practiced in the "book of the law," still visible here. Both heroes thereby deepen their love of mankind, as do the Socratic

[217]

rulers, who are also loving and kind and hold sway by winning over the multitude gently and soothingly.[27] Rousseau is walking in the very footsteps of the master at the same time as he passes beyond him. For in Socrates' case the multitude is an orderly one, corresponding to necessary desires within the moral person or city, whereas the modern disciple, under the influence of Christian charity, appeals on behalf of the "indigent," "oppressed," and "unfortunate" amid a dusty and sordid humanity. Indeed, Rousseau virtually says that Christian and classical traditions are herein intermingled by comparing his hero at this stage both to medieval knights-errant and illustrious young Romans "who spent their youth bringing criminals to justice and protecting the innocent." After their example and that of the Socratic kings, Emile takes care not to alienate people or cause contention among them, for he loves peace and harmony[28] that are implicit in the common good. Gradually, his active compassion lavished upon all alike reveals to his mind what makes or mars the happiness of men, including his own felicity as a man of virtue. The love of humanity that results from his beneficence is identified as the love of justice, although he practices it only externally and is not yet obliged to "set in order his own inner life." The same qualities would be essential for the formation of the society of friends described in the *Contract*.

Rousseau warns that such good works permit no acceptance of persons. Like his masters he pleads strongly against partiality in soul or city. As we know, in both his books the sovereign will that favors justice has no particular object. Unlike those whom Socrates, in the very context here used by his disciple, styles "false philosophers" or "pretenders," the hero of the novel is concerned not with personalities but with principles.[29] He is taught that justice is the virtue most conducive to the common good of all men equally, for it secures the bond of peace and unity among them. Since the same bond is symbolized by his friendship with Jean-Jacques, their fellowship is obviously not an ex-

[218]

clusive one. As we saw long ago, it is open to everyone, springing as it does from general concepts that lie at the basis of Rousseauist and Socratic order. Even in his personal life, the writer professed to be a friend of all men, however disordered, as well as a citizen of the new Geneva,[30] although he understood too well the discipline required to reconcile one's private affections with a generous fairness to mankind as a whole. The warnings against partiality in *Emile,* paralleled by those in the *Contract,* are prompted by personal experience as well as Socratic and biblical models.

Rousseau stops at this point to admire the effects of Emile's formation and in doing so, continues to follow the sixth book of the *Republic* so closely that I must continue to handle the two together. The youth, with a heart free of exclusive inclinations and a mind absorbed by inner truth, beholds a Socratic ideal world "fixed and immutable," the true principles of justice, the real prototypes of beauty all moral relationships of beings, and the orderly disposition of things. Conversing with a reasonable and sublime order within the Aemilian city and practicing virtue in a chaotic world outside, he becomes orderly and sublime as far as the nature of man allows. These are the very terms in which Socrates too in the corresponding text describes his future philosopher-kings. Next Rousseau, again like the Greek sage and in the same context and similar words, faces the incredulity of his readers, as he also did in the *Contract.* He suspects that we have long since relegated him to the land of chimeras in company with his master.[31] People are skeptical, says he, because Emile is the man of nature and not of man.[32] Once more he is almost quoting the sage, who admits that by comparison with his ideal "all other things whether natures of men or institutions are but human," "conventional imitations," whereas he is molding "a human being" into the "proportion and likeness of virtue." Rousseau does the same. In doing so, he professes, with his master, to be adhering faithfully to his vision of human

[219]

nature sanctified by its divine origin. In the Greek text here reflected in *Emile,* Socrates explains further that he is fashioning his "image of a man . . . according to . . . the form and likeness of God," or according to the truth that is akin to the highest good as he sees it.[33] Rousseau hardly strays from the model that culminates with the great similitude of the sun or vision of the idea of good now matched in the creed of *Emile* contained in the "Profession of Faith of the Savoyard Vicar."

The author finally has recourse to the saving power of religion when the hero is eighteen years of age. Before doing so, he remarks meaningfully that Emile is no longer one of the "vulgar herd," although he started as one. The point is that his religion will exceed theirs.

According to the writer, most men are unable to commune with the Supreme Being, even in our confined degree. Consequently he would not have them study the catechism or Christian mysteries, which allegedly mean nothing to them.[34] If we protest that one must believe in God to be "saved," he agrees, on condition that the precept does not imply the notion "outside of the church no salvation." He believes that religion is necessary, at least for men living within the fabric of the social order. But he draws a distinction between the religion of the thinker or leader like Emile and the coarser instruction of the common people, who are so engrossed in physical needs that they hardly think at all. He does so even in his ideal order since many men are insensitive to the harmony of the universe that now enchants and mystifies Emile. For this reason he would instruct them in religion all the sooner, as he does in his dream of a perfect city that comes to the birth at the end of both books.

The distinction between the faith of leaders and that of followers brings to the surface the functions of Rousseauist religion. The latter provides further against sophisms and passions that were the themes of the previous pages of *Emile* and the *Contract.* For example, we are told that, as the hero's mind becomes more cultivated, religion would in the end be an intellectual necessity for him. That is one of its functions in the lives of leaders. But Rousseau is convinced that nature is slow to stir curiosity about the deity even in their case. Jean-Jacques, we are told, anticipates the moment slightly since he must impart instruction early enough to arm the will against the passions, accelerated by society, and maintain a balance among the faculties. The flames of passion constitute the sacrificial fire of the temple, offered to the Godhead to purify the soul. Religion serves this need for purification in the lives of both leaders and followers.[35] It therefore has a double purpose for leaders, though not for most men. At last Emile is to know the great lawgiver, whose sacred laws are already the substance of his childish faith. He is to acquire the essential elements of all religions without being associated with any particular one until he can choose for himself.

These views that scandalized Rousseau's contemporaries are far from new. One might cite the example of the *Republic*. From their earliest childhood Socrates' guardians are taught what is called a popular version of religion that is quite simply the practice of the virtues under the aegis of Apollo. But the reason of philosopher-kings is not even oriented toward the study of "true being" and the idea of good until after they are twenty years old, and only at fifty do they attain to the sight of God.[36] In addition, the sage formulates a practical profession of faith as a guide to conduct for all men in Plato's last book. Thus he too sees religion as fulfilling a double role. Rousseau, in his view of the subject as everywhere else, remains close to the master without, however, forgetting the founder of Christianity, even though he remains skeptical about Christian dogmas and mysteries.

One need not conclude that the religion of leaders and that of followers are incompatible, any more than the faith of guardians and kings in the *Republic* is incompatible with the practical religious dogmas formulated at the end of the great dialogue. The articles of popular faith in the Rousseauist city are likewise defined at the end of *Emile* and the *Contract,* and identically so in both cases. Later I shall compare them with Emile's. The latter is now presented in a long profession of faith that has no corresponding chapter at this point in the appendix. It prepares for an inner adjustment that is not included in an exteriorized version of the nascent city, upon which religious dogmas are superimposed after birth as the coping-stone of social order as in the case of the *Republic.*

The Aemilian creed has an apparently objective form. The writer professes to transcribe a document composed by a fellow-citizen who recounts the adventures and religious instruction of his youth.[37] To see the reason for the change in form, one must examine the introductory narrative.

In the latter as in the creed itself there are two figures, just as there are in the rest of the book. But they are not the same ones. Rousseau suddenly abandons the ethereal Emile and the mysterious Jean-Jacques and replaces them by two very earthly human beings, a young exile who remains nameless and an equally nameless Savoyard vicar who becomes the youth's mentor. In circumstances reminiscent of the vision of Er at the end of the *Republic,* two pilgrims ascend from the earth "dusty and worn with travel " and confront two other souls who have come down to our midst by the heavenly way, "clean and bright." The vicar and his protégé, who are obviously exiles from the blessed city or sphere of absolute beauty to which Emile and Jean-Jacques belong, are meant to exemplify the safest course open to men who must live in a world not their own.

The events of the introduction serve to show how enlightening an interpretation of art forms can be. Thirty years ago, we are told, a young Calvinist exile reduced to poverty became a fugitive in Italy, where he changed his religion for a morsel of bread. He was admitted to a hostel for converts, where controversy raised doubts in an unsuspecting mind and evil was made known to an innocent heart. He longed to escape but was locked up. In the course of time he contrived to consult privately a poor but worthy visiting "ecclesiastic" who favored his escape at the risk of creating a dangerous enemy. Thereafter a little good fortune led him to forget his benefactor. But his hopes for the future soon vanished with romantic illusions. At last without food or shelter, he returned to the priest, who welcomed and comforted him.

I must pause here for a moment before concluding the story. The outcast is, of course, the young, unregenerate Rousseau. The same child we saw groping about in the darkness of a Calvinist temple in search of the holy book is still groping about at a critical point in the writer's past, but this time in the Catholic church. The author here evokes the moment when, at the age of sixteen, he sold his Protestant birthright for a mouthful of food. The story is told in the second book of the *Confessions;* and if we compare the two accounts, we can easily see the symbolism of the one in *Emile,* which is usually taken for "romance." In the autobiography the abandoned youth runs away from Calvinist Geneva and takes refuge in a Catholic hospice for converts in the city of Turin. The hospice is transformed in *Emile* into an image of the Catholic church, in whose bosom he saw nothing but moral and intellectual disorder. In that inn for the pilgrims of life he was morally a "prisoner" for about twenty-six years, from 1728 to 1754. Within its precincts, though only after he had left the building in Turin (where he probably remained no more than a few weeks at the most), he met a visiting priest, Father Gaime, who was one of the vicar's two models in life. In the *Confessions* the vicar favors his escape from the mythical hostel by advising him to return to his own country and faith, advice which, as the autobiographer says, did not take effect until later. The youth's fleeting happiness with its promise of deliverance is also narrated in the *Confessions.* After its eclipse he remembers the vi-

car's words and associates them with another voice heard a
year later when, as a young seminarian at Annecy in Savoy,
he receives guidance from Father Gâtier, the second model
for the Aemilian vicar.[38]

In the rest of the story the vicar's life parallels the outcast's, and in the end the two are recognizable as one. A
youthful adventure caused the priest to lose favor with
his bishop, much as the exile's folly led him to break faith
with the religion of Calvin. Consequently both are outcasts
in Italy, where the vicar is almost as destitute as his protégé. From this point on his story identifies him not
merely with the exile of the context but also with the hero
of the *Confessions* and the writer of *Emile*. The priest was
once tutor to the Count de Mellarède's son, as Rousseau
later became tutor to the count's daughter. Moreover, he
desires to be restored to favor with his church and retire
to a parish in the mountains, like the writer who in 1754
resumed his Genevan religion and then made plans to
withdraw to the Swiss mountains once *Emile* ws complete.
Besides, when the book was published he was the same
age as the vicar he impersonates, the age of fifty when the
Socratic philosopher finally attains to a beatific vision of
God. The priest's method of reviving a youthful conscience
is also the author's. He begins by arousing self-esteem in
the embittered outcast to lead him to the practice of virtue.
For instance, he refuses to give him a deposit of money entrusted to him "for the poor," even though the youth protests that he is one of their number, for, says the vicar,
"we are brothers; you belong to me, and I may not touch
this deposit for my own use." The two are one, and the
writer identifies himself with both exactly as he does with
their heavenly prototypes, Jean-Jacques and Emile. Moreover, like him the two exiles favor dogmas contrary to
the Roman church, although they remain faithful to its
rites. In the end both appear as disguised Protestants.
When the vicar or "man of peace" finally succeeds in awakening the youth's reason and compassion for mankind, he

promises to confide to him the secret of happiness but warns him first that all is vanity under the sun and that peace of mind lies in detachment from the world. His secret entails that of "man's fate and the true value of human life." This is the Socratic theme of *Emile,* the *Contract,* and the *Republic,* which is now to be evolved in a religious context that adds power to the author's philosophy. For the profession of faith is really a religious statement of the principles of his companion volumes.

The figures of Ecclesiastes and the outcast evoke the most decisive events in the writer's religious experience. The voice that speaks in the creed is really that of his own conscience, which was once heard through the lips of two priests but was ignored. It is finally impelled to speak again by a consciousness of remorse embodied in the young scapegrace of thirty years before who still lives within him at this moment of truth. In other words, the voice is actually inspired by the mute presence of the hapless figure to whom it is ostensibly addressed. There can be no "revelation" until that voice is heard. It formulates a profession of faith that, like the whole of *Emile,* is really a conversation of a man with himself on the subject of good and evil. Mingled in its accents is that of Rousseau the grave Calvinist, the rebellious Catholic, the renegade "philosopher," and the disciple of Christ and Socrates. All combine to plead on behalf of a vision of moral truth that springs from the writer's deeper impressions of some of our oldest traditions.

If we still wonder why, in such an intensely subjective phase of the work, he declines to speak in his own person, we might suspect that, as I have shown elsewhere,[39] the objective form lends itself better to a public confession of the kind. But why put on the person of a skeptical Catholic priest? There are several reasons why he dons the priestly mantle. One is that his theme is theology. Besides, he always longed for the life of a village curate although he was judged unsuited to that vocation after two months'

[225]

probation as a seminarian at the age of seventeen. There is still another reason. Since the voice that speaks is that of conscience, regarded as the spokesman of God, and since his conscience is unquestionably Christian, he quite naturally poses as a vicar of Christ, whose home is the promised land of Savoy, the scene of an idyllic phase in his life. We may infer that he himself presides as high priest in the temple of the soul where, in the life of Emile until the age of discretion, Jean-Jacques is ministrant or Levite in an office upon which his disciple's fate largely depends.[40]

As for his skepticism, Rousseau maintains that, unlike that of the young fugitive and the writer's contemporaries, it does not affect the essential truths of religion.[41] Skeptics like those, he says, have more to gain than lose by adopting the vicar's views. Thus he uses his unregenerate and regenerate selves respectively as an image of the society of his day and its supposed hope of redemption.

But why choose a Catholic priest as spokesman instead of a Protestant, for whom doubts are permissible? He explains in the *Letters from the Mount* that the form of the work favors the Reformation, since a skeptical though pious Catholic priest advises a former Calvinist to return to the religion of his birth. However, according to a letter addressed to him by a friend after a long conversation together, the word *Catholic* is used in its etymological sense of *universal*.[42] As has been suggested, he probably wished to underline the non-confessional character of his faith and its value for the safe conduct of human life wherever men may dwell.

The setting of the discourse is adapted to its ideological function. The author describes a gracious summer dawn, beheld from the heights of a hill that rises beyond the confines of the city of Turin and overlooks the long-drawn, gently sloping valleys of the Po. The scene is crowned in the distance by the immense chain of the Alps singularly clear in the transparency of the air and the flood of early morning sunshine. The aesthetic qualities of the description are heightened by symbolic implications that are intentional, for

[226]

the writer openly acknowledges the ideological value of suitable surroundings for any serious form of instruction.

The choice of a mountain scene is especially appropriate. The mountain represents the summit of his thought. In Socratic terms it is the highest sphere of knowledge in the ascent of the soul toward moral truth. But it has many other resonances in the traditions combined in the book. It might be Mount Sinai, where God spoke to Moses as he does to the exile in the vicar's voice; or Mount Nebo, whence the prophet beheld the Promised Land here presented to our imagination; or even the hill of Sion, where Solomon paid homage to divine wisdom in the sanctuary of the Lord. On the other hand, it might also be some Greek acropolis or Mount Olympus itself, where the Delphic shrine now stands in ruins amid a landscape suggestive of the presence of the deity. But then again it may be that other mount in Galilee where Christ's "finest discourse" was pronounced, for the Christian overtones of this new sermon on the mount were accentuated in the final revision of the work.[43] In fact it is probably all of these, evocative of the various traditions that solicit the author's thought.

The sun is also symbolic.[44] Indeed, it corresponds, as I have said, to a Socratic similitude prefigured in the third part of *Emile*. In the image that occurs at the end of the sixth book of the *Republic*, the sage uses the sun to convey his idea of the goal of the education of kings: the supreme principle of the good whose light is moral truth and imparts visibility to the sight of reason. This idea dominates the Rousseauist text where however biblical reminiscences are also implicit. For example, in the apocryphal book of Ecclesiasticus, a favorite with the writer, Wisdom, having spoken of God's covenant, the law of Moses, and its duties and promises, boasts: "Teaching is here like the dawn for brightness, shedding its rays afar." The New Testament too is full of similar images of light to which Rousseau alludes elsewhere. In the brilliant mountain setting of *Emile* the blind boy of Bossey has come to be healed of his blindness.

[227]

The rays of light are a revelation illuminating reason and conscience that dawn like the sun upon the temple of the soul and lead man to an IDEA of good, which, for Rousseau, as for Socrates, is the "cause of knowledge and of truth."

The landscape confronting the vicar is also an inner one, representing in artistic form his own complex state of soul, both "romantic" and "classical" at once. The orderly cultivated valleys of the Po, remote from urban chaos, are an image of life as it has already been visualized, a well-organized, harmonious, largely "classical" vision. It is now superelevated by powerful lyrical aspirations that are bodied forth in the Alps in the background of the picture to form a "romantic" image of eternity and infinity, concepts that are also in the background of the speaker's mind. As the ultimate object of his thought, they poeticize it and sanctify it in his own eyes, thereby supposedly ensuring the safety of the simple order of life it propounds.

CREDO

"The Profession of Faith of the Savoyard Vicar" is, so to speak, the tabernacle of the living God in the very heart, or central nave of the cella, of the mythical shrine, where it is set apart by its own superscription and the cunning use of spacing. Rousseau himself called it "the best and most useful piece of writing of the century," meaning "useful" in the Socratic sense. The work is indeed a landmark. For the first time in modern culture, the author of a literary masterpiece uses all the resources of his craft to handle his entire creed as a major theme of art.[45]

Throughout the piece the blending of Greek classical and Judeo-Christian elements is visible. Rousseau's own statement that his books were mere commentaries on the scriptures is to a fair degree applicable to the profession of faith. Apart from numerous biblical echoes in its content, the ideological framework closely resembles that of the Solomonic book of Ecclesiastes, beginning with the theme

[228]

"Vanity of vanities; all is vanity," and ending in much the same way as King Solomon in the sacred text which is paraphrased by Christ and his apostles: "Fear God, and keep his commandments: for this is the whole duty of man." The Old Testament book shows how far a man, richly endowed with knowledge and experience, may go by the light of natural revelation alone, and in this respect is related to Rousseau's purpose. But its conclusion leads straight into the New Testament, which also reverberates in the Aemilian creed. Rousseau acknowledges a special debt to Christ not merely by choosing a mountain setting but in other more convincing ways. For example, he calls his work a "discourse," the word applied in French to the Sermon on the Mount. Besides, he quotes from that and other of Christ's sayings. And in the central tableau of the piece he portrays the divine master towering far above Socrates. But in the same tableau and elsewhere, too, he hints at his indebtedness to the Greek master and to pagan tradition in general. Indeed, as I have said, he calls his creed a canticle or hymn of Orpheus. Whether or not the reference to the Greek musician was inserted at the last minute to accommodate an engraver as seems to be the case, it is a felicitous image nevertheless. Just as Orpheus, the son of the Delphic Apollo, was empowered to tame wild beasts with the music of his lyre, so the son of man, who in the creed is "lord of the earth and the beasts thereon," appears in the vicar's person as the new Orpheus taming what Socrates and his disciple call "the wild beast" or "multitudinous monster" within the soul or city; and he does so far more effectively than the Sophist lion tamer of the sixth book of the *Republic,* who flatters the beast instead of taming him.[46] In fine, the writer is obviously conscious of fusing the great streams of our culture in his "hymn."

The creed is indeed a "hymn" as defined in the *Dictionary of Music:* a song in honor of gods or heroes. Moreover, just as a hymn is also a prayer, so is the whole profession of faith: not a prayer in the sense of a petition but an act of worship, of admiration, contemplation, and submission, such as the writer favored in his personal life.[47] It is a long meditative dialogue, or rather monologue, offered in homage to the divine prototype of justice and wisdom and therefore to the soul or city made in that likeness. This prayer, like many another, is filled with imagery that in the present case serves to illustrate the author's philosophy of life, as is usual with him.

The profession of faith begins and ends, as does *Emile,* with a defense of the "true" laws of basic social institutions, like love and marriage, that respect the rights and duties of humanity and are rooted in the universal principles of nature, unlike the "false" decrees of existing man-made religious and political systems that allegedly shock her ordinances. Indeed, Rousseau says in his letter to the archbishop of Paris written to vindicate the book that that is the primary purpose of the vicar's creed and of *Emile.* According to the writer of the epistle, existing institutions that tyrannize and mutilate nature force her to claim her rights by stealth and thereby create an abyss between reality and appearances. He exemplifies the strife between them by the contemporary laws of celibacy and marriage. The latter would be the laws whereby the French government refused to recognize the validity of Protestant marriages in France and also forbade the intermarriage of Catholics and Protestants. As we saw in the beginning of *Emile,* the author defends marriage as a civil contract upon which any society stands or falls. As such it wins the support of "enlightened" faith.

Accordingly, the spokesman of the Aemilian creed commences by confessing his own moral dilemma concerning marriage and celibacy. By virtue of a Freudian, or rather Platonic, method of using the sentiment of love to convey attitudes toward life, he expands his perplexity into a spiritual problem of good and evil. He begins with the reflection that he was destined by his estate to till the earth. This, of course, is man's true vocation in the book and the one to which the author felt that he was born.[48] The vicar's parents, however, decided to make him into a priest, much as Rousseau's resolved to "wed" him to an exclusive communion, without considering whether it respects the rights of humanity or does not. The "parents," in Socratic or Rousseauist language, are the country and its laws. This engagement is a false contract, corresponding to the falseness of a society that violates nature. The vicar is bound to it by a vow of celibacy whereby he promises "not to be a man." Again he is the writer pledging himself not to take any other "bride" outside the communion to which he is committed. This vow represents in the context a spurious rule, comparable with existing laws of marriage that cause a man to be at war with himself. The result of such rules is their inevitable infraction. In literary terms the vicar-writer is faithless to his "bride." He intuitively follows conscience and well-ordered nature, which disregard "false" man-made decrees and lend their support only to the laws of reality. The spokesman breaks his vow of chastity, as the writer strays from the faith of his fathers toward "natural religion."

But the priest, in taking to himself another "bride," reveres marriage as "the first and most sacred institution of nature." In other words, though violating the mythical marriage forced upon him, he remains deferent to the commitments of other people. He therefore forms a connection with an unmarried woman. She becomes for the author a biblical and Socratic symbol of the natural religion of man that is the vicar's faith, called "the pure Christianity of the Gospel." She is recognizable in the bride of the Levite of Ephraim, to whom Rousseau by his own free will is now espoused, at the same time as he professes to respect all established religions seen as private engagements like those honored by his spokesman in the Aemilian creed.

The consequences in both cases are the same. The vicar's infidelity to a "false law" leads to scandal, arrest, dismissal, and exile. This was the fate reserved for the author as a result of an analogous apostasy. His words here are prophetic and proved to be true enough. But worse disaster lay in store for both men who are one. The vicar explains that the enforced infraction of arbitrary laws that trouble the order of nature causes strife and disorder in the soul, to which he is remorsefully a prey. The disorder in question is typified by that of the senses and is said to impair the happiness of the human creature, which depends upon unity and harmony and can be assured only by a truly moral engagement and laws based upon man's natural constitution. with its hierarchy of faculties. Such are the allegorical implications of the exordium of the Aemilian creed.

Before proceeding, it is necessary to consider it in the light of the *Contract* and other texts. The alleged violation of nature's ordinances by our institutions is traced to its origin in a historical survey at the beginning of the chapter of the *Contract* "Concerning Civic Religion," which practically concludes the book.[49] The survey helps to underline the vicar's plight. In pagan antiquity, says the writer, the gods were identified with the laws of the city, which were regarded as divine. For him, of course, this would be desirable only in a perfect social order governed by "true" laws. Then, he continues, Christ came—to a "degraded" society, as we see later—to establish upon earth a spiritual realm or kingdom of the other world. This realm, which puzzled the pagans, is the one to which the vicar withdraws; and so conceivably would Emile, but for an allegorical *coup de théâtre* at the end. The survey in the *Contract* ends with the advent of dogmatic Christianity that allegedly replaced the realm of the other world by a violent despotism in this, and caused a conflict of power between religious and political authorities. The conflict, as illustrated by the vicar, is due to the presence of the same tyrannical aspirations in both systems that Rousseau regards as equally arbitrary and hostile to human nature, creating victims of "false" laws like himself and his spokesman. The conclusion to be drawn from the passage of the *Contract* is that, although the social and politico-moral unity essential for a good constitution requires the support of religion, yet if the laws of society are not in fact "sacred," then the only solution is the spiritual kingdom proposed by Christ as a refuge from the world and at the same time a guide to life therein.

In these pages of the *Contract* and *Emile* where the writer is haunted by Christianity, he has not forgotten his Greek teacher. In his preoccupation with moral law, he approaches religion in the same way as Socrates approaches both his similitude and practical creed at the end. In the former case the sage proposes to show his student kings the virtues "in their perfect beauty" to make those heroes into true guardians of the laws, and lovers of the idea of good. In the final creed, he seeks a remedy to the evils of actuality described in the eighth and ninth books where he traces the process of decline from the ideal order of things to the tyranny of lust and lawlessness. In those books he shows how moral and social chaos arise when desires, instead of being tamed by true law, are constrained by necessity and fear until they create "war" in the soul and then escape control, and a master passion, concupiscence, becomes tyrant absolute. In the tenth and last book he finds a solution in a religious profession of faith. The spiritual disorders, in the context of which its doctrines evolve like the vicar's do, are in his view fostered by tragic poetry, which flatters and glorifies false opinion and tyrannical passion. He combats those exhibitions of evil by his own concept of the great artist and the divine plan of life. His avowed follower does likewise in the vicar's creed as well as in its popular version at the end. Presumably the Rousseauist "hymn" is meant to be an example of the only kind of poetry that the sage would admit to his city, the kind that honors gods and heroes and is "useful" to states and to human life.[50]

I come now to the creed itself. Although the vicar's at-

[233]

titude to speculative reason is far from Cartesian, he begins with what Descartes regards as a necessary first step in the way of truth: a denial of habitual impressions and a conscious opposition to the current mode of thinking. From that point he sets out to determine his bearings on the vast "sea of human opinions," without benefit of helm or compass and with no other guide but "an inexperienced pilot who does not know his way, who knows neither whence he comes nor whither he goes." Here the Socratic image of the ship of the soul recurs by implication. The pilot without helm or compass is the untrained intelligence visualized as such in a passage on the philosophical nature in Plato's sixth book, as we know. In the Socratic text he "is a little deaf and has a similar infirmity in sight, and his knowledge of navigation is not much better." He is nevertheless the true helmsman and must attend to "what belongs to his art" if he means to be "qualified for the command of a ship."[51] In conformity with this idea the Aemilian vicar searches about anxiously for some positive light of doctrine to guide him to "the cause of his being and the rule of his duties."

Bereft of the ancestral Roman religion as a guide, he contemplates the variations of philosophy and derives therefrom a renewed conviction that we know neither the first principle nor ultimate issue of things. He therefore disquiets himself only concerning those matters that it is important for him to know and reposes in profound ignorance as to all else beside, says he in the very words of the book of Ecclesiasticus.[52] These limitations and the avowed weakness of reason envelop his creed in intellectual uncertainty and doubt.

In order to learn what concerns him, he takes as his guide "the inner light," called "inner feeling or persuasion." It is really insight or intuition regarding his own true interests, confirmed by reason and experience and expressed in conscience, which later appears as the voice of the enlightened human will. Consequently it is a moral and intellectual guide as well. Following this tutelary genius within, he is at once led to reject materialism in favor of the "Being of beings and dispenser of things," honored by the theologian Clarke, who, like Socrates, rises to the idea of a Supreme Being. In other words, the vicar begins with an a priori choice in favor of God or Providence. By comparison with the rest of the book this choice is all that is ideologically new in the creed, but that is a great deal.[53] The profession of faith proceeds like the convenant from a deliberate act of the will, as indeed it must do if, as we shall see, religion is to be a law in his city and invigorate all other laws. He defends his choice as being more consoling and presenting fewer difficulties and more proofs than any other system. But intellectually it still remains a hypothesis. It appears as a self-conscious assent to a presupposition without which life would be absurd as well as intolerable. He obviously finds sufficient ground of evidence in that very fact. Thus the will or inner feeling, used as an instrument of knowledge, provides him at the outset with a "reasonable" belief, tokens of which he now seeks in the world about him.

Next, after using inner feeling as a guide to discover God as the source of moral truth, he sets out on his search for that truth and examines the guide he follows. The feeling in question must be essentially love of self since it entails a consciousness of his own existence and regulates the use of the senses as organs of cognition to acquaint him with the outer world of beings and things insofar as the latter act upon him. Thus he relies heavily upon sensitiveness and impressions, and his knowledge is largely subjective.

Then he considers the structure of the intellect. He discovers within himself the active power to compare the objects of his sensations by "shifting" them, "transporting" them, and "superimposing" them upon one another to form judgments about their mutual relationships. The motive images convey the idea of activity on the part of the subject and imply both volition and intelligence. Accordingly he concludes that he is an active, thinking being, capable of attributing meaning to existence and judging it. He denies

[235]

that he is merely sensitive and passive, as the materialists say. He distinguishes between the sensible and visible on the one hand and the intelligible on the other. In doing so, he shows that comparative and numerical ideas belong to the sphere of the intelligible. He gives the examples of a big and a little stick and the fingers of the hand, which the eye may see without counting them or making relative estimates about size. Socrates, too, in proposing the great revelation for student kings in his own similitude of the sun, makes meticulous distinction between the visible and intelligible. Later he cites examples of impressions that stimulate the mind and invite thought as opposed to those that do not, and his examples are the very ones chosen by Rosseau, who also resembles him by claiming the freedom to respond or not to the stimulus. But the mind is subject to error. To train it, both thinkers favor the mathematical sciences, as we know.[54] But Rousseau's vicar, unlike Socrates, refuses to renounce the senses in favor of speculative reason alone to attain to a vision of a reasonable order in human life. On the contrary, like Jean-Jacques hitherto, he corrects faulty apprehension of the outward world by having further recourse to them, for, says he, they never really deceive us about themselves, and we need no proof that we feel what we feel. We go astray, he explains, only when the judgment mingles its errors with the truth of sensations. The corrective proposed is to refiñe and perfect the instruments of intuition by passing from confused to unconfused sensation, as Emile did, always remembering that the truth is in things and not in the mind that judges them. He concludes that the rule to follow inner feeling instead of speculative reason when the two disagree is confirmed by reason itself, which for him is basically a reason of sense, or rather, common sense. The rule of insight thus confirmed is conceived as the bulwark of education and legislation.

After making the choice of God and analyzing the organs of knowledge, he uses the latter to search for clues to justify his faith and rescue him from chaos. Lost in a universe whose bounds escape him and amid beings whose nature and relationships to himself mystify him, he suddenly realizes, by the grace of inner feeling alone, that whereas he is able to move his limbs spontaneously and at will, the sun rising in the Alpine sky before him in its regular progress through the heavens lacks that very power. It obeys fixed laws, even as a watch does. This is a wonderfully suggestive image, more Rousseauist than Cartesian or Voltairean, as it has been called, since the writer is the watch-maker's son—and I am not referring to Isaac Rousseau, who was a master craftsman in that capacity. Inner persuasion tells the vicar that movement is foreign to matter and that the heavenly bodies are responding to some external first cause, comparable to the power felt within himself. There is, he concludes, a sovereign will diffusing itself through the world, whose action sets the universe in motion and gives life to nature. The vicar is convinced that there can be no action, as distinct from movement, without will. The argument is a traditional one, of course. But the point to observe is the literary parallel with man, who experiences the action of the will not merely in spontaneous bodily motions but in the covenant and its oath that give life and movement to the city or the soul. Indeed, we are obliged to see this since, according to Rousseau and in view of the exordium of the creed, such is the main point of his dogmas, which are intended to sanctify his whole philosophy.

The vicar confesses, however, that he knows neither the nature of the will nor how spirit acts upon matter. But to confuse the two substances as the materialists do, with their ideas of "blind force" or "necessary movement" in nature, is even more incomprehensible for him.

Proceeding with his meditation, he deduces from the laws of order imposed upon the world of matter that there is also a supreme intelligence, an active, thinking being like himself "behind this vain show of things," an argument as old as the first. He sees this being in the harmony of nature to which he belongs and in the ordered relationships of things

[237]

that he perceives, even though their common purpose—of whose existence he feels inwardly assured—escapes him for the moment. He can do this just as a man who sees a watch for the first time can, without understanding its use, admire its mechanism and even see the workman therein. The familiar image recurs. In fine, the orderly spectacle before him discloses to the vicar's mind the intelligence of a master craftsman comparable to the Socratic artist of artists. Again we must see a literary analogy with man. The divine intelligence and its laws are visualized as a pattern of the operations of the human spirit and acts of the reasonable will that impose laws upon the city or soul and order all parts of the whole in accordance with a common object. Here the vicar on the mountaintop receives the tablets of the law from the hands of God, and the law is the Rousseauist one, of course.

Once more he attacks materialists like Diderot, with their theories of chance combinations of atoms. How could nature and human life be the work of chance, he asks, any more than Virgil's *Aeneid* could result from fortuitous combinations of printed characters? His arguments are as old as time. "No," he cries, "the world is governed by a wise and powerful will: I see it, I feel it, and it concerns me." It is a very personal intellectual and moral need for him.

He does not say here that the Being of Beings created matter, an idea unintelligible to him. However, he later uses the work *creator* to signify that the artist who formed and ordered all things is the creator of order and therefore of the idea of good in Socratic terms.[55] What matters to him is that divine wisdom exists, one with nature and with man, disposing the system of creation in such a way that every part contributes to a common end. The purpose now descried is the preservation of the whole in the established order. Since this is also man's object in the disposition of city or soul, the aim of *Emile* and the *Contract* is herein hallowed. The vicar gives the name of God to this being whose will and

[238]

power are equally boundless and balanced and who is, he infers from the perfect order of his work, possessed of goodness too. For Socrates and many other thinkers goodness is the first attribute of the divinity. But Rousseau cares less to show that God is good than to show *how* he is good; what concerns him is that goodness results from a balance of power and will and is manifest in order, an idea applied to man in *Emile* and the *Contract*. Accordingly the vicar concludes that what really matters are God's relations to him, and not a knowledge of the creator's essence or that of the human spirit either. Thus his recognition of God takes the form of conscious effort on his part to order his own soul or city after the divine pattern. God is he in whose image man or the city is made.

This is confirmed when the speaker turns his attention directly to human beings. In lyrical passages of a biblical quality he proclaims the royalty of man, who is king of the earth like Adam and can tame the beasts at will. The new Orpheus uses words that hardly differ from those of the Psalmist or Socrates. His eulogy of human powers culminates in an angry apostrophe to the materialist Helvétius, who by establishing continuity between man and the animals is said to "liken himself to the beasts" instead of to God.[56] By contrast, the vicar's convictions result in a sense of human self-esteem that arouses gratitude to the deity. This acknowledgment implies a flutter of conscience analogous to Emile's early gratitude to the "superhuman" Jean-Jacques, the recognition of a debt to be repaid according to the law of justice, which is, after all, Rousseau's primary concern.

Thereupon the vicar looks about him to find his place among men. It is then that he discovers evil and disorder, as Emile did in the portraits of Plutarch, but here it appears as a violation of the divine order of the cosmos: "The beasts are happy. Their king alone is wretched! O wisdom where are thy laws? O Providence is this thy rule? I behold the earth and there is evil upon it." The phraseology here re-

[239]

sembles that of the Pauline passage: "O death, where is thy sting? O grave, where is thy victory?"[57] The resemblance is appropriate, since we are about to learn that despair is to give way to hope since the disorder here revealed is to be adjusted in death. That adjustment depends, of course, upon his concept of the soul, which he discusses next.

It is the discovery of evil that leads to the discovery of the soul, whose powers, according to Socratic doctrine, are called into play in the presence of evil. Thus the spokesman becomes aware of the soul when he observes and then personally experiences strife between two principles in our nature corresponding to the aforementioned active, thinking being and the sensitive, passive one. He discerns that the active principle conducts him to truth and justice, whereas the passive one, at issue with it, makes him a slave of the senses and passions, "the wild-beast nature" within, threatening to overthrow the balance of faculties. To describe the inner conflict, he follows Socrates but again borrows the language of the apostle Paul: "No, man is not one: I will and I will not; I feel myself at once a slave and a free man; I perceive what is right. I love it, and I do what is wrong; I am active when I listen to the voice of reason; I am passive when I am carried away by my passions; and when I succumb, my greatest agony is the feeling that I might have resisted."[58] The opposition of apparently incompatible elements, felt with the birth of moral bonds and passions in society, convinces the vicar of the dualism of his nature arising from the coexistence of a material and spiritual substance within him.

Again he defies the materialists, who, in an effort to prove that there is only one substance, try to reconcile thought and feeling with qualities of matter like extent and divisibility. His arguments are less persuasive than the forms that clothe them. He accuses such men of being deaf to the hidden harmonies of the spirit that now reach a lyrical crescendo, not merely audible to the reader but also visible in that prospect toward the Alps: "Something within thee

[240]

strives to break the bonds that confine it; space is not thy measure; the whole universe does not suffice to contain thee...."[59] The passage evokes many another in Rousseau's works. But as a poetic tribute to the vast harmonies of the inner world, it is also evocative of Socrates' discussion of harmony, wherein the sage disparages those who hear only with their ears and not with their understanding.

The vicar, attentive to the reverberations within, formally announces his belief in the soul. He declares his faith in the power of the human will to resist slavish passions and torment us if eluded. He further declares his faith in the ability of its ministrant, the active human intelligence, to formulate judgments and liberate the will, whose nature is to pursue the good of the entire moral person, and not to seek its harm. Man, he concludes, is free to act, animated by an "immaterial substance." This belief enables him to suggest a solution to the problem of death hereafter. But he does so in a new development in the creed, for the first series of dogmas ends at this point with the same emphasis on volition with which it began.

We come now to another class. The transition occurs when the vicar suddenly declines to enumerate his doctrines, as he has done hitherto. The pretext is that we can do so for ourselves. But we could also have counted the others. The real reason is that he is on less solid ground. This is also indicated by the presence of prayers. There are five in the creed if we include a footnote, and but for one at the end they all occur in the passages we are now approaching. Even though the whole creed is a prayer, the prayer form here assumes great artistic value to express the writer's timorous "hope against hope." So does his increasing recourse to scripture to justify his persuasions.

Since man is active and free, he alone is held responsible for evil. The greatest ills he endures, we are told, are moral ones and are his own doing in a supposedly enlightened social state since he abuses the freedom and intelligence that dignify him and enable him to scale the heights of virtue

[241]

and wisdom. The antithesis drawn in the text between the excellence of man's nature on the one hand and the responsibility for evil on the other is suggestive of a certain vexation of spirit that deters many a man from belief. But the vicar rises above his difficulties in a first prayer and thereby testifies that he does so by virtue of a conscious act of the will: "God of my soul, I will never reproach thee that thou hast created me in thine own likeness to be free, good and happy as thou art."[60] In these words the spokesman renews his vow of faith in the very presence of evil and in spite of his awareness of a certain inherent desolation in things, caused not only by the wicked deeds of men but also by the presence of death that he now faces.

To show that life is prolonged after death, he quotes the words of Christ to the Sadducees, who say there is no resurrection, and declares that "God is not the God of the dead." In his own reasoning the Omnipotent, whose goodness imposes the laws of order, will in his justice restore order in death by bestowing happiness upon the virtuous man whose heart reassures him with the words: "Be just and you will be happy." Here the vicar deliberately rejects any suspense of judgment regarding further stages of being possible for the soul. But to proclaim his faith in a future life, he breaks free of dialectic to take refuge in artistic imagery by fancying a speech of God with the soul of Brutus, who cried out upon the plains of Philippi where he lay dying, "Virtue, thou art only a name." The image is momentous since here for the first time we behold a personal deity who intervenes in human life. In spite of the charming image of the watchmaker, God seemed until now more like the eternal reason of the Greeks than the Judeo-Christian Father of men. Suddenly the latter stands compassionately over pagan humanity in the person of Brutus and promises new life to the dead. "O Brutus! O my son!", says he, "why dost thou say, 'Virtue is naught,' when thou art about to taste its reward? Thou shalt die? Nay, thou shalt live! And thus my promise is fulfilled!" In this context the writer appropriately cites Plutarch, who uses the allegory of the races to explain that we must finish the course before we can win the crown of victory. The apostle Paul says the same and so does Socrates.[61] This is a race in which Emile must be an active participant and not a mere spectator. The prize this time is life after death, in which the vicar professes to believe.

"If the immaterial soul survives the body," says he, "Providence is justified." On this condition, he adds, the appalling discord in the universal harmony, the triumph of evil over good, is resolved. At death, he reasons, when the two substances in man's nature are separated, the true life of the liberated soul begins. But, as someone has observed, he defends the idea negatively; for he explains that although he does not know the soul's essence, he cannot imagine how it could die, and so his reason assumes for moral purposes that it lives, not merely until order is restored, but forever. The life he anticipates is a consciousness of his own identity prolonged by memory, a Fénelonian notion favored by Rousseau, who took pleasure in recollection. Our suffering or our joy, we are told, will be born of the remembrance of our deeds upon earth, contemplated in the light of God, truth, and the beauty of order.[62] At this point the author adds a pious supplication hidden away in a footnote that again betrays the role of will in his creed. It is taken from a translation of Psalm 115 in the Genevan Psalter of 1698 and reads: "Not for us, not for us, O Lord,/ But for thy name, for thine own honor,/ O God! may we live again." Reflecting upon that life, the vicar frames another prayer to express his doubts that the torments of the wicked never come to an end. But if the future life consists of a new vision of the present one upon earth, logic is again threatened by an effort of volition to behold perfect harmony beyond the grave, at least ultimately if not immediately, although in the end he suspends judgment on the subject.

In these reflections upon the origins and consequences of

evil, pagan images are intermingled with Judeo-Christian. Indeed, quite apart from Plutarch, pagan antiquity can hardly be ignored in the context. Socrates teaches his guardians from the beginning that God is the author of the good only and not of the evils that occur to men, and in addition he commends to them "the world below." Later in his great similitude he proposes to lead his student kings to see the divine as the idea of good. Moreover in the creed at the end he presents the great artist or workman as the creator of real things existing in nature, especially justice and virtue or rather order. In the same context he also teaches the immortality of the soul and the rewards of justice here and hereafter, comparing life again to the sacred games wherein the true runner wins the prize and is crowned—even by men and upon earth, at least in his ideal order. When he shows the meed of virtue in another life, in the culminating vision of Er, Socrates, who professes to believe in hell as well as heaven, declares that such rewards and punishments are just, since men choose their own life and their own destiny: "Virtue is free," says he, "the responsibility is with the chooser. God is justified." These are Rousseau's very words. The sage concludes: if we discern well between good and evil and choose ever the better life that suits the nature of the soul and makes her just, then we shall be happy here and in another state of existence when, "like conquerors in the games who go round to gather gifts, we receive our reward." The passages in the vicar's creed, inspired by the spectacle of evil and the mystery of death into which it plunges him, turns out to be a fusion of biblical texts, Plutarch, and the Socratic myths.

We are now approaching the high point in the canticle of Orpheus. After the "monument to the unknown God" whose presence is seen in the eternal processes of nature and especially in the life of man, the vicar still disclaims any knowledge of the divine essence or even of our own, and in a fourth prayer surrenders his reason before the mystery of the deity. Yet for him the mystery is partly unveiled when he goes in search of rules of conduct and finds them written in his heart and uttered by his conscience. For him conscience implies consciousness of a power outside the self that approves or disapproves of our conduct. It is in a sense the oracle of God testifying to the Socratic idea of good and the laws that it ordains. In the imagery of *Emile* it is the Pythian oracle in the midst of the mythical temple that again recalls the shrine of the Delphic Apollo. There stood the tripod at the navel of the earth where the divine voice spoke to men, as it allegedly does in the vicar's creed. According to the latter, it addresses each one of them and affords the only revelation that the speaker accepts unreservedly.

The vicar defines conscience as a natural feeling of good and evil that bids men seek their own good but not at the expense of others. For him it is generated by the antagonism of bodily passions in inner life that made him first conscious of the soul. Indeed, he calls it "the voice of the soul," which is the enlightened will as we know. It is therefore the voice of that "inner feeling" or insight that formulates the creed as it does the rule of life in *Emile* and the *Contract*. The speaker regards it as a kind of moral instinct that is as natural to the heart as reason is to the mind, and as "normal" as the law of Rousseauist society, which of course does not mean that it is a spontaneous, subjective, and arbitrary moral sense. On the contrary, he calls its enlightened feelings "judgments," which are always on the side of justice. Hence he infers that justice suits the nature of man and reflects a state of health in the soul. Socrates said as much, and Rousseau did too when he spoke of the reasonable will that favors the virtue of justice.[63] The vicar undertakes to prove it in literary terms. For example, he imagines men's reactions to the spectacle of good and evil in the situations of actual life, in the theater, or in the pages of Plutarch. What is the explanation, he asks, for their admiration of heroic deeds and their indignation at wickedness? "Why," he inquires, "should I choose to be Cato dying by his own hand, rather than Caesar in his triumphs?'' And again: "What are the crimes of Catilina to me? I shall not be his victim.'' Incidentally, the example of the Roman conspirator also inspires the writer of the civic creed in the *Contract* when he comes to defend the dogma of a future life. The Aemilian vicar cites more instances of men's love of moral beauty and of its frustration in our society through the injustice of false laws. Even wicked souls, he adds, cannot entirely quench human feelings of mercy, loyalty, or friendship. He contrasts their remorse with the serenity of the sage who obeys nature's ordinances. Although most of the images here are selected from pagan antiquity, the writer obviously possesses a Christian conscience that throbs painfully before the spectacle of cruelty and suffering. Yet at the same time he contends that basically the precepts of good and evil are everywhere and always the same. He therefore concludes that men possess an innate sense of justice called conscience, even though it is felt only in a social and moral order that activates it in the presence of passion.

As usual at each stage in his meditation, he challenges his adversaries among the philosophers. This time they include a dissident friend, Montaigne, of whom he asks in Ciceronian terms: Is it ever a crime to keep one's plighted word, to be merciful, beneficent, and generous? If not, then righteousness allegedly befits the nature of man.

If we ask whether he means that men are naturally selfless, or how he defines the principle of conscience or the will it expresses, he admits as usual that men must obey its laws for their own good.[64] But he explains that there is a spiritual good to be found in virtue, the grace sought by men like Socrates and Regulus. The principle that bids us pursue moral order is, therefore, for him self-love, which, as we were told long since, impels us to seek what pleases, suits, or perfects our nature. In social life, however primitive, it is moderated by compassion for others; and with the rise of discernment it dawns upon us in the form of conscience, like the break of day that is the scene of this meditation.

[246]

Without that light, which is the light of moral truth, the rational power in social man is lost, in his Socratic view. The vicar bursts forth in oracular accents in a hymn to the unfailing monitor within, called "divine instinct," the "celestial voice," the guide of an intelligent and free being, "the infallible judge of good and evil, making man like unto God" and alone raising him above the beasts. This Socratic "divine wisdom within" supposedly dispenses us from metaphysical speculation and suffices to reveal the goodness that befits the human self, unless we wilfully suppress it.

In defining the principle of conscience, the spokesman has also suggested its aim. According to him, the moral good it favors by favoring our own "true" nature requites our natural love of beauty, justice and truth and thus entails pleasures of soul like those enjoyed by the Socratic heroes in the sixth book of the *Republic*.[65] In fact, his ideas on conscience as the voice of the soul are reminiscent of the philosophic nature described at the beginning of that book. Finding wisdom and happiness close by, he asks what sweeter felicity there is than to obey the duties of the natural law ordained by God's justice and to acquiesce freely not merely in a love of order but in a love of the perfect order divinely established? The Rousseauist philosopher resembles the Socratic by imitating that "heavenly pattern" in his life, and he does so, we are told, by ruling over the passions of a body maimed by disorders and thereby rising to a sphere above the angels, in the words of the vicar and the apostle Paul as well.[66] The happiness that results gratifies man's "first will," the constant and unalterable one that bids him be good and wise according to his nature.[67] In brief, felicity implies the orderly action and interaction of human faculties working together in harmony according to their proper functions.

The Rousseauist order and its laws now consecrated are violated by the "false" law of celibacy, to which the vicar alludes again at the end of the first or affirmative part of his

[247]

creed. He does so by referring to the irregularities of his life, including an illusion of happiness supposedly bred in him by that law which allegedly reverses nature's decrees. He goes on to condemn all "rash vows" that aspire to trouble the order of nature, including prayers for special spiritual graces or miracles of any kind. He himself refrains from praying for bounties, and the last invocation of his faith is the Lord's Prayer: "Thy will be done." For him that will is best expressed in the human conscience and the laws of the constitution that is the great artist's handiwork. The choice of the prayer form here to protest against what he considers selfish supplication has great literary merit, as the author says in the *Letters from the Mount*. Moreover, the prayer selected is ideologically appropriate, for, however we choose to classify his philosophy, his conscience is essentially Christian and even transfigures his Socratic laws. The affirmative part of the meditation that ends here has amply demonstrated this. I shall come to the so-called negative part in a moment.

First it remains to be shown that the dogmas of civic faith stated in the penultimate chapter of the *Contract,* as they are at the end of *Emile* and the *Republic*, are wholly contained in the vicar's creed. I have commented upon the historical survey with which the chapter opens. When the author comes to formulate the faith of his citizens, he begins by considering the relationship of religion to both social and civil order and defining the virtues and flaws of the religion of man and that of the citizen, with a view to combining their resources and avoiding the pitfalls of each. The creed he proposes is thus designed, like the vicar's, for society in general as well as for an exclusive association. Consequently the popular idea that the Aemilian faith is the religion of man and is irreconcilable with the other[68] casts doubt upon his success in carrying out his intentions.

The religion of man or of social order in general is, says he, true Christianity, not the dogmatic variety but the evangelical, which he identifies with the vicar's so-called theism, or natural religion. He names it "natural divine law," meaning that it sanctifies the universal and eternal principles of natural and political law. It is confined to the inner cult of the heart and the moral duties of men, teaching them that they are all brothers. However, it adds no force to civil laws as we understand them, and even detaches men's hearts from the earth. The attitude of detachment is that of the vicar and the one Emile would logically adopt in an alien society where, in Rousseau's view, there is no other hope of happiness.

Next the writer considers religion in its relationship to civil order, whose laws it serves to consecrate as it does his own. Such is the citizen's faith that he calls "positive divine law" since it adds divine authority to the positive laws of an established government. He favors the union of divine cult and love of the laws, providing, of course, that the laws are "true" ones based upon universal principles; but he fears superstitious ceremonial that disorders men and intolerance that destroys them. When he comes to define the civic creed of his own mythical city, he tries to avoid both perils by forbidding intolerance and recommending a simple cult reduced to public ceremonies that dignify the moral law. This religion would result from a sense of friendship, or fellow-citizenship, with others and would allegedly provide most men with a more powerful incentive for the performance of civic duty than the vicar's "evangelical Christianity," whose principles are, however, basically its own but are directed to leaders and thinkers. In a provocative passage he shows how those lofty principles, which foster detachment in the anti-society of actuality, would among the common people of an imaginary, impossible ideal city, serve as a pretext for indifference to civic duty and submission to tyranny. Such men require only the practical dogmas derived therefrom.

His idea of using religion to hallow the general principles of natural and political law as well as positive civil laws has far-reaching implications. Religion, far from fabricating arbitrary enactments like the contemporary laws of marriage and celibacy, which he regards as such, must be the strongest support of "true" ones presumably like his own, and for him as for Socrates it is itself one of them.[69] Consequently like all the laws of his city this one too is framed by the sovereign will of the people, which has no lawful superior, religious or political either. Moreover, since his laws envisage the common good and may require nothing useless or unessential to the entire moral being, the law of religion cannot evade or exceed these limits. It can sanctify only such commandments as those of Moses, Numa, or Lycurgus. And the vicar's "evangelical Christianity" provides for him a revelation of their source.[70]

The articles of faith proposed in the *Contract* and later at the end of *Emile* are a popular exposition of the vicar's dogmas. The positive ones are briefly defined thus: "The existence of a powerful, intelligent, beneficent, foreseeing, and provident deity; the future life; the happiness of the just; the punishment of the wicked; the holiness of the social contract and the laws." There is also a negative dogma forbidding civil or theological intolerance of the kind exemplified in contemporary enforcement of the precept "Outside of the church, no salvation," which, so the writer declares in the *Confessions*, leads people to lie against the Holy Spirit." This precept is good, says the author of the *Contract*, only in a theocratic state that is in fact a church, whose pontiff is the prince. Yet like Socrates he himself applies it in his own city in the form "Outside of the city or temple of the soul, no salvation," meaning that the human constitution cannot otherwise be saved. In a word, he excludes dissenters who reject the faith, as they are free to do, just as he exiles those who repudiate the covenant. Men who profess to believe it and then behave as if they did not are punished with death. But he tolerates all religions that are tolerant of others and respect his own, even if the latter can never be an established faith any more than his city can see the light of day.

[250]

The death of the apostate has aroused a great deal of controversy. To understand the writer's thought, one must capture the spirit of the text, which reads: "Let him be punished with death; he has committed the greatest of crimes, he has lied before the laws." Now to lie before the laws that proclaim the constant will as conscience does means, in the Aemilian faith and in the words of the *Confessions*, to "lie to the Holy Spirit" that speaks to men in that "celestial voice." Such is Rousseau's interpretation of blasphemy against the Holy Spirit, called by Christ "the unpardonable sin." This is "mortal" sin that brings death to the sinner, the spiritual death of one who is "cut off" from the moral person like the sacrilegious soul in the Mosaic law who is "cut off from among his people" as a limb is severed from the body. If life, freedom and salvation are to be found, as Rousseau says, only in his system, then to cut oneself off from it after being integrated in it is in his eyes spiritual death. We are reminded of the controversial "right of life and death" as applied to apostates of the covenant in an earlier chapter. The sentence of "death" is not only Judeo-Christian but Socratic too, as we know. In speaking of spiritual "warfare," the Greek sage says: "And he who allows himself to be taken prisoner may as well be made a present of to his enemies [meaning passions]; he is their lawful prey and let them do what they like with him." Rousseau too means that such a man is doomed to die, which does not alter the fact that he teaches mercy and tolerance, as we have repeatedly seen.

But he knew well enough that legislation will never prevent intolerance, for human beings are always inclined to favor "friends" or kindred souls in preference to aliens or "strangers." He betrayed this awareness when he spoke of the difficulty of reconciling "positive divine law" with "natural divine law." He betrays the same awareness in the *Letters from the Mount* where, speaking of the problems of civic faith, he says that "patriotism," or love of a man's own city, and "humanitarianism," favoring human rights, are two virtues incompatible in their energy and especially in a whole nation.[71] Many of us may be tempted to infer from this text that the popular antithesis between man in *Emile* and the citizen of the *Contract* actually exists. But we have already seen that the principles of both are the same, though they are not applied with the same "energy" in the great society as in a small one, except by a few lofty souls as opposed to "the body of a nation." Of course, in actuality the problem posed by patriotism is academic since for the author no authentic city exists anyway: there are only disordered states that foster nationalism or love of one's birthplace at the expense of human rights.[72] However, he imagines the unlikely case of such a city existing, not only at the end of *Emile* as we shall see, but also in the *Letters from the Mount* where he evokes a society of the Savoyard vicar's Christians. They are surely freemen of the city of the *Contract* since, as he says, their creed—or, rather, the vicar's— "is affirmative and conclusive in all the main points of civic religion," which is that of his ideal citizens. He adds that it "contains all dogmas really useful to both universal and private [or exclusive] societies."[73] Hence it teaches the duties of both man and citizen. The vicar's Christians are presumably both and so is Emile, as opposed to most men.

But some critics still contend that Rousseau fails to reconcile the two. They argue that he tries to do so by integrating the religion of both but that the civic creed has dogmas absent in the vicar's, these being the holiness of law and condemnation of intolerance.[74] But these two articles are the very essence of the Aemilian faith. The affirmative part of it is nothing else but a vindication of the holiness of all "true" law. As to the negative part on revealed religion that we are now approaching, it is simply a denunciation of every kind of intolerance. The difference between the two creeds is more artistic than ideological, although the one explores principles and the other simply defines conclusions, as I have shown.

[252]

In the second part of his meditation Rousseau in the person of the vicar confides his doubts to a doubting world on the subject of dogmatic revelations. For him these are the "artificial" laws of established faiths that violate both "natural and positive divine law," including "evangelical Christianity." He speaks mainly of Judeo-Christian dogmatism and is inspired by personal experience. For example, his doubts are entrenched within the negative dogma of civic faith that condemns the maxim "Outside of the church, no salvation." This maxim vexes his conscience, audible in the vicar's voice and visible in the exile, who calls to mind a moment in the writer's conversion to Catholicism when he was allegedly asked whether, in his judgment, his deceased mother of the Protestant faith was damned.[75] But although that memory never leaves his thoughts, his skepticism really extends far beyond the Roman church and embraces the whole of dogmatic Christianity, including Calvinism itself, as we saw in the story of the blind boy of Bossey groping through the darkness for the sacred text.

The attack upon dogmatism is banal in its argumentation but is presented in an original form. If the writer regards his own faith as "evangelical Christianity," then authentic Judeo-Christian revelation as he sees it is to be found in the affirmative part. It is his inheritance and has left its mark upon his conscience and in the qualities of his imagery. He cannot then intend it as the object of his rebellion, which is directed rather against so-called obscure dogmatic interpretations of its message. Consequently his art now consists in wresting it from the hands of sectarians and claiming it for himself by arraying on his side all the prophets of Judeo-Christian tradition, including Moses, Isaiah, John the Baptist, and the divine master himself. He does so by strengthening his arguments with words and phrases borrowed from their sayings.

In his view private esoteric or "artificial" dogmas, as opposed to true revelation, lead to abuses that cause strife

[253]

among men. To illustrate this, he uses the very words of Christ's prophecy that his coming would bring not peace to the earth but fire and the sword. For Rousseau, who ignores the militant side of Christ, this is a warning that the spiritual kingdom of the divine missionary would turn into a violent despotism in the present world, as events proved according to the *Contract*. The vicar protests—again using the master's words recorded in revelation—that the cult required of us is that of the heart and not simply the external formalities of a system of ritual. He adds that God wishes to be worshipped in spirit and in truth, thereby repeating the lesson of Christ to the Samaritan woman at the well: "God is a Spirit: and they that worship him must worship him in spirit and in truth." For the vicar these phrases from revelation prove that to exceed its literal teaching is to violate it. For him a doctrine that does so is not merely unnecessary but harmful since it disorders and divides men.

Looking about him at those who are eager for private supernatural enlightenment, he assumes a tone recognizable as that of Solomon in the book of Ecclesiastes, the preacher: "I beheld the multitude of sects that hold sway upon the earth."[76] He implies that sectarians use the supernatural to "hold sway over the earth." Apart from this impropriety, the multiplicity of sects varying from country to country makes religion of that kind an effect of chance dependent upon one's birthplace. If, says he, adopting a commonplace argument, there is only one of these churches outside of which there is no salvation, it possesses universal and eternal signs obvious to all men. This argument leads him into a discussion of miraculous signs and wonders used by dogmatizers to support their pretensions.

The prodigies in question, unlike those of the first part of the creed, are the kind that every man cannot verify for himself. They are discussed in three lively dialogues. Whether or not we share the writer's views, we can still appreciate the mythical form with which he clothes them and acknowledge its suitability to impart his message.

[254]

The first dialogue presents Ecclesiastes and a so-called apostle of truth who seeks to prove his mission by portents and prophecies recorded in books by human beings. In a formula that most critics find the only original one here, the skeptical vicar protests: "How many men between God and me!" In a similar vein the author of *Emile* and the *Contract* virtually exclaims: "How many men between the law and me!" And again: "How many men between nature and me . . . and between the world and me!" In the same spirit he asked the archbishop of Paris whether it was natural for God to go looking for Moses in order to speak to Jean-Jacques Rousseau.[77] The vicar demands to know how it is possible to verify ancient chronicles of prophecies and prodigies and to distinguish the latter from the unknown laws of nature that best reveals the Supreme Being. Nature itself is therefore the greatest of all miracles. Admittedly the writer contends in the *Letters from the Mount* that the marvels of chemistry and physics are not miracles, but he means in the usual sense of the word, a point of view already implied in the conjuror scene of *Emile*.[78] The speaker of the creed suggests the paradox that the real miracles and true revelation are to be found in the affirmative part and that they support him against the dogmatizers.

In the next dialogue he converses with a real apostle and does not exclude the possibility of authentic miracles in the popular sense. But he uses revelation to contrast them with the supposed miracles of zealots. The envoy of the Most High comes forward to announce undeniable ones that bear a conspicuous resemblance to those of Joshua stopping the sun and Moses making the waters of the Red Sea part to let his people cross. They are also reminiscent of others in a passage of Isaiah applied to Christ by John the Baptist and describing the Messiah's coming and the supernatural phenomena to accompany it for "all flesh" to see. Such miracles, says the vicar, are decisive and are not to be confused with the fraudulent ones of false prophets. Discussing the latter, he again borrows freely from Judeo-Christian revelation. For example, he cites the testimony of Moses in Genesis and Deuteronomy that puts us on our guard against the wonders of magicians and strange prophets. Moreover, he expresses doubt about miracles wrought in deserts or chambers, alluding almost textually to the words of Christ: "If they say unto you, Behold he is in the desert, go not forth: behold he is in the secret chambers, believe it not." Hence, Rousseau in the person of the vicar uses the words of the divine master himself to justify his incredulity. True miracles, he says in a note to the creed, must be evident even to the "poor in spirit" for whom the kingdom of heaven is reserved, according to the Sermon on the Mount, whose message he defends against the dogmatists. The vicar rebels against the alleged obscurities of the latter on the grounds that the God he adores is not a God of darkness. Consequently the speaker appears paradoxically as the defender of revelation against those who malign the "Great Being" by what Socrates calls unworthy representations of the Godhead. Such men are contrasted with the true apostle of the dialogue.

The third dialogue is between Inspiration and Reason, both of which are personified—or, as some people say, caricatured—although the two figures are evocative of Fragonard's Inspiration and Study (circa 1769), which can hardly be so described. This dialogue differs from the others in that here the spokesman takes refuge in Socrates instead of revelation. Apparently hinting at the dogma of transsubstantiation and other mystical beliefs, Reason challenges them with the mathematical axiom that the whole is greater than the part.[79] By having recourse to mathematics to combat mysticism, Rousseau like the Greek master summons the arts of calculation to his aid to resolve the perplexities of the soul and virtually refers to a passage at the end of the *Republic* that I mentioned at the close of the previous chapter. In that passage the sage, speaking of optical illusions, observes that the confusion created within us is "that weakness of the human mind on which the art of conjuring and ... other ingenious devices imposes, having an effect upon us like magic ... and the arts of measuring and numbering ... come to the rescue of the human understanding ... and the apparent greater or less ... no longer have the mastery over us, but give way before calculation ... ."[80] The germ of the dialogue of Inspiration and Reason can be found here and so can the whole attack upon so-called false miracles, as well as the conjuror scene. The same Socratic passage also deepens our appreciation of the myths of *Emile*. Although the author has recourse to abstract mathematical sciences as he does in the *Contract* to evade what he regards as obscurity and deception or pious illusion, yet he personifies ideas and uses figures and dialogue to animate sheer logic, however misplaced the latter may be in spiritual matters. The device is less subtle and more provocative than the paradox hitherto employed.

He returns to the miracles and his defense of revelation as he sees it in the second and third of the *Letters from the Mount*. Again he uses the Bible to find support for his view, but this time he does so even more openly. Like his vicar he refers to the Old Testament, especially Genesis, where the feats of Pharaoh's magicians are said to be the work of the devil who performs false miracles. He adds that in the New Testament the divine master not only warns against false signs but rejects miracles altogether as a proof of doctrine. Here he almost quotes Christ's words to the Pharisees: "A wicked and adulterous generation seeketh after a sign ... ."[81] Again the scriptures are on the writer's side against the dogmatizers. Although in his youth as a Catholic he once testified to a miracle, he now claims the right to personal interpretation of the sacred writings on that subject as on every other. This right, he says, was originally the cornerstone of the Reformation but was being demolished by his intolerant coreligionists. It was to them that he addressed the *Letters*. By what authority, he demands, do they deprive him of a liberty that they themselves have wrested from the mother church? But his main concern in the *Letters*, as in

[257]

Emile and the *Contract,* is not religion at all but a system of law to which it belongs. His attack upon dogmatizers is really an indictment of what he regards as arbitrary enactments like contemporary laws of celibacy and marriage or those threats of damnation against dissenters like himself.

The precept "Outside of the church no salvation" and its pendant the negative dogma of civic faith banning intolerance are still the prevailing ideas in the last part of the meditation. Rousseau's personal experience with the maxim, to which he twice alludes in these pages, lends warmth to his images and intensity to his thought.

Assuming the dogma to be valid, his spokesman confronts us with the perplexities and fanaticism generated by it. Like many another man before him, he argues as follows: If there is only one true religion that all must follow under pain of damnation, how can the "lover of truth," who knows that she is one and not many, make a perfectly safe choice, since there are many guides among men proposing an infinite variety of beliefs? He cannot study the doctrines of one sect without the others, for a judge may not listen to one party only but must hear them all. He must also read their writings. And if he decides to trust one of them, surely it must be one who has a thorough knowledge of all systems of thought, beginning with the three great European religious philosophies. Even so, what is the fate of those whose lives lie beyond the span of any of these? The vicar imagines a pagan listening to a missionary preaching mysteries that men must know unless they would "be damned." The pagan replies: "And my father is damned . . . he who was so good and kind . . . " The thought is hardly original, but the tone is very personal. This is a direct allusion to the question allegedly asked of the author in life at the moment of his conversion,[82] a moment eternized in the homeless exile of *Emile.* The dismayed pagan decides that he must journey abroad to inquire about these mysteries. So, says the vicar, must all men. But since a lifetime would not suffice for such labor, he refuses to believe that it is necessary to be so learned "under pain of hell fire."

[258]

To resolve these perplexities, the vicar suddenly breaks free of theological erudition, scientific reason, and their inhuman demands to take refuge in the heart and plead in favor of evangelical Christianity. In a famous tableau of its founder he surpasses himself to portray the peaceful soul of Christ in life and in death that set him apart from the men of his time and our own. He compares him with the "statue" of the just man proposed as a type of the Socratic sage at the beginning of the *Republic*. But then he proceeds to draw an impressive contrast between the divine master and Socrates, who, we are told, found among the Greeks close by examples suggestive of his teaching, whereas Christ appears as an image of the "loftiest wisdom amid the fiercest fanaticism." That wisdom is supposedly also the vicar's since his song of Orpheus is designed to tame the wild natures of men, and he is therefore called "the man of peace." Socrates, of course, sought to do the same by means of his laws and, although in the end he voluntarily submitted to "false" ones, died for the sake of the true; and so in the vicar's eyes his death redeems him. Yet Rousseau draws a distinction between the Socratic ideal of justice and virtue practiced among friends and the Christian ideal of compassion and charity for the wicked, exemplified by its founder, who blesses those that persecute him. Moved by admiration for the latter, he calls him a "God" among men. It matters little whether this divinity is of a substance, an adoption or a function. What matters is that, in conformity with his stance as the defender of Judeo-Christian revelation, he identifies his faith as an evangelical one. I have already said much about his cult of Christ in his personal life and in his work, which moreover includes two other portraits of the divine master.[83] In the vicar's meditation he uses a mythical image born of great intimacy with the Gospels to convey his moral inclination toward Christian revelation in spite of his persistent doubts. In accordance with that inclination he is persuaded that true worship is indeed of the heart and is visible in propriety of life and virtue.

[259]

The vision of sublime charity amid the madness of the multitude is followed by a new protest against the excesses of intolerance. The vicar refuses to preach damnation "outside the church" on the grounds that to do so is to blaspheme the justice of God and lie against the Holy Spirit. Again he alludes to Christ's words about the unpardonable sin and subtly uses revelation on his own behalf against its professed exponents. Moreover, the allusion, like the pagan's words above, shows again that the writer is indeed moved by that moment in his life when he abjured Protestantism and "lied to the Holy Spirit" by violating his conscience.[84] It is wrong, says the vicar, to ask anyone to leave the religion of his birth, not because it may after all be the true one, but because by doing so we ask him to disobey the laws of his country that prescribe a uniform cult for all. This association of religion and law— as forceful in *Emile* as it is in the *Contract*—is one reason why the writer opposes Diderot's distinction between civil and ecclesiastical intolerance in both the Aemilian and civic faith where the language is the same in each case.[85] It is also why the vicar, who has confided his faith to one who embodies a skeptical age, counsels him to return home and practice the ancestral cult prescribed by law in his own country, even though he may not share its beliefs. For, says he, quoting John the Baptist, "if God is able of the very stones to raise up children to Abraham, every man has a right to hope to be enlightened when he is worthy."[86] Again he appears as a defender of revelation, confident that doubts will be dispelled not by a miracle but by a man's worthiness of enlightenment. And for him such worthiness can best be fostered by the faith of one's fathers, to which the heart most naturally responds. This is a practical solution of the dilemma posed by the multiplicity of sects, any one of which a "man of peace" must somehow inwardly adjust to the principles of natural divine law. He may do so by using those principles to exercise his spiritual freedom and rise above intolerance and the external con-

[260]

formity prescribed by quite another law, as Emile does politically in the end.

In conclusion the vicar suggests, as he did in the beginning, that faith is at the outset an act of will or of hope or desire. He adds, quoting Seneca, that it springs from a righteous heart, which is the true temple of the Godhead. The temple is also that of *Emile*. The righteousness it safeguards is synthesized by the new Ecclesiastes in the words of the old, which are also those of Christ and his apostles: "To love God above all and one's neighbor as oneself is the summary of the law."[87]

The meditation closes with a little colophon in the form of a literary paradox. It is a skeptic's protest against skeptics. The vicar, having condemned fanatical, intolerant believers, denounces fanatical, intolerant unbelievers, although he professes to reconcile the two and tame the fierce natures of both. Dogmatic atheists, says he, led on by their own wild imaginings, make a mockery of the old morality. In doing so, they exile themselves from the Aemilian city and that of the *Contract*.[88] By contrast with their "desolate" doctrines, his own moderate skepticism is intended to favor a decorous and venerable system of manners and morals that lends grace and harmony to human life. He sees it as the fruit of the human mind through the centuries, sanctioned by a great throng of distinguished spirits led by Christ and Socrates. But in his final words the Socratic "Know thyself" with which he commenced is transformed into the Christian "Forget thyself:" "When we forget ourselves," says he, "we are really working for ourselves."

THE OATH OF KINGS

The last "nave" of the vast temple chamber matches the first one and is the inspiration of the remainder of the *Contract* with the exception of the final brief chapter. In *Emile* the author now comes to closer grips with the problem of evil, this time not besieging the soul from without, as in the first "nave," but checked from within by Jean-Jacques. In

[261]

subtle ways the latter uses religion as an ally in his work of government.

Emile's faith is called natural religion or natural divine law; and although, like natural and political law, it will ideally guide him to favor its civic counterpart, namely the "positive divine law" of the citizen's creed, yet in practice he will presumably follow that of his birthplace and reconcile the two in the manner suggested above. Meanwhile, the governor takes advantage of the intellectual and moral value of religious studies and research on the author of nature to cultivate the youth's reason and moderate his sensitivity with a view to balancing the faculties, providing against inner strife and strengthening the ruler's hold upon the heart. As a result Emile is impelled to do good "without being forced by law," for love of God and himself or, if we wish, for love of the Rousseauist and Socratic divine order of things, so that he might one day enjoy lasting happiness in another state of existence reserved for the soul hereafter. For him the yoke of incipient reason is that of manhood, and its burden is no heavier than the cult of the heart upon which it rests.

For Emile is on the verge of manhood. The latter comes with the full awakening of reason as the light of conscience, and therefore with the consciousness of a root of evil within himself to be felt intuitively and averted through his own volition. We are prepared for this awakening by a discourse directed by Jean-Jacques to imaginary critics among us. The governor explains that only at that moment do his own rights, which are those of reason, begin for the youth since only then will the latter recognize them. Hitherto, the law of duty was imposed so unobtrusively that it was as unknown to him as passion in his person. So was the minister through whom he was subject to its rule. It seemed to be in the very nature of things, as indeed it is in Rousseau's view. But since Emile is to ratify and obey it consciously, he must feel the need to do so and be made aware of the mediatorial action of his governor in the past as executor of the law as well as a friend to man. This step in his progress will be

[262]

made simpler by the fact that, as we are told once again, Jean-Jacques has bound chains about the heart of his disciple. As we have seen, the chains are meant to be the lawful fetters of ideal social relationships. Their appeal to Emile is described thus: "Reason, friendship, recognition, a thousand bonds of affection speak to him in a tone that he cannot fail to acknowledge."[89] Again the Socratic leitmotiv recurs in a fresh expansion of the basic theme. The idea is that, as reason sheds its light more brightly upon the bonds of friendship, his reaction will be the Socratic one anticipated in the first "nave." He will recognize and salute his familiar friend as the law of reason and duty incarnate. This means as before that he will acknowledge a social debt of gratitude to be repaid, a reaction that symbolizes the law of justice at work in the inner realm of conscience. His gratitude, says Jean-Jacques still preparing us for the crisis, is based upon natural self-love, regarded as the only permanent feeling (as opposed to the flux of vagrant desire) and recognizable as love of the human or higher self befriended by the governor.

Since the moral order thus visualized respects nature, when the youth's desires begin to expand, Jean-Jacques continues, they will not be treated as "crimes," even though they are of course potential "enemies," passion having already been defined as a perversion of natural feeling. The governor of the ideal city is nature's minister, not her "enemy." In this capacity he does not, however, favor an early marriage but reconciles nature's decrees with the law that ought ideally to "befriend" them, and employs "a great deal of art to prevent social man from being quite artificial." The paradox is by now familiar to the reader.

When nature's time comes, says Jean-Jacques in concluding his discourse, the governor must make the youth responsible for himself by enlightening him about their mutual relationships and moral engagements, the crisis he has reached, and the perils he must face. Whereas, hitherto, vicious passions seemed alien to him personally, he must now face the threat of evil in himself, the "enemy" within, and he can do so only if the notion of evil developing with instinct is clear to him. Like the Socratic heroes, who in this respect are said to resemble a well-bred dog, he must know his "enemy" as well as his "friend" and be able to distinguish between them.[90] In fact, that is all the Socratic and Rousseauist philosopher needs to know in life. Consequently, the Aemilian governor proposes to draw the youth into a larger consciousness of the spiritual obligations implicit in the order of friendship or moral order. In this wise we are led to the crisis.

The shift of moral responsibility from Jean-Jacques to Emile is inevitable since the autonomous action of the inalienable sovereign power is indispensable. In the author's eyes it is all the more so since the Rousseauist social order never has materialized and never will, and the hero is doomed to live in a disordered world. And, of course, even if the ideal order were to descend upon us from the empyrean, every human being must still consciously and voluntarily commit himself to the IDEA of man, whose essence is his own and upon which that order is supposedly founded. He must himself apply its laws as those of the human constitution and be governed by "divine wisdom within." The just society must first exist in the heart of man if it is to exist anywhere at all and if, as Socrates says and Rousseau teaches, true justice pertains not to the outward man but to the inward, "the true self and concernment of man." Now that Emile's passions are quickened, he who knows how to create order in the external world must be induced to prevent the elements within him from interfering with each other's work, to "set in order his own house," be his own master and his own law and at peace with himself. This is all the more true since he is presented as a leader who will hold sway over his fellows by the force of his example. In Rousseau's Socratic view men who are ruled by external authority and rely upon the enforcement of law by others as agents of an inactive will and dormant reason are childish

[264]

and could at best practice only "images of virtue" by force of habit or necessity like Emile heretofore. The youth later observes that they are like blocks of wood instead of men, and Socrates calls them "posts."[91]

Jean-Jacques makes meticulous preparations before awakening his ward to the real struggle between good and evil: "Before we sow," says he, "we must till the ground; the seed of virtue is hard to grow; a long period of preparation is required before it will take root." Indeed, he has been cultivating the soil from the first where the book opened with the same image, which then recurred in the myth of the Socratic and Christian husbandman.[92]

Before making the great disclosure, he wards off the imminent onslaught of passion. The youth is compared to a somnambulist who is led away from the brink of a precipice before being awakened. He is then briefly distracted from the presence of peril by the violent exercise of the chase popular among Genevans. In a new Socratic myth elucidated by the author himself, he becomes a huntsman, a follower of Diana, the chaste goddess of the hunt and enemy of love, and rides through woods and fields and rugged countryside. He was prefigured by the child astray in the shadows of Montmorency forest who exclaimed, "O my good friend!" when he was led forth into the light as the youth is about to be, only this time the light will be a brighter one. The myth of the hunter is, like that of the forest, evocative of the one in the fourth book of the *Republic* where Socrates and his friends go hunting for a quarry that is justice. Emile's quarry is the same.

The scene of his awakening to the true nature of justice in the form of spiritual order is also that of the governor's transfiguration before him. It is hardly less dramatic than Mentor's metamorphosis into the goddess Minerva in Fénelon's *Télémaque*. The setting is chosen in accordance with Rousseau's usual respect for the language of signs and is an impressive one of woods and rocks and mountain slopes. Like that of the vicar's creed it is symbolic of a state

[265]

of soul in the midst of the temple as much as it is a landscape outside. It is, we are informed, a place fit for solemn oaths and the recognition of ruling powers, since it suggests the presence of the deity as the judge of mankind who sanctifies "covenants," "alliances," and "promises." The writer recalls the awesome scenes of biblical oaths and sacred contracts. He also calls to mind the august signs of royal power that won men's allegiance in the past, and gives the example of the ancient Romans and their use of symbolic expression adopted in the Aemilian text. He admires the care with which they chose a suitable time and place for the great assemblies of the people, and ordained that candidates for government office go clad in appropriate robes. From all these observances he draws a lesson: "Clothe your reason with a body if you would make it felt" and let it speak the language of the heart. Indeed, the tableau in *Emile* is inspired by the solemn rites described, whose purpose was the same as that of Jean-Jacques.

The dramatic action follows. The governor, animating the voice of reason "with images and figures" to appeal to the emotions, speaks first about friendship and then about marriage, but his discourse is not verbally recorded as the vicar's was. In the light of this collation of texts and in view of the author's own warning about "images and figures," we might be justified in seeing in his handling of the two themes a portrayal of Rousseauist social and civil order, which does not, however, exclude the possibility of a literal interpretation as well.

The motif of friendship takes precedence, of course. The speaker finally reveals who he really is and shows Emile all that he has done for him but talks as though he had done it for himself, motivated by affection. Instead of appealing to the youth's interest as he did previously, he appeals to his own. Yet he is really identifying the two, if the common happiness is secured by the Socratic and Rousseauist law that "friends have all things in common," which is the law of the covenant. He explains: "I shall kindle in his young

heart all the sentiments of friendship, generosity, and recognition that I have already begotten.'' Again the famous
words of Socrates are audible in the text that underlines
the identity of thought between the two. Jean-Jacques concludes the first part of his discourse with more Socratic
speech: "You are my wealth, my child, my handiwork, my
only hope of happiness." He implies that the law of reason
or its spokesman begets the nobly ordered soul or city[93] and
is a man's true father and friend, who are one as we were
told at the beginning of the book.

Continuing the discourse, he allegorizes about marriage.
He reveals both the natural laws and exclusive moral affection that consummate it, and depicts it as "the sweetest
form of society" but also as a "sacred bond" and "the most
holy and inviolable of covenants." He contrasts the horrors
of debauchery with the blessings of chastity, which symbolizes purity of will or love of the law—as in the vicar's
case—and promises health, strength, virtue, love, and all
the true goods of humankind. In this way he associates the
good with happiness and evil with misery, "enemies," and
death in the mind of Emile.

This passage is full of allegorical elements. The bond of
marriage, which for Rousseau as a Calvinist was, as we
know, a civil contract,[94] is "begotten" of the laws of nature
and realized by love. Now he has already said that love in
the civil order is an exclusive affection born with reason,[95]
and in this respect it resembles a man's devotion to his own
city. Indeed, the conjugal ties that consummate it poeticize
for him the conventional bonds of a private civil order that
harmonizes with the natural one. Hence while the vicar
called love and marriage "the most sacred institutions of
nature," Jean-Jacques calls the conjugal bond "the most
sacred of covenants." He used the same words to describe
friendship, which binds a man to the laws of justice and social order and is here applied to an exclusive object. There
is no contradiction between the two texts. For Rousseau the
civil covenant is founded upon the universal and eternal

[267]

principles of the great covenant or social contract, which in his view are the laws of human nature. When they are observed in the intimacy of private life, intensity of affection gives powerful unity of motive to practical rectitude. Here as in the fifth part of the book, the primary institutions of love and marriage are used to portray the "wise order" of the Rousseauist city and its laws that are about to prevail in the innermost sphere of human action. The image is appropriate since in marriage love becomes a law. If the author here regards matrimonial ordinances as "sacred" and their violation as a crime, it is largely because for him they symbolize those of his own city and are the very reverse of the arbitrary decrees against which the creed was mainly directed.[96] Again Freudian or Platonic methods serve to impart his thought.

Emile's response is typically Socratic. The Rousseauist huntsman, like the child emerging from Montmorency wood, exlaims "O my friend!"—recognizing in reason or the light of the human will the Socratic "companion of his life and education" and discovering the law of justice as nearby as the Greek huntsmen found it. Aware of his responsibility, he pleads with his "master" to resume the authority that, endorsed by his own will, is now all the more sacred to him. "Defend me," he implores, "from all the foes that besiege me and especially those I bear within myself." His constant will, he says, is to obey Jean-Jacques' laws, or rather the dictates of his own reason that alone can save him from the slavery of sense and make him master of himself. At this point the enlightened will is fully formed in him, and he sees his governor as an outward equivalent of that faculty whose voice, like the vicar's, is heard in conscience. By promising obedience, he consents to share actively in the society of friends. He also performs an act of self-government by begging his friend to be what Socrates calls his "minister of education" or governor. He contends with evil autonomously in this way until he can finally cope with it alone. The pledge to which he proposes to subscribe in this context is not merely a pedagogical contract that evokes the great covenant, as has been said, but actually translates that covenant into literary terms.[97]

Jean-Jacques' reaction to the plea for his ministry is as typically Socratic as the plea itself. He hesitates. In a city of good men, says Socrates in Plato's first book, to avoid office would be an object of contention, for they would know —as Christ also teaches—that true kingship is of the nature of a service to others. Rousseau says the same in the *Contract*, as we know and shall again be reminded. To restrain the passions of men is no easy task. Emile, says Jean-Jacques, will be like Ulysses, who could hardly resist the singing of the sirens even by entrusting himself to another. But in this case the "other" is the wise Ulysses or great helmsman, to whom the speaker himself was formerly compared and whom the youth must ultimately become. Rousseau, by identifying each of his characters with the same hero, confesses that both are himself, not merely Jean-Jacques. The confession is made in a moment of crisis, as is also the case twice in the next part. Furthermore, the use of the image of Ulysses for the two shows that the man of nature, by recognizing and choosing Jean-Jacques as the true pilot, already becomes for a moment his own helmsman. The imagery represents concretely and in a literary manner the way in which a governing power is lawfully instituted according to the *Contract*. The two friends together momentarily symbolize a democratic governing body into which the sovereign or collective moral being temporarily transforms itself in order to decide upon a ruler. Jean-Jacques, in spite of his reluctance to guide Emile, to "forget himself" in devotion to his friend and wage unceasing war against the vagrant desires of both, accepts the double burden of the ruler who is also subject to the laws.

After the disciple has "signed the covenant" and the friends have reached an agreement that, throughout the crisis of expanding passions, the wiser of the two will execute the laws on behalf of both, Jean-Jacques at once takes precautions against acts of blind obedience. For instance, he observes that Emile can understand his governor's motives if he waits to be free of passion before judging. "Always obey me first," says the ruler, "and then ask me to account for my commands." Here the friends poeticize the ideal Rousseauist and Socratic relationship existing both within the sovereign people and between them and their rulers: real governors are always answerable to those whose felicity they serve. Jean-Jacques' professed purpose is, as usual, to make Emile happy in the present as well as in the future, in accordance with nature's designs. He does so by representing true love as the supreme happiness of life, but he uses it to symbolize the love of wisdom and win Emile to his side: "I shall make him into a sage," says he, "by making him into a lover."

These pages of the novel, where the sovereign appears in a quasi-religious atmosphere to accentuate the majesty of sovereignty, and where the governing power receives his mission at the hands of the moral being over which he is to preside, are closely allied to the corresponding ones of the *Contract*. They are the third, fourth, fifth and sixth chapters of the fourth part, and mainly the third and fourth.

The third chapter is entitled "Concerning Elections." Here the idea that kingship is a form of self-sacrifice, already implied in the third book, recurs in a passage on election by lot. In a true democracy, says Rousseau, the magistracy is not an advantage but a burdensome office that cannot justly be imposed upon anyone, the difficulty being to prevent the government from changing form. He adds that the law alone can impose that burden upon the man on whom the lot falls. The outcome is allegedly indifferent in such a society since absolute equality is in its very nature and in fact the lot falls upon everyone. But he concludes that the matter is purely academic since he has already said that such a government is too precarious to exist unless people were gods, in which case they would not need to be governed at all.

In an aristocracy such as we see in *Emile* the writer prefers election by choice therein typified: "The Prince," he

says "chooses the Prince." In the novel we have just beheld the prince in the union of Emile and his friend, deciding together upon Jean-Jacques as ruler, a choice favored
by reason. The author of the *Contract* adds what the Aemilian governor also illustrates, namely the Socratic and Christian idea that in an aristocracy too magistracy or kingship is
a ministry to others.

In the same context he artfully contrives a pretext for referring to the assemblies of the people where rulers are
elected, and thereby prepares us for his treatment of that
theme in the next chapter. But the assemblies here are very
different from the idealized ones to follow. They are exemplified by Venice, which he says, however, is not an aristocracy at all but a republic, a term suggestive not only of
the ideal city-state but also of his birthplace. Knowing full
well that Venice was no such thing in his definition or any
other, he proceeds to draw a parallel with Geneva. The
irony lurking in the preposterous analogy was lost upon the
world. We are right to question its validity,[98] but the tragedy is that it was valid enough to convey his caustic criticism of the Genevan assemblies and the election of magistrates therein. The impoverished Venetian nobles, says he,
excluded from the magistracy and possessing only the right
to attend meetings of the great council, which he compares
to the Genevan one, have no more privileges than his own
fellow countrymen. Since the real theme of the chapter is
elections, he clearly means to impugn the election of magistrates in the council of his native city and discredit the council's assemblies. Here we are very remote from the ideal relationships portrayed by Emile and his chosen "ruler."

The author of the *Contract* next turns his attention to
utopian assemblies of the sovereign people, where social
order is born and elections take place, as in the case of Emile
and Jean-Jacques. They are the theme of the first of four
chapters partly inspired by primitive Roman institutions.
Political theorists object to them, alleging that they have
only a remote connection with the principles of political law

and are the work of a historian instead of a moralist, or rather, philosopher. They suspect the author of padding at the cost of a digression for the purpose of inserting the chapter on civic faith, drawn up at the last minute. The same charge of padding has been laid against the second and third parts of the work, where it has proved unfounded.[99] In the present instance, quite apart from the fact that throughout the treatise he has consistently illustrated his ideas with historical examples and that the chapter on civic faith would probably have been inserted anyway in imitation of the Socratic model, a collation of texts shows that these chapters are as much an integral part of the book as the earlier ones that are also regarded as superfluous and yet define his laws. They are not a mere review of Roman institutions, and they bear a close affinity to the corresponding portions of *Emile*.

The first one is entitled "Concerning Roman Assemblies." Rousseau was obliged to introduce a chapter here on popular assemblies to show how the moral being he has been carefully constructing *ab ovo* might finally come to the birth and enjoy the grace of life as in *Emile*. As he said in four chapters of the previous part, the realization of his system hinges upon the exercise of sovereignty that occurs only when the sovereign manifests itself. It is inconceivable that in the final book there would be no tableau of the society of his fancy and no picture of a popular convocation that alone could transform the dream into reality.

But he knew well enough that modern readers would regard popular assemblies as chimerical. To show that they are not, he affects to give a historical illustration instead of a purely imaginary one, although he virtually confesses that it is indeed mythical.[100] If we failed to grasp the irony of the previous chapter directed against Geneva, we should expect him to cite the example of the general council there, especially since he professes to eternize that city in his book, at least as it existed in his heart. But a picture of the new Geneva would have been as disquieting here as it proved to be in the case of the dedication of the second *Discourse*.

Instead he chooses ancient Rome as an image of the ideal city and retires to the era of Aemilius to bring that city to life, for it does not belong to his century any more than the heroes of the novel do.

Before he broaches the subject, the author of the *Contract* inserts a note about the transition from the rule of force to the rule of law effected by such assemblies. It reads: "The name of Rome, said to derive from Romulus, is Greek and means 'force'; the name of Numa is also Greek and means 'law.' Is it likely that the first two kings of the city bore in advance names so well suited to what they did?"[101] Apart from providing new evidence of Rousseau's interest in the symbolism of names, the note relates to the whole purpose of *Emile* and the *Contract,* which was to show how the prevailing rule of force can be replaced by that of law through the exercise of sovereignty. The idea does not merely apply to the existing order of things where anarchic individualism would have to give way to humanism. Even in the presumably lawful order of his books, until the awakening of reason as a moral guide, the educator-legislator was obliged to resort to force, necessity, or Socratic lies or myths to win obedience on behalf of that ideal, but henceforth the moral being is to be consciously and voluntarily governed by law. The writer of the *Contract* suspects that the evolution that presides at the birth of his own city also presided at the birth of Rome, whose traditions exemplify for him the proper handling of the sovereign power in solemn assemblies of the people. Many elements of the chapter inspired by those assemblies, the high point of the book, are also present in the scene where Emile's reason is roused from sleep to enlighten the will.

The chapter is composed of two parts. In the first the author describes the character of the Roman people by recalling the various classifications into which they were divided: first the military tribal divisions of Romulus; then the many rustic tribes created by the legendary King Servius in the mid-sixth century B.C. He reflects that the rustic tribes far

[273]

outnumbered the urban ones and won honor by reason of the predilection of the early Romans for country life, a taste that they combined with their traditional dedication to the duties of war. He then ponders upon a further partitioning of the people by King Servius into centurial divisions graded according to wealth. In Rousseau's system these gradations might correspond to the Socratic men of gold, of silver, of brass, and of iron, answering to a natural hierarchy of human faculties,[102] especially since he shows how the simple manners of the early Romans were effective security against the seductions of riches. Such was the character of the nation that he significantly studies first since, in his view, it determines the nature of the laws to be enacted for its moral and spiritual life. The same rusticity and austerity of life characterize the freemen of the Rousseauist city including Aemilius, who is later reminded by his governor that he must always be ready to serve his country like the early Romans who passed from the ploughshare to the consulate. Of course, for he is their heir.

In the second part of the chapter the author imagines assemblies, corresponding to the various divisions, that met to sanction laws, elect magistrates, and make the nation truly sovereign. He dwells upon the careful choice of time and place for solemn convocations, as he did in the awakening scene in *Emile*. In spite of the imperfections of the centurial divisions, he expresses admiration for their assemblies and uses them to show how aristocratic and democratic elements, which after all exist in the human constitution, can be balanced in practice to achieve a close approximation of absolute justice. He concludes that they alone were endowed with all the majesty of the Roman nation since no one was excluded. On the other hand, he disapproves of the tribal assemblies, called "the real council of the Roman *populace*" (italics mine), since they were confined to the commons, or "motley multitude" in Socratic speech, and excluded the aristocracy. In spite of such abuses he is inspired by republican Rome to conceive of a sovereign nation that not only exercises sovereignty in its own person but also assumes some of the powers of government that it has a right and duty to control. The same ideas are present in the monumental scene of *Emile* where the hero participates personally in both sovereignty and government, the latter by his choice of an agent whose conduct he is bidden to supervise. Such is the controversial chapter of the *Contract* whose principles belong to the Socratic city in that book as well as to the mythical Aemilian one.

It is followed by others equally controversial. One is entitled "Concerning the Tribunate" and the other "Concerning the Dictatorship." Both deal with powers related to government, but lying outside the constitution. The reason for the presence of these chapters is that the powers in question are extraordinary ones necessary for education, which is the real problem of the *Contract* and only true law.

The Rousseauist tribunate is not to be confused with the early Roman one, whose function is, however, included in its own. It is designed to maintain the proper balance of faculties and prevent them from meddling with one another's work. For instance, it serves to protect the sovereign against the encroachments of government and the government against the resistance of subjects, preserving the famous "mean proportional" between them. But it possesses neither legislative nor executive rights. As defender of the laws, its action is largely negative, like that of the educator-legislator hitherto, but it is the strongest support of a good constitution. These are the author's professed convictions. Yet in choosing examples from historical institutions to clarify his intentions, he illustrates intolerable abuses, instead of the uses just enumerated as one might have expected. The implication is that though the powers of any constitution must be balanced and harmonized, it is perilous to rely upon alien agents to do the work. This shows that he is thinking mainly of inner life and education, where the authority of the Rousseauist tribunate is indispensable. In the novel we see its action in the explicit provision made for

[275]

Emile to supervise Jean-Jacques' government and for the governor to account for his commands, both of which tasks serve to maintain the balance of faculties threatened by the false opinions and evil passons of worldly society. The provision in question thereby ensures the safety of the constitution by training Emile to be detached enough from himself to scrutinize the inner workings of his own powers to that end.

The chapter on the dictatorship deals with the suspension of normal processes to save the city from disaster. The suspension is brought about by concentrating the governing power in fewer hands and thus intensifying it under the sway of the laws, or else by naming a supreme commander to suspend the laws and sovereign authority momentarily to meet the crisis. The writer shows how the institution was effective and without danger for the ancient Romans. But he also knows how hazardous it would be today. Again he betrays the fact that he is thinking of the law of education, which is suspended by this extraordinary device in the next part of *Emile* for the benefit of the human constitution.[103]

The following chapter of the *Contract,* "Concerning the Censorship," is the last of the chapters that are alleged to treat of Roman institutions but are really devoted to Rousseau's own system, with the usual historical illustrations. Its theme is that of the remainder of the fourth part of *Emile.*

His censorship proclaims the "law of public opinion" and applies it to individual cases, in the same way as the governing power makes particular applications of the law of the general will. The law of opinion, says he, defines moral and aesthetic tastes and affections by formulating what we find pleasing or beautiful as well as honorable. Such beliefs are an outgrowth of the spiritual or "political" constitution, and are fostered by education or legislation. Once they are fully formed, the censorship can preserve them by making wise applications of them, or it can fix them while they are still faltering. But according to Rousseau this institution, like public opinion itself, admits of no constraint, and cen-

[276]

sors cannot do what legislation or education has failed to do.

In both books the latter is presumed to have imparted the habit of order, true opinions, sane tastes, real pleasures, and lofty morals. Indeed, for Rousseau as for Socrates that is the main part of education or legislation, since both thinkers see men as products of the law of public opinion; and both regard lawful opinions, tastes, and pleasures as the source of all lawfulness. Consequently, the educator or legislator has sought from the first to provide for the cultivation of true opinion as opposed to false in the matter of what is pleasing. He was, we were told, "secretly" concerned with manners, customs, and opinion that are engraven on the heart to secure the habit of order and are therefore the "keystone of the vault" of fortress or temple. This was illustrated at the end of the second part of both books, which concluded exactly like this one does in each case. His work was even then seconded and safeguarded by a censorship of some kind as is the case in the *Republic*[104] and as I remarked in the third chapter above. With the formation of the city the institution emerges into the light to save that work. In the novel this task too as well as government is delegated to Jean-Jacques, but in the end both will be Sophia's—that of wisdom within Emile and perhaps also outside unless a combination of the two is impossible.

To revert to the context of the novel where the ideas of the chapter on censorship are finely illustrated, after the youth has pledged himself to the covenant, we are told that he is not made to live alone but to fulfill his duties as an active member of society. In other words, he is now to be prepared for the civil contract symbolized in marriage. He must therefore learn "the art most necessary to man and the *citizen*," (italics mine) which is that of living with other people.[105] Hence, he goes to reside for a year in the French capital.

Before exposing him to the ways of the world, Jean-Jacques in the censor's role takes precautions to fix his opinions of what is beautiful and honorable, Socratically bound together here as in the *Contract*. As I have said, these opinions, the fruits of his education, are assumed to be true since that education has bred in him an orderly constitution. The governor preserves them intact in the disciple's heart by molding them into the visible likeness of the future bride "who is suited to him," and proposes that they seek her out together. The verbal portrait he paints of her is designed to entrance Emile and secure him against danger. For the charms of the woman who is destined, through the efforts of his friend, to be his betrothed embody, we are told, all the qualities he must love and honor. Again, morals and aesthetics are linked.

Jean-Jacques' portrait of her is curiously enigmatic. She is "imaginary," for true love is all "fancy, falsehood, and illusion"; and we love only the image we create, clothed "in a veil of prestige." Yet she is not "a model of perfection that cannot exist," although he would not lie by saying that she really does. He calls her Sophia, meaning "wisdom," a name dear to the author in his life and work.[106] In fine, Emile "thinks that his destined bride is purposely concealed from him and that he will see her in good time." Meanwhile, her image prepares him for his entrance into worldly society by protecting his taste and morals from defilement. Or so we are informed.

Symbolism is suggested here by the mystery of the phraseology, which, however, in any case never excludes a literal reading. Since Sophia is able to safeguard Emile's ideas of what is pleasing and honorable, she must be Rousseauist wisdom, allegedly suited to the perfect man and belonging to the same ideal imaginary order that may conceivably exist, although in the case of both of them one may have to look here below for the nearest approach to the model. She crowns the whole purpose of the book, which was from the first to gratify nature's aspirations to what pleases, suits, delights, and perfects us, or rather, to find the wisdom that secures our happiness. At last Emile understands how the "happiness of the sage is suited to the nature of his being."[107] He becomes thereby a philosopher, or "lover of Sophia," and is impelled to go in search of her though the governor has long since found her. He must personally engage in the search, since by binding himself to the covenant that provides a basis for his love and promises to fulfill it, he has dedicated the mythical temple to her. Besides, his virtue must be autonomous. Small wonder if her portrait is perplexing.

Rousseau's personification of wisdom is reminiscent of many another in biblical and Socratic tradition. Take, for example, his favorite Old Testament books like Wisdom, and especially Proverbs, which closely parallels Ecclesiastes and contains the passage: "Get wisdom. . . . Forsake her not and she shall preserve thee: love her and she shall keep thee . . . she shall bring thee to honor when thou dost embrace her. . . . Say unto wisdom, thou art my sister, and call understanding thy kinswoman: that they may keep thee from the strange woman . . . which flattereth with her words." Finally wisdom herself speaks, promising "knowledge rather than choice gold . . . durable riches and righteousness."[108] This imagery is increasingly reflected in Rousseau's text. So is the Socratic and medieval personification of the Muse of Philosophy and companion of reason, the queen of the republic who appears in Plato's sixth book, for whom Socrates' rulers have renounced all other wealth and to whom the sage is finally wedded. Following such examples as those, Sophia is to preserve intact Emile's ideas of beauty, honor, and wisdom.

Jean-Jacques finally introduces the youth into society using the precautions he has taken in order to guard against the attacks of passion and error. His object is therefore the same as it was in the first "nave" of the temple chamber where he had recourse to Plutarch and the fables to achieve it. The themes are identical, but now temptations beset the inner man. In Socratic terms the governor henceforth relies upon "Sophia" to save Emile from sophists

[279]

and their allies, lawless desires.

As in the earlier treatment of passion and error, Rousseau still has in mind Socrates' warnings about the corruption of the philosophic nature in the sixth book of the *Republic,* but also alludes to the eighth and ninth where the sage describes the decline of the state. I might point out that in the central pages of this part he has shown more independence than usual in handling his material. This is true even though, as we have seen, the similitude of the sun and profession of faith are largely Socratic, as are the myth of the hunter, the covenant of friendship, and the personification of wisdom. He is perhaps slightly less original in dealing with the passions and sophisms that, according to Socrates, too, threaten the philosopher-king in our midst, but even here he draws heavily upon his own personal experience.

The problem of sophisms is handled first. The governor shows how an ideal love typifying the spirit of wisdom can preserve a man from false opinion and the proverbial "strange woman" who, under the pretext of teaching youths fine manners, dishonors them. The text is autobiographical as well as scriptural in inspiration. One of the victims of such women was the model of the Savoyard vicar's protégé in life who was also the protégé of another Savoyarde, the Baroness de Warens. The young Rousseau's love for her was allegedly a shield of virtue in his life until she decided "to make a man of him."[109] Her contribution to his "education" was supplemented after 1742 by that of Parisian society, which also furnishes the writer of *Emile* with another example of the dangers against which the hero is protected. He describes a young man well raised in the provinces but transformed within six months in Paris by the distorted opinion of a disordered society that vitiates him and gives him "a second education the very reverse of the first." This is the education of the public who, in Rousseau's Socratic terminology, fashion him according to their taste, discrediting his parents and teachers as dispensers of pedantic jargon and childish morality, until he finally succumbs to their insidious sophistry.

In undertaking to save his disciple from that fate, Jean-Jacques takes up Socrates' challenge in the sixth book of the *Republic*, to which I have alluded. The sage avers that under alien conditions the finest natures become preeminently bad, "whereas weak natures are scarcely capable of any very great good or very great evil either." Of course, Emile has not been reared in a completely alien soil, and is to live in such a place only briefly. But for the Socratic thinker even transplantation for a year is not without danger in a city like Paris, where the public, "the greatest of all sophists," are always ready to educate him anew. The Greek sage is convinced that no private training can enable a young man "to stand firm against the overwhelming flood of popular opinion." Every type of character, says he, is formed by it. He adds that, in our present evil plight, whatever is saved is saved "by some divine power," which for Rousseau would be the reasonable will heard in the "celestial voice." But according to Socrates, few are ever redeemed. For most men, says he, wisdom consists of popular notions of good and evil, justice and injustice. It is quite simply the discernment of the tastes and tempers of the multitude, who do everything possible to prevent a well-endowed youth from "yielding to his better nature" and do even more "to render his teacher [reason] powerless by private intrigues and public prosecutions." Consequently "philosophy is left desolate with her marriage rite incomplete...."[110] Such is Socrates' challenge to mankind, and Rousseau's is not very different.

Nevertheless, in *Emile* Jean-Jacques accepts it. As the youth goes abroad with his governor in the French capital, he is allegorically armed from head to foot. The word *armed* is used in the text, reminding us of the medieval knights-errant that he emulates, "girt about with truth and wearing the breastplate of righteousness." He is also shielded by the aegis of Minerva in the persons of Jean-

[281]

Jacques and Sophia. Moreover, he has two other "guardians" as well called "shame and fear," the very ones that watch over Socrates' citizens in the fifth book of the *Republic*.[111] And so he is allegedly invulnerable to public opinion that is false and foreign to his nature. The future Ulysses is insensitive to the siren voices of the children of foolishness. According to the text, their call is muffled by the voice of a "faithful and true friend" whose attachment of twenty years' standing has already been revealed to him as the "sublime" and saving power of reason in the service of the human will.

That voice which is conscience makes an impassioned appeal to rescue him from provocative young sophists, foreshadowed by the flatterers and seducers of the earlier lessons of experience and fables in action who were reflected in the *Contract*. But here the tempters represent false opinion assailing the temple of the soul from within as well as without. They do the same in the sixth book of the *Republic*, in the passages on the corruption of the philosophic nature mentioned above, and again in the eighth. In the latter fierce natures beset the youth, oppose parental influence, and besiege "the citadel of the soul," driving away its best guardians, here identified as modesty, temperance, and moderation, and replacing them by a "rabble of evil appetites" such as insolence, anarchy, waste, and impudence that masquerade as "breeding," "liberty," "magnificence," and "courage."[112] Emile finds himself in a similar plight. His governor pleads against such sophisms in the name of the hero's true interest that is his own and is alien to that of self-indulgent youths who seek only to control him, and have renounced the so-called prejudices of their fathers based upon love and experience to adopt those of other people. Thus Jean-Jacques carries on his task as the spokesman of reason and true opinion, of Emile's father the law, which begot him, appealing for discipline in the name of paternal affection seen as the truest image of friendship.

[282]

In Emile's response the haunting Socratic phrase from which the whole book sprang recurs like the fundamental theme of a great symphony: "He recognizes the voice of friendship, and knows how to obey reason."[113] In doing so he obeys Jean-Jacques, who has the mastery of his will through the friendship of reason, and who governs him continually. So the text implies. Even when he leaves the youth among "strangers," he hints that he is mystically present within him. Emile, by heeding his governor, heeds his own conscience. In both plea and response, artistic and literary methods empower the author to make the inner workings of the human spirit both visible and audible to the reader.

Next the governor faces the problem of passion also beleaguering the inner world, instead of appearing only externally as in the pages on Plutarch and the related ones in the *Contract*. The presence of the inner foe is indicated by fresh precautions against the instinct of sense, "which cannot be trusted in the midst of social institutions." Guided by sad personal experience, Rousseau warns against the so-called dangerous supplement.[114] If Emile is to be delivered up to a "tyrant," that tyrant will be women's wiles rather than himself. The image is well chosen to portray what Socrates calls the tyrannical soul in whom the best elements are enslaved to the beast within. The same image also conveys the idea that lawlessness does not necessarily have anything to do directly with other people. Here, for instance, it does not appear as a form of rebellion against external authority. That was the main concern in the first "nave" of the great chamber of the spirit, where the youth witnessed outward impropriety in ancient biographies without having any personal knowledge of inner disorder. Here lawlessness appears as a violation of the proper inward disposition of all faculties, a disposition that requires unlawful appetites to be allayed and better desires and rational or spiritual powers to prevail in a harmonious ordering of the entire person. In fine, as in the vicar's creed lawlessness is represented by sexual aberration, whereas

[283]

love of law, purity of will and self-mastery are symbolized by chastity and continence. Rousseau implies as much by saying that until twenty continence is in the order of nature, and after that it is a moral duty indispensable for one who would "rule over himself" and be "master of his appetites."

The precepts followed by the governor to combat error and evil within are the same as those employed hitherto in the external world. In both cases there are two. First, if the youth goes astray, his mentor remains at his side to guide him in his errors. The writer cites the historical case of a diplomat who became inebriated in the service of a prince. The example stands in counterpoise to that of the Roman captain in the first "nave" who, like the Socratic "leaders," led his army even in retreat. The second rule was also formulated there. The governor refrains from affected blindness or false dignity and feigned perfection that foster abuses and lead to "the overthrow of all order and contempt for every law."[115] The law here is not merely that which governs external behavior in society but the one whereby the disciple's inner life is kept in order by Jean-Jacques. This interpretation, imposed by the context, is confirmed by an appeal to every governor to provide a model of one who must withstand his lower nature in order to remain "master of himself." The appeal accentuates the difference between the two "naves," for in the former he refrained from showing his weakness to the youth. The object here is professedly to save the latter from the fate of modern men whose shriveled souls and corrupt bodies allegedly make them incapable of any very great good or evil either, words echoing the Socratic ones quoted above. Emile is to be a good and temperate man who, if he chose, might like the child of the second part "become master of all with far less trouble than it cost him to become master of himself."

At this point the author sketches the hero's portrait as he did at the end of the second part, except that now the setting is worldly society. The one prefigures the other, as it

[284]

should. The emphasis is still on moral and spiritual qualities. Although at the age of twenty Emile is as ignorant of the formalities of politeness as he was at ten, his attitude toward others has deepened. He feels a common bond of sympathy and affection for them, which is the mainspring of his conduct in their regard. Yet the rule of his conversation has not essentially altered. The youth of twenty confines his words to what is "useful," much as the child of ten uttered only the simple truth as far as he knew it. Emile does not cultivate eloquence until after he has entered society, when grace of speech results from a new desire to please that is the secret of his cordial ways. His bearing is "that of a citizen"; and his politeness, being a spontaneous manifestation of human feeling, likewise proclaims "the citizen." Obviously this must be so since, as we were told, he is learning the art necessary to "man and the citizen." In a word, he appears as an inhabitant of the city of the *Contract*. When the author adds, "All this demands... no great stock of precepts from me; it is all the result of his early education,' he reminds us again of Socrates, whose laws are as few as his own. In Plato's fourth book the Greek sage too declined to legislate about such matters as the respect owed to elders, the honor due to parents, modes of dress, deportment, and manners in general, since "the direction in which education starts a man will determine his future life." His very words are matched in the present context of *Emile*.[116] Since the Aemilian city is hardly different from the ancient Greek one, it is not surprising to learn that the hero appears among men as an "agreeable foreigner." His spiritual growth is shown in the qualities of his mind, whose former embryonic moral ideas have expanded to include all that is useful for his own happiness and that of others. It is also shown in the pleasure he finds in the company of those who possess his own taste in moral matters. Thus the association of taste with morals recurs as it did in the portrait of Sophia and the chapter on censorship, as well as in the second part of both books.

The last pages of this part of *Emile* are devoted to the further cultivation of good taste or true opinion that is to save the constitution according to the texts just enumerated, wherein beauty is conceived to operate as a moral ' influence. If I refer again to the said pages, already referred to in my first and third chapters,[117] it is to accentuate further the linking of aesthetics and spirituality. For example, although Rousseau now defines taste as the power of judging what is pleasing to most men in matters indifferent or amusing, we know that he means materially but not Socratically indifferent since pleasures determine the fate of his city. Moreover, according to him "what is pleasing" is ascertained by "the majority of votes" if, as in an ideal order of things, each man expresses his real sentiment, which means that the canons of taste are formulated in the same way as the laws that govern the ordering of city or soul and that the same rule produces both virtue and the beauty of harmony. The affinity of taste and morals is everywhere implicit, even when he tries to distinguish between taste in moral and physical matters, for he observes that there is always a moral element present in everything involving imitation such as the plastic arts. Take for instance, traditional art, whose model is his own and which offers an idealization of nature such as we see in *Emile* or ancient Greek sculpture.[118] For him the natural model constitutes a universal moral and aesthetic pattern. But he also says that taste is modified by local circumstances, as he said of laws as well. He adds that perfection of taste is the fruit of frequenting numerous societies of amusement on condition that they possess a fair degree of equality to moderate the influence of false opinion, a condition also required by his system of legislation and government. He goes further. Since good taste is in his eyes realizable in the company of the sexes wherever lofty moral standards intensify the desire to please, he concludes that good taste is related to good morals. He links the two again by observing that we must know how to please others if we would do them service. In fine, in the present context he illustrates the idea of the *Contract* that aesthetic taste is connected with moral taste and motivates the conduct of human life, and that both are the main responsibility of education and legislation. Consequently Jean-Jacques, who professes to teach nothing but the duties of man, gives lessons in aesthetics. This makes the perfecting of taste a very serious business.

Rousseau's ideas on the subject are expressed in Emile's aesthetic training, which began with his education but which he now consciously pursues. The governor familiarizes him with models of taste in nature by training his judgment in Parisian society until he acquires a discriminating insight into the complexities of the heart. His knowledge and love of nature are further deepened by a study of ancient writings like Plato's *Symposium* and Virgil's *Aeneid*. Unlike the Socratic philosophers and contrary to Rousseau's own teaching in the *Letter to d'Alembert*, Emile also frequents the theater and delights in all manner of beauty designed to please the heart and stir the feelings. For he is to be a sensitive man as well as a sage. Imaginative sympathy, Christian in its origin, lends a lyrical tinge to Rousseau's basically "classical" tastes as it does to his moral convictions.

The avowed purpose of the hero's aesthetic formation is to fix his affections and tastes and prevent the decline of natural inclinations so that he will seek his happiness not in wealth but in the good things of life that lie close by. This means that his felicity will depend largely upon his own personal resources. Rousseau suggests the extent of the hero's inner wealth by sketching a great tableau of happiness and the good life that contrasts with the earlier spectacle of human suffering but matches the fair sights and sounds at the end of the second part. However, this tableau is supplied from the writer's own experience, including biblical and Socratic readings, on the pretext that Emile's pure heart "can no longer serve as an example for anyone."

He calls the admittedly autobiographical conclusion an "essay." He imagines therein how he would enjoy all the truest pleasures of life if he were rich, although he has just said that happiness is not to be sought in wealth. Thus he appears to take up the challenge of his divine master, who, without excluding the rich from the heavenly paradise, teaches that "it is easier for a camel to go through the eye of a needle than for a rich man to enter into the kingdom of God." The self-styled Gospel commentator is perhaps emboldened by the master's subsequent reassurance that "with God all things are possible," as well as by Socrates' conviction that in an alien state "whatever is saved, is saved by the power of God,"[119] which for Rousseau is expressed in conscience. However that may be, the rich man in the essay wins happiness, but the delights he enjoys have nothing to do with vanity and false opinion. They allegedly spring from realities.

In actual fact, although the writer is too much of an artist to say so bluntly, he indicates clearly enough that the wealth he possesses in the essay, far from being a threat to happiness, is paradoxically its source. It is the only kind he considers worthy of a disciple of Christ, or of Socrates and the Greek heroes, who were wedded to poverty as is he. In the language of his favorite "discourse," his coffers, like theirs and Emile's, are not laid up on earth but contain only the "gold" of spiritual and aesthetic experience that suffices to make felicity possible for a nature like his. That wealth is his concept of wisdom as it has been presented in both books.

Accordingly, the concluding tableau of wisdom and happiness synthesizes Rousseauist social and civil order beheld in the ideal city or moral being, and anticipates the enchanted world of the fifth part of *Emile* and of certain passages of the *Confessions* and *Dialogues*. That order is conceived as already existing within him, since he begets it in his work. The dream becomes reality. This interpretation is suggested at once by the tone of the essay, which is that of the dedication of the second *Discourse* addressed to the new Geneva existing in his heart. There the motif "if I had had to choose my birthplace" serves as a pretext for sketching his "own city," much as the motif "if I were rich" serves as a pretext for depicting his own inner riches,[120] which are those of that mythical realm.

The essay is divided into two parts. The first contains a panorama of Rousseauist moral and social order. With Socratic sobriety and restraint the essayist depicts his idea of the outward fabric of a well-disposed life seen in the context of actuality and exemplifies the main principles governing the relationships of a spiritual being with the world as we know it. He follows the same sequence as Socrates does in the construction of his city, just as he did throughout the book. He begins by saying that if he were rich, he would first purchase freedom and then acquire health by the practice of temperance, since he still regards these two assets as the basic ingredients of happiness. In his appetites and tastes as well as in the adornment of his dwelling, he would take nature as his guide. Observe how he hardly distinguishes between physical and aesthetic taste. In all things he would favor simplicity of life. Like the Socratic kings who lived like servants in their own houses, he would have no footman stand between the world and himself. Nor would he dwell in a palace any more than they, for like any other traveler in life he needs, so he says, no more than a chamber at an inn. Besides, the world "is a palace fair enough for anyone." In that habitation and untrammeled by the furniture of other men's dwellings, he is as free as his thought. *Ubi bene, ibi patria* is his device, and for him both goods and city lie within the spirit that permits him to enjoy the true pleasures of mind and of heart. To prove that he is a lover of these rather than of wealth or power, he makes a sudden sally against gaming that, according to him, turns thought toward arid combinations. In other words, he would not resemble the lover of gain in the *Republic* who

[289]

compels reason to think only of how lesser sums may be turned into larger ones, and who forces the human spirit to be ambitious of nothing else but the amassing of gold.[121] Indeed, Socrates can hardly be far from his mind since he depicts himself like a Socratic prince, professing to regulate bodily habit, property, and clothing in such a way as to remain, as he says, "master of his conduct" in all states and conditions of life and especially among the common people. In that case he does not covet power over others any more than wealth. This idea leads him to broach the theme of friendship and subsequently that of love, to which he accords the same symbolic values as he has done hitherto. His friends would be bound together not by dependence upon him but by mutual attachment and conformity of taste and character, in a relationship based upon freedom and equality. The main elements of the Aemilian city of the *Contract* and the Socratic one too are present in this first part of the essay.

The stark realism of the above tableau heightens the quasi-mystical "ravishing contemplations" that follow to provide a literary antithesis and foreshadow the dénouement. Significantly enough, they are introduced by a long discourse on love. Thereupon we are admitted to the "inner sanctum" of the mind, corresponding to the ideal civil order or private society that would presumably materialize if the general principles of the *Social Contract* were applied in the sphere of an exclusive alliance. The writer appears in an idyllic setting evoked in the most enchanting language. "On the slopes of some pleasant shady hill-side," he writes, "I should have a little country cottage, a white house with green shutters." There he would gather round him a chosen company of friends who know what pleasure is and how to enjoy it. Each meal would be a banquet of the simplest things served in careless array on the grass: "We should be our own servants, in order to be our own masters; each would be served by all." These inhabitants of the city of the blessed who live together in freedom and equality share the fruits of the earth with one another and their neighbors and do no harm to any man. Although the writer imagines himself living like a "prince" on his little farm *(métairie)* with its white dwelling-place, yet he would not indulge in the pleasures of other princes who hunt upon their estates and destroy the work of defenseless peasants. In the society of his dream he would enjoy only pleasures accessible to all men.

Paradoxically he admits that, however mythical that society may seem, it is a reality for him and that he has simply portrayed therein the life he lives in poverty. That being the case, the essay swarms with symbols beginning with his imaginary "riches" as we foresaw. His wealth consists in his capacity to inherit the earth like the meek and take spiritual possession of it. That is how he possesses the white house with green shutters, the spectacle of which is set within the city of Paris and contains many allusions to it.[122] Since he has just refused to occupy more than a chamber at an inn, one can only surmise that the mysterious abode with its nebulous inhabitants is a state of soul or philosophic mood and the visions that this mood induces. It is the house of the writer's thoughts and emotions, which he "sets in order" in the Socratic manner by bringing it into harmony with itself and the world round about. There he retires into what the Stoic philosopher calls "the little farm of his own mind," and ministers to the genius within him, taking advantage of its "princely" power over circumstance to foster fancies that express his idea of beauty, wisdom and happiness.

The high point of the ecstatic meditation is the banquet scene. The very theme is enough to bring to mind Plato's *Symposium,* whose repercussions in Rousseau's novel reach a crescendo in the next part prefigured here. Meanwhile we may observe that the host in that dialogue complains in a phrase echoed in the present text that on feast days his servants become his masters. But the same theme is also Judeo-Christian, as we shall see hereafter. The

[291]

Christian elements transform the idyll into something re-sembling an evangelical parable. Not only the meal on the grass but also the charity extended to others outside the fold have Christian overtones. As Rousseauist wisdom is both Christian and Socratic, so is the dream of happiness with which it culminates in the realm of the inner man.

In this part of the essay Socratic elements are not con-fined to reminiscences of the *Symposium*. If, as the Greek master says in the *Republic,* every genuine philosophy pro-vides men with a better life than the one we know, the life of "beatific vision"; if, as he says, philosophy really "con-cludes in an ecstasy" that affords full fruition to all human faculties, then the essay in *Emile* foreshadows the fulfill-ment of Rousseauist wisdom in consummate happiness in the next part. That happiness is presumably born of a So-cratic "knowledge of beauty and goodness" in the absolute sense, implying the sanctification of law and spiritual har-mony transfigured by Christian influences. It crowns the author's philosophy in the same way that the blessed vision anticipated in Plato's sixth book and realized at the end of the seventh crowns Socratic education. And just as the latter inspired Emile's earlier formation set amid images of grace and harmony as counterparts of goodness and vir-tue,[123] so it inspires his future progress that leads him be-yond the "things of beauty" where he played in childhood to the ecstatic contemplation promised here. But for him those "things of beauty" will always be caught up into the larger vision whose object they reflect.

Rousseau concludes by affirming that the happiness just described is accessible to anyone in actual society pos-sessed of freedom in the sense of self-mastery, health, and the necessities of life. Such a man, he adds, is rich in the gold of Horace's "aurea medocritas." He is rich because he finds within himself and round about him in the present moment some traces of the lost golden age of beauty that Emile recovers at the end of the book.[124] Rousseau's thought has in fact led him to a vision of this perpetual "age of gold"

[292]

enshrined in the poetic essay. But the degree to which any man can attain to the same felicity depends upon poetic genius as well as the cultivation of powers of insight and volition necessary to transmute the dross of existence into gold and metamorphose ordinary human experience into an earthly paradise. Of course, the cultivation of such powers is the very object of the two books herein collated.

The finest passages of the essay are reflected in many of Rousseau's works but nowhere better than in four letters written by him at Montmorency village to Malesherbes in January 1762 while the novel and its appendix were being printed.

In the letters he tells his correspondent of his search for happiness that led to the discovery of wisdom too. That search impelled him to abandon the French capital for the countryside, where he could indulge his love of solitude, freedom, and ideal companionship. He traces these inclinations to his earliest years when the disorders of actuality, including those of his own life, led him to escape to an imaginary world of his own creation. The same inclinations were further nurtured, he says, by a vision of spiritual "truth" vouchsafed to him in 1749 on the road to Vincennes when he beheld in a single revelation both the present evil plight of governments and the essential goodness of human nature. That experience, he explains, moved him to compose his major works and change his life. Seeing the root of all evil as false opinion about the "just and unjust," the "honorable and dishonorable," he fled its yoke and found in the solitude of Montmorency new wisdom and happiness for himself, without doing harm to others.

His solitary blessedness is that of the essayist in *Emile*. Asked by his correspondent what he enjoys, he replies "myself, the whole universe, everything beautiful in the visible world and everything imaginable in the intellectual world."[125] He delights in wild places where he can, so he says, be master of himself and where none can come between nature and him. He rejoices in the company of chim-

[293]

erical beings and creates for himself "a golden age" of his fancy not in the past or in the future but in the present. With a void still left in his soul, he strives to fill it by rising to enraptured contemplation of the universe and the "incomprehensible being who embraces all," until at last he reaches a state of ecstasy comparable to that of the "celestial intelligences." But he denies that his love for the good life is incompatible with the love of humanity. He professes to practice the "duties of man" toward his neighbors and to preach them in his writings for the happiness of mankind and his compatriots. In such terms he depicts his own personal discovery of wisdom and happiness, which is the real inspiration of *Emile* and the *Contract*.

And yet, according to the author, the felicity described in the essay of the novel is not Emile's nor is it comparable to his. The essayist, who poses as such in the whole book and not merely at the end of the fourth part, began by forbearing to define the ultimate ideal. Likewise at the same point in the *Republic* and in the similitude of the sun, Socrates pleads that "to reach what is now in my thought would be an effort too great for me." In Rousseau's case we may, however, consider the essay as a kind of prophetic dream of Emile's mythical happiness in the fifth part. It anticipates the imaginary civil order in the novel even if, as the author would have us believe, it provides only a shadowy image of the ecstasy that Sophia promises to those who live as closely with her as Emile does in the end.

Needless to say, the beatific vision has no place in the hypothetical exteriorized version of the city in the *Contract*, which is, however, patterned after its object as is the whole of *Emile*. We have seen that the entire fourth part of both books is essentially and substantially identical and that both echo faithfully the fifth and sixth books of the *Republic*. This is true throughout, beginning with the pages on sophisms and passions and the kind of "warfare" that must be waged against them until the "light of truth" dawns and the ideal moral being is born. It is also true of the measures prescribed to balance, control, and preserve the powers of that being and save the human constitution, whose nature always remains the criterion of Rousseauist and Socratic moral and social order.

1. I have chosen the chapter title to suggest the main body of the structure in both books. I am emboldened to use it by the thought of Romanesque churches, which were in fact medieval strongholds. It has the added advantage of combining the Socratic image of the "citadel of the Soul" and the Christian image of the spiritual temple.

2. For reflections on birth, the brevity of life, and the passions, see "Emile," pp. 301, 306-8, and cf. 489 and 495. The question of happiness is also raised in each part: pp. 313-16, 512-17. So is the matter of delay: pp. 323, 518-19. In both parts there is an alien society round about: pp 329 ff., 517 ff.

3. For the image see ibid., p. 388; cf. chap. 2, n. 10, above.

4. Cf. The Republic 5. 450. Burgelin sees that for Rousseau positive education begins here: O.C., 4:490 n. 3. For the allusion below to the "know thyself" of the Delphic shrine, see the first paragraph of the fourth promenade of Les Rêveries du promeneur solitaire, where Rousseau refers to "le connois-toi-même du Temple de Delphes": O. C., 1:1024.

5. "Emile," pp. 511-12. Cf. chap. 3 above, n. 40. Cf. Fénelon, Les Aventures de Télémaque (Liège: Grandmont-Donders, 1865), books 16, 17, 18, 21, 23 (especially pp. 410-11). In Fénelon's thought the example of Plato is tempered by that of Christ, and the tutor Mentor-Minerva links justice and pity, reflecting that "Sans cette compassion on n'a ni bonté, ni vertu, ni capacité pour gouverner les hommes." Such compassion is extended to all men without exception.

6. The treatment of the theme in both parts concludes with similar phrases about method: "Emile," pp. 315, 316, and cf. p. 517. For the misery caused by indulgence cf. pp. 313-315, 512-15. Starobinski remarks upon this in "J.-J. Rousseau et les pouvoirs de l'imaginaire," Revue internationale de philosophie, no 51 (1960), p. 9.

7. See note 2 above and chapter 3, note 30.

8. He does so since he is persuaded that the age of innocence can be prolonged.

9. See The Republic 5. 461, where Socrates speaks of a scheme whereby his guardians have their wives and families "in common," meaning that the latter are subject to universal human faculties rather than the lawless wild beast nature.

10. Ibid. 5. 462.

11. They are defended in the "Contrat social": see "Emile," p. 837. To see that the friendship of Jean-Jacques and Emile does not represent an exclusive affection between individuals, see ibid., pp. 547-48. The symbolism of friendship and love has escaped our notice in the past.

12. The leitmotiv occurred in the previous chapter: see note 20. See also the covenant of friendship in chapter 2 above and note 35.

13. For the attitude of Socrates'heroes toward "enemies," see The Republic 2. 375-76; 5. 468-71. With the latter passage cf. 7. 537.

14. For the moral function of history in the eighteenth century, see G. May, *Le Dilemme du roman au XVIIIe siècle* (New Haven, Conn.: Yale University Press, 1963), p. 146.

15. *The Republic* 10. 606. Cf. 3. 398 cited in Latin in the "Lettre à d'Alembert," *O. C.*, Hachette, 1:259 n. 1 For Rousseau's images of the stage in this part, see "Emile," pp. 515, 525, 526, 527, 530, 532, 551. The work "De l'imitation théâtrale," which is also reminiscent of Plato's *Laws,* was undertaken in connection with the "Lettre à d'Alembert" and was completed shortly afterward, though it was published only in 1764.

16. For these two expressions see "Emile," pp. 352 (men are changed into "bêtes féroces") and 535 ("vous êtes des fous"); cf. *The Republic* 6. 496 (regarding "the madness of the multitude" and "wild beasts").

17. Here the governor behaves exactly like Mentor in *Télémaque,* where the language is very similar, especially in book 1, pp. 14-15: "Le sage Mentor m'aima jusqu'à me suivre dans un voyage téméraire que j'entreprenais contre ses conseils. ... Une noire tempête déroba le ciel à nos yeux.... Mentor parut, dans ce danger, non seulement ferme et intrépide, mais plus gai qu'à l'ordinaire: c'était lui qui m'encourageait." Burgelin implies that the governor symbolizes reason in the text of "Emile" to which I refer in this note: *O. C.*, 4:539 n. 1. Cf. chap 2 above, n. 28.

18. *The Republic* 2. 382.

19. Cf. ibid., 10. 590-92.

20. Ibid. 5. 463. For Rousseau's "constant will," applied both to the general will and to conscience, see "Contrat social," chapters 1 and 2; and "Emile," pp. 583-84, 594 ff., 652. Their identity is commonly recognized.

21. *O. C.*, 3:830. If some readers still protest that he does not give "the people" sufficient chance to debate proposals but only to ratify those of "leaders" who have "discovered" what the general will is, the misunderstanding would be due to his use of Socratic symbolism. For him the "people" or "subjects" represent desires to be disciplined by the rule of the enlightened human spirit, which leads man to "moral truth."

22. *The Republic* 6. 505-6; 9. 577.

23. Cf. "Considérations," *O. C.*, 3:996-97.

24. E.g., J.-J. Rousseau, *Du Contrat social,* ed. M. Halbwachs (Paris: Aubier, 1962), p. 355 n. Cf. Broome, op. cit., pp. 66, 68. C. Eisenmann sees in Rousseau's recourse to majority vote the collapse of the whole system: "La Cité de J.-J. Rousseau," in *Etudes sur le Contrat social de J.-J. Rousseau* (Paris: Les Belles Lettres, 1964), pp. 197-98.

25. "Emile," p. 849 ("rois et sages").

26. Cf. the present text of "Emile" and *The Republic* 6. 484-95 (definition of the philosphic nature and the dangers it faces); 503 (aspirant tested in labors and dangers); 7. 517 (fights in courts of law); 519 (partakes of labors and honors); 537 (trained in labors, lessons, dangers).

27. Cf. "Emile," pp. 543-44, and *The Republic* 6. 497 (the "living authority"); 499-500 (the philosopher is "gentle" and "soothing" and "loves" mankind).

28. For Emile the paladin: pp. 544, 743, 770. For his duties and love of peace: pp. 544-46, and cf. *The Republic* 6. 500. Rousseau's note on pp. 544-45 alludes to *The Republic* 5. 464-65. Burgelin discusses it without reference to Plato: *O. C.*, 4:544 n. 2. But later he compares Emile to a Platonic philosopher: ibid., p. 548 n. 2.

[296]

29. *The Republic* 6. 500.

30. See, for example, *C. C.*, 5:181 and 6:78: letters to mme de Créqui and T. Tronchin, 13 October 1758 and 28 April 1759.

31. "Emile," pp. 548-49; "Lettres de la montagne," loc. cit., p. 810. For the reader's incredulity: "Emile," p. 548, and cf. *The Republic* 6. 498, 500.

32. For natural man in the civil order see chapter 4 above, note 40.

33. For the "conventional imitation" cf. "Emile," p. 549, and *The Republic* 6. 501-2. Cf. p. 498. For the perfect model of the Socratic artist cf. "Emile," pp. 549-50, and *The Republic* 6. 501-2. Cf. Rousseau's concept of the ascent of the soul to the idea of good and *The Republic* 6. 503-5.

34. "Emile," pp. 554, 722-28. For the catechism cf. "Julie," *O. C.*, 2:582-83.

35. P. D. Jimack sees the usefulness of religion rather as a result than an object: *La Genèse et la rédaction de l'Emile de J.-J. Rousseau* (Geneva: Institut et musée Voltaire, 1960), pp. 161-62. In either case Rousseau cannot imagine virtue without faith.

36. *The Republic* 6. 498. Cf. 7. 540. For popular faith: ibid., books 2, 3, 4. Cf. book 10. For the distinction between "leaders" and "followers": ibid. 5. 474; for religion as "a popular exposition of the virtues": ibid. 6. 504.

37. Rousseau, of course, often admits that the creed is his own: see, for example, *C. C.*, 9:342, letter to Moultou, 23 December 1761; cf. "Lettre à C. de Beaumont," *O.C.*, 4:960; "Lettres de la Montagne," 1-3; "Lettre à M. de Franquières (25 March 1769). *O.C.*, 4:1134 ff.; cf. "Rêveries," *O.C.*, 1:1015-18.

38. "Confessions," *O.C.*, Pléiade, 1:46 ff., 90-92, 117-19.

39. *Rousseau's Venetian Story: An Essay upon Art and Truth in Les Confessions* (Baltimore: Johns Hopkins University Press, 1966).

40. Cf. Exod. 19:6: "Any ye shall be unto me a kingdom of priests and an holy nation." Cf. also Rev. 1:1 regarding Christ who "hath made us kings and priests unto God."

41. "Emile," p. 630, and cf. p. 607. He professes to sacrifice a few branches of the tree of faith to preserve the trunk: *C. C.*, 8:236, letter to Malesherbes, about 10 March 1761; cf. ibid., p. 338, letter to Moultou, 29 May 1761; 10:113, letter to Néaulme, about 22 February 1762; "Lettres de la montagne," loc. cit., p. 802.

42. *C. C.*, 16:75, letter from Usteri, 16 April 1763. For the "Lettres de la montagne," see loc. cit., pp. 719-20.

43. For Rousseau's revision briefly stated: *O. C.*, 4:lxviii, lxxix lxxx, cxxxviii.

44. Burgelin sees that the sun is symbolic but does not connect it with the Socratic similitude: ibid., p. 565 n. 1, and cf. p. 430 n. 1.

45. Rousseau believed that he had a mission as the only eloquent defender of God at the time, and sought to make religion attractive and speak of death with more hope than all the moralists: *C. C.*, 15:305-6, letter from mme de Chenonceaux, 20 March 1763. For his judgment of the creed: "Lettre à C. de Beaumont," loc. cit., p. 960. Cf. *C. C.*, 11:24-25, 36, 39, 44, letters to Nèaulme, Moultou, mme de Créqui, and m de la Pouplinière, 5, 7, 8 June 1762.

46. *The Republic* 6. 493. For man's rank among the creatures see "Emile," pp. 582-83; cf. pp. 587, 601. In assuming the person of Orpheus, Rousseau has recourse to the Lydian or sorrowful mode banned by Socrates and akin to Christian pathos: see "Dictionnaire de musique," *O. C.*, Hachette, 7:152. For the introduction of Orpheus see J.-J. Rousseau, *La Profession de foi du vicaire savoyard*, ed. P.-M. Masson (Paris: Hachette, 1914), p. 299. Cf. "Confessions," loc. cit., p. 207, and "Dialogues," ibid., p. 681.

47. "Lettres de la Montagne," loc. cit., pp. 751-52. Cf. "Confessions," loc. cit., pp. 236, 642, and "Lettres à m. de Malesherbes," *O. C.*, 1:1141. For an example see "Emile," p. 594.

48. See, for example, "Confessions," loc. cit., pp. 277, 492; and "Dialogues," ibid., p. 727.

49. For Rousseau's civic faith see *Lettre à Voltaire* (18 August 1756); *Julie; Lettre à C. de Beaumont;* and *Lettres de la montagne.* Some scholars fear it breeds intolerance, which it is intended to avert: e.g., R. Derathé, "La religion civile selon Rousseau," *Annales de la Société J.-J. Rousseau* 35 (1959-62): 161-80. Cf. Ronald I. Boss, "Rousseau's Civil Religion and the Meaning of Belief: An Answer to Bayle's Paradox," *Studies on Voltaire and the Eighteenth Century* 84 (1971): 150-53, 157, 173-74, 179-81, 187. To Rousseau's Socratic way of thinking his intolerance is directed against "disorder in the soul."

50. *The Republic* 10. 607.

51. Ibid., 6. 488-89. Burgelin also identifies the inexperienced pilot as reason, but traces the image to Locke and Condillac without recalling the Platonic myth, where the language is much closer to Rousseau's: *O.C.*, 4:567 n. 1.

52. Ecclus. 3:22-26; "Seek not to know what is far above thee... beyond thy range... dwell upon duty.... content to be ignorant of all God's dealings besides.... Leave off thy much questioning about things as little concern thee, and be content with thy ignorance.... By such fancies, many have been led astray and their thoughts chained to folly."

53. Starobinski finds nothing new in the creed: *J.-J. Rousseau: la transparence et l'obstacle* (Paris: Plon, 1957), p. 180.

54. See chapter 4 above. Cf. *The Republic* 7. 522-27, 531, 536; 10. 602.

55. "Emile," p. 593. Cf. "Lettre à C. de Beaumont," loc. cit., p. 976, where he uses the word *creator.* He discusses the difficulties of the idea on pp. 956-57 in the same work. At the end of *The Republic* Socrates teaches that God or the idea of good is the great artist, maker, or creator "of all the works of all other workmen," meaning that he is the creator of the idea of their works.

56. He does not name Helvétius or Voltaire: e.g., *C. C.*, 13:37 and 191, letters to Comparet and De Luc, about 10 September and 10 October 1762.

57. 1 Cor. 15:55-56.

58. "... Non, l'homme n'est point un; je veux et je ne veux pas, je me sens à la fois esclave et libre, je vois le bien, je l'aime, et je fais le mal: je suis actif quand j'écoute la raison, passif quand mes passions m'entraînent, et mon pire tourment, quand je succombe, est de sentir que j'ai pu resister." Cf. Rom. 7:15 and Gal. 5:17.

59. "Quelque chose en toi cherche à briser les liens qui le compriment. L'espace n'est pas ta mesure, l'univers entier n'est pas assés grand pour toi.... " Cf. for example "Lettres à m. de Malesherbes," loc. cit., p. 1141. For Socrates on harmony: *The Republic* 7. 531, the words of which are echoed in Rousseau's text in the paragraph preceding the one quoted here.

60. "Non, Dieu de mon ame, je ne te reprocherai jamais de l'avoir faite à ton image afin que je pusse être libre, bon et heureux comme toi!"

61. 1 Cor. 9:24-27 and *The Republic* 10. 613, 621. Cf. 3. 403 and 5. 465-66.

62. Cf. "Confessions," loc. cit., pp. 619-20; the first of the "Dialogues" and second and fifth of the "Rêveries." For the psalm below see *O. C.*, 4:591 n. 2. When Rousseau says later that death is the end of life for the wicked, he means that that is their opinion and that they live as if such were the case: ibid., p. 820.

63. *The Republic* 4. 444 (justice is as natural as health); 6. 505-6 (man's whole quest is the good); 10. 612 (justice in her own nature is best for the soul in her own nature). For the idea that feelings may be judgments see "Emile," p. 484. Cf. p. 584 n, where the same idea is suggested. It is obvious from the context that in the present case the subjectivity of conscience does not favor moral anarchy.

64. For the complex idea of "interest" see *C. C.*, 9:143-45, letter to d'Offreville, 4 October 1761. Cf. "Lettre à C. de Beaumont," loc. cit., p. 936.

65. Cf. the text of "Emile" and *The Republic* 6. 485. Cf. also Rousseau's idea of divine wisdom within and *The Republic* 9. 589-92. For the imitation of the "heavenly pattern" mentioned below; ibid., 6. 500.

66. 1 Cor. 6:3; but cf. Psalm 8:5 cited in Heb. 2:7, where the apostle recalls that man was made lower than the angels but was raised above them by Christ.

67. "Emile," p. 599, and cf. p. 583, where the delights of the sage are compared with the torment of the man who succumbs.

68. See, for example, *O. C.*, 4:614 n. 2 and 636 n. 1. According to these notes, natural religion is excluded from the city of the *Contract*.

69. Cf. *The Republic*, books 2, 3, 4. See especially 4. 427.

70. The connection between the two creeds is discussed by S. Cotta, "Théorie religieuse et théorie politique chez Rousseau," *Annales de philosophie politique* 5 (1965): 171-94. Crocker agrees with Talmon that they supplement each other: *Rousseau's Social Contract: An Interpretive Essay* (Cleveland: Case Western Reserve University Press, 1968), pp. 100-101. Cf. J. L. Talmon, *The Rise of Totalitarian Democracy* (Boston: Beacon Press, 1952), p. 24. These writers see in the civic creed a support for totalitarianism. Broome, who also notes that the two creeds are reconcilable (op. cit., pp. 105, 114), is perhaps closer to the truth when he sees in Rousseau's notion of the General Will sanctified by religion "an attempt.... to propose a meeting-point between Man and God, in the concept of Law...." (ibid., pp. 122-23). Boss (loc. cit., pp. 130, 139, 144) also connects the two creeds: see note 74 below.

71. Loc. cit., p. 706 n.

72. "Emile," p. 250. He says the same of religion: "Contrat social," p. 469.

73. Loc. cit., pp. 695, 705.

74. See, for example, K. D., Erdmann, *Das Verhältnis von Staat und Religion nach des Sozialphilosophie Rousseaus* (Berlin: Verlag Dr. Emil Ebering, 1935). Boss (op. cit.) concludes that the vicar's spirit of tolerance is violated in the civil creed. He allies himself with Bernard Groethuysen, *J.-J. Rousseau* (Paris: Gallimard, 1949), p. 259, and C. W. Hendel, *Jean-Jacques Rousseau, Moralist* (London: Oxford University Press, 1934), p. 243. Yet the idea of religion as law and of atheism as lawlessness and spiritually fatal is present in the vicar's creed. Since law, like conscience, is conceived as the spokesman of the sovereign human will, a morally committed man submits because he wants to, whether he is a leader like the vicar or a follower like the citizens of the *Contract*, even though the laws to which he submits are those of a city that can never exist on earth.

75. His reply was that he would hope that she was not, and that God had been able to enlighten her at her last hour.

76. "Je considerois cette diversité de sectes qui régent sur la terre."

77. The quotations are from "Emile," pp. 311, 610-11, 680, 848; "Lettres à m. de Malesherbes," loc. cit., p. 1140; cf. "Lettre à C. de Beaumont," loc. cit., pp. 986, 987. The protests against men who separate him from the law and from God are intentionally analogous: see "Confessions," loc. cit., p. 567: " ... La Relig-

ion raisonnable et morale ôtant tout pouvoir humain sur les consciences, ne laisse plus de ressource aux arbitres de ce pouvoir." That is the object of law in *Emile* and the *Contract,* which are supposed to defend "the rights of humanity."

78. Burgelin sees this: *O.C.,* 4:611 n. 2.

79. In the "Lettres de la montagne," loc. cit., pp. 749-59, Rousseau maintains that neither he nor the vicar approves of the "Raisonneur" but that the dialogue shows the dangers of mysticism and its vulnerability at the hands of scientific reason.

80. *The Republic* 10. 602. This is a likely source in spite of Voltaire's feeling that the real one is his poem on natural religion and letter to Urania. See Bernard Bouvier, "Notes inédites de Voltaire sur la Profession de foi du vicaire savoyard," *Annales de la Société Jean-Jacques Rousseau* 1 (1905): 279.

81. Matt. 16:4.

82. Burgelin suspects this: *O. C.,* 4:623 n. 1. See "Confessions," loc. cit., p. 70; E. Ritter, *La Famille et la jeunesse de J.-J. Rousseau* (Paris: Hachette, 1896), p. 202.

83. "Lettres de la montagne," loc. cit., pp. 753-54; "Lettre à m. de Franquières," loc. cit., pp. 1145-47. Cf. "Morceau allégorique sur la révélation" (*O. C.,* 4:1053-54) where Rousseau (circa 1755) prefers Christ to Socrates, whose submission to false laws after his revelation of true ones still puzzled him. I deal with Rousseau's perplexity about Socrates in the next chapter where I handle the famous comparison of Socrates and Cato.

84. "Confessions," loc. cit., p. 63; cf. Matt. 12:31. See Masson's edition of the *Profession de foi* (see note 46 above), p. 425.

85. Cf. "Emile," p. 628 n, and "Contrat social," p. 469; cf. also "Lettre à C. de Beaumont," loc. cit., p. 978.

86. Matt. 3:9; Luke 3:8. Cf. Rousseau's plea for enlightenment and that in Mark 9:24. The problem of adjusting theism and one's ancestral faith, to which I propose a solution below, has been raised by various critics.

87. "Aimer Dieu par dessus tout et son prochain comme soi-même est le sommaire de la loi. . . ." Cf. Eccles. 12:13; Prov. 21:3; Matt. 22:37-39; 1 Cor. 13; Gal. 5:14. For faith as an act of the will, in addition to this context of "Emile," see *C.C.,* 9:342, letter to Moultou, 23 December 1761.

88. For attacks upon "Philosophers" and materialists in the creed: "Emile," pp. 568-69, 576-78, 579-80, 582, 595 n, 598-99, 601, 632-35, and Rousseau's note. For the latter, refuting Bayle's idea of virtuous atheism, see Boss, op. cit., pp. 123 ff. The "philosophers" are also attacked elsewhere in "Emile": pp. 253, 256, 350 n.

89. "Mais voyez de combien de nouvelles chaines vous avez environné son coeur. La raison, l'amitié, la reconnoissancè, mille affections lui parlent d'un ton qu'il ne peut méconoitre." For the Socratic leitmotiv see note 11 above. The phrase recurs often in "Emile": pp. 522, 539, 639, 648-49, 653, 660-61. For "lawful fetters" mentioned above, see "Contrat social," p. 351.

90. *The Republic* 2. 375-76.

91. Ibid., 7. 534. For virtue practiced by habit, force, or necessity: ibid., 2. 358-59; 7. 519-20; 9. 590; 10. 619.

92. Ibid., 6. 491-92. Cf. 497 (Socratic parable of the sower). For the husbandman: ibid., 9. 589. Cf. the Christian parable in Matt. 13:1-8. Rousseau writes: "Avant de semer il faut labourer la terre: la semence de la vertu léve difficilement, il faut de longs apprets pour lui faire prendre racine."

93. Cf. *The Republic* 7. 520 ("we have brought you into the world"); 8. 548 ("running away like children from the law, their father"). Rousseau writes: "... J'enflamerai son jeune coeur de tous les sentimens d'amitié, de générosité, de reconoissance que j'ai déja fait naitre et qui sont si doux à nourrir.... Je lui dirai: tu es mon bien, mon enfant, mon ouvrage; c'est de ton bonheur que j'attends le mien...." The Socratic leitmotiv is quoted above just before my discussion of Plutarch's biographies and again a few pages later apropos of the so-called lessons of experience; see also the last section of this chapter, "The Oath of Kings."

94. "Contrat social," p. 469 n, and "Lettre à C. de Beaumont," loc. cit., p. 979 n.

95. "Emile," pp. 494, 764. For the distinction between what is natural in the savage state and civil order, see chapter 4 above, note 41. For the vicar's words quoted below: "Emile," p. 566.

96. "Lettre à C. de Beaumont," loc. cit., p. 979 n, and see the fourth paragraph of the section of this chapter entitled "Credo." For the law of love that replaces the rule of necessity mentioned above, see Plato, *The Symposium* (Agathon's speech).

97. Emile is asking to be "forced to be free." Failure to see the Socratic symbolism here leads to the impression that the hero, in order to be free of the slavery of sense, renounces his own free agency: David Cameron, *The Social Thought of Rousseau and Burke* (Toronto: University of Toronto Press, 1973), pp. 101-2. An awareness of symbols and literary correspondences shows that the "ordering agent" is in fact Emile himself, who is engaging a minister or servant to externalize the governing power existing within him until he can serve himself. He does so in the fifth part, whose ideological content we can no longer afford to ignore. See chapter 6 below.

98. *O. C.*, 3:442 n. 4 (here we can see that even Voltaire missed the point) and 443 n. 1. With regard to elections it has been said that in Rousseau's system magistrates are chosen by lot. But this would be so only in an impossible democracy where the lot falls upon all, not in the elective aristocracy that he prefers.

99. The chapters considered out of place are "Contrat social," part 2, chapters 8, 9, 10; part 3, chapter 8; part 4, chapters 4, 5, 6, 7; loc cit., pp. 384 n. 6; 414 n. 1; 444 n. 1; cf. 458 n. 1. See chapters 3 and 4 above and chapter 1, note 55. Many thinkers believe that the book contains confused historical discussions of institutions of little importance today.

100. In the opening words of the chapter he admits that all he knows about the origins of Rome are "fables," "conjectures," "traditions."

101. "Le nom de *Rome* qu'on prétend venir de *Romulus* est Grec, et signifie *force;* le nom de *Numa* est grec aussi, et signifie *Loi.* Quelle apparence que les deux premiers Rois de cette ville aient porté d'avance des noms si bien rélatifs à ce qu'ils ont fait?"

102. *The Republic* 3. 415.

103. There Jean-Jacques exercises some mysterious power to force Emile to leave the beatific contemplation of wisdom for a time and engage in active life in the "false" kingdoms of this world.

104. Cf. *The Republic* 2. 377.

105. The italics are mine. We were previously told that he was not "an active member of society": "Emile," pp. 421, 467. Even when his pity becomes "active," he is still a spectator: pp. 542 ff. The references to the "citizen" in this context are on pp. 655, 667 and note, 669. Cf. pp. 262, 469. It must be understood

[301]

that when Emile enters our society, he is literally going down into the Socratic den, on a level far below the lofty idealism of the *Contrat,* which always remains within.

106. In addition to being mme d' Houdetot's name, it is also that of a character in his play "Les Prisonniers de guerre" and of one of the mendicanti orphans in "Confessions," 7. Cf. the Princesse Raison in "La Reine fantasque," *O. C.,* 2:1189-90.

107. He learns to seek what was beyond him in "Emile," p. 453: "On voit à quinze ans le bonheur d'un homme sage, comme à trente la gloire du paradis."

108. Prov. 4:5-8; 7:4-5; 8:10; 8:18. For the banquet of wisdom in 9:1-5 see chapter 6 below.

109. "Confessions," loc. cit., pp. 193 ff. For love as a shield of virtue: ibid., pp. 7, 109.

110. *The Republic* 6. 492-95. Cf. 8. 560 ff.

111. "Emile," p. 659: "...Tous deux [Emile and a young girl] auront au moins pour gardes la crainte et la honte...." Cf. *The Republic* 5. 465: "For there are two guardians, shame and fear, mighty to prevent him...." "Fear means fear of breaking the law bred in him by education.

112. *The Republic* 8. 560-61.

113. "... Il reconoit la voix de l'amitié et il sait obéir à la raison." "Emile," p. 661. See note 89 above.

114. Cf. "Confessions," loc. cit., pp. 108-9.

115. The parallel passages are in "Emile," pp. 537-40, 663-64.

116. "Emile," p. 669, regarding manners, deportment, and taste in dress and concluding: "On voit que tout cela n'exige point de ma part un étalage de préceptes, et n'est qu'un effet de sa prémière éducation." Cf. *The Republic* 4. 423-25. All Socrates' regulations are trifles of the one great thing, education. And he too declines to "legislate" about "when the young are to be silent before their elders; how they are to show respect to them by standing and making them sit; what honour is due to parents; what garments or shoes are to be worn; the mode of dressing the hair; deportment and manners in general." His heroes will discover these rules for themselves, through the force of their education. The same is true of laws about markets, police, harbors, law-suits, and so on. See chapter 3 above, note 39.

117. See above, pp. 16 ff. and 135 ff.

118. His taste is also shown in his admiration for Raphael that is characteristically combined with a love of the neo-classics of Bologna, who added emotion to Rapheal's classical ideal: "Emile," p. 790. For the importance of amusements cf. *The Republic* 4. 424. Rousseau associates virtue and beauty as the object of laws in the "Fragments politiques" as well as in the chapter of the "Contrat" on the censorship.

119. For the evangelical challenge: Matt. 19:23-26. For the Socratic phrase corresponding to "with God all things are possible": *The Republic* 6. 492-93.

120. Cf. *O. C.,* 3:111 n. 4.

121. *The Republic* 8. 553. Cf. 550-51. Cf. also "Contrat social," p. 429 (the word *finance* is unkown in the city).

122. See pp. 680, 683, 686, 691.

123. *The Republic* 3. 400-402. Burgelin notes the connection of taste and morals in Rousseau: *O. C.,* 4:671 n. 2.

124. See pp. 782, 820, 859, 861. Observe that for Rousseau the golden age belongs neither to the past, as with the ancients, nor to the future, as with the moderns, but to the eternal present.

125. "Mais de quoy jouissois-je enfin quand j'étois seul? De moi, de l'univers entier, de tout ce qui est, de tout ce qui peut être, de tout ce qu'a de beau le monde sensible et d'imaginable le monde intellectuel...."

VI
Inner Sanctum

The fifth part of *Emile* leads the reader into the innermost
chamber[1] of the mythical temple dedicated to divine wisdom. Although there is no corresponding part in the *Contract,*[2] the principles of the treatise on citizenship prevail
throughout this section where they are also summarized. I
shall therefore discuss the novel in the light of discoveries
to which the collation of the two books has led. Indeed,
here it affords a new vision of Rousseauist wisdom in its
most intimate relations to the human spirit. In addition, the
writer shows clearly enough to what degree he dared hope
that the city of his creation might have real existence in
some form of civil order or exclusive communion of men.

The inner sanctuary of the temple of the book matches
the second chamber of the Greek pattern, adjacent to the
other and somewhat smaller, but also divided by rows of
columns into three symmetrical naves. In accordance with
Rousseau's consistent symbolic adherence to this architectural form, the last part of *Emile* is therefore a little smaller
than the previous one and also has a tripartite shape, the
three "naves" varying only slightly in magnitude.

It covers the hero's life between the ages of twenty and
twenty-five and contains the story of Emile and Sophia in
three parts, the first and last being marked by titles, and the
middle by the spacing of the text. They deal respectively
with the nature and formation of woman and presentation of
Sophia; the courtship of Emile and Sophia and the promise
between them; and finally a comparison of the Rousseauist
covenant with the historical one, culminating in Emile's
pledge to the former and marriage to Sophia. Henceforth
the symbolism becomes increasingly obvious. Indeed, fail-

[305]

ure to cope with it and to take account of the literary—as well as literal—aspect of the work especially here is the reason for most of our misunderstandings in the past. Often we are so shocked by the "reactionary" or traditional character of Sophia's formation that we can hardly see much else, or are tempted to pass lightly over the "storybook ending" as if the romance were simply that of a man's love for a woman. It may indeed be that, but it also turns out to be much more. Rousseau himself has said so, as we know. In painting her portrait, the Aemelian governor explained that the aesthetic and spiritual or social ideal existing in Emile's mind and heart is embodied in her, and that his love for the moral truth and beauty of that order of wisdom assumes the form of love of Sophia, whose name befits her. That was the very reason for the portrait. This love supposedly makes autonomous action possible for a man and releases him from "his tutor the law," to use the author's Socratic and biblical phraseology. And so we need not protest, as we have done hitherto, that this part whose theme in the original plan of the work was to be wisdom is replaced by a love story.[3] As in the case of friendship, Rousseau handles the theme of love as freely as he did before and no less freely than it is handled in the Platonic dialogues, particularly the *Republic* and *Symposium*. He uses it to dramatize the idea that wisdom is suited to the human spirit, and to exteriorize his thought in figures and events that may be taken literally but must be taken symbolically.

SOPHIA

In the first nave of the mythical inner shrine, where he begins with the nature and formation of woman, he makes statements that have a double meaning and hint at both a philosophical and love drama. For example, he quotes Genesis, "It is not good for man to be alone," and then formulates a query that may have a much broader scope than we think, like the biblical text itself. It reads: "Where

[306]

is Sophia? What is she?" These words conspicuously echo the oft-repeated phrase: "Where is wisdom? Where is happiness?"

He considers first the nature of woman, since her formation must be suited to the constitution of her species and sex if she is to fulfill her role in life, which for him is that of wife and mother. He dwells especially upon the moral effects of the affinities and differences between men and women and the role of both in their union, wherein each concurs in the common object in a different way. His meditations run as follows. Man is active and strong, endowed with power and will, whereas woman is a passive being, made to please him and activate his strength. In their reciprocal reactions he is governed by the law of reason, which makes him free and master of himself. She is as subject to that law as she is to him, but is further restrained by the modesty imposed upon her by nature and also by a gradually acquired aesthetic taste for right conduct. Moreover, although the stronger of the two seems to be master, he really depends upon the weaker and must please her as much as she does him if he would woo her. In this way, according to the author, the moral aspects of their interrelationship give rise to "the sweet laws of love" and have consequences that influence the whole of life. By the power of love, says he, she binds men's hearts to herself, educates her children, and is the link between them and their father. Her fidelity to the covenant from which the miniature society of the family springs is therefore more indispensable than man's for the purpose of maintaining "the bonds of nature." Again as in the first part of the book, he sees her faithlessness as the source of all evil. Indeed, in his view she must not merely be faithful and chaste, but deemed so by public opinion as well as by her husband. For Rousseau these are the moral effects of the peculiar place that nature herself assigns to women in regard to men.

These opinions about the nature of women are as relevant to the "perfect city" or "wise order" of the covenant

[307]

as equivalent ones about a mother's duties in the first part.[4] And rightly so, since in the book it is through a man's alliance with her that the city materializes. The special destiny attributed to her in the pursuit of that object proves to be that of the ideal state, passive as such, created to please him and impel him to moral action or obedience to the law of reason that is rooted in his noblest self and empowered to release it. A woman subject to such a man is, as it were, a "state" ruled by "true laws," and a state ruled by true laws is the ideal city. The charm of its institutions is also hers, which he must honor.[5] By her persuasive influence Jean-Jacques' law of reason, of necessity and freedom, of utility or Socratic "usefulness," and of the constitution—which is as subject to human nature as she is—becomes "the sweet law of love" that makes the city a reality. That law, like the one that takes the form of friendship, may also bring others into the fold and win their hearts to the Socratic "father." Fidelity to the latter, who is the law, ensures peace and union—the blessings of the common good and of the covenant—by securing "the bonds of nature" that are the spirit of all law. Since the moral order that takes shape in this way and without which man is presumably lost is Rousseauist wisdom, public judgment that safeguards it is seen as true opinion, which prevails in the Aemilian city and whose approval the heroine must win while her lover, beset by the sophisms of false opinion, despises them in favor of her. These distinctions convey in an imaginative way the idea that she must move him to be what he essentially is and fulfill himself through her in the mythical city whose image she exteriorizes, however small or large it may be.

Before dealing with her formation, Rousseau himself draws attention to the symbolism of love and marriage in a passage in which he appears to part company with Socrates. He challenges the sage's disregard of the family as an educational institution and repudiates his ideas on the education of women contained in Plato's fifth book, from whose content the author of *Emile* nevertheless borrows later on. As we know, the Greek sage allots the same exercises and duties to both sexes in the republic. His modern disciple protests that women are not made to go to "war," meaning that they cannot engage in active life in the world like men can. We may judge from the name of Sophia that for him their domain is "politics," or citizenship and education. He complains that the speaker in the *Republic* turns them into men because, having removed private families from his system of government, he has no place for women as such, and consequently no other alternative.[6] This "civil promiscuity" leads, says he, to the subversion of the sweetest sentiments of nature, meaning family affections, which are sacrificed for the sake of an artificial sense of loyalty to an outward city that could exist only through their effectiveness. For him, as we saw in the first part, these bonds furnish a natural foundation for the conventional bonds of patriotism that they also serve to portray. It is "through the miniature city of the family that the heart grows attached to the large one." It is "the good son, the good husband, the good father who makes the good citizen." Accordingly, as before, the writer uses conjugal or family affection to allegorize the orderly disposition and felicitous expansion of the soul wedded to "wisdom" or the ideal city.

In that case his thought remains as Socratic as ever, whatever form it assumes, especially since he really has no more hope for the family than he or the Greek thinker has for the city. Consequently, even in this context the ideal probably remains as confined to the inner realm of the sage as it does in the *Republic*. The truth is that Rousseau does not take leave of his model at all. However much he makes an issue of disagreeing with the sage's views in Plato's fifth book on the nature and formation of woman—a real disagreement that we anticipated in the previous chapter—he nevertheless continues to be deeply indebted to the master in another context of the Greek classic for the image of Sophia or woman as the embodiment of wisdom and the

[309]

ideal state whose lover is a "philosopher" in the etymological sense. We saw this too in the previous chapter above, as well as in the second, where we studied the symbolism of the father, mother, and family. But in this respect, as we know, he is inspired by Plato's sixth book where woman plays a symbolic role and personifies the Muse of Philosophy or queen of the republic who has watched over the early education of its heroes and is finally revealed as the philosopher-king's destined bride. Indeed, that book, together with other Socratic recommendations at the end of the *Republic* dealing with the choice of wisdom in life, is one of Rousseau's two chief sources in his treatment of the formation of woman, which is not, however, Socrates' real theme therein. The other source is Plato's *Symposium* or *Banquet*[7] to which he directed us earlier by including it in Emile's readings and which has no more to do with feminine education than the texts in the *Republic*. He appropriates the Socratic ideas and allegories of his models freely enough to show clearly that the main subject of the present part of his work is not what it appears to be. The reader is by now familiar with the symbolism of the first Platonic dialogue. I must briefly review the other before proceeding further.

The theme of the work is love. Socrates is again the chief speaker but takes his turn with others in discoursing upon that subject. In fact, it is the only one of which he professes to have any knowledge at all since, in his opinion, there is only one love and that is the love of wisdom, as Rousseau too implies by naming Emile's beloved "Sophia." I shall combine all the discourses into one except that of the sage, which I shall handle separately.

Love, we are told in the *Symposium*, is a source of virtue and honor, since lovers would be pained to be dishonored in each other's eyes. Consequently, "if there were only some way of contriving that a state or an army should be made up of lovers and their loves, they would be the very best governors of their own city.... Love will make men dare to

[310]

die for their beloved." Such love is, however, far from common. It is love of the good, that of intelligent beings who "are a law unto themselves," and is incompatible with tyranny [a cipher of the power of evil passion]: "The interests of rulers [meaning tyrants or tyrannical passions] require . . . that there should be no strong bond of friendship or society among their subjects [corresponding to desires that ought to be harmonized by reason and true opinion] and love, above all other motives, is likely to inspire this." But such a bond can be formed only by "love of the noble mind," subject to law, as opposed to love of wealth and power. Now since both noble and ignoble love are to be found in all things, only a skillful physician or musician can discern the love that harmonizes temperate and intemperate elements, "is concerned with the good," "is perfected in company with . . . justice," and leads to happiness. This love that is "lord of the good" is every man's desire and so "if all of us obtained our love . . . then the human race would be happy at last." But under present circumstances, the nearest approach to consummate felicity would be the attainment of a congenial love. And that achievement depends upon ourselves, for acts of love must be distinguished from those of necessity: "all serve love of their own free will and where there is love as well as obedience [the Rousseauist correlatives too], there, as the laws which are the lords of the city say, is justice," and temperance, courage, wisdom, and poetic inspiration. The latter is included since love is love of the beautiful as well as the good.

Before dealing with Socrates' part in the dialogue, I might observe the relevance of these ideas to Rousseau's thought, even though the connection becomes clearer henceforward. Woman, as he has described her, inspires that love of the good which wins obedience to the laws, which is manifest in wisdom and all virtue, and tempers ignoble passions to create harmony and peace among the powers. Indeed, such a love which is that of the beauty of a divine order of things allegedly becomes the only law in the

[311]

end, making all other ordinances superfluous and creating a
state where honor reigns and the lover knows "for whom
he must die." So we are told later, as we shall see. The government of love or honor ultimately replaces that of reason,
both being subject to the same law of the human constitution. The speakers of the *Symposium* help clarify the symbolic value of Rousseau's text.

But Socrates, who incidentally attributes his ideas to a
"wise woman," Diotima, is the most enlightening of all. He
explains that if love is defined as love of wisdom, truth,
beauty, and goodness, to which he adds immortality, it is
not because that all-powerful creature posseses them, but
because he feels the need for them and hence pursues them
for the sake of happiness, bearing fruit thereby in thought,
word, and deed. Thus the sage sees love not as possession
but as poverty or an awareness of need, and this leads him
to emphasize the pursuits and labors of love to the same
extent that he emphasizes those of study, which are identical. Creative souls, says he, who engage in an active
spirtual life, are moved by love to beget wisdom and poetic
fervor. "But," he adds, "the greatest and fairest sort of
wisdom by far is that which is concerned with the ordering
of states and families and which is called temperance and
justice." That wisdom of the ideal city is not only Emile's
whole quest in life but is the very essence of Rousseau's
conception of the education of woman, since for him the
ideal can materialize, if at all, only through a woman thus
formed. And that miracle would be possible only if she won
the love of a lover of wisdom like the hero, or the ones
exemplified in the master's words in the Greek dialogue.
Socrates adds that such a lover has in him the seed of temperance and justice, and in his maturity desires to generate
both: "He wanders about seeking beauty that he may beget
offspring [the aforementioned virtues] . . . and when he finds
a fair and noble and well-nurtured soul, he gladly embraces that soul, and to such an one he is full of fair speech
about virtue, and the nature and pursuits of a good man,

and he tries to educate his beloved: and, at the touch and presence of the beautiful, he brings forth the beautiful which he conceived long before . . . and they have a closer relationship than those who beget mortal children." As we shall see, this is precisely the homage for which education is intended to prepare a woman in the Rousseauist order of things. The sage concludes by tracing the course of love from beautiful forms and fair thoughts to beauty of institutions and laws, culminating in the love of absolute beauty, which enables a man to bring forth not mere images of beauty but realities or true virtue and to become the "friend of God" and enjoy immortality. It is impossible to ignore the affinity of his words and of the whole work to the text of *Emile* where the author portrays his own view of the beauty of a wise order of life that wins love and moves a man to beget virtue.[8]

The personification of wisdom and the ideal state in woman is, as I have previously remarked, Judeo-Christian as well as Socratic. Quite apart from the Solomonic personification of wisdom, or the idealization of chaste womanhood discussed earlier,[9] other biblical imagery to which I alluded in speaking of the covenant is visible in Rousseau's handling of the theme of Sophia and accentuates its symbolism. For example, in the Old Testament the covenant people Israel is represented as a spouse whose spiritual husband is God. In the New Testament the society of the church, Ecclesia, appears as the bride of Christ, united with him in a single "mystical body," and again as the "holy city prepared as a bride adorned for her husband." In both cases the city is ideally shaped by the laws of the mystical bridegroom. These ancient myths combine to cast light upon Rousseau's miniature city of the fifth part that suddenly becomes accessible in woman.

Broaching the question of her education, he defines first the principles of the process, that spring from the distinctive traits of her nature as analyzed at the beginning of this part, with their symbolic flavor. If she is to be suited to

[313]

man, to please him and direct his strength as she must in accordance with her alleged destiny, inclination, and duties as wife and mother, which are surely Sophia's, her education must be devised to that end. The writer sees no other possible vocation for her. He accentuates her dependence upon man but paradoxically admits that the latter depends upon her for everything: his education, morals, passions, tastes, and happiness throughout life. As we foresaw in the previous chapter in reference to Sophia, she is entrusted like Socrate's Muse with what Rousseau called, in the second and fourth parts of the *Contract,* the laws whose domain is the heart, which replace authority by manners, customs, and opinions and which determine the success of all other laws, shaping men's morals, tastes, and lives for all time. In that case Sophia has been mystically present in *Emile,* in company with Jean-Jacques, from the dedication onward.

The education of Rousseauist woman, which I shall trace briefly to show how the symbolism evolves, is both aesthetic and spiritual according to the character of Rousseauist wisdom, and, together with the story of Sophia that follows, is sketched within the bounds of Paris like the philosophic ecstasy induced by the same wisdom. In every phase of her evolution the model proposed is the example set by her sisters in the ancient cities of Sparta and Aemilian Rome, cities whose character is reflected in their noble women as it is in her. Moreover, the order of her formation is that of the "true" state ruled by the reasonable will or law of the constitution, which she must learn to activate and for which she must win obedience by the power of love alone. Thus as in the case of Emile provision is made for the training of physical attributes first of all, and then the will and the reason in that sequence.

In the first stage of her education the author directs his attention to the cultivation of personal charms and a strong constitution required for the fulfillment of her vocation as he sees it. He gives the example of Spartan maidens who

[314]

sang and danced at public fetes and pious rites, which he elsewhere recommends for his own city. With that ideal in mind he begins by recommending outdoor games and amusements. He combines these with simple "useful" lessons in sewing and design, the physical side of the art of pleasing, and also in traditional studies like the three Rs. In prescribing the latter, which he ignored in the case of a leader like Emile, he applies to her the rule of the common people or ideal state. In this context he likens her to the goddess of wisdom, whose role she plays in the end as protectress of a supposedly wise order of human life symbolically identified with her.

There are further signs of the presence of symbolism in the treatment of her early moral formation. She is industrious like Emile, but always under constraint since all her life long she must submit to the will and judgments of men as to law. Such, of course, is the nature of Rousseauist and Socratic wisdom, as we have seen from the beginning. The author adds that she must be devoted to her duties and — like the Socratic muse, we may observe — must guard against lawlessness in amusements, although she is permitted to use her natural ingenuity to evade the rules in matters of indifference.[10] She learns thereby to reign in obedience and make man's dwelling-place an abode of happiness. Jean-Jacques has done the same. The functions assigned to her in the most intimate sphere of life are those of wisdom or the imaginary city where the laws of reason prevail as they did in the order of friendship, and the laws are the same in both cases.

The second phase of her education is suggestive of the same symbolism. The new Minerva emulates Venus by favoring Spartan simplicity of adornment to accentuate her natural graces. Her charm is therefore that of the new Sparta. From the age of ten she also follows the example of Spartan maidens by acquiring talents already extolled in them, such as singing and dancing, that enhances private life. In Rousseau's view the lawful amusements of harmony

[315]

and rhythm are the palladium of marriage and the family as they are of the Aemilian city and Socratic republic. He never loses sight of the principle that the city stands or falls upon the nature of its pleasures, and greatly emphasizes it in the present context.

Obviously for him the art of pleasing extends far beyond the sphere of appearances. Taste, he says again, opens the mind to all beauty, including that of moral ideas. Accordingly he is led to speak of ethical instruction at this stage. It is largely imparted by way of conversations on moral themes that, besides teaching the art of polite speech, show the child "what qualities men esteem and what makes the true glory and felicity of a good woman." She learns, in fine, where wisdom and happiness lie.

To lead her thither and foster in her a growing "taste for good morals" that combines ethics and aesthetics, Rousseau borrows the support of religion when she is presumably ten or twelve years old. He explains that since the concepts of religion are beyond her reach, she must learn them all the sooner. Here, as in the case of the three Rs, he again applies to her the rule of the common people, which is that of the state subject to law. Before doing so, he defines her cast of mind. In his opinion it is practical, oriented toward human relationships, and it conducts her to the goal proposed by man, who in turn reaches that goal through her. The goal, as we know, is that wise order of things called the city. He admits it. The society of the sexes, says he, produces "a moral person of which woman is the eye and man the hand . . . . " This idea brings into higher relief the symbolism of the text and of the names Aemilius and Sophia, "industry" and "wisdom," the latter conceived as pertaining to the sense of sight. The composite creature thus formed, upon which both are completely dependent, is an image of the rational being born of a man or association of men wedded to "divine wisdom" by the covenant of peace through an act of the enlightened human will intensified by love. Reflecting upon the society of the sexes,

[316]

Rousseau explains that man discovers principles or laws but his companion possesses the spirit of detail and observation that leads to their execution. Hence, "each contributes to the common purpose . . . each obeys and both are rulers." Here again their reciprocal correspondence resembles that of the citizen to the subject or the sovereign to the state, which is really the solemn engagement of a man with his own noblest faculties.[11] This pledge could hardly be better portrayed in its innermost and only really effective form than by the conjugal union. In the past we have been aware of the analogy without seeing that the one is a literary image of the other. The author himself suggests the politico-moral similitude by quoting from the Pauline chapter on the mystical body born of the union of Christ with his bride Ecclesia: in matters of religion, "women must receive the decision of fathers and husbands as that of the church,"[12] or the holy city they symbolize in the context. They must do so because religion is a law in a presumably wise order of life governed by the covenant.

That he does indeed allude to the ideal city is even more evident when he defines the faith prescribed, which is the law of the civic creed in the *Contract*.[13] He replaces the catechism and mysteries by dogmas "important to human society" that bid us do our duties toward our neighbor and ourselves. The dogmas he recommends here as in the *Contract* proclaim the existence of God, our judge and common father; they ordain in his name the practice of justice, charity, beneficence, mercy, and fidelity to our engagements with others; and they promise a future life where the Supreme Being will reward the good and judge the wicked. These dogmas, we are told, are compulsory for all "citizens," and expressly preclude any others that breed intolerance. Their very nature lends more weight to the figurative or literary interpretation of woman in *Emile*, which, however, does not exclude a literal reading as well.

Rousseau's conception of the third and last degree in her formation has even more allegorical overtones than the pre-

[317]

ceding ones. It is ushered in by the awakening of reason in conscience. The rational faculty is given a twofold ministry to discharge. In a very simple form it enjoins duties of obedience and fidelity to the covenant upon which the diminutive city of the family stands. In a more complex form it reconciles the voices of conscience and public opinion whenever possible, in which case a woman must learn to make wise applications of the law of true opinion like the censor in the *Contract*. And as the latter defines opinions when they waver, so she too must learn to anticipate them and win their favor for herself by wooing them to wisdom. For her domain, like his, is a sort of government, as I have said, and is analogous to that of the prince, whose work she makes superfluous in the end. The symbolism is unfolding more insistently.

It is carried further when Rousseau considers the training of her reason. Before doing so, he reflects again upon the intuitive discernment of a woman who knows the art of pleasing men by virtue of subtle observation of the heart. He gives the example of Galatea in a Virgilian eclogue, who resorts to cunning wiles to induce a shepherd to follow her. We may infer that in Emile's case Jean-Jacques' earlier artfulness will soon be replaced by Sophia's, or even by his own since, according to the projected work on *Sensitive Morality* described in the *Confessions,* a man may invent such devices for himself to regulate his conduct. The writer of *Emile* adds that the practical tendency of a woman's mind with its firm grasp of human reactions not only enables a man to implement the moral laws found by himself, as we were told before, but even leads him to find them. She discovers "experimental morality" or psychology, while he reduces it to a system. Both together attain to "the most complete knowledge accessible to the human mind, that of oneself and of others." But this indispensable knowledge that is the fruit of their union is already bred in Emile, betrothed to Rousseauist wisdom from the beginning. His

[318]

education, presided over by that wisdom through the agency of Jean-Jacques, culminated in the previous part in the conscious cultivation of taste and discernment, making him sensitive to the beauty of an ideal order presented in a form to win his love and ultimately moving him to act and exteriorize it.

In the author's opinion that mythical order can assume visible form in a woman only if her mind is trained according to his concept of its nature and if the fine psychological observations of which she is capable are exercised, like Emile's hitherto, in worldly society, which also provides for the acquisition of agreeable knowledge and the formation of taste, as we know. Rousseau follows the example of the ancients by favoring the frequentation of polite society for young girls of marriageable age rather than for married women. But first, by way of precaution against evil, he would provide them with common sense, a love of honor, and a taste for the simple charms of family life and the little city of the home, the sanctuary of woman. If he succeeded, the woman he has in mind would give outward expression to virtues and a society regarded as impossible at the beginning of the book.

For experience furnished by social life teaches her the answer to the questions that were the theme of her childish conversations: "What qualities do men esteem? And what makes the true glory and happiness of a good woman?" Or if we prefer: Where is wisdom? Where is happiness? She learns what the *Symposium* teaches, namely, that propriety of life wins love and honor in the sight of men and moves them to seek honor for themselves in her eyes, since she is the natural judge of their merit as they are of hers. But for Rousseau the burden rests primarily with woman if the miniature city is to exist at all. He again holds up to her the example of her Spartan and Roman sisters of a heroic past. The love she must win is a love of the good and of the wisdom exemplified in them and is akin to that of the

[319]

Platonic dialogue, whatever other implications it may have.

But like Socrates weaving his myths in that work, he goes further. That love is not passive, any more than the Spartan's love for Sparta or the Roman's love for Rome. In Socratic speech it is the love of creative souls and impels them to pursue wisdom and all virtue. In the phraseology of *Emile* it arouses in the lover's heart natural fervor for perfection and beauty, visualized in the beloved, and begets sublime acts in himself, leading him at last to the supreme sacrifice. For the author asks, in the language of the *Symposium* or even of Christ: "What true lover exists who would not lay down his life for his beloved?"[14] Once more evoking the shades of medieval paladins, he observes that a chaste and virtuous woman wins devotion like theirs from all mankind as well as the love of a good and noble-minded man. Again using the language of the *Symposium,* he explains that "a lover serves his beloved as he serves virtue." He adds that a virtuous woman, like her Spartan sisters — and he might have said like Sparta herself—rules over great and strong souls and "sends her lovers to the end of the world, to war, glory and death at her behest." Moreover, we are later told, in a passage occurring after Emile's meeting with Sophia, that he must study a citizen's duties in order to learn "for whom he must die," a phrase to which I alluded above. The Aemilian texts as well as their analogy with the Platonic one suggest again that the hero's love for the heroine is really a love of wisdom involving "political" responsibilities and the risk of death. If passages like these are mystical jargon, as some of us in the past have been tempted to suppose, then so is the whole *Symposium,* for the great concepts of the latter are recognizable therein. Without ignoring Judeo-Christian tradition, Rousseau hints broadly that here woman is for him a symbol of the Socratic "greatest and fairest sort of wisdom by far" and an image of "the beauty of institutions and laws" that generated the fervor of the Spartan patriot in the opening pages of the book.

The foregoing survey of her education in *Emile* shows that the writer uses the theme to convey his thought in a new and imaginative form. His statements may be taken literally if we wish. But he has already said that women will never again be mothers, as he also said that the city will never exist in the world. And so while he takes pains to record his thoughts upon such grave issues, he frames them in figures equally suited to convey the main message of his work, the Socratic ordering of a man's inner life through effective modes of self-direction to make the mythical city a moral reality at least.

The allegorical character of the fifth part becomes even clearer in the brief portrait of Sophia that follows. The writer illustrates therein his previous treatment of the theme of womanhood. And yet there are subtle distinctions between Sophia, who is "woman," and woman in general as wife and mother. In the case of the latter the exteriorization of the ideal city in the sphere of conjugal and family relations, however hypothetical, seems less so than in the portrait of Sophia, which appears to belong more obviously to the world of the spirit. Moreover, the mingling of Judeo-Christian elements with pagan is more highly accentuated in her. For example, she bears a striking resemblance to Antiope, heroine of *Télémaque,* whose Christian and Platonic qualities reflect the scholarship of her creator, the priestly Fénelon. In that treatise of education, written a half century before *Emile,* Antiope is betrothed to the hero Télémaque and like the latter's governor Mentor is said to be "Minerva herself in human form."[15] Sophia too is Minerva, and her affinity to Antiope is hardly surprising since Télémaque is later reborn in Emile as Mentor is in Jean-Jacques, the Rousseauist figures being further christianized in the process. Such affinities as well as the portrait itself, like the earlier one, indicate that a purely literal and positivistic approach to the heroine and a neglect of literary values would be inadequate for an understanding of the author's meaning.

[321]

In the portrait the fusion of Greek and Christian elements is evident in both physical and spiritual attributes. Describing the former, the writer, having said that Sophia does not at first appear beautiful, betrays the fact that he has in mind his own "classical" definition of beauty as the sum of the most common features, or eternal and universal traits. Yet he also ascribes to her a gentle, touching expression that belongs to Christian tradition in art and literature. Besides, he visualizes her in flowing garments that reveal the charm of her person and are as evocative of both traditions as the imagery of the book that enhances his concept of natural wisdom. Moreover, he endows her with talents that are both Platonic and Fénelonian. For example, she is deeply sensitive to cadence and music and grace of movement, qualities that are as characteristic of Fénelon's Antiope-Minerva as they are of the "true Muse" of the *Republic,* who is "music," the companion of reason and philosophy, and who guards against corruption of soul by the potent influence of beauty and of order. Sophia too exemplifies the beauty of harmony that saves the constitution of soul and of city.[16] Rousseau imagines her "setting her house in order" like Antiope and thereby displaying the same love of grace, purity, and discipline as the Fénelonian heroine and a cast of mind like hers, bereft of "vain" ornaments, but pleasing, penetrating, and substantial. He bestows upon her an abundant capacity for practical observations that can translate all principles and powers into acts. He enriches her with other qualities too that in his view facilitate the same operations, such as Christian sensitivity, imaginative sympathy, patience, and charity. These moral virtues are, he says, the essence of her faith and life. Indeed, he sees her enamored of virtue by reason of its aesthetic appeal and the glory and happiness it promises a woman by winning her the love of a man of merit "whose character is written in her heart," as it is in the ideal city and as, conversely, the hero like the author bears her likeness and the city in his soul.

[322]

Having completed her portrait, Rousseau tells the story of her tragic fate. Suddenly the allegory becomes so translucent that an exclusively literal interpretation would be immensely perplexing.

Sophia, having grown to maidenhood, receives from her father instruction about the purposes of marriage and the principles to be followed in the choice of a bridegroom. In accordance with Rousseauist imagery the theme of marriage serves to convey ideas about the nature of the soul that may be "wedded" to wisdom and in whom the latter, in the language of the *Symposium,* may "walk and dwell and have her home." The purpose of the sacred covenant, says her father, is the common happiness, that of her parents, herself, and the bridegroom of her election. The principles prescribed to guide her are simple. She is to choose a man who would be honored by her and would also do her honor, being suited to her. The author's words are those of the *Symposium,* and the meaning is Rousseauist and Socratic at once. If she is indeed supposed to portray a wise order of human life, by her very nature she honors that of man and is honored thereby. But a man will be suited to her only if he typifies humanity at its best and in its pristine purity, not "disfigured by ten thousand ills." Such is the object of her search.

To guide her further, her father proposes an ideal of love, setting aside all other considerations. In other words, her bridegroom is to be a Socratic "lover of wisdom." The speaker urges her to seek a union of hearts, conformity of tastes and inclination, and thereby alludes to what were called the keystone of the vault of a "unanimous and harmonious" city or soul. He also alludes to the city by declaring that the law of love is that of nature, which civil laws may not oppose except at the expense of happiness and good morals. It is, however, a law or act of the will for Rousseau, as it is for the speakers of the *Symposium.* Sophia is therefore bound to obey it and remain "mistress of herself" in choosing her lover. Her task is all the more

[323]

difficult, she is told, since although she possesses spiritual riches, in the eyes of the world she is poor—as poor in popular esteem, we may add, as wisdom or the ideal city, where the word *finance* is unknown. Hence she is now bidden to follow the law of reason rather than the inclination of the heart. The apparent discrepancy in the text is a matter of semantics. The inner feeling favored above is based upon real conformities, and consequently it is enlightened by intelligence and distinguishable from sentimental dispositions that lead us, in the vicar's words, "to do other than we will." Sophia is to avoid this pitfall by consulting her parents before making her choice. In a word, that choice is obviously to be governed by the laws of poverty or necessity and freedom, which are those of the Rousseauist city and of the wisdom it serves to symbolize.

If readers are skeptical, Rousseau is aware of it. To convince us of the truth of his words, he declares that she is not imaginary and that her name alone is of his invention; for she really existed, and her memory is still mourned by a whole honorable family. Then he decides to finish the story of a girl so similar to her that it might well be her own, and so he continues to use the same name. It is necessary to finish it with him in order to grasp his meaning. This new Sophia is sent to the town in search of "a master for life," a "lover" to be her bridegroom. But her errand is vain: "she sought a soul and there was none to be seen." Consequently she chooses none. On her return home she confides to her mother that she could enjoy love and happiness only with him whose "charming image is written in her soul." The image turns out to be that of Fénelon's Télémaque, son of Ulysses and prince of Ithaca in Greece who, according to legend, died many centuries ago. Sophia justifies her choice by saying that she was not formed for a man of her century and asks whether it is her "fault" if she loves "what is not." Yet she adds: "I am not mad . . . . I am not a visionary: I do not want a prince, I am not looking for Télémaque. I know that he is only an imaginary person. I am looking for one who resembles him. And why may he not exist, since I exist, I who have a heart like his? No, let us not dishonor humanity; let us not think that an amiable and virtuous man is merely chimerical. He exists, he lives, he is looking for me perhaps . . . . But what is he? Where is he?"[17] These questions echo Jean-Jacques' "Where is Sophia? What is she?"

According to the author, her search is futile to the end. She slowly draws near death, like her prototype, while "others are thinking of forcing her to the altar." He admits at last that such love as hers is based upon notions of merit and beauty that are not to be found in nature. But, of course, neither is wisdom nor the spiritual state or city evoked by the love theme in the book, or the patriotic fervor it would generate if it ever took shape "under the sun."

Obviously an exclusively literal reading of the story would be puzzling to say the least. As in the first presentation of Sophia, here too the element of mystery is too conspicuous not to be intentional. If we use our collation to solve the enigmas, the original Sophia who really lived would be the wisdom of Socrates as Rousseau sees it. In our confused world, says the sage in the sixth book of the *Republic,* the Muse of Philosophy, beloved of the lover of wisdom and queen of the republic "is left desolate, with her marriage rite incomplete: for her own have fallen away and forsaken her, and . . . other unworthy persons . . . enter in and dishonor her . . . . Persons who are unworthy of education approach her and make an alliance with her who is in a rank above them." This passage, which inspired the fragmentary sequel to *Emile,* vividly describes the fate of Socratic wisdom in actuality, where she is mourned by a "small remnant" of "worthy disciples of philosophy."[18] The latter would be the grief-stricken "honorable family" of Rousseau's text.

The new Sophia who loves Télémaque is, of course, his own understanding of wisdom. She is the heir of the Socratic one, but is also descended from Judeo-Christian tradi-

[325]

tion. Like her forebears she honors poverty. And her fate in actuality is conceived to be as tragic as that of her Socratic predecessor since she cannot exist in the abstract but must dwell in a soul worthy of her, and none is to be found. Or rather, the new Sophia finds one in Fénelon's Télémaque and will wed only a man who, like him, is "prince" of himself and a disciple of Minerva or divine wisdom. But such a one is not of the author's century. Nor is Aemilius or the Aemilian city of the *Contract,* which do not exist, probably never did and never will. In all cases he portrays "what is not." But although he admits that he is writing about an ideal, he borrows Sophia's voice to protest with Socrates that it is not an impossible one and that he is not a visionary after all.[19] Nevertheless, since the existence of the hero and that of his city, taken in the usual sense or as a family, is far more problematical than Sophia's, her lot in life is the lot of the Socratic Muse, as we saw in the case of her counterpart in the *Levite of Ephraim.*[20]

And so Sophia dies. But the author resurrects her at once. He also resurrects Télémaque in the person of Aemilius, upon whom he bestows her. Consequently he abandons actuality altogether in evolving his myths where the lovers come to life within the world of art and thought.

This is the very theme of his "lyrical scene" or prose-poem *Pygmalion,* which is universally regarded as an important work for a study of his psychology and aesthetics.[21] Since it is textually derived from the foregoing story of Sophia and, like it and the *Levite* too, casts light upon Rousseau's view of *Emile* —facts hitherto unrecognized in published works— I must examine it briefly. Although he was not the first of the moderns to seize upon the ancient theme, which was treated in an opera-ballet by Rameau in 1748, yet later versions were inspired by the fame of his work.

Its protagonist, the sculptor Pygmalion, is obviously the author himself. In the opening lines of the poem he appears in his atelier surrounded by his works symbolized by pieces

[326]

of sculpture, only one of which is finished and that one is veiled. Similarly the *Symposium* has been compared to a statue, and in the *Republic* Socrates, the son of a statuary, uses the same comparison to describe the portraits of his heroes,[22] as we have seen. He does so because, as we know, the Greeks of his era expressed inner harmony in their sculpture and painting, not in their literature—with some exceptions like the Platonic dialogues. There is only one of Rousseau's works that in his eyes has the beauty of a finished statue, and that is *Emile*. It would therefore be designated by the single completed piece in Pygmalion's studio. In his masterwork, as we have observed, he behaves like a Socratic artist and avoids images of moral deformity that abound in his other writings. The latter, which he calls "pamphlets" by comparison with this, would be the rough casts of other carvings in the prose-poem. These sculptures have reduced their creator to a state of discouragement and apathy comparable to Rousseau's reactions after the completion of his magnum opus.[23]

The only object capable of stirring the sculptor's emotions is his "immortal work" that stands veiled like the holy of holies. In it he professes to have "surpassed the masterpieces of nature" that were the models of his art. Likewise for the writer, nothing in nature is comparable to the moral beauty expressed in his *Emile*. Pygmalion exclaims: "When my extinguished spirit no longer produces anything great, beautiful, worthy of me, I shall show my Galatea and say: 'This is my work.' " It is, he adds, "the most lovely of my works... the sanctuary of a divinity."[24]

The name Galatea reminds us of the incident in Virgil's eclogue used in the novel to illustrate the feminine mind. In the lyrical monologue or dialogue, she becomes, like Sophia herself or the bride of the Levite, a new personification of Rousseauist wisdom, which, like its Socratic and Christian origins, has an element that is called "divine" and which, later abiding in the soul of Emile, is presented in very deed as a "divinity" whose sanctuary is the temple of the book.

[327]

In the prose-poem she is a "goddess," "lovelier than Venus." As the artist raises the veil to admire her graces, he declares again: "Nothing so beautiful has ever appeared in nature; I have surpassed the work of the gods." His adoration of his own masterpiece recalls Jean-Jacques' enigmatic words in the first portrait of Sophia: "We are in love with the image we create," meaning an image of virtue and moral beauty such as the writer professes to offer in *Emile*. In this spirit Pygmalion cries out before the statue: "What! so many beauties have come from my hands... My mouth was able to... " The suspension points, which are in the text, and the allusion to the mouth confirm my suspicion that marble is used to symbolize the medium in which the artist really worked. He is dealing with language that, in the words of Socrates, "is more pliable than wax or any similar substance." Suddenly the hero of the piece wonders whether the vesture covers the nude too much, just as the author of *Emile* says that Sophia's robes are not made to conceal her charms. The sculptor decides to cut the garments lower to reveal more hidden seductions, but his hand trembles and the palpitating flesh rejects the chisel. This work, says he, is consecrated to the gods. Rousseau's Greek master says the same of the art he favors in the *Republic*.

Like Emile's Sophia, who sought a soul "written" in her heart and could not live without it, Galatea, says the sculptor, "lacks a soul" and needs one suited to her beauty. Impulsively he looks into his own and "the veil of illusion" falls, a phrase lifted right out of the first portrait of Sophia. He finds within himself a spirit where she might come to life, much as Rousseau liked to imagine that his own was worthy of the Aemilian heroine. At last Pygmalion borrows the speech of the unhappy admirer of Télémaque, though Sophia is moral beauty in love with humanity instead of the reverse as here: "Such is the noble passion that leads me astray." Moreover, as she protested that she had not lost her sanity, so he too denies that he is a madman or a visionary: "I am not in love with this dead marble, but with a living being who resembles it." This is almost a quotation from Sophia's words applied to the Fénelonian hero. Again in terms suggestive of hers, he inquires whether it is folly or a crime to be sensitive to beauty's spell. She poses the same question by asking whether it is a fault in her to love "what is not," meaning a soul made in the image of absolute beauty to which Rousseau refers later in the phrase "there is nothing beautiful but *what is not*." (Italics mine.)

Pygmalion like Sophia rejects the idea that the object of his love cannot live. Impelled by sudden hope, he calls upon the gods to give life to Galatea, invoking Venus especially, "the sublime essence" of true love, felt not by the senses but by the heart. "See this object; see my heart," says he, much as Sophia asked: "Why may he not exist since I exist, I who have a heart like his?" Pleading for a hearing, the sculptor cries: "Where is the law of nature in the sentiment that I feel?"—words echoing the author's about Sophia's love for Télémaque. The artist then offers his own life to the creature of his hands: "It will be enough for me to live in her... Goddess of beauty, spare nature this affront, that such a perfect model should be the image of what is not."[25] These are the very words of Sophia, who also rebels against the dishonor done to human nature by those who regard her noble ideal as imaginary. The same terms lend themselves to both texts since to say that the sage is unreal is to say that moral beauty cannot live.

Just as the writer resurrects Sophia to inhabit the soul of Emile, so he brings her to life in the poem, where she reappears as Galatea. The statue, moving from the pedestal, recognizes herself only in Pygmalion, while his other works with their images of a disordered world are alien to her. The scene closes much as it began, and the artist exclaims: "Yes, worthy masterpiece of my hands, of my heart and of the gods, ... I have given you all my being: I shall no longer live except through you." This means that paradoxically she resurrects the dying artist and becomes the everlasting

[329]

reflexion of the soul that fashioned her.

This interpretation of Rousseau's poem, derived from the texts of his writings, can hardly be reconciled with that of Goethe.[26] According to the German poet, Pygmalion, having put part of himself into his creation, refuses to allow the work to enjoy an autonomous existence, but insists that it be reabsorbed into his earthly life, with the result that art is dissolved in nature. Literary criticism shows that the opposite is more nearly the case and that though the artist's work owes its life to him, he, on the other hand, lives and has his being only in his art that eternizes his own apprehension of moral beauty. At least, such is the author's hope and intention, lyrically expressed in the poetic "scene" and powerfully manifested in *Emile*.

To recur to the novel, the death and resurrection of the heroine bring us to the end of the first "nave" of the inner sanctum of the Aemilian temple. Rousseau conveys the idea by spacing his text at this juncture and introducing a horizontal stroke of the pen to conclude the section devoted to Sophia or woman, where Emile's name appears significantly at the beginning and end.

EX-VOTOS

In the next or central nave, which unlike the other two bears no label, the author reverts to the hero. This section is appropriately dedicated to the latter's homage and offerings to Sophia. I say "appropriately" because, although we do not know for certain the function of the Greek chamber upon which Rousseau's is herein modeled, archeologists have surmised that it was chiefly a treasury where things of value were kept such as votive gifts made to the divinity or plunder from famous battles among men. In the central part of its equivalent in *Emile,* the young man is to make choice of Sophia and place all his inner wealth at the feet of her in whom wisdom is reborn.

Just before the friends set out in search of her, Jean-Jacques addresses the reader in a discourse matching her

[330]

father's. It too is presented by way of precepts about the principles of marriage. After wisdom's quest for a noble soul comes the soul's quest for wisdom. This one is more practical since it must take account of the conditions of life in a man's bodily abode and earthly dwelling-place. That is the real difference between the two discourses that complement each other, without being redundant.

Since in choosing a bride Emile chooses a life for all time, the matter is a solemn one. The rules he follows relate to natural affinity, institutional distinctions based upon natural ones, intellectual formation, and finally physical beauty.

In recommending "natural" affinity, Sophia's only rule, Jean-Jacques like her father emphasizes the importance of reason in its application. For just as he previously distinguished between what is "natural" in the savage and social state, so he now distinguishes between what is "natural" in the savage and civil state. Whereas in uncivilized life all women suit all men, in society love is born of a perception of diversities in character and intellect and is therefore enlightened by reason, as we have seen,[27] although it still remains a natural bond in the civil order. Consequently enlightened love must be the basis of the civil contract of marriage if the latter is to dramatize the formation of an ideal "political" association. Jean-Jacques points out that an alliance of that kind rather than one based upon distinctions of wealth and power, ensures human happiness by ministering to harmony of feelings and tastes, and the speakers of the *Symposium* say the same. The freedom of choice herein defended, unhampered by the sway of riches or prestige, corresponds to that which unites the freemen of the Rousseauist city. But in Emile's case the ruler claims the right to discover "nature's choice" since he who has made a man of the youth is in reality his father. His claims, which are also those of the Socratic ruler in the fifth book of the *Republic*, are valid since he is the law of reason that begets natural man in society. As we know, he has not waited until now to find the bride. He finally admits his

[331]

Socratic "duplicity": "this feigned search is purely a pretext for acquainting him [Emile] with women so that he may feel the value of her who suits him. Sophia was discovered long ago."[28] So was the city or wise order of the *Contract* for which the hero has been fashioned from birth as he has for her. The city, like Sophia, is supposedly suited to his nature as an active, thinking being, and the choice that favors both is primarily determined by this principle.

However, the speaker does not set aside institutional distinctions altogether, especially if they reflect natural ones like the moral and spiritual distinctions already mentioned. With respect to institutional considerations, Jean-Jacques prefers that Emile's bride be his equal in birth though not in fortune, as we know, since the author means to honor poverty in her as he does in the ideal city. But since the hero's property is probably his birthplace as his inheritance is the earth, his real wealth is herself and is the same as the essayist's in the previous part. As for equality of rank, if in actual practice it were impossible, then the ruler would select a bride in a station below her husband rather than above, so that civil order would accord with the natural one that "bids woman obey man." Symbolically this would mean that wisdom must serve human nature. If she governs man, as we have been told, she does so "as a minister [meaning "servant"] reigns in the state." In objecting to a bride of higher rank, Jean-Jacques may also mean that Emile is worthy of his consort, unlike the "unworthy persons" of the *Republic* who make an alliance with Socratic wisdom in a rank far above them. On the other hand, the governor does not favor a bride of very lowly station either, on the grounds that it would be difficult to find in the dregs of society a woman with an appropriate idea of what is beautiful and honorable, which is supposed to be her special domain.

He thereby reverts to the moral and spiritual class distinctions that he admits. But he denounces lady pedants as he does all pedants, at the same time as he exalts Sophia's

[332]

vocation in the spheres of aesthetics and spirituality. He insists that she has only moderate instruction, as she has moderate personal beauty, for moderation is the key to both beauty and wisdom. He intends her bridegroom to adorn her mind with the talents and knowledge she needs to enhance her natural gifts.[29]

Such is the governor's discourse on marriage, which, as I hinted in the antepenultimate paragraph above, has the same allegorical elements as Socrates' treatment of the same theme in the fifth book of the *Republic*.[30] The Greek sage too has his rulers secretly arrange marriages between guardians of the city and women of like nature and of similar capacity and character, both guardians and rulers representing faculties of soul related to Rousseau's reasonable will that is entrusted with the choice rather than desire. But as I have said, the master's recommendations about the choice of a bride have influenced the Rousseauist governor far less than the idea of the mythical marriage of the sage to wisdom. To this influence we must add that of other subsequent admonitions of the sage about the choice of a life. The latter occur at the end of the great classic in the vision of Er, to which I have alluded in discussing the creed. In that vision souls, in the act of choosing their lives, are advised by the sage to observe the very rules that determine the selection of Sophia. A man must, says he, seek and follow wisdom only, which teaches him to discern between good and evil, so as to choose always the better life. In making his choice, he must consider the bearing of all things upon virtue, such as the effect of beauty combined with poverty or wealth. He must study "the good and evil consequences of noble and humble birth, of private and public station, of strength and weakness, of cleverness and dullness, and of all the natural and acquired gifts of the soul, and the operation of them when conjoined; he will then look at the nature of the soul, and from the consideration of all these qualities, he will be able to determine which is better and which is worse; and so he will choose . . . ." That is exactly what Jean-Jacques has done in deciding in favor of Sophia, to whom his own philosopher-king will be wedded.

It is therefore time for the hero to find and "recognize" her. The friends begin their "journey" in search of her by bidding farewell to Paris, for, says the author, she is very far from there. Since he has already said that happiness is always close by and since it is to be found in her, the distance here must be spiritual rather than spatial and the "farewell" a symbolic one to the spirit of worldliness. Indeed, the travels of "our paladins"—for the two companions are thrice pictured as such in this context—have the same mystery about them as have all art forms. The theme can hardly be travel in the literal sense, which is treated later under that very title. The journey in this case would be a high point in the pilgrimage of life,[31] projecting the explorations of the spirit as it follows the call of an ideal of happiness and wisdom that Emile must know for what it is.

The story of his progress contains a description of the conditions of the journey that may be taken as an imaginative definition of the three requirements for the attainment of wisdom. The first is to live in the present, making the most of every experience and adorning the days with a vivid appreciation of things and the performance of good deeds. The second is to make the pilgrimage on foot, since nothing but our own effort can transport us to the goal. Rousseau, describing Emile's delight in walking, is mindful of his own pedestrian expeditions, recorded in the *Confessions,* that enriched his knowledge of men and of things.[32] Indeed, he momentarily identifies the young hero with Jean-Jacques when he writes: "If I am tired . . . but Emile is never tired." The suspension points, which are in the text, suggest that the two are one, who is the author himself recounting his own journeys in search of wisdom and happiness. He recalls ancient philosophers who were engaged in the same search and traveled the same way, as he also does in a note to the second *Discourse.* Those named are Thales, Plato, and Pythagorus, and he might have added Christ and Socrates too. "How," he asks, "can a philosopher travel otherwise?"[33] The "philosopher" is etymologically the "lover of Sophia" in the text, and the word implies the third requirement for the successful pursuit of wisdom: the love of learning. It is illustrated by the youth, who reads the book of nature and studies husbandry and natural history. All these clues suggest that the writer is describing a way of life that leads to wisdom and clothing it in myths to cover the nakedness of unembodied ideas, although he leaves us free to look no further than the myths if we so choose.

Lest we imagine that men do not go astray in the quest for wisdom, Jean-Jacques and his spiritual companion, that other and purer self, lose their way in valleys and mountains where there is no path to guide them or food to appease their hunger. The scene is reminiscent of the one in Montmorency wood at dinnertime. Here, as in the earlier one and in the allegory of the hunt in the previous part, the object is the same as in the myth of the *Republic* where Socrates and his hunting party are lost in a wood that is "dark and perplexing," in search of their quarry justice, called "the cause, condition, and preservative" of wisdom and all virtue. Once again we have the feeling that Jean-Jacques is no more lost than the sage. Suddenly a peasant appears to direct the pilgrims to a "house of peace," which happens to be Sophia's. He describes it as the dwelling of a good and generous family that is blessed by all the countryside. After more vicissitudes[34] they reach their destination, which turns out to be on a nearby hillside like the white house with green shutters in the previous part.

The reception of the wayfarers is full of mystery, suggestive of symbolism. "The house of peace,"[35] a phrase reminiscent of the "man of peace" who is the vicar, is later called a "castle," perhaps because it is a castle in Spain that suddenly appears like a mirage in the desert. But in reality it is hardly more than a farmhouse, like the Stoic's "little farm of the mind," which I recalled in connection with the essay on wealth. The pilgrims, craving hospitality,

[335]

are welcomed by the goodman of the house and conducted
to a modest guest chamber, comparable to Emile's rustic
room elsewhere in the book, or the essayist's simple lodg-
ing at an inn. There they find fresh linen garments laid out
in readiness as though this were indeed some curious
shrine. Soon thereafter supper is prepared. The scene
brings to mind the Gospel story where the disciples make
ready for the Lord's supper, as well as the *Symposium,* or
even the feast of Dido and Aeneas in Virgil's epic. But
memories of these famous banquets are all eclipsed by the
recollection of another in the Book of Proverbs where we
are told that "wisdom hath builded her house . . . : she hath
mingled her wine: she hath also furnished her table." It is at
the table that Sophia suddenly makes her entrance like an
apparition. When Aemilius weeps over the fate of her parents, who may be identified with the two main Rousseauist
laws that govern her life, she sees him as a reincarnation of
Télémaque arriving in this new isle of Calypso with his
governor Mentor-Minerva. For his part he recognizes her,
not only by her name, but also by the sound of her voice.
This is another allusion to her role as the Muse or Socratic
guardian of virtue, companion of philosophy, and counterpart of Antiope-Minerva, whose charms she combines,
however, with some of the emotional seductions of the
nymph Eucharis in the Fénelonian story.[36] The hero behaves like a man in a trance: "It is the soul of Sophia that
seems to animate him." The words may be taken literally if
we understand that, in the phraseology of the *Symposium,*
divine wisdom takes up her dwelling in the soul and receives therefrom the life that she in her turn quickens and
safeguards. The whole tableau has an emblematic flavor
that can hardly be ignored.

Rousseau himself invites us to look beneath the surface
by warning that all these details are no frivolous amusement
on his part and that this is the most valuable phase of the
book, which is "the romance of human nature" and ought
to be the story of the race. He adds characteristically that

[336]

Emile's mind, feelings, and tastes are fixed for all time by this lasting passion. In saying so, he is simply quoting from his earlier reflections on a woman's vocation that secures the most essential part of the *Contract*. The cipher of Sophia's name,[37] already emphasized in the previous part, and the mystery of their meeting serve, we are told, to intensify the hero's love of her charms, which is represented as a noble one, fostering in him a sense of propriety and honor and disposing all his inclinations towards what is good. This love of the beautiful and the good is that of the *Symposium*. The symbolism of the text is unmistakable.

It is increasingly accentuated in the story of Emile's courtship, which assumes the form of homage to a divinity. Subject to Sophia and docile to Jean-Jacques, he is, we are told, "subject to the law of wisdom" and "docile to the voice of friendship." In that state at the age of twenty he is about to experience what is described as "an intoxication ... a delirium ... the supreme happiness" of life and a foretaste of "paradise upon earth." In the light of the essay upon wealth this would be a foretaste of the ecstasy of philosophic vision that crowns the education of kings at the end of Plato's seventh book and of which they too are given a foretaste at the age of twenty, as we shall see.

This view of the "courtship" is confirmed by a second visit of the friends, who take lodgings for the summer not too far away. Emile and Sophia converse together in a garden which, we are informed, is that of the visionary white house of the essay. This earthly paradise is a suitable setting for their quasi-mystical discourse. The theme is Jean-Jacques' or the reasonable will, of which Emile speaks to Sophia as passionately as the lover of wisdom in the *Symposium* who, having found and embraced a noble soul, is "full of fair speech about ... the nature and pursuits of a good man." The power extolled by the Rousseauist hero is to preside over his union with the heroine, as it does over the enchanting city of the essay and that of the *Contract* and Socratic republic.

[337]

There is further evidence that the essay upon wealth anticipates this part and therefore casts light upon it. The courtship encounters an obstacle, in Sophia's eyes, caused by Emile's reputed fortune. Of course, since, as Socrates says in the *Symposium,* love is poor and must engage in many labors in the pursuit of good and fair things. The young man, apprised by his governor of her feelings in this respect and hitherto unaware that he is "rich," is ready to renounce all else for her sake, to have the honor of being as poor as she is and worthy of her hand. Jean-Jacques protests that she cannot be "purchased" in that way, and that what she fears is not wealth itself but its effect upon the possessor.[38] Hence Emile is bidden to offer her the treasures of his spirit by loving and serving her and her parents, for the sake not of passing fancy but of indestructible principles written in the heart. The latter are the laws of the city of the *Contract,* where the word *finance* is as unknown as it is to Emile or the essayist.

It is helpful to be conscious of the Socratic and Christian tonalities of the thought in this advice of Jean-Jacques, as well as in the essay. For example, in both cases the mood is close to that of the Sermon on the Mount. Like the essayist, Emile has presumably "laid up for himself treasures in heaven" rather than upon earth, and his heart is where his treasure is. There lie the coffers whose contents Sophia must see. The governor's advice also contains other recognizable evangelical echoes. For example, the warning that the hero may not "purchase" her seems to imply disapproval of the merchant man in the parable of the kingdom of heaven who, having found one pearl of great price, "went and sold all that he had and bought it." The same admonition conflicts with Christ's exhortation to a rich young follower who sought to attain eternal life: "Go and sell that thou hast, and give to the poor, and thou shalt have treasure in heaven." We can hardly ignore these famous parables in the context.[39] Jean-Jacques, fearful lest Emile try to buy the right to enter into paradise, adheres more closely than

[338]

they do to the divine master's conclusions that it is hard for a rich man to enter the kingdom of God. It is scarcely necessary to repeat that Socrates was obviously of the same opinion. In *Emile* the treasures offered to Sophia are of a Socratic and evangelical order.

After she is reassured, there follows the promised foretaste of paradise or of the philosophic ecstasy that provides more clues to the myths. It comes about through the intervention of Jean-Jacques, who, wearing the mantle of Mentor-Minerva, is mediator between the lovers.[40] He is the link between the heart and the object of its longing, defined as "the good that every soul of man pursues," and it is he who fulfills the aspirations of the sovereign will. Through him Sophia finally takes possession of Emile instead of the reverse, as the Socratic soul is said to be "possessed of wisdom." The effects are the same in both cases. The author portrays the "raptures," "intoxication," and "delirium" in which the ruler shares as he leads the lovers toward "the happy bond that is to unite them until death." The myth of the sage and the wisdom that suits him is becoming increasingly obtrusive.

It is highly accented from here to the end of this section. In the treasure house of the mythical shrine, Emile cultivates "music" in company with the Muse by dedicating to her all the agreeable talents he has developed, these being the arts over which the Muses preside and that preserve harmony in the soul. Rousseau writes: "As an idolator enriches the object of his worship with the treasures he loves best and decks out the altar of his God," so the lover pays homage to his beloved. He adds: "It seems to him that all beautiful things find their place only when they adorn the supreme beauty."[41] The distinction between beautiful things and absolute beauty is expressed in the words of the *Symposium* and is by now familiar to the reader of this study of *Emile* and the Platonic dialogues where the supreme beauty is the idea of good and the ultimate object of love, manifest in divine wisdom. In his tribute thereto

[339]

Emile, like the lover of wisdom in the *Symposium* who "tries to educate his beloved," offers to Sophia a summa of his studies, which are "useless" in his eyes unless they pertain to her. So we are told in words recalling those of Socrates in the *Republic*, who also calls the same studies "useless" unless they are sought after with a view to the beautiful and the good. Accordingly, the Rousseauist hero dedicates to the heroine his knowledge of philosophy, physics, mathematics, history, and religion, which at this stage are to be brought together and interrelated. In doing so, he is on his knees before her and "imagines he sees the heavens open" above him. In the rarified atmosphere of the book, with its close affinities to the purity of the *Contract* and its correspondences in antiquity, the writer's phrases have an entirely different emphasis and broader scope than similar ones in love scenes elsewhere in his other works, where images of disorder abound. Love here appears as a myth for the conveyance of philosophic experience at its best, which does not exclude a literal reading as well.

The youth's formation at this stage is patterned after that of philosopher-kings at the end of the seventh book of the *Republic* where their education is completed. There the sage insists that his heroes, trained in physical and intellectual discipline, be "industrious" in the pursuit of philosophy or moral truth. To them, as I have said, he grants a foretaste of wisdom at the age of twenty when their studies have reached "the point of intercommunion." This foretaste takes the form of a comprehensive view of their entire education and its "relationship to true being," and hence, to wisdom. The Rousseauist hero enjoys an analogous privilege, represented as the delirium of love but adhering strictly to the author's original plan for the fifth part of his book, which we have in the past accused him of ignoring. His adherence to that plan is still more obvious henceforward.

If the foretaste of ecstasy described in *Emile* with such abandon results from the fulfillment of the soverign will or law under the rule of Jean-Jacques, then, paradoxically, the condition of such blessedness is austerity. Rousseau invents more myths to emphasize this. Sophia is, he says, morally severe for the sake of preserving her integrity. For instance, she objects when Emile dares to kiss the hem of her robe in private, although her father permits him to kiss her lips in his presence. That is precisely because the natural feeling uniting them is governed not by the law of instinct or desire but by the law of reason that gratifies a man's heart by gratifying his entire nature. Indeed, in this context we are told again that civilized love, in spite of its natural origin, is very different from "the gentle habit" of nature's ways: it is based upon a perception of beauty and merit, betokened by exclusive preferences. According to the author, that is why it quickly grows into an unbridled ardor full of illusions of perfection in the beloved. Again we are free to observe that in this respect it is like a man's love for the city. The remark is all the more valid since Rousseau adds that love, giving in return as much as it exacts, begets justice. We may also draw a parallel between the austere demands made upon both patriot and lover by the object of their love. Their fervor is, in the writer's view, a betrayal of nature and of virtue only if it is accompanied by jealousy born of vanity. In that case pride replaces love, as nationalism replaces patriotism. Hence the Rousseauist myths emphasize the idea that there is a discipline or law of love and that Emile can win Sophia's esteem and find happiness only by increasing his merit in her sight.

Subsequently the author develops further the double-edged Socratic idea that in all probability suggested the foretaste of wisdom and happiness now granted to the hero: the idea that throughout the book the latter's studies all pertain to wisdom and that they are now brought together and interrelated.

[341]

To show first that Emile's education has led him toward wisdom from his birth, Rousseau proves that the youth's present passion, far from marking a break with the past, is a sign of continuity in his formation.

The writer broaches the matter by asking whether the hero, who was subject only to the laws of wisdom, is now — at the age of twenty — living an idle life at the discretion of a child. Since the word *child* is written in the masculine gender, it may refer to himself. Yet the context suggests that it refers to Sophia. The reply to the question reads: "Happy is he that is conducted to wisdom in spite of himself!" To conduct him thither by winning his love is Sophia's role in the book, and in a mythical sense she has fulfilled it from the first through Jean-Jacques.

To illustrate this, Rousseau continues to employ literary methods. He explains that the governor is like a clever artist under whose direction early inclinations, good habits, and tastes are carried forward from childhood and adolescence into "the yoke of manhood" that is docility to reason and the love of Sophia. This love, we are told, has been contrived by the "artist" because it embodies the very qualities he has been molding in the disciple at every step of the way so that the latter has only "to be himself" in order to woo her. Again Rousseau admits that the youth's passion is the governor's work. According to the text, it is not by chance that the lovers find and suit each other, that they live far apart, and that Emile's visits are few and tiring. The latter remark shows that he is not idle at all, but must work as hard as the Socratic heroes and be "industrious," or rather, "Aemilius," to court his bride. For this reason he is separated from her, we are informed, as Leander was from Hero, which incidentally explains why he learned to swim the Hellespont in the second part: otherwise, asks the writer curiously, how would he be willing to die for her? The question implies that she does indeed embody the values for which he has been taught to live and die. The symbolism of the heroine is as transparent as that of Jean-

Jacques. Emile, recognizing the latter's part in his felicity, calls himself in gratitude "the child" of his mentor. Sophia is even more aware of the governor's role as she follows his secret advice regulating the austere circumstances of their visits. In him the law of the reasonable will presides visibly over a relationship that promises to crown his work.

Rousseau next provides a summa of Emile's education so far—such as the one offered to Sophia—and thereby exemplifies concretely Socrates' idea of granting his heroes a comprehensive view of their entire education in its relationship to wisdom. He thus brings together and integrates some of the most striking images in the book, which are, however, not merely Socratic but Judeo-Christian too.

First he evokes Emile the husbandman. The youth works with peasants round about and then is suddenly transformed into an image of the Socratic[42] and Judeo-Christian "good husbandman" through the practice of beneficience and charity among them. For the object of his zeal is not simply the cultivation of the soil but especially that of the soul.

The image of the mythical husbandman is followed by a new image of the equally mythical Olympic victor of the second part who reappears in the youth of twenty. The latter can still run for cakes like other men. But like the Socratic heroes, and the apostle Paul too, he also runs a very different race with Sophia herself, who volunteers for this exercise. She is compared to Atalanta, who consented to marry only a suitor able to outstrip her in a race, and who incidentally appears at the end of the *Republic* too. Emile pursues her as he has done all his life long, though now he does so consciously. Then he lifts her in his arms and carries her to the goalpost, crying "Victory to Sophia!" as he kneels before her and confesses himself vanquished. This is surely the race for wisdom that a man may win only by his own autonomous efforts and that leads to the imperishable crown promised by the vicar in words worthy of both Paul and Socrates. In fact, we may reasonably see in Emile the

[343]

sage's "true runner [who] comes to the finish, receives the prize and is crowned" at the end of the *Republic,* winning wisdom and with it a paradise here and hereafter. Of course there is a link between the childish races and the manly one, as we foresaw in the earlier context. Indeed, Rousseau's very purpose here is to show the interrelationship of past and present. In the scene with Sophia he is saying, as clearly as subtle literary methods would allow, that the early training of the mind and will through those childish contests, and the practice of a shadowy form of justice therein, was the beginning of a race along a course culminating at the high point of spiritual formation now reached. To ignore this would be to ignore the substance of his art as a litterateur.

After the tableau of the "true runner" comes another of the mythical carpenter. Again we behold Emile "doing his own work" under a master craftsman, paying his debt to society with the sweat of his brow, and providing a new image of human justice. The text itself suggests that his real work is not the carpentering that builds material things, but rather the work of the Socratic or evangelical carpenter, namely, the practice of virtue that builds the city or temple of the soul. The deeper meaning emerges further into view when Rousseau points to the hero and exclaims "Ecce homo!" in remembrance of the carpenter of Galilee. It is even more conspicuous when Emile, visited at the workshop by Sophia, forbears to pay the master workman to release him from his contract in order that he might escort her home. By refusing to substitute money for duty, he recognizes the sacredness of contracts and proves that he is not a slave of wealth but a "lover of Sophia." So she herself says in the text. The artist is doing his utmost to draw attention to his myths and show that his real theme here is that of his original plan.

The Socratic "intercommunion" of studies ends with a tableau to show that the lover of Sophia is and ever will be the same lover of all humanity that we knew before. In-

[344]

deed, we are told that, if he would win her, he must prefer humanitarian duties to the private object of his love, although she is otherwise jealous of her rights without, however, failing to be reasonable and just.

The ideas are conveyed in another well-devised myth or parable. One day the friends are summoned to the heroine's presence but do not appear until the following morning. When they finally arrive, she betrays resentment of their apparent neglect. Jean-Jacques then relates the unhappy events that delayed their coming. They were detained by the performance of acts of Christian charity toward men of disordered life, notably an intemperate peasant—the very one who had originally guided them hither—and his unfortunate family, whose needs and sufferings they relieved on their way. When the tale is told, Emile declares courageously that Sophia cannot make him forget the rights of humanity, which are more sacred to him than hers. The just Sophia recognizes in her lover one who vindicates the universal claims of all mankind as well as her own. This brings her to consent spontaneously to become his bride. Then she too sets out, with "the zeal of charity," to minister to the afflicted family that belongs to another order of things in the world. She is called "an angel from heaven sent by God," since she too serves the "rights of humanity" by combining Christian mercy with Socratic justice. "Ecce femina!" says the author in a phrase that again calls to mind the divine master, whose wisdom is visible in her.

This allegory throws new light upon the great problem of humanitarianism and patriotism that I discussed apropos of the two creeds. Although Emile's love for Sophia is an exclusive one like a man's love for his own city, yet it does not exclude or overlook the "sacred rights" of humanity that are its source—which does not, however, make it compatible with cosmopolitanism, the love of "false" states that violate them and might even include his birthplace.[43] The rights in question spring from natural law in the sense of the law of human nature, and have hitherto been portrayed in two different spheres. In the foregoing scene they are implicit in the claims to pity made upon the friends by men of disordered life, victims of a "false," anti-social and uncivil state that frustrates human rights. Obviously a state of that kind also frustrates the laws of the just Sophia, who, however, has the same compassion for erring mankind as her votaries have. Human rights have further been portrayed in the guise of ideal Socratic friendship used as a cipher of universal natural and political bonds that are allegedly the basis of all Rousseauist society including an exclusive one like Sophia's. In that shape they generate a love of humanity in its pristine state that is as reconcilable with patriotic fervor as Emile's affection for Jean-Jacques is consistent with his passion for the heroine. For Rousseau both are essentially a love of human nature at its best, however difficult it may be for the average person to practice that love with equal intensity in its various forms.

The author touches upon the same question in many another work. In particular, his article on *Political Economy* contains a well-known passage where he contrasts Socrates and Cato, the sage and the citizen.[44] When the former lived, says he, Athens was already lost and the sage had no "patria" but the world; whereas Cato bore his in his heart, challenged Pompey and Caesar on its behalf, and died when he saw no country left to serve. The writer therefore prefers Cato. But he knows full well that Socrates too bore his city within him and that neither one had a true city anywhere else. Only the Greek master bore his in his mind instead of his heart. Moreover, he confined his patriotic fervor to that inner realm and therefore declined to challenge the gods of this world in vain. According to his words, if a man of understanding tried to resist the beast-like natures about him, "he would have to throw away his life [as Cato did] without doing any good to himself or to others." This being so, he lives apart. But if he found a state suitable to him, he would favor the life of a patriot and would have a larger growth therein,[45] although such a state would not be

[346]

best for most men. In fact, it would be a city of sages. Thus what really distinguishes him from Cato is first the quality of his "patriotism," which is intellectual rather than emotional, and then his aloof attitude toward the world as it is, as opposed to the Roman's sublime act of laying down his life in an élan of enlightened love for a city and its laws that still existed in his heart five hundred years after they had ceased to exist anywhere else. But the great sage passed beyond his theories and died a willing victim of a mere semblance of law in a state as disordered as the Rome of Cato's time. His voluntary submission after a lifetime dedicated to the discovery of true law long perplexed Rousseau; but since he died for the sake of his teaching, his death redeems him in the Savoyard vicar's sight, even though in the creed it is not considered comparable to Christ's. The writer obviously does not consider it comparable to Cato's either, since Socrates is moved by the dialectical intelligence as opposed to enlightened feelings. That is Rousseau's real quarrel with the master, which does not minimize his debt. We noted the cleavage between them in their attitude toward justice and sympathy. But in this respect the modern writer's teaching transcends not only the thought of Socrates but also the example of Cato, by the breadth of its Christian charity extended to men of ignoble life, visible in the foregoing myth of Sophia and the peasants. In Rousseau's view love of one's own city must somehow be reconciled with love of mankind, however disordered men may be, and the two are in fact as reconcilable as love of self and pity.

In other works, as we have seen, he deals with various aspects of the question of humanitarianism and patriotism. One might cite, for instance, his letter to the archbishop, where he complains that national political and religious systems do not respect the rights of humanity as they ought to do. One might also cite the *Letters from the Mount* where he is solicitous about doctrines useful to both universal and private societies and warns that in practice even the purest

[347]

patriotism, as opposed to national prejudice on behalf of the land of one's birth,[46] can still lead to the neglect of mankind. Nevertheless, he regards love of a man's own city as a more powerful motive in human conduct than love of humanity. He does so long after renouncing his Genevan citizenship, for instance, in the *Considerations upon the Government of Poland* where he favors an exclusive society based upon human rights, even if it exists only in the hearts of men as Sophia exists in the heart of Emile.

The scene where Emile sacrifices the ecstatic contemplation of Sophia to heed the call of humanity brings to an end the Socratic foretaste of wisdom and happiness and the "intercommunion" of studies entailed therein. In literary terms the lovers are to be separated for a time. One day the governor abruptly asks the youth what he would do if Sophia were dead. Since she has already been resurrected from the dead as the spirit of wisdom in the book and since, according to Rousseau, that spirit will never again be seen in the shape of a city or family, she probably has only a mythical material existence anyway, like the ideal creatures that filled the author's life in solitude. Nevertheless, Jean-Jacques reassures his disciple and then addresses him in a long discourse designed to win his consent to leave his present state of blessedness and go abroad among the "false" states of the world.

In the discourse, which has puzzled many of us in the past, the writer again handles in a literary manner the great problems of education at this stage, problems magnified by the necessity for a transfer of government from Jean-Jacques to Emile. The youth is now to be taught that the object of his love does not exist among men in the sphere of his travels, but that the energy and intensity of that love must never impair his love for our poor humanity, although it must preserve him from the unworthy passions of others.

The governor begins his discourse by asking again where happiness lies, although he has obviously found it in wisdom, even if both have reality only in a Rousseauist world of chimerical beings. He recalls the covenant of friendship to which he engaged himself at Emile's birth for the sake of his disciple's happiness that is his own. That felicity is now threatened, he says, by the enemy within, in the guise of exclusive affections with which the young man has not yet learned to cope alone since he still has a "minister of education" upon whom he relies. Jean-Jacques explains that the youth was previously subject only to the human bonds of friendship, but that now he is subject to personal attachments that give him a much more relative existence—like the Spartan's, for example—by concentrating his growing sensitivity into a smaller private whole. These attachments, says the speaker, will threaten the former ones if they are governed by the law of desire exemplified in the theater. In that respect, one might infer, they are like a man's love for the ideal city that threatens his love for mankind as it is, except in a few rare souls. Rousseau is presumably one of the exceptions according to his aforementioned statement to Malesherbes that his own love for the society of imaginary perfect beings is not incompatible with the love of humanity. Emile, who has successfully reconciled the two under the sway of Jean-Jacques, must now learn to do so himself.

In that case, according to the discourse, he must learn to rule his own heart by subjecting to the bond of necessity all desires that exceed human strength and cause misery and vice, such, one may fancy, as the desire for a corporeal Sophia. To rule himself in this way he is bidden not only to accept involuntary privations, as in the past, but also to sacrifice his feelings deliberately whenever the law of reason demands it, in order to practice an autonomous virtue.[47] He is told that he will thereby learn to follow reason and conscience, be his own master, and not only govern his passion for Sophia[48]—as Jean-Jacques has done hitherto— but subjugate all other loves, these being in all probability worldly passions for sensual gratification, gain, or glory. He is therefore advised that he must be skilled in "warfare" to face the aforementioned "enemy within," or vagrant de-

[349]

sire, especially since he runs the risk of losing Sophia, as the speaker may lose Emile or, we might add, as any man may fall from grace or fail to attain the object of his love. The thought of losing Emile prompts the governor to ask: "What would be left of me then?" By posing this question, the author hints that the hero is natural man within himself redeemed by the pledge that induced these meditations.

Jean-Jacques concludes the discourse by asking once more; "Where is happiness? Where is wisdom?" The answer implies that they do not exist in the world of actuality, to which the heroes are about to repair. For Emile is told that he must love only imperishable beauty, which in Socratic terms would be that of wisdom or the heavenly city. By virtue of an inward adjustment to the law of necessity, he must detach himself like the vicar from everything else but the object of that love which liberates the spirit and permits a man to rise above vexations and enjoy the transitory graces of this life while he awaits a better one beyond the grave.[49] In that case it is problematic whether those fragile beauties, even though they are a reflection of the absolute and constitute the Rousseauist "age of gold," include a corporeal Sophia. It is all the more problematic by reason of the governor's conclusion that, with the exception of the being "that is," "there is nothing beautiful but what is not." Surely we must infer, as we were told before, that in our disordered world she "is not," she who loves "what is not." She is meant to be not a reflection but "supreme beauty itself," as we were told, the love of which may conceivably be crowned only in death. And so, after a "foretaste of paradise" mysteriously vouchsafed to Emile in a blaze of summer sunshine, as the ghostly season approaches he is bidden to go down into another and different world to make his own practical and laborious effort toward the ideal.

The speaker of the discourse adheres closely to the advice of Socrates in the final pages of the seventh book of the *Republic* following the "foretaste" of wisdom and integration of studies discussed above. The sage, introducing his heroes to the study of philosophy—or, if we wish, initiating them into the love of wisdom—also fears lawlessness. Since that study is intended (as in the Rousseauist text) to lead them to discover the true law of justice in the inner man and to practice virtue in the highest sense, he takes precautions lest they come to regard as an amusement what ought to be an orderly and steadfast pursuit. Even later when they finally reach the "beatific vision" itself (as distinguished from the "foretaste") and are unwilling to descend to human affairs, for their souls are ever hastening into the upper world where they desire to dwell, he still ordains that they take their turn at "politics" as a matter of duty, although they do so only in "the good and true city," as he shows at the end of the seventh book. Thus Rousseau concludes the section on Sophia much as the sage concludes his study of that city. Moreover, in the next two books Socrates too embarks upon a review of evil and false states and shows how easily his kings could become slaves of passion therein. And as he sets out, he poses the question of the relative wisdom and happiness of his own state and of others, the very question framed by Jean-Jacques when he proposed to Emile that they engage in a similar survey. In both cases the answer is the same. Wisdom and happiness are not to be found among the disordered states of this world. The sage decides that his kings must be content to cultivate "divine wisdom" within or "the city within," and live accordingly. Its "pattern" is absolute beauty— Rousseau's "supreme" and "imperishable beauty"—that is not to be found on the earth and is the ultimate object of Socratic and Christian love. Hardly anything could be so valuable as the ancient text to heighten the symbolic quality of Rousseau's, since their affinities are undeniable and are abundantly disclosed in intimate correspondences of thought, word, and image.

To revert to Jean-Jacques and Emile, the latter is as reluctant as the Socratic heroes to leave the better life, and

[351]

suggests marriage as an alternative. It is rejected for three reasons. First, he wishes to wed Sophia because she "pleases" him. He has yet to understand as well as Jean-Jacques does that she "suits" him. Again the love of wisdom is governed not by pleasure or desire but by the law of the enlightened will that secures happiness. Second, he is too young for marriage. We may take this literally to mean that he may not enter the conjugal state before the age of his majority, then twenty-five,[50] or figuratively to mean that he may not be wedded to wisdom until he is ready to be released from his governor's custody, which would be at the same age. However we take it, he will be united to Sophia two years later when they are twenty-five and twenty years old respectively, the age favored by Socrates for his heroes' nuptials in the fifth book of the *Republic*. The third reason for delay is that before he enters a private civil order by way of marriage and seals his pledge to the covenant that secures it, he must know his place as a citizen therein. He must study the pattern of the city, its laws and government, as compared with existing evils, and learn "for whom he must die." These words, suggestive of the *Symposium*, refer to Sophia as though she were in reality the image of a realm for which he must live and die, as I have observed. They echo earlier ones about his tiring visits that teach him to be willing to die for her, and are related to others on the formation of the woman for whom a man will lay down his life and who sends him "to war, glory, and death at her behest."[51] Throughout the whole context here, the heroine emerges as more mythical than corporeal.

At this juncture the influence of the Christian Fénelon is again combined with that of Socrates. Emile's reluctance to face the earthly warfare necessary for virtue is so great that the governor is obliged to exercise the dictatorial authority vested in him and force him to be free, to do not his pleasure but his will. And so at the moment of parting, when Sophia has given Emile her *Télémaque* as a guide on his travels, he is "drawn away" by the superior power of

Jean-Jacques. Likewise, in Fénelon's book Mentor-Minerva is obliged to use extraordinary means to force his disciple to leave the nymph Eucharis and the enchanted island where she lives. The young prince never again sees either one. But as I have said, Sophia resembles not only the nymph but especially Antiope, the hero's betrothed, from whom he must also part for other reasons, namely, to become worthy of her by following the call of duty. The latter idea is present in the scene of Emile's departure. He leaves Sophia in order to find her again by Socrates' "longer and more circuitous way."

VIATICUM

The last nave of the mythical inner chamber of the spirit bears the title "Voyages." There are only three subtitles in the whole book, including "The Profession of Faith of the Savoyard Vicar" in the middle of the previous part, whose tripartite shape is thereby emphasized. As I have said, the other two occur at the beginning and end of the present part and have the same effect. The entrance to the first nave bears the rubric "Sophia or Woman" and is matched by this one that contains a summary of the *Contract* or a political profession of faith, essentially identical with the religious creed.

There are several reasons for the title. For example, Emile now relives the wanderings of Télémaque on a modest scale. Just as that Greek hero goes upon his travels in search of his father, Ulysses, whom he finds at last in his own city of Ithaca, so his modern counterpart goes abroad looking for the city of his heart, whose prince he recognizes at last as his own father, the new Ulysses. The title is likewise suggestive of the epic journeys of Ulysses himself, whose adventures in quest of his island home Emile has long since read in the *Odyssey*. It is also evocative of the wanderings of Aeneas, who goes through the world seeking a site for his city and finally settles in Latium where the Rome of Aemilius was born. But, as I have already pointed

[353]

out, the main source of inspiration here is Socrates, who surveys the "false states" of this world in the eighth and ninth books of the *Republic* before taking refuge in "the city within" whose "pattern is in heaven" and whose laws govern the sage's life upon earth.

The title has other implications. It is derived from the Latin "viaticum," meaning "provision for a journey." This journey in quest of the ideal city on earth is an image of the pilgrimage of life like the earlier one in quest of Sophia, where the author defined the conditions indispensable to attain that object. Here the "provision" in question is his whole philosophy, which, according to the preface, is necessary for those who wish to prosper on their way through the world and find happiness here and hereafter. To establish a psychological link between the search for the city and the search for Sophia, he has recourse to the artistic device of parallelism that always helps to clarify his meaning. For instance, in each one he warns that travel must be undertaken for love of knowledge. And in both he cites the example of Plato and Pythagoras, whose pedestrian expeditions were a form of study. Moreover, in the same way that Jean-Jacques on the former occasion engaged in a "feigned search" for Sophia, who had already been found long before, he now goes looking on earth for a city that has already been found in the place where she too exists, the domain of the heart and the mind. And just as the previous search was simply a pretext for acquainting Emile with women so that he might feel the value of her who suits him, so the present one is a pretext for acquainting him with "false" states that he might cherish the one that suits him and is "his own." These facts, combined with the presence of mystery in both texts, suggest the need for a literary rather than an exclusively literal reading.

The purpose of this second peregrination is further elaborated as the parallelism continues. As on the former journey Emile studied the great book of nature and natural history, he now studies the nature of mankind and the natural his-

[354]

tory of the race to avoid national prejudice. At the same time he examines his civic relations with his fellow citizens and consciously analyzes the nature of government and its various forms including that of his birthplace to see whether or not it is "suited to him." For, as in the case of the covenant of friendship that prompted this Odyssey, at twenty-five years of age he is free to confirm or abjure, by his choice of residence, the historical contract to which he was pledged by his ancestors. The combination of the study of human psychology and political philosophy at this stage shows that he is looking for a city patterned after the nature of man.

The difficulties confronting him are set forth by Jean-Jacques. The latter explains to Emile that the youth is soon to be released from the external authority of his governor and must rule himself independently, for the "laws" are about to make him "master of his property and of his person." Yet in the next breath the speaker warns the future "master" that he now runs the risk of depending upon everything, including his patrimony, which is presumably his birthplace. After these admonitions he is advised that he must choose his own life. Of course, he has already done so by choosing Sophia, but that was through the complicity of powers unrecognized by him until after the choice was made. And so he is told that he must decide for himself what kind of man he intends to be, how he means to spend his days and earn his livelihood, which is not, however, the main business of human life. Will he be a lover of gain or glory and seek his fortune in commerce, offices of power, the army, or finance, where he must cater to the vices and prejudices of others and fall a prey to them himself? In this vein the speaker describes the dilemma of a man trained in Socratic law to become guardian and ruler of his life, and now faced with the risk of living in a lawless society full of slaves and tyrants.

Jean-Jacques' speech to Emile virtually alludes to Plato's eighth and ninth books where Socrates describes the evil

[355]

plight of men who live in "false" states. These are the military state, the oligarchy of wealth, the democracy that in his view indulges multitudinous desires, and the tyranny where passion prevails. Such states threaten ruin to his kings. Until their majority, says the sage, their safety has been assured by the authority that the law has exercised over them "and the refusal to let them be free until we have established in them a principle analogous to the constitution of a state, and by cultivation of this higher element have set up in their hearts a guardian and ruler like our own [to give life and movement to the city within], and when this is done they may go their ways." This is the crucial point now reached by the Rousseauist hero. Jean-Jacques follows the master to the letter.

The question is, Which way will Emile go? He replies that his employment will be the practice of beneficence and justice, which, incidentally, is the employment of the Socratic and Judeo-Christian carpenter king. It is also that of Jean-Jacques, whose "work" is often said to be Emile, the cultivation of the ideal man within us. As for the "play" that men call "work," the hero chooses husbandry in order to be happy and live independently with Sophia by acquiring each day the ingredients of felicity that are health, strength, and the necessities of life. He longs only for a little "farm" in some "corner of the world" to be his own. The word "farm" (*métairie*) was also applied to the visionary white house of the essay on wealth. In the context of the book his ambition is puzzling. One of the first lessons he learned was that there was "no corner" of the world that he might call his own. If there is and it enslaves him, as he has just been warned, can he be more than a symbolic husbandman, like Jean-Jacques, cultivating his spiritual powers under the guardian and ruler that is said to deliver men from the disorders of gain and prestige?[52] On the other hand, one might also ask whether Sophia's solitude is not the farm of his fancy; and if so, why is he looking for another? The logical reply to that question is only one more

reason for suspecting that her retreat is as mythical as Fénelon's enchanted isle, especially in the light of Emile's forthcoming vain search for the object of his desire.

In his response Jean-Jacques commends the choice of
wisdom in preference to power and wealth. But he
wonders — logically enough after the parable of the
sower — in what "corner of the world" a man of property
can live free and independent, in peace and justice, without
compromising his honor, and yet manage to escape the fate
of the biblical Naboth dispossessed of his vineyard and his
life by the wicked King Ahab and his wife Jezebel? Contrary to Voltaire in the conclusion to *Candide*, Jean-
Jacques doubts whether to "cultivate one's garden" really
ensures happiness, if the famous phrase be taken literally.[53]
One may infer that if Emile is to rule his own life, he cannot
possess anything or live after the manner of the earthly cities
where he dwells. That is why the governor now sketches for
him the ideal city of the *Contract*, where the orderly relations of powers allegedly reflect those of human faculties.
This is the "pattern" to which Socrates too reverts at the
end of Plato's ninth book, and with which the sage, both
Socratic and Rousseauist, strives to conform his life.

It is not surprising that the idyll of Aemilius and Sophia
with its summa of the hero's education, implying all the
principles of Rousseauist wisdom of *Emile* and the *Contract*, is interrupted by a frank synthesis of the latter or of
Political Institutions, interposed between images of the
heroine in the innermost chamber of the mythical temple.
Rousseau could hardly say more clearly that the city to
which Emile aspires is formed by a man's pledge to wisdom
and is made to suit him as she is. The demands she makes
upon him are, like those of Jean-Jacques, set forth in its
principles and precepts that are his own. He now acquires
an awareness of their particular application to his present
circumstances.

These precepts, says his governor, are those of "political" law, called "natural and political" law to emphasize

[357]

the anthropological and ethical implications of Rousseauist citizenship. He admits that the study of true law is a "useless" science except for someone like Emile, for whom, we recall, the only useless knowledge is whatever does not pertain to Sophia. This obviously does. It is therefore comparable to Socrates' "useless" studies that are popularly so-called since they relate to the beautiful and the good instead of to shopkeeping. It is also useless since it discloses "what must be" but, alas, "what is not," and never will be except in the inner realm where the hero and heroine of the book have their being.[54] As I have said, in all cases the writer proposes a canon of moral truth that is "the nature of things" as he visualizes it. The mythical Emile is, we are told, far from indifferent to his new studies, for it is not immaterial to him to know whether the outer and inner worlds meet in one or do not. On the contrary, he who cherishes human rights is eager to find a government that safeguards them, as that of the *Contract* supposedly does, so that he might live under its rule. He is stimulated in his search by a love of justice and (moral) truth to which the author of the treatise professes to devote his work. Its principles are now to be defined by Jean-Jacques as a standard to judge the positive laws of established civil societies and guide the hero in his present plight. I shall give a simple exposition of them to underline their relationship to the context here.

The young man, about to be "set free," is told that all men by birth naturally free and independent. And he who intends to dispose of his freedom by entering into a union with Sophia is made to realize that human beings can be united only by an act of the will (or law), since force cannot produce any permanent bond between them. This instruction about the nature of a genuine union among men is equally true of an integration and correlation of faculties within the soul. Emile is himself intended to be an example of such a harmonious whole, of one whose virtue is not what Socrates calls an enforced virtue. He may therefore

[358]

conceivably achieve happy self-expansion in the exercise of paternal rule, which Jean-Jacques discusses in his synthesis. Of course, that rule is an image of the rule of law that is as rooted in the nature of man as fatherhood is, and that the disciple is now to exercise autonomously. According to the governor, a father—the Socratic symbol of law—has the same restrictions as that organ of the human will and his authority over his children is limited to what is "useful" to themselves. He adds, moreover, that at the age of reason they become the judges of such "usefulness" and masters of self, as his own disciple is destined to be. If they continue to obey the father or submit to another in his place, as Emile defers in the end to the laws of which he is begotten and which, in the person of Sophia, preside over his whole life, it is of their own free will. According to the speaker, slavery pertains not merely to the thralldom of bodies but to the repression of the human person and of inner life or morality that springs from the free operations of conscience and reason required of us by nature herself. It is she who ordains that men govern themselves as Emile is now bidden to do.

Men bear rule, the governor continues, or delegate it to others freely according to their will, by favor of a prior conventional bond or covenant that creates civil society, as it also does moral man. He formulates the familiar words of the covenant of promise. By its terms, as we know, individuals—like individual powers and desires within man—subject themselves and all they have to the sovereign power or active thinking being and become an indivisible part of a moral collective whole that represents civilized or humanistic man born of the act of union. Since Emile exemplifies the engagement in himself, he will see it as that of Rousseauist moral man who is social and civil man. Such a man, the governor explains, is committed to the sovereignty of his own higher being and applies this principle in the disposition of his life. Although the hero's personal commitment has been freely assumed in en-

[359]

lightened forms of love and moves him spontaneously to seek his happiness in that of the objects of his love, or rather, in the gratification of conscience and in the service of wisdom, he must now learn that the bonds formed by that commitment are a law, the one and only fundamental law of the moral being. The pledge can be renounced, says the governor, only if it proves harmful, which, to his mind, is preposterous. The human will it hallows and exalts seeks only the good of the integrated person as a whole and can have no other object, for, as the vicar said, men are free to will their good but not to harm themselves according to their "pleasure."[55] Injury, says Jean-Jacques, could hardly come to the various parts from inner adjustment to the spiritual sovereignty proposed, which need therefore give no guarantee of fidelity to the pledge. Harm could come only from a betrayal of the engagement by the parts themselves, such, for example, as might arise through the desire for gold or glory that enslaves the soul. Emile, who has been taught to respect his promises as sacred and to rule by obeying his own sovereign will, has already learned the advantages of doing so. One of these, says the governor, is freedom, meaning freedom to obey the self that is made to rule, and to pursue the human spirit's loftiest aspirations. Another advantage, which would allegedly ensue, however, only if the human will were enshrined as law in objective reality, is the protection of Rousseauist property. But since this is not the case, Emile's coveted vineyard is not safe; and, as we shall see, he will have to find the necessities of life in some other way. Such is the bearing of the first part of the *Contract* on the hero's present problems.

Jean-Jacques synthesizes more briefly the following two parts of that work. He ponders over the nature of law as an act of the sovereign will applicable to the entire moral person, as opposed to the acts of partial factions that divide a kingdom against itself.

This raises the question of the application of law in particular cases. The moral person, says the speaker, may transform itself into a democratic governing body for the purpose of appointing leaders to do its will, if it so chooses. But, he warns, such leaders are neither sovereigns nor representatives of sovereignty in which they share but which can never be alienated to them as individuals. They are merely officers of the people, and as subjects of the law are entrusted with its execution and the maintenance of civil and political freedom. By emphasizing the importance of self-government in rulers, he suggests that it is perilous for a man to entrust the "helm" to anyone but himself, or rather, his own best faculties, if he is to be properly governed and his freedom safely ensured. Emile exemplifies this. To show the hero the need for objectivity in acts of the governing power, Jean-Jacques, like the author of the *Contract*, represents the ruling faculty in geometrical terms as intermediary between subject desires and sovereign will, all of which must do their own proper work indicated by the nature of each. He exposes the perils of government in far-flung realms where a man hardly shares in sovereignty at all and where manners and customs are at variance with law. Analogously the same evils would arise in the soul of one who, instead of expanding spiritually, extends his being through time and space in search of wordly benefits. He explains that in such cases the governing power is necessarily intensified for purposes of active life, but then it allies itself with lawless elements and private interests to silence the moral will of man. Proceeding from these considerations, he summarizes the ideas of the *Contract* on the various forms of government, their rectitude and effectiveness, and suggests that aristocratic rule, which is that of the reasonable will, suits a state—or a man—whose range is that of neither giant nor dwarf but is of natural and normal proportions like his disciple's. At the same time he warns that government is capable of as many forms as the state has citizens, implying that the only true one is self-government, for which the young man has been trained from the first, and which is of course entirely consistent

[361]

with aristocratic but not democratic rule.

He crowns his discourse by developing the brief "Conclusion" of the *Contract* that was to be treated in the work *Political Institutions*. This is the only chapter of the fourth part of the treatise to which he alludes and the only one that remains to be included in this collation. The writer of the *Contract* states simply that his book, to be complete, would have to take account of the external relations of the ideal city in war and peace. These relations, he says, would be governed by international laws enforced through federation. As we have observed, the idea is extravagant if he envisages an affiliation of many mythical cities, since the existence of one is hard enough to imagine. And how could he suppose an association of his "true" state with the "false" ones of this world, to use his own Socratic expressions? Or in his favorite Pauline terms, can there be any accommodation of his covenant of promise to the covenant of bondage allegedly prevailing in our midst? He has consistently rejected the idea. Hence in the *Contract*, where the city appears miraculously materializing as such, the problems of external relations seem purely academic and are not developed. Of course if we pierce the imagery, they are as real as they are in *Emile,* since the city seen as a magnified image of a well-ordered life might indeed come to the birth in a human soul as it does in the novel, where the matter of external relations is critical. Emile, though bound to great spirits of the past and present, must also live among "false" states and learn not only what his relations with them might be but also what their own are with each other. Jean-Jacques illustrates these problems in the conclusion of his discourse.

He paints a melancholy picture of what he and his disciple have beheld in the world and what we can see for ourselves not merely in life and history but also in the eighth and ninth books of the *Republic:* the wretched state of men perpetually buffeted in their internal and external contacts with each other, and subject not to law but to tyrannical

[362]

passions that create a state of warfare within and among them and expose them to foreign conflicts as well. Their misery, he says, is the result of an imperfect historical evolution that combines the evils of an allegedly "natural" state of independence with those of a so-called "civil" condition of slavery. In his eyes this combination of evils explains the futility of past attempts at federation, since he can visualize affiliation only among "true" states possessed of sovereignty. By contrast with this course of events, the Aemilian order is presumed to combine the supposed advantages of the Rousseauist natural and civil order, freedom and morality.[56] But Emile has learned that to expect to find his city and its laws in the sphere of actuality is both absurd and undesirable, for then virtue would be a matter of habit and necessity and men would be like blocks of wood, or "posts," as we remarked. He says so, observing that he and his governor seem to be "building" their "edifice" with wood instead of men. On the other hand, any sort of alliance of the Aemilian city with our disordered world is just as absurd and undesirable, although Emile will not withdraw altogether and a society of friends or city of the heart is never impossible.

After the pattern of the *Contract* has been revealed, the ruler identifies the city of his fancy with the Fénelonian one in *Télémaque*, transfigured not only by the wisdom of Mentor-Minerva but also by Christian charity. According to him, if the friends search for it in vain that is because, unlike Fénelon's heroes, they are neither God nor even king in the usual sense of the word and so they cannot imitate those models by re-creating cities and their rulers but must content themselves with doing the good that is the work of men. Indeed, they would decline to rule over others even if they could: "If we were kings and sages, the first good deed we should do for ourselves and for others would be to abdicate our kingship and become ourselves again." Of course they *are* kings and sages; but their kingship is not of this world, and the Rousseauist philosopher-kings do not rule in objective reality. Nor do the Socratic ones, as we see at the end of Plato's ninth book where the sage reverts to the soul. The Rousseauist philosopher-king, like the Socratic, rules over himself and his own city or inner realm without trying to convert other people living outside the covenant except by the force of his example. To try to change them in any other way would, in his eyes, be not merely unrealistic but unlawful and immoral, a violation of all the principles of *Emile* and the *Contract*, as well as of the *Republic*. For him the impulse for reform must come from within the human spirit. Men cannot be "forced to be free" unless they are already committed to the covenant and its laws by an act of their own enlightened will and are themselves the ordering agent.

Apart from this basic difference, Jean-Jacques' city is indeed the Fénelonian one. The travelers examine the tokens of good government, defined by Fénelon exactly as they are here and in the *Contract* and related works.[57] A good administration in the sight of both writers favors population by encouraging marriages. This criterion accentuates the value of the governor's work in *Emile,* which fosters marriage as an image of the autonomous inner bond of a man with his highest self. The same criterion also provides Rousseau with a new pretext to underline the primacy of volition in the contract by specifying that the conjugal union, like any other, must not be an effect of force, or laws against celibacy, which are as bad as those enjoining it. He protests against such enactments, even though, in his *Project on Corsica* — in the region of imperfect actuality — he discriminates against celibates by limiting them to the class of aspirants to citizenship.[58] A further sign of good government for himself and Fénelon is the even distribution of population over the whole territory in agricultural districts outside the urban center of the city-state. This is illustrated by Jean-Jacques' rule in *Emile* that is represented as particularly effective in rural surroundings, as we know. The friends on their travels verify the author's fond illusions

[364]

that men closer to nature are also closer to goodness. In the society of country folk the young man's virtues are supposed to run less risk, although his aegis at all times is his love for Sophia.

The denouement of the novel begins at this point, as Rousseau indicates by the use of spacing and a horizontal line. The last conversations of the travelers refer back to questions posed when they set out in search of wisdom and happiness. With that object in mind, what conclusion has Emile reached about his future? This is tantamount to asking which is more conducive to his goal: the Rousseauist covenant that aims to secure the life and liberty of persons, or the historical one that consolidates property? Or how can fidelity to the one be reconciled with the demands of existence under the other? Such is the theme of the hero's dialogue with his governor, treated not abstractly but through cunningly contrived myths.

Since this is the case, and since the myths are largely inspired by the second half of Plato's ninth book, it would be helpful to recall the latter before broaching the Aemilian text. I was obliged to allude to it earlier since, in the preamble to the separation of Emile and Sophia and again at the outset of the peregrination abroad, Rousseau reviewed the *Republic* cursorily from the end of the seventh book to the end of the ninth. In the present context he exploits the latter more fully and leaves me no alternative but to revert to it. There the sage solves the problem of wisdom and happiness posed by himself as well as by his modern disciple, as I have said, when they began their survey of false states. He concludes that the happiest of men is the lover of wisdom who is master of himself and knows a felicity that the votaries of gain and glory do not know, which is the fulfillment of the human spirit according to its nature. Speaking of the others who engage in injustice to indulge their lusts, he warns them that it is ignoble and unprofitable to happiness to enslave the god in man to the beast. He contrasts them with the sage who is ruled by divine wisdom within that

[365]

suits his nature and who preserves his freedom of action by regulating his property and prestige so as to guard against the sway of wealth or power, which cause disorder in the soul. Such a man is statesman and ruler in the aforementioned "city... within him." It is not the land of his birth but a city that "exists in idea only" and whose "pattern" is laid up in heaven. He "will live after the manner of that city, having nothing to do with any other." This Socratic text is the inspiration of Emile's dialogue with Jean-Jacques.

The hero, like the Socratic sage, finds happiness in the wisdom of the "true" covenant and remains as his governor has made him, faithful to "nature and the laws." Thus he ratifies the pledge of friendship again, before applying it in the intimate domain of the soul, and promises to be loyal as man and citizen to the "natural and political law" of the *Contract*. He discusses the two theoretical advantages: freedom and security of life or Rousseauist property. The freedom he enjoys is the Socratic liberation of his noblest faculties. But in the present order of things it entails detachment from all property. This includes his coveted vineyard or "corner of earth," which would, he says, threaten his spiritual freedom through the intrigues of covetous desire. It also includes his mysterious inheritance which, as I have said, is probably his birthplace and would constitute, in the terminology of the *Contract* "the public domain of the sovereign," if men were indeed sovereign in the land of their birth. But in the book they are not. And under the covenant of bondage a man's needs (Rousseauist property) are at the discretion of other men's passions. He explains his dilemma thus to his governor: "When you wanted me to be at once free and without needs you wanted two incompatible things for I cannot withdraw from dependence upon men except by returning to dependence upon nature."[59] Hence in an earthly society the two objects of the "true" covenant are incompatible, as we suspected from the first. In choosing the covenant that frees the spirit even for the

victim of other people's passions, Emile is forced to renounce security in the matter of needs, which would in-
volve dependence upon men that enslaves. He withdraws
from such dependence and declines to rely upon his inheritance. If it subjects him, he will abandon it, providing for
his needs as best he can and facing privations and death
itself under nature's law of necessity. In his view submission to that law frees him from enslavement to men, so that
his faculties can perform their appointed tasks, the wise will
exercising its natural sway over desire. The same law is, of
course, also that of Jean-Jacques, whose disciple again recognizes him as the "father" who begot him. Emile concludes that all he needs to be happy is Sophia or what
Socrates calls in the analogous text "divine wisdom dwelling within." Such are the hero's conclusions about wisdom
and happiness, imparted in the form of highly suggestive
allegories that naturally lead a classical scholar to the
Platonic myths.

In his reply Jean-Jacques again commends the choice of
wisdom. In his opinion the disciple is wise not to seek freedom under the sway of the laws of passion or property,
which are those of bondage. It is to be found, says the
governor confirming the young man's words, in obedience
to the eternal laws of nature and of order, or rather, of
conscience and of reason written in the heart of the sage
and replacing all others in his life. Thus he describes the
laws of the *Contract,* as readers are beginning to suspect,[60]
and the sage is Emile. Those laws are kept, after the example of the Mosaical stone tablets, in the ark of the covenant
within the mythical temple where the city exists and Sophia
resides. The hero, like Socrates and Cato or the citizens of
Rousseau's new Poland, bears his city in his person. Indeed, the author says in the *Considérations* that the true
sanctuary of laws and government is not to be found in
fortresses, which will forever be taken by tyrants, but in
citadels within,[61] by the effects of education or legislation
answering to man's nature and the decrees of his highest

[367]

faculties. So far the ideal is basically the one in the *Republic,* however suffused with emotion.

Subsequently Jean-Jacques appears to modify his disciple's Socratic attitude. Unlike the Greek heroes Emile is not to withdraw completely to the city within. He *must* have something to do with other states. He has duties as a citizen in his birthplace, even if "his own city" and its laws do not exist in external reality. Here the speaker observes the Socratic distinction between the two: *pays* and *patrie.* The former allegedly has only a caricature of a contract, semblances of laws and appearances of government that are nevertheless traces of order to be found in actuality, reflections of the IDEA of harmony. They have therefore served to make him love the good and abhor evil. Moral action of that sort is possible only in human society, however imperfect. Of all men, says Jean-Jacques, the hero alone will sacrifice his interests to the common good, be just among the wicked, and rule like a philosopher-king over himself. If we ask why a man would practice virtue among anarchists and immoralists, the reply is to be found throughout *Emile,* the *Contract,* and the *Republic* and is restated by Socrates in the text that inspired the dialogue of Emile and his governor: the sage, unlike most of us, is convinced that justice and wisdom, by their very nature, suit the nature cf the soul, since he regards them as an orderly disposition of human faculties according to the proper or normal function of each, and finds happiness therein. The Rousseauist governor, in representing his disciple as "the just man" among the wicked, implies like Socrates that injustice suffered by such a one is as powerful a motive for the harmonious and felicitous operations of the soul as justice obtained.[62] Nevertheless, the ancient sage favors withdrawal, whereas Emile is bidden to live among his compatriots and there to practice virtues fostered by the "true" covenant of whose nature and existence they are unaware. Unlike the writer, he is told, he need not live in exile since he has not assumed the sad task of speaking the truth to men, but his "example

[368]

will serve them better than all our books.'' That example is, however, enshrined in a book that is intended to provide an image of a kind of wisdom and happiness accessible to anyone.

The hero's return to his birthplace is explained in the novel not only by the need for the presence of a pattern of well-ordered life in a haphazard society but also by the hope that that pattern may materialize in visible form beyond the person of Emile. This faint hope is founded upon two unlikely hypotheses: that the family may in some exceptional case become what it could be but paradoxically never will be, and that it may in turn expand its influence through a patriarchal pastoral life that Jean-Jacques now mysteriously recommends to his disciple, who, however, has no farm in the material sense and never will have. Indeed, the governor having admitted that there is no corner of the earth where Emile may live in peace with Sophia, and having counseled him to return to the land of his birth, paradoxically directs him back to that corner where she abides, although we know that they had to "travel" far from his birthplace to find her. In the country where she dwells, says he, gentle natures are still to be found, benificence may yet bear fruit, and men may revive the desert solitudes. But the hero must always be ready to emulate his Roman forebears and leave the ploughshare to serve his *patria*. Together with Fénelon,[63] Rousseau clung to his dream of a golden age of rural and family bliss. Yet the paradoxes in the text betray his skepticism and make a literal reading virtually impossible, though some readers may disagree.

The question arises as to whether there is a real cleavage between him and Socrates in this context. Admittedly the Socratic philosopher withdraws altogether from our unruly world whereas Emile does not, although sometimes the latter's desert solitudes dangerously resemble withdrawal. Nevertheless, the Rousseauist hero does indeed have relations with a chaotic world, as we have seen; and their nature, as illustrated earlier, underlines the other distinctions

[369]

between his creator's thought and that of the Greek master: Emile's city and its laws are enshrined in the heart as well as in the mind; they extend justice to include mercy, and enlarge the scope of sympathy to embrace enemies and men of lawless life. These are serious differences between the two thinkers. Moreover, the Rousseauist hope of material expansion through family or rural life and the emotional images of both are obviously quite foreign to Socrates. But even for the sage's modern disciple they are unrealistic and paradoxical; and in any case, as I said earlier in the chapter, images and settings do not change the essential identity of thought, which is, however, greatly christianized in Rousseau's case.

To bring out more forcefully the close relationship between his concept of the good life and the master's, despite their differences, we must look to the end of the tenth and last book of the *Republic* where the love of simplicity and "golden mediocrity" is also exalted. There in the Socratic vision of Er, Odysseus or Ulysses is reborn, as he and Télémaque are in *Emile*. Indeed, he is the last of a host of souls to be reborn into the world and to choose a new life among the "samples of lives" set before them. And he chooses the same simple life as the Rousseauist hero. The ancient text reads: "... Disenchanted of ambition... he [Ulysses] went about for a considerable time in search of the life of a private man who had no cares; he had some difficulty in finding this which was lying about and had been neglected by everybody else; and when he saw it, he said that he would have done the same had his lot been first instead of last, and that he was delighted to have it." The choice of the wise Ulysses is also Emile's, though in the former case there is no question of family or farm. Rousseau's affinities with Socrates are visible even when he pretends to oppose him.

Jean-Jacques' circumspect advice to his disciple resembles that of the vicar to the exile and further justifies my comparison of the religious and political creed. The similarity is impressive. In a far land the vicar confessed his natural faith to the outcast and disclosed a celestial pattern for the ordering of human life. But at the same time he urged his protégé to return to his own land and faith even though neither conformed to the heavenly model, there to practice the lesson of detachment. Jean-Jacques teaches the same lesson. In some distant clime he reveals to the exiled Emile the principles of natural and political law, divinely inscribed in the heart of the sage, as a source of harmony in human affairs. Yet he sends him back to his own country where chaos allegedly prevails, that he might rise above it. The two texts are perfectly symmetrical. Moreover, the conservatism of both, which is, of course, that of the *Contract,* is striking. Nothing could be less revolutionary than they are.[64] There is no question of changing material things in objective experience but only of changing life by the action of the spirit. The writer's conservatism is further accentuated by his lofty idealism and use of mythical forms, as well as by his skepticism. Not that he doubts the reality and feasibility of the version of moral truth proposed. But he has no faith in men's willingness to achieve it.[65]

To conclude the story, the governor's happiest day dawns when his work is consummated and Emile is wedded to his bride. They are united "in the temple" by an indissoluble bond, after having loved one another for three years and sought one another for a lifetime. The "temple" is surely not the place of darkness in the second part, nor yet the symbolic hostel in the fourth. It must be the mythical one of the soul and of the book where the betrothal originated. As for the ceremony, it may be taken as a marriage in the literal sense if we wish. But *Emile* is a literary work wherein the symbolism of marriage, which has already emerged into the highest possible relief, can hardly be ignored in the present context, especially since for the writer there is only one "indissoluble bond," namely, that which sanctifies all others and upon which fidelity to every other engagement depends. This is the Rousseauist covenant or

[371]

social contract, which finally takes the form of a civil contract externalized in marriage in accordance with the Calvinist view.[66] These considerations are enough to make us
suspect that we are now witnessing the sacred nuptials of
the sage, corresponding to the mythical "marriage rite" of
the Socratic philosopher-king and the Muse, his queen, anticipated in the sixth book of the *Republic,* where the Greek
master broaches the education of his kings, and consummated at the end of the seventh. Indeed, we can hardly fail
to see that Rousseau is portraying an initiation into the
ultimate beatific vision of wisdom, a "foretaste" of which
was previously granted.

This interpretation is confirmed by the marriage ceremony itself, of which we have, in fact, a detailed account.
The latter is to be found in a discourse of Jean-Jacques
addressed to the lovers, wherein some of us have in the past
accused the writer of questionable taste.[67] In reality there is
nothing salacious or unsavory in the text. The reason for
the misunderstanding is that we have failed to recognize the
monologue as an imaginative projection of the marriage rite
performed by the ruler, as is the case in the *Republic*. Indeed, it concludes with a sacramental "treaty." The word
occurs twice as it did in the first part of the book in reference to the covenant of Jean-Jacques and Emile.[68] It accentuates the link between the beginning and end and is
another clue to the mythical quality of the present scene
where the governor himself presides over the "sacred"
union of the true prince and wisdom, which is visualized in
an allegorical manner outside the "temple."

The controversial solemnities begin when he proposes to
the bridal pair a way of prolonging the happiness of love in
marriage to create a paradise, a diminutive city of the
blessed, upon earth. The object can be achieved, he says, if
those who engage themselves forever to "the most sacred
of contracts" perpetuate their commitment by the constant
action of enlightened love. In other words, Emile must continue to be a "lover of Sophia," or philosopher, while she,

[372]

for her part, must continue to suit and please him by preserving the integrity of her nature. Socrates is of the same
opinion.[69] The Greek sage, having said that licentiousness is
forbidden in his city where matrimony is sacred in the highest degree, contrives marriages between the best men and
women at the prescribed age who "breed only with the
sanction of the rulers," or rather, ruling faculties in the
soul. These faculties, which have been formed in Emile to
make him ruler of himself, are still personified in Jean-
Jacques, who is performing the last act of his Socratic mission. He still embodies the enlightened will that governs
desire in the union of hero and heroine. And so he formulates the covenant anew whereby Emile enters a select society of just men who hold sway over themselves.

It contains the same "clauses" as the one in the first part,
which is definitively ratified now that the hero is of age.
First, he and his bride are to remain faithful to the covenant
that unites them since fidelity is "the most sacred of all
rights." That is because it signifies obedience to the one
and only fundamental law. But this clause has an essential
corollary to provide for the correlative of obedience which
is consent. The union of Emile and Sophia is not an effect of
force. To illustrate his meaning, the governor objects to the
"constraint" of so-called conjugal rights and contrives to
make each of the consorts exclusively dependent upon the
covenant's law of love or enlightened feeling. He would
thereby avoid all "subjection." In that way, says he, a
man's lawful love for his bride will be stronger than any
lawless desire for the "stranger." That is the theme of an
Old Testament passage already cited in the previous chapter. It is also the theme of the Pauline allegory of the two
covenants represented by the free woman and the
bondmaid who are the covenant of promise and of bondage
to which I have alluded, corresponding to the Rousseauist
and historical one. Jean-Jacques' allegorizing expresses the
idea that "hearts are bound" by the former "but bodies are
not enslaved," for the enlightened love or act of consent

[373]

that gives rise to it becomes itself the only law.[70] Under its sway, according to his words, the contractant remains "master of his person" and exercises his will freely in order to win for himself the only lawful happiness that leaves the human spirit intact and springs from wisdom herself. Such are the two clauses of the "treaty," which is not for that reason a "double" one as we have hitherto supposed.[71] Emile subscribes to it, and this may be taken as the "marriage" ceremony. Since the covenant is in the very nature of Rousseauist wisdom whose spokesman is Jean-Jacques, he answers for Sophia without consulting her. He says so. The allegory portrays in a literary manner the civil rights of the Rousseauist citizen.

After establishing the sovereignty of the will in his first discourse, the speaker institutes the ruling power in a second one, addressed to Sophia alone. In the past it has met with the same fate as the other on our part. This time he is curiously careful to make a distinction between the usual relationship of a man and his bride and that of Emile and Sophia. Emile is the head whom the woman obeys, but since, in this case, she is Sophia, he is to be "led" or "conducted" by her. The word is the same one previously applied to Jean-Jacques' government of his disciple. The reason is clear enough, as we have seen. As the governing power of a city or moral person executes the sovereign will to give movement to the active thinking being, so Sophia makes an appeal to the heart to implement the commands of reason and ultimately secures them by fostering the habit of order as a principle of moral growth. The speaker exhorts her to reign over herself as well as Emile, for then she can recall him to "wisdom," to "virtue and reason," or rather, to herself, if he chances to stray. For the governor warns that the ecstasy of love does not last forever. One may observe that it lasts no longer than that of philosophy or virtue, which it is suited to symbolize. It is not a permanent state of soul, and in the end is replaced, says he, by a "sweet habit" that unites a man for all time with the bride

[374]

of his choice, corresponding to the Socratic "life of his choice." Such is the dialectic that leads to the establishment of Sophia's reign, which may or may not be that of a woman but is surely that of Rousseauist wisdom. Again the basic "treaty" is confirmed and the little city set in motion, certainly within the soul and perhaps also within the family.

Once the moral person is autonomous and the habit of order is secure enough to replace laws, Jean-Jacques withdraws, like Mentor in *Télémaque,* the Socratic image of law in the *Republic,*[72] or the Pauline one in the Epistle to the Galatians. He does so, he says, in favor of "another." The word is in the masculine gender, like the "child" that ruled Emile in an earlier text. Moreover, the governor, in retiring, says to the hero: "Today I abdicate the authority you entrusted to me and here is your governor." The latter word, too, is masculine, *gouverneur,* instead of the feminine equivalent.[73] Nor is the name of Sophia even mentioned at this juncture. Again one is inclined to see in her a mystic companion who has entered the mythical temple where alone she belongs. Jean-Jacques' transports of emotion and tears of joy as he beholds his work in the fullness of its consummation are comparable with those of Pygmalion. In Sophia he abides with Emile all the days of his life, like Télemaque's Mentor, who disappears into the empyrean promising the hero: "My wisdom will never leave you . . . It is time that you should learn to walk alone." One suspects that Emile too is now walking alone in the midst of an invisible company of lofty spirits evoked in the essay on wealth, the letters to Malesherbes, the *Confessions,* and the *Dialogues.*

However, the imagery of marriage provides the author with an opportunity to express once more his preference for private education. The book closes with Emile's announcement that he hopes soon to have the honor of being a father. Unlike other fathers he will educate his own son, to make him into a man and citizen. Again the ending stands in counterpoise to the beginning where Rousseau proclaimed

[375]

unequivocally that it is a father's duty to educate his children and raise up citizens to the state, and that domestic training is the only hope of salvation for modern society. Yet even this turn of events may be taken in a literary rather than exclusively literal sense. It may be interpreted in the light of Socrates' discourse in the *Symposium*. If so, it would mean that Industry wedded to Wisdom begets not merely mortal children but an autonomous spiritual being generating the moral beautiful, temperance, justice, and all the virtues that may spring from such a union to perfect human society. In that case domestic education would represent the self-discipline of the autodidact, which transformed the young scapegrace of the central pages into the wise Savoyard vicar and now promises to bear fruit in the life of some new disciple reborn of Emile.

Before concluding, I should like to recall the role played by the *Republic* and the *Symposium* in this part, in order to accentuate the theme as that of the original plan. Under the title "Sophia," Rousseau objects to Socrates' ideas on the education of woman in the fifth book of the *Republic* but like the sage in another context uses her to personify wisdom as the object of his hero's love, a theme that he handles according to the teachings of the *Symposium*. He then reverts to the same fifth book to show that it is the ruler who decides upon the choice of Emile's bride. Since that decision implies the choice of a life that is the subject of the vision of Er in the conclusion to the *Republic*, he turns to the famous text for further inspiration. In the middle part where he deals with the courtship of Sophia, or foretaste of the beatific vision, he finds his point of departure in the climax of the formation of kings at the end of the seventh book of the great classic. In the pages on travel and the pattern of the city unlike all others, he goes to the eighth and ninth books to show that the world is full of false states and that the only true one is the "city within" where the hero finally takes refuge, though he lives in the world as we know it. At the end, where there are more echoes of the vision of Er, the nuptials are those of the Socratic ruler and queen of the city, presided over by a true philosopher-king according to the Greek sage's advice. These affinities are impressive. Yet the substance bears the stamp of Rousseau's spirit wherein the heart and feelings play a role not accorded to them in the model. The sphere of action in his case is therefore less abstract and more familiar. He takes the Socratic world of dialectic, animates it with feeling, and brings it into the domain of ordinary life, transfigured by insight and poetic genius.

Besides, however deeply his myths and ideas are rooted in Socratic tradition, they are just as deeply embedded in Judeo-Christian imagery and belief. An example of particular relevance here is the idealization of woman that is Judeo-Christian in tone and implications, in spite of the close affinities between Sophia and the Socratic Muse. The woman to whom *Emile* is dedicated is a combination of both strains of our culture. She is the mythical Sophia, that "chimerical" spiritual and social order of the *Contract* which, in the eyes of Rousseau, could alone restore peace to human life, but never will.

1. Here we are led into what George Eliot, in *Romola*, calls "the inner chamber and sanctuary of life" or "the inmost cell of consciousness" (The World's Classics [London: Oxford University Press, n.d.], pp. 256, 347).

2. One chapter of the *Contract* remains to be discussed: see the section entitled "Viaticum" in this chapter in the conclusion of the summary of the *Contract*.

3. *See, for example, O. C., 4:lxxxvi.*

4. See chapter 2 above. In the past, few of us have connected the beginning of *Emile* with the end, or taken the latter seriously. Broome, in *Rousseau: A Study of His Thought* (London: Arnold, 1963), pp. 100 ff., shows that past interpretations border on the ridiculous.

5. Cf. Plato *The Symposium* (Diotima's speech reported by Socrates).

6. Rousseau was seduced by the idea as he interpreted it in his early youth, but in his literary debut was already wondering about its value thus interpreted: see, for example, the dedication of the second "Discours." Cf. the discussion of the family early in chapter 2 above.

7. In this context Burgelin, commenting upon the linking of love and perfection, refers to the *Symposium* and *Phaedrus: O. C., 4:743 n. 1.*

8. In connection with the fifth part of "Emile" Burgelin recalls the Platonic theme of pedagogical love, but does not develop the idea since that is not his task: *O. C.*, 4:cxxvi.

9. Cf. *The Republic* 4. 424; 6. 499. Cf. also Prov. 8:22-30, ending thus: "Then I was by him, as one brought up with him.... "

10. Rousseau's guide is always the nature of things as he sees it: "Emile," p. 837; "Contrat social," pp. 378, 393. In the present context (p. 712; cf. 714 and 732) he quotes the maxim of Leibnitz and Pope: "Whatever is, is right." Cf. "Lettre à Philopolis," *O. C.,* 3:233. For Socrates' warning against lawlessness in amusements see *The Republic* 4. 424.

11. "Emile," p. 720. Cf. "Contrat social," pp. 360-61. Broome sees the symbolic significance of the moral person formed by the union of the sexes: op cit., pp. 99-100. Cf. Burgelin, *O. C.*, 4:720 n. 2, who also speaks of an analogy between the conjugal and social pacts. Cf. M. B. Ellis, *Julie or La Nouvelle Heloïse: A Synthesis of Rousseau's Thought (1749-1759)* (Toronto: University of Toronto Press, 1949), p. 68.

12. Cf. "Emile," p. 721, and Eph. 5:22 ff.

13. We have hitherto observed the similarity of the two creeds but have not yet explored their relationship and its symbolic implications: see, for example, *O. C.,* 4:729 n. 1.

14. See "Emile," p. 743. See also pp. 745 and 823. Cf. p. 599 where the vicar speaks of the man who dies for the public good. Cf. also p. 249 where Rousseau begins by depicting Spartan patriotic fervor in a context comparable to this concluding passage upon feminine education. References in this note include all quotations in the paragraph.

15. Fénelon, *Les Aventures de Télémaque* (Liege: Grandmont-Donders, 1865), bk. 22, and especially p. 400.

16. Cf. *The Republic* 3. 400 ff.; 4. 421-25. Cf. *Contrat social,* pt. 4, chap. 7. See chapter 5 above and note 123.

17. "Est-ce ma faute si j'aime ce qui n'est pas? Je ne suis point visionaire; je ne veux point un prince, je ne cherche point Télémaque, je sais qu'il n'est qu'une fiction: je cherche quelqu'un qui lui ressemble; et pourquoi ce quelqu'un ne peut-il exister, puisque j'éxiste, moi qui me sens un coeur si semblable au sien? Non, ne déshonorons pas ainsi l'humanité; ne pensons pas qu'un homme aimable et vertueux ne soit qu'une chimére. Il existe, il vit, il me cherche peut-être; il cherche une ame qui le sache aimer. Mais qu'est-il? Où est-il?... "

18. *The Republic* 6. 495-96. Cf. *Emile et Sophie ou Les Solitaires.*

19. The Republic 6. 499.

20. In the sequel to the novel Rousseau, like Socrates, envisages the dishonoring of the Lady Philosophy and the decline of the little city, with the result that Emile, like the Socratic philosopher, is thrown back upon the order of friendship, and reason again replaces the habit of order.

21. See P. Burgelin, *La Philosophie de l'existence de J.-J. Rousseau* (Paris: Plon, 1952), pp. 168-80; J. Starobinski, *Jean-Jacques Rousseau: la transparence et l'obstacle* (Paris: Plon, 1957), pp. 90-92. We have not in the past recognized the affinity of the piece with "Emile." See also L. Millet, *La Pensée de Rousseau* (Paris: Bordas, 1966), pp. 160-62. In the latter the unfinished statues are unidentified, but Galatea is seen as "Absolute Beauty," which is, of course, true since Rousseau's apprehension of absolute beauty is to be found in *Emile.* The musical score of Rousseau's "Pygmalion," unworthy of the monologue, is, with the ex-

ception of his own overture and andante, the work of Horace Coignet. The first Parisian performance is mentioned in the "Dialogues," *O. C.,* 1:964. For Rameau's work see "Confessions," *O. C.,* 1:383.

22. *The Republic* 2. 361; 4. 420; 7. 540. For the Socratic artist: *ibid.,* 3. 401. Note that the *Symposium* is said to possess a beauty "as of a statue."

23. Pygmalion complains that his genius has deserted him, that the marble comes cold from his hands. Cf. *C. C.,* 15:132, letter to Rey, 29 January, 1763: "Les disgrâces ont achevé de m'ôter le peu de génie qui me restoit... je le [cet ouvrage] trouve si froid...."

24. "Quand mon esprit éteint ne produira plus rien de grand, de beau, de digne de moi, je montrerai ma Galathée, et je dirai: Voilà mon ouvrage!... la plus belle de mes oeuvres.... Je ne sais quelle émotion j'éprouve en touchant ce voile [qui le couvre]... je crois toucher au sanctuaire de quelque Divinité.... Pygmalion! c'est une pierre; c'est ton ouvrage. Qu'importe? On sert des Dieux dans nos temples... qui n'ont pas été faits d'une autre main." The latter words and the "sanctuaire de quelque Divinité" are particularly significant in the light of the mythical temple of "Emile."

25. "... Voyez cet objet, voyez mon coeur... céleste Vénus... où est la loi de la nature dans le sentiment que j'éprouve... il me suffira de vivre en elle [Galathée].... Déesse de la beauté, épargne cet affront à la nature, qu'un si parfait modèle soit l'image de ce qui n'est pas." The last words cited below read: "Oui, digne chef-d'oeuvre de mes mains, de mon coeur et des Dieux... je t'ai donné tout mon être; je ne vivrai plus que par toi."

26. *Aus meinem Leben: Dichtung und Wahrheit,* 2:ii. Starobinski and others follow Goethe. See note 21 above. It is not generally known that Goethe follows a rather flippant judgment of Diderot in the first of the latter's two *Essais sur la peinture* translated by the German poet. See Carl Hammer, Jr., *Goethe and Rousseau* (Lexington: University Press of Kentucky, 1973), p. 40.

27. "Emile," pp. 493-94, 798.

28. "Cette feinte recherche n'est qu'un prétexte pour lui faire connoitre les femmes, afin qu'il sente le prix de celle qui lui convient. Dès longtemps Sophie est trouvée...."

29. Cf. "Confession," loc. cit., p. 421.

30. For this paragraph see *The Republic* 5. 458-61 (laws of marriage); 10. 619 (regarding the choice of a life).

31. The pilgrimage of life is mentioned in "Emile et Sophie," *O. C.,* 4:914. The "paladins" are mentioned above, chapter 5 and note 28. For the statement that Sophia is far from Paris: "Emile," pp. 691, 770, 773, 801-2.

32. "Confessions," loc. cit., pp. 45-48, 57-59, 101-3, 143 ff., 161-73.

33. Cf. Socrates' definition of the philosophic nature in *The Republic* 6. 485-87. A philosopher must love truth and learning, delight in "pleasures of soul" and be a spectator of all time and all existence." With regard to the Greek philosophers, see note x to second "Discours," *O. C.,* 3:213.

34. "Emile," p. 783, where on their second visit they go astray for the third time.

35. In this "house of peace" wisdom has sequestered herself in a secluded retreat where, according to the "man of peace," the vicar, the voice of conscience may still be heard: "Emile," pp. 601, and cf. 506-7. The Gospel story mentioned below is in Mark 14:13-16. For the banquet of wisdom: Prov. 9:1-5.

[379]

36. Burgelin also sees in Sophia a combination of Eucharis and Antiope: *O. C.*, 4:775 n. 1, 778 n. 1, 798 n. 2. For the beauty of the virtues that is Sophia's: *The Republic* 6. 504. Cf. 7. 518: " . . . The virtue of wisdom more than anything else contains a divine element which always remains."

37. Rousseau often alludes to the symbolism of the book. Apart from the many examples already given there are two in the present context: pp. 777-78, where he calls his book a "novel" and refers to an earlier passage on the symbolism of Sophia's name. Cf. p. 657. Even the governor's comments on the name in the present case lend themselves to a symbolic interpretation: "N'y a-t-il qu'une Sophie au monde? Se ressemblent-elles toutes d'ame comme de nom? Toutes celles qu'il verra sont-elles la sienne?" To the reader of Plato these words contain veiled allusions to what Socrates calls the many "false forms" of wisdom as opposed to the one true form.

38. For the effect of finance upon human faculties see chapter 5 above and *The Republic* 8. 553.

39. For the parable of the pearl: Matt. 13:45-46; for that of the rich young man: Matt. 19:21.

40. Burgelin explains the role of the governor here in a similar manner: *O. C.*, 4:789 n 1.

41. "Comme l'idolatre enrichit des trésors qu'il estime l'objet de son culte, et pare sur l'autel le Dieu qu'il adore, l'amant a beau voir sa maitresse parfaite, il lui veut sans cesse ajouter de nouveaux ornemens . . . . C'est un nouvel homage qu'il croit lui rendre . . . . Il lui semble que rien de beau n'est à sa place quand il n'orne pas la suprême beauté." Rousseau adds: "Il se figure d'avance le plaisir qu'il aura de raisoner, de philosopher avec elle, il regarde comme *inutile* tout l'acquis qu'il ne peut point étaler à ses yeux: il rougit presque de savoir quelque chose qu'elle ne sait pas." The Socratic distinction between *useful* and *useless* studies, the latter unrelated to wisdom, further confirms the symbolism of Sophia. (Italics mine.)

42. The references for the Socratic images are as follows: the good husbandman is at the end of book 9 (referring to the method used from the first); the carpenter is in books 3 and 10; the Olympic victors appear in books 4, 5, and 10, and the lover in books 6, 7, 9, and 10. Observe how Socrates too reviews his images.

43. This is Rousseau's doctrine, however impractical it may be: "Emile," p. 548 (opposes exclusive friendship). Cf. "Lettres à m. de Malesherbes," *O. C.*, 1:1144-45. He praises cosmopolitanism in the second "Discours," loc. cit., p. 178, allegedly under Diderot's influence, but disapproves of it in "Emile": p. 249. It is important to define terms here. Patriotism is love of a man's "own city" in the Socratic sense; nationalism is love of one's birthplace; cosmopolitanism is love of the "false" states of this world. It is impossible to understand Rousseau without making the Socratic distinction between a man's "own city" and the land of his birth.

44. *O. C.*, 3:255. For Rousseau's perplexity mentioned below see "Morceau allégorique sur la révélation" in ibid., 4:1053.

45. *The Republic* 6. 496-97.

46. For nationalism: "Emile," pp. 635-36 (no concession is made to "national prejudice" in matters of religion), 828 and 831-32 (Emile travels to avoid the influence of national prejudice), 855 (he maintains correspondence abroad for the same purpose). For the problem of patriotism and humanitarianism see "Lettres de la montagne," *O.C.*, 3:706 n. See chapter 5 above, n. 71.

47. Rousseau is opposing the "inner (or secret) doctrine" of his contemporaries that favored the inclinations of the heart: cf. his "Observations" on Stanislas' reply to the first "Discours"; *O. C.*, 3:46 n. Cf. "Confessions," loc. cit., p. 468. He condemns it too in the first and third "Dialogues" and in the third of the "Rêveries": see, for example, *O. C.*, 1:1022. Cf. *C. C.*, 4:162, letter to T. Tronchin, 27 February 1757, where he opposes the idea of following the inclinations. Cf. "Lettre à m. de Franquières," *O. C.*, 4:1143.

48. Jimack finds this turn of events strange: *La genèse et la rédaction de l'Emile de J.-J. Rousseau* (Geneva: Institut et musée Voltaire, 1960), p. 202. But, of course, he interprets the book exclusively literally. The problem is greatly simplified by an appeal to Socrates. See below.

49. Cf. "Rêveries," loc. cit., pp. 1046-47.

50. For the age: *O. C.*, 4:lxxxv and 833 n. 3.

51. See note 14 above.

52. *The Republic* 9. 589-92. When Jean-Jacques asks Emile what kind of man he intends to be, he is quoting from ibid., 2. 365.

53. Burgelin proposes the comparison: *O. C.*, 4:836 n. 1.

54. The phrase "what is not" is applied to Emile, Sophia, and, by implication, to the city of the *Contrat* in "Emile," pp. 762, 821, 836-37.

55. Cf. p. 586, and "Contrat Social," pp. 369, 394.

56. See p. 311. Cf. "Etat de guerre," *O. C.*, 3:610. For the question of federation and sovereignty, raised by Rousseau in this context ("Emile," p. 848), see "Contrat social," p. 431 n. 2.

57. *Contrat social*, pt. 3, chap. 9. Cf. the second "Discours," n. ix, in *O. C.*, 3:206; "Discours sur l'économie politique," loc. cit., pp. 258-59; "Fragments politiques," loc. cit., pp. 527-28; "Projet de constitution pour la Corse," *O. C.*, 3:904; "Considérations," loc. cit., p. 1005. Cf. Fénelon, op. cit., bk. 22. The fact that the travelers find no good government or laws has been used to illustrate the weakness of Rousseau's system. It is meant, of course, to illustrate the weakness of our "anti-society."

58. Loc. cit., p. 919; cf. p. 941.

59. The whole passage reads: "Je me souviens que mes biens furent la cause de nos recherches. Vous prouviez très solidement que je ne pouvois guarder à la fois ma richesse et ma liberté, mais quand vous vouliez que je fusse à la fois libre et sans besoins, vous vouliez deux choses incompatibles, car je ne saurois me tirer de la dépendance des hommes [in the matter of the necessities of life] qu'en rentrant sous celle de la nature."

60. See, for example, *O. C.*, 4:858 n. 1. But the laws are not defined.

61. See "Considérations," loc. cit., pp. 1013-29 (especially 1018) on the military system and the plan to subject members of the government to a very gradual system of promotions.

62. Rousseau finally solves what seemed to him like a contradiction in Socrates, who reveals true laws to men and then submits to false ones.

63. Op. cit., bks, 2, 17, 22; pp. 38, 293, 300, 402, 438.

64. Rousseau shows the same moderation in the "Considérations," regarding the admission of the middle classes to government and the freeing of peasants in Poland: loc. cit., pp. 1024 ff.

65. He says this of the city and the age of gold: "Emile," pp. 250, 859 (beginning and end of the book).

[381]

66. See chapter 5 above, note 94.

67. See, for example, *O. C.*, 1:201 n. 1. Burgelin, in *O. C.*, 4:866 n. 1, is right to observe that "reason must necessarily play a part in everything."

68. See pp. 267-68.

69. *The Republic* 5. 459.

70. Cf. "Considérations," loc. cit., pp. 960-61. Cf. Gal. 4:22-26.

71. See, for example, *O. C.*, 4:863 n. 1.

72. *The Republic* 9. 590-91. The "habit of good order" that is Rousseau's object is also that of Socrates: ibid., 4. 425.

73. See p. 867 and cf. p. 799, " . . . Ici finit ma longue tâche, et commence celle d'un autre. J'abdique aujourd'hui l'autorité que vous m'avez confiée, et voici désormais votre gouverneur."

VII
Conclusion

This commentary of *Emile* and the *Social Contract* reveals Rousseau in a new light by dwelling upon several aspects of his work that have not previously been explored. Yet they are significant enough not merely to modify rather seriously but also to enlarge and clarify his personal image and his place in the history of both literature and ideas.

The collation has entailed study from three points of view; historical, ideological, and literary or aesthetic including the mythological. I now propose to define briefly the advantages derived from each of these aspects in turn. At the same time, in every case I shall recall once more that we have the authorization, or rather, invitation, of the writer himself to approach his books, and particularly those under discussion, in the ways enumerated. I have examined them on the basis of his own evidence in order to learn whether his words are true or false, and I have discovered that they are abundantly true.

Let me deal first with the historical implications of my research. This comparison of *Emile* with the *Contract*, while accomplishing the initial purpose of investigating the Aemilian myths and their value to express the author's philosophy translated into abstract terms in the companion volume, has come upon and brought to attention some rather startling affinities between him and antiquity that help to situate him more precisely in the main currents of occidental civilization. The discoveries in question are a major feature of the collation and can hardly be lightly dismissed. That is especially true if, as Rousseau himself says, knowledge is mainly an awareness of relationships; for in that case not to know his affinities, herein revealed to a vaster and fuller extent than ever before, is not to know him. The foregoing inquiry shows how scrupulously he cultivates his classical and religious inheritance, especially in the two books it fuses into one. It demonstrates that he belongs to Greek and biblical tradition far more intimately than we have hitherto supposed. It proves that he who has been called "the first modern man" preaches a doctrine as old as Christ or Socrates or, rather, Solomon. I emphasize all three since, although his ties with Socrates. Plato, and classical Greco-Roman literature and philosophy emerge rather impressively from a collation of this kind, so do his aesthetic and ideological associations with Solomon and Christ. The Platonic dialogues, the Solomonic books of the Old Testament, the Gospel stories and apostolic epistles have all left their mark on his thought, which has profited thereby as much as his art as a writer is enhanced by Socratic and biblical imagery. These are facts that we can no longer overlook and to which we can hardly remain indifferent. It is imperative to know that some of the greatest works of our culture are inseparable from one another and that Rousseau is a vital link in the chain extending from ancient Judaical and classical pagan civilizations to their modern Judeo-Christian and romantic counterparts.

By heeding his own admissions, we might long since have come to a better understanding of his affiliations, which, incidentally, I do not pretend to have exhausted in all their depth and immensity. Or we might at least have been alerted to their gravity, if we were too uninformed about Socrates, Plato, or the Bible to recognize them for what they are. For example, when he says that his writings are mere commentaries on the Scriptures, and that his masters are Plato, or Socrates, and Christ, to whom he repeatedly pays tribute in his books, we might have listened more solicitously or taken him more seriously. But in order to fathom his meaning, it is not enough to scrutinize passages in his work where such open acknowledgments occur. It is necessary to go much deeper and commit to memory the acknowledged sources so that we might discern their verifiable presence in Rousseauist texts where they are barely mentioned or not at all.

Most readers will be especially struck by the enormous extent of his debt to Greek philosophy. Of course, this debt has not been completely ignored in the past. For example, the Spartan strain coming through Plutarch has always been known. But that is because it is so conspicuous and lacking in subtlety that it could hardly be disregarded. Some notice has also been taken of the influence of Socrates and Plato upon him, and small wonder since in the second *Discourse* that heralds his future he virtually begins thus: "I shall suppose myself in the Lyceum of Athens, repeating the lessons of my masters, with Plato and Xenocrates for judges, and the whole human race for my audience." This phrase might well be applied to his entire career as a writer. Yet the influence to which it testifies has never been probed and measured in its complex, far-reaching, and widespread ramifications throughout the very warp and woof of his greatest works. The main reason is probably that its immense scope is most easily visible through an evaluation of myths; and although the Platonic and Socratic ones have been carefully appraised, Rousseau's have gone almost totally unobserved. Unfortunately for us, since the similarity of his imagery to that of Socrates permits a most enlightening comparison of texts.

In *Emile* he confesses his debt to Socrates or Plato at crucial points in every part of the book. We have hitherto closed our eyes to this fact, but it is nevertheless true. He begins with a moving tribute to the *Republic* and calls it the finest treatise of education that has ever been written. True, he puts us off the scent by saying that it gives one an idea of public education and then failing to add that in the dialogue the latter is merely an image of private education, which is the real theme of the book as it is of his own. But it behooves us the readers to see that, for it is obvious to anyone who takes the trouble to familiarize himself with the great

[385]

classic. In the second part he makes an unmistakable ges-
ture of gratitude to his Greek master at the very moment
when he is preparing to broach the education of his "guardian of the constitution" and the laws. Suddenly he stops to
hold up for our admiration the example he follows: "Plato
in his republic who is considered so stern teaches children
only through festivals, games, songs, and amusements."
We have only to proceed from there and take the hint furnished by himself to see that the Socratic guardian is the
model of the Rousseauist and that their education is the
same. At a critical juncture in the third part Socrates himself
materializes in flesh and blood to teach Emile the most
solemn lesson he has to learn, namely, that he requires to
be governed by superior powers. As if this clue were not
enough, at another turning point in the same part where the
author proposes as a rule of instruction whatever it is useful
to know, he goes out of his way to tell us that he is imitating
Socrates. He says so undeniably. For, having induced
Emile to want to know only what is useful and to ask, at
every step taken by himself and his governor, "What is the
use of that?", the author comments: "Anyone who is
taught to want to know only what is useful interrogates like
Socrates." This is a frank, outspoken assertion that he is
using the word *useful* in the Socratic sense. He is actually
referring to the Platonic text where the sage himself establishes this law of learning and defines what he means by it.
If we go to the text indicated, as we are virtually invited to
do, we literally fall upon the source material of his whole
third part. It is disastrous to pass over these telling signs of
the master's presence in *Emile*. There are more in the
fourth part. In the pages on Plutarch we are told that Emile
imitates no one, not even Socrates or Cato. We ought to
have seen that Jean-Jacques does and so does the author,
especially since throughout the book the former consistently undertakes studies usually assigned to children. In
the same fourth part, in the profession of faith, Socrates
stands at the summit of both the affirmative and negative

[386]

phases of the piece. For instance, in the affirmative one, where Rousseau tries to identify the principle of consience, he professedly avoids any doctrine that, like La Rochefoucauld's, for example, would degrade Socrates or Regulus by attributing virtue to selfishness. Moreover, in discussing revelation in the negative phase of the creed, he reaches one of the greatest heights of eloquence in the book in the famous contrast between Christ and Socrates. Besides, again in the fourth part, in facing the vital issue of aesthetics, he has recourse to Plato's *Symposium* as well as to Virgil and Tibullus to perfect Emile's taste. In the fifth part he begins with a new tribute to the master, however ambiguous. Again he makes a pretense of differing from him, this time in the matter of feminine education as discussed in the *Republic;* but then he proceeds to display quite plainly that their differences in this case are simply a matter of imagery since he, unlike Socrates, uses the home and family to exteriorize the city. At the same time he borrows Socratic imagery to show that supposedly wise order of things embodied in the heroine. Later, when his heroes set out first in search of Sophia or wisdom and then in quest of the Rousseauist city, they are said to "travel" like Plato, which in both contexts is tantamount to admitting symbolically that they follow him, as in fact they do. Thus throughout the novel Rousseau loudly proclaims his debt to Socrates and the Platonic dialogues, especially the *Republic* and *Symposium.*

His own sayings are amply verified by an analysis of texts, where the evidence of close relationships between him and his Greek masters is overwhelming. The similarity of Socratic and Aemilian images, that first stirs the mind to suspect links between them, necessarily leads the classical scholar from one book to the other, and then the perception of ideological identity follows apace. Admittedly, many writers and thinkers have said the same things as Rousseau or Socrates. But it is by no mere coincidence, especially after the repeated avowals recorded above, that Socrates in

[387]

the *Republic* and Rousseau in *Emile* — and less obviously in the *Contract* — consistently convey the same ideas, usually in identical words and metaphors, and always according to an analogous pattern, with only the slightest variations from title page to colophon. The points of contact between them are too numerous to be accidental. Rousseau's debt turns out to be massive. From a confrontation of texts comes the astonishing realization that *Emile* in particular might well be taken for a Rousseauist version of the *Republic*.

To admit this, it is enough to reflect upon only a few of the vast correspondences between them, even without including the identical myths that I shall discuss below. The main problem of *Emile* and indeed of all Rousseau's works is Socratic. I refer to the sphinx-like riddle of wisdom and happiness that he makes a point of formulating four times in the novel, as Socrates does in the *Republic,* and each time he does so in exactly the same context as the sage. Moreover, in *Emile* and the *Contract,* as in the *Republic,* early reflections upon so-called morality and justice in our confused world lead to the institution of an ideal order of things. In addition, in the case of all three books the latter is presented by way of an analogy between the soul and the city. And in all cases the formation of the moral being is almost identical. More still: as we have seen, the three great "waves" that Socrates must first overcome before he can establish his city are closely linked with the triple-tiered foundation of the Rousseauist order of city or of soul. In fact, the dominant leitmotiv of *Emile,* which is greatly expanded in the fourth part, is taken from the *Republic*. This is the idea of the friendship of reason for nature, used to represent the bonds that unite the freemen of the Rousseauist city. Finally, the entire fifth part is inspired by the Socratic lover of wisdom who alone can make the city a reality. These affinities are only a sampling of the many to be gleaned by following Rousseau as he makes his way through the *Republic* in the pages of the companion volumes that form the central work of his career.

[388]

Again these are facts that we have never before suspected and can hardly go on ignoring. If we continue to expound his philosophy without taking them into account, we renounce fruitful possibilities of comprehension, whether or not he construes his sources correctly. For here I must insist that, in pointing to his dependence upon Socrates and Plato, I do not mean to imply that his interpretation of the Greek thinkers is orthodox. It may not be. That is for philosophers and political scientists to decide. My task is rather to add to our knowledge of the modern writer by bringing out affiliations hitherto unseen.

Indeed, a perception of them leads to a new understanding of *Emile* and the *Contract,* and broadens, deepens, and enriches our appreciation of both. We have formerly treated *Emile* as a pedagogical manual and the *Contract* as a political handbook in the narrowest sense of the words, whereas in fact both are philosophical works. They are quite as philosophical as the *Republic,* which, according to Rousseau, is not a political work at all but a treatise on education or, if we wish, on legislation. So are his own books.

Let us consider the *Contract* first to see how our knowledge of the book has been expanded by an awareness of its Socratic origins. There the author's purpose is not to provide the pattern of an earthly city for founders to follow. By imagining that it is, we reduce the scope of the treatise and minimize its value. It is true that, like Socrates and for the same reasons of clarity, he fancies the city mythically taking shape in the book. It is also true that, in other publications and at the invitation of statesmen, he adapts his principles to a new constitution for Corsica and a government for Poland. But it is he himself who assumes the formidable task, he who is the legislator of his own city of the *Contract,* as Socrates is of his, or so he claims, and who alone knows the philosophical implications of his "system." Moreover, in doing so, he is obliged to make concessions and modifications to adjust the scheme to a sphere for

[389]

which it was not really meant. Furthermore, he has no illusions at all about the practical or pragmatic usefulness of his ideas in that sphere, even in a mitigated form. In their original idealistic cast they would be useful only in the Socratic sense. And so he says repeatedly that his city does not exist and never will, and that if it did, men would be like blocks of wood or, to use Socrates' word, like posts. He even says that, if he were a philosopher-king ("sage et roi") in our world and could found such a city and change men accordingly, he would decline to do so.[1] In other words, he does not seriously visualize a city in the ordinary sense of the word governed according to his abstract principles, any more than his Greek master does. The Rousseauist city, like the Socratic one, exists in idea only. Since its pattern is a concept of the soul in its pristine purity and made in the image of God, it is itself proposed as the true sage's pattern of educational or legislative processes, a pattern that is several times evoked in the *Republic* and in matching passages of *Emile*. It is intended to reflect a sublime prototype or mythical model of civil or civilized life that "he who desires may behold, and beholding, may set his own house in order." The Rousseauist sage, like the Socratic, does precisely that. He orders, preserves, and governs his own life after the manner of that ideal city, as God orders, preserves, and governs the universe. He is a creator of order like the Maker or, rather, like the Socratic and Rousseauist carpenter who in the *Republic* is only once removed from the Artist of artists.

He accomplishes his purpose, in the view of both Socrates and his disciple, by no other means than an act of his own enlightened will. Nothing else can liberate a man's powers or "force him to be free" in Rousseau's own phraseology. For him as for his master nothing else is even lawful. To impose such restraint upon others is lawless, unless those "others" correspond Socratically to a man's own faculties imaginatively exteriorized. Such action is also futile since no one can be changed from the outside. Rousseau's whole philosophy is built around this idea, which is entirely Socratic. In the vision of Er in the *Republic,* which I must again recall to the reader's mind, the Greek sage too shows the great danger of having men behave like posts. There we see souls, about to be reborn, ascend from earth and descend from heaven to a place where they are bidden to choose among samples of lives set before them and thus assume responsibility for their own destiny. Socrates explains that those who came from heaven and in a former life had dwelt in a well-ordered state made an unwise choice; their virtue was a matter of habit only, and they had no philosophy: "They had never been schooled by trial whereas the pilgrims who came from earth, having themselves suffered and seen others suffer, were not in a hurry to choose." Rousseau sees the same danger in any outward authority, except in the case of children, who must be taught to be sages and to need neither external laws nor government but only those of the *Contract.* That being so, what is the use of complaining, as we have been doing, that a city like his cannot exist on earth, since he was the first to say so, and that our fate would be worse if it did, since no one could agree more completely than he does? And what is the use of arguing about his demand for a unanimous whole and about the effects of such a demand upon majority rule, since he is simply saying that a true sage must be single-minded?

As for *Emile,* it too now appears in a fresh light since a study of its intimate affinities with Socrates throws into new and larger perspective the real theme of the book and true preoccupations of the author, which, as in the case of the *Contract,* are self-discipline and self-government. In the fifth of the *Letters from the Mount* Rousseau declares that, in the preface to the novel and several times in the text thereof, he indicates that such is his subject. There he writes: "It is a question of a new system of education [in the sense in which he applies the term to the *Republic*] whose plan I submit to the inspection of sages, and not a

[391]

method for fathers and mothers, which never even entered my mind. If sometimes, in common enough imagery, I seem to address them, it is to make myself better understood.... " As we have witnessed, he makes himself thoroughly clear, whatever imagery he uses. For example, he says in the opening pages of *Emile* that his system would be effective only if employed by someone who had himself been educated according to it. The governor, he contends, must be formed for his pupil and may undertake only one education and no more. This can only mean, as Socrates says, that the governor, who is the embodiment of reason taught by experience, must foster and cultivate natural man within the human creature of which he is a part. The only education a man may pursue is his own. That is the lesson conveyed in *Emile*. There Rousseau appropriates this Socratic conclusion in a very personal way as we have seen. In speaking of the inner life of the sage, he is speaking of his own as well as ours, and his ideal story of the race is that of his own spiritual pilgrimage. Emile is natural man within himself and supposedly in us all, conceived on the road to Vincennes in 1749, or later in the forest of Saint-Germain, and finally born or reborn at Montmorency. Jean-Jacques is the "helmsman," or reason in the service of human nature, who has learned the secrets of spiritual life "in the school of misfortune" and who undertakes to guide the whole moral being to wisdom and happiness. As we now know and need not prove again, the writer admits the autobiographical value of his work at every critical turning point in the novel: when the governor subscribes to the oath of the covenant that commits him to respect the constitution and rule accordingly; when Emile for his part is drawn into the same conscious commitment; and finally when the moral or social person applies these principles in the conduct of life and particularly in the innermost recesses of the spirit where Sophia, or wisdom, abides. Rousseau implicitly admits it again when his hero, searching through the world for a city where alone he can live happily with her, is shown a pattern of the writer's own city of the *Contract* whose laws and government, he learns, are enshrined within the sage since it is in fact a pattern for his formation.

That formation, Socratic in almost every respect, goes much further than we have formerly thought. Usually, the first two parts of the book are understood to deal with the nature of the sensitive being, the third with the development of judgment in the active being, the fourth with the growth of the reasonable being, and the fifth with a love story. This interpretation is, of course, true as far as it goes. But it overlooks the training of the Rousseauist will whose acts are Socratic laws and are defined accordingly, as it also overlooks the training of reason in the application of those laws or in the art of Socratic kingship. It overlooks too the fact that the author follows step by step the education of the Socratic guardian and philosopher-king, which is the discipline imposed by the sage upon himself. Besides, its exclusively literal and even positivistic approach has led us to complain that he neglects to follow his original intention and deal with wisdom in the love story; but in truth there, as much as anywhere, he speaks of little else, although he does so in Socratic imagery. Any work on Emile that ignores this, as well as the laws and acts of kingship, requires to be supplemented by fresh study. We *must* come to terms philosophically with the fifth part. We must treat it as if it were as essential to the story of the Rousseauist sage's education as the corresponding phase in the case of the Socratic, since it really is. It is all the more so, not only because it contains more than a quarter of the book, but because it relates to the most important phase, namely, manners, customs, and opinion, which are the "keystone of the vault" of the *Contract* as they are in the *Republic*. It is therefore necessarily connected with earlier parts, notably the early training of taste through beautiful sights and sounds, the Socratic orientation of reason, Sophia's first portrait, Emile's studies in aesthetics, and the essay on wealth, or rather, on happiness. wisdom, and beauty. We

[393]

may conclude that insight into the historical relationships of the work enlarges our knowledge of it to the same extent as is the case with the *Contract*.

Our knowledge of both is also increased by a comparison of the two books with one another. For this approach, too, we have the writer's authorization in his correspondence as well as in *Emile* itself. And his authorization proves to be justified. It is quite true, as he says in a letter of 23 May 1762, that the *Contract* is a sort of appendix to *Emile* and that both together make a complete whole. With equal justification Jean-Jacques in the text of the novel implies the same thing. When he sets out to provide the hero with an archetype of the ideal city that is really a pattern to lead him autonomously to Sophia, he explains that he is motivated by an oath sworn at the beginning of Emile's education and binding him to find wisdom and happiness for them both. The results of that search are therefore to be found not only in his work heretofore but also in the synopsis of the *Contract*, anticipated by his words and following thereafter.

These assertions of the author have been verified in the foregoing collation. The two productions, far from representing a cleavage in his mind, as we have thought in the past, are essentially one and are consequently more closely bound together than has been supposed even by recent critics who have pointed to links between them. In fact, the affinities of both to the *Republic* are enough to arouse suspicions about their mutual connections. The same affinities make the reader more sensitive to the myths of *Emile*, which provide easier access to the ideas they convey and help to bring out the identity of the latter and those of the appendix. Indeed, the parables and myths of the novel consistently turn out to be an allegorical version of doctrines of which the *Contract* is merely an abstract. The latter reduces the allegories to a state of disembodied ideas that in their turn are infused with fresh life by a collation with the imageries of the master work. My primary purpose herein has been to demonstrate this rather than to evaluate ideas

[394]

as such. I have sought to achieve that purpose not abstractly but as concretely as possible by means of a juxtaposition and comparison of texts, a method suited to detect and reveal their kinship. The results constitute another major aspect of this study. They show that both treatises evolve according to a single plan—which is that of the *Republic*—the *Contract* following the novel step by step and carefully respecting the order of its composition as the two move together through four parts without ever taking leave of each other. My research also proves that the fifth part of *Emile* is a synthesis and consummation of all that precedes. Moreover, the intimate relationship of texts has emerged as self-evident. In other words, the texts have lent themselves freely to collation and comparision without being beaten into submission or tortured in any way. That is further proof that they do indeed match one another perfectly, as the author says.

It is, of course, important to be aware of this. Not that it matters in an absolute sense whether his thought actually possesses unity or does not. But it concerns cultured persons in general and scholars in particular to know the facts of the case.

The realization that the two books are basically one modifies our view of both as much as an understanding of their associations with the *Republic* does. It confirms that *Emile* is as certainly a treatise on citizenship, law, and self-government as the *Contract* is. It also discloses that the latter, even though its principles are as universal, eternal, and therefore as static as those of *Emile*, presents them by way of a gradually evolving educational process as much as the so-called pedagogical work does. Rousseau like Socrates "imagines the State in process of creation" to see "the justice and injustice of the State in process of creation also."[2] Both his books describe one and the same process. A consciousness of this shows further what their affiliations with Socratic thought accentuates, namely, that each one deals with faculties of soul, their alleged natural or normal

[395]

constitution and proper administration to which every man of understanding is invited to accommodate his life. In both Rousseau proposes to sages a solemn spiritual commitment that integrates the entire person or human creature into a closely knit whole, subjects all its parts to the reasonable will, and thereby brings it into communion with great leaders of the past and present, especially his own chosen masters. The intricate and presumably well-balanced moral relationships that result in the inner realm are those of an ideal city, and for him they must prevail in civilized life, although they do not and cannot materialize in a political order in the external world. His ultimate and proper domain, like that of Socrates, is the soul, from which, in his eyes, all social reform must come. Consequently, the only remedy he favors to heal the disorders of the world is integrated, humanistic man as opposed to the amoral savage or his immoral modern counterpart. Any other scheme is, in his opinion, sheer quackery. He proposes that solution even though such a man has never been seen since the time of Socrates or Christ. He is exhorting men to come out of the woods and abandon their primitive, unsocial, or antisocial ways not by changing material things in the sphere of actuality but by changing life through the action of the spirit, as we have seen. For him that is the only way to create a real bond among them and to generate sympathy, friendship, and love in their midst, at least theoretically. Through that bond alone the unearthly new Geneva, Sparta, or Aemilian Rome of his desires really existed in his imagination and filled him with characteristic ardor for "his own city" or ideal image of the soul. His patriotic fervor, undiminished after the renunciation of his Genevan citizenship, has nothing to do with the Calvinist republic or national prejudice on behalf of the land of his birth. Theoretically it may be combined with the love of human nature in mankind since that love is supposedly its very source, however difficult it may be in practice for most of us to embrace the race of men, including the most disordered souls, and

[396]

love them all with equal energy. On the other hand, the same fervor can hardly be reconciled with cosmoplitanism, which for Rousseau means a love of the false states of this world, states quite alien to his own view of the true one as seen in the two books under discussion. The interrelationships of the companion volumes greatly clarify his philosophical and psychological aspirations in both.

The consciousness of their intrinsic identity increases our knowledge of them in other ways too. For instance, a collation of the *Contract* with *Emile* explains the presence in the former of certain chapters in the second, third, and fourth parts hitherto deemed repetitious or regarded as useless padding. In fact, it reclaims for readers eight chapters of the treatise, formerly as lost to criticism as most of the fifth part of *Emile*. It reveals that, far from being expendable as we have always believed, they are among the most significant of all. For example, in the past—and this applies to all critics without exception who have written on the subject—we have been setting aside and eliminating from serious consideration chapters 8, 9, and 10 of the second part. Since in those chapters Rousseau defines his laws, as a study of the texts shows in the light of a collation with *Emile* and comparison with the *Republic*, we must now admit that we have heretofore failed to recognize the laws for what they are. In the third part we have hitherto been willing to dispense with chapter 8, where he discusses the effects of wealth on government and maintains that the freest men are those with fewest needs and equivalent material resources. That is one of the most vital and central chapters in the book, for he formulates therein a fundamental rule of the Rousseauist and Socratic order of life. In the fourth book we have in the past been disposed to treat lightly chapters 4, 5, 6, and 7. We have dismissed them as affording a rather irrelevant essay upon primitive Roman institutions. We may as well lop off the heads from what Socrates calls in the *Republic* the statues of his heroes. For in chapter 4 Rousseau brings his Socratic city to the birth, as we can see if we decipher the imagery and compare it with *Emile*. In chapters 5 and 6 he deals with very real powers necessary for good government and indispensable to preserve a balance of faculties, which, in his Socratic view, is the mainspring of a felicitous inner life. The same may be said of chapter 7. Indeed, if we ignore it, we are ignoring what he himself calls the most important laws of all—manners, customs, and opinion, which are the "keystone of the vault" not only of the *Contract* but of *Emile* too, or rather, of his whole philosophy. The reader can see for himself how urgent it is for political scientists and philsophers to be informed of the bearing and scope of these chapters that correspond to some of the most significant parts of *Emile*. As a collation shows, the said chapters must be accepted as an integral part of the treatise, and their relevance and effectiveness must be recognized if we are to achieve even an elementary knowledge of the work and its author.

There is still more to be said about the value of a collation of the two books in question. As we have seen, the method leads to a clearer conception of the subject of each part of *Emile*. The main themes are as follows: first, reflections upon the covenant of friendship; second, the training of the will and other powers through the application of the laws of necessity and freedom, the latter being that of negative education and including the one about the natural bent; third, the training of reason in the art of government or kingship; fourth, initiation into social order; and finally, the foretaste of wisdom and civil order, all within the precincts of inner life as in the case of the *Republic*. In the end the social contract of friendship is perfected by the civil contract of marriage, which brings to fulfillment all principles and powers called into play from the first and symbolizes initiation into the ultimate beatific vision of wisdom.

As I have said, the associations of *Emile* and the *Contract* with one another and the *Republic* can best be recognized by approaching Rousseau's masterwork through his aesthetics, including his use of myths. The examination of this aspect of the novel is another basic contribution of the present study to Rousseauist scholarship. In the past what I have called the artistic, imaginative content of the book has been overshadowed by ideological theorizing or stylistic, positivistic analysis. To my knowledge it has never been the subject of a published commentary. The fact that it has been overlooked results in a serious lacuna in the Rousseauist bibliography. The omission is serious not only because the matter is interesting in itself but especially because a treatment of it leads to worthwhile historical and ideological disclosures. The omission is all the more grave by reason of the author's own statements in the text of the book where he underlines the role of aesthetics in his philosophy and also says quite frankly that he is using the language of symbolic expression in his writing. "All my ideas are in images," says he in the fourth book of the memoirs in a phrase comparable to others in *Emile*. His own words are an open invitation to consider the novel from a literary and artistic standpoint and to cope with the problems entailed therein. In order to see how imperative it is to do so, one has only to formulate a few conclusions from the foregoing study relating first to his aesthetics in general and finally to his use of myths.

The aesthetic approach is authorized in both *Emile* and the companion volume, where Rousseau teaches that taste guides the course of human life. He does so especially in the second and fourth parts of each and in the fifth part of *Emile*. In the *Contract* his aforementioned "keystone of the vault" or law of opinion defines what is beautiful or pleasing, and honorable or admirable, and thereby shapes manners and customs of which the censor is custodian. For the author the secret of what we judge good or evil is to be found in what we believe beautiful and honorable or the reverse. The doctrine is that of Socrates, who contends, by an identical process of reasoning, that the city stands or falls on the nature of its pleasures. The same doctrine reappears in *Emile* where the law of opinion governing the beautiful or honorable is regarded as determining the success of all others. For example, Rousseau is guided by this conviction in the second part where he broaches the education of his guardian of the laws, and makes ethics and aesthetics as inseparable as they are for his master, who never dissociates the two. In the third part he professes to teach what is "useful" but openly admits that he is employing the word as does the Greek sage, for whom the only useful knowledge is whatever is related not to shopkeeping but to the pursuit of the beautiful and the good. In the fourth part the social and moral order is Socratically crowned by aesthetics, which are again linked with ethics in the first portrait of Sophia, and in Emile's studies in taste, culminating in the essay on the ecstatic contemplation of the beautiful and the good where the whole fifth part is foreshadowed. Obviously beauty is of primary concern to Rousseau in both *Emile* and the *Contract*.

For that very reason he is far from indifferent to the imaginative content of the masterwork in particular. He takes to heart his own precept that it is important to please men in order to serve them, and that "the art of writing is no idle [or useless] pursuit when it is employed to proclaim the truth."[3] The latter maxim is a Rousseauist form of the Socratic one that the useful is whatever leads toward truth, meaning moral truth or the beautiful and the good. In pursuing this object and seeking to please, the author of *Emile* intends to behave like a Socratic artist. He never loses sight of the context of the *Republic* from which the leitmotiv of his book is taken. There the sage exhorts all artists to express in their works that grace and harmony which, like goodness and virtue, are said to depend on "the true simplicity of a rightly and nobly ordered mind and character." He expels from his republic those who depict images of moral deformity and admits only the ones who are gifted to discern the beauty that is "the effluence of fair works" and draws the soul into likeness and sympathy or friendship with the beauty of reason. This passage and its sequel, to which Rousseau was so deeply indebted for the main theme of his book, was also decisive in shaping its artistic character, at least in his own intentions. As we saw in *Pygmalion,* he liked to imagine that his work was as faultless in beauty as the "statues" of Socrates' kings in the great classic. The Socratic concept of the artist who portrays only the beautiful and the good is clearly the ideal to which he aspires in *Emile*.

The question arises as to how it is possible to reconcile those aspirations with the professed aim of his literary art, which is to portray the human heart in its folly and its misery, as well as moral and psychological truth in the absolute sense. The difficulty is more apparent than real. Everywhere in *Emile*, and even in the last part, we are constantly alive to the presence of an alien world that, although it never becomes obtrusive enough to overshadow the ideal order or usurp the center of the stage, is still the background of the story. Rousseau shows how its existence stirs the soul to life and moves it to exercise its powers, of which we are never really conscious until they are challenged. For example, the Savoyard vicar becomes aware of the soul only as a result of the contradiction between man's evil plight and the excellence of his nature. In *Emile* that contrast is something with which the human spirit must contend, and this fact accentuates the psychological realism of the book in spite of its lofty idealism.

For the author does, in fact, adhere therein to the main purpose of his "classical" aesthetic doctrine. He uses a variety of visual forms to portray his concept of universal and eternal human qualities and especially the inner world, its principles, orderly processes, threatened deviations, and existing and ideal relationships with the material and moral environment. The same is necessarily true of the *Contract*. In both, notwithstanding the rarified atmosphere that distinguishes them from his other works, he betrays exactly the same interest in human psychology as he does

[401]

everywhere else. In all of them he makes a profound and comprehensive study of inner man (including the actual and the "true"), which, like the "classical" writers of antiquity or of the French seventeenth century, he regards as the one theme worthy of literature. And in the two books in question the results are as valid or as invalid as they are anywhere else in his work, since they are no different. It is only the external form that varies from the early *Discourses* to the last autobiographical compositions, his researches being presented in a variety of disguises. They may take on the air of a historical survey or a philosophy of religion or citizenship or a pedagogical treatise or even a story of his own life. But behind the disguises there is always a preoccupation with man in general, which was consistently a prime motive of his writings however we may evaluate the results. In this respect, as in many others, he stands in direct antithesis to his famous contemporaries. The abyss between them lies largely in a difference in attitude toward literature. They use it as a pretext for moral, religious, or political theorizing and turn it into a glorified kind of propaganda. He takes the opposite course. For example, in *Emile* he uses the social, religious, and political preoccupations of the day as pretexts for artistic creativity, and turns them into the mythical substance of literature in the traditional sense of the word with its psychological and spiritual implications.

In doing so, he is guided not only by his readings but especially by a personal intuitive vision of man and the world, based upon observation and experience and supplemented by what we call "classical" common sense. His appeal to that faculty in the pedagogical novel and elsewhere also sets him apart, at least in his own eyes, from some of the other great literary men of his time. According to him, they constructed their theories and "philosophical" systems by means of speculative reason frequently divorced from the facts of reality. Consequently he complains of their lack of psychological realism. By contrast he pro-

[402]

fesses to rely upon knowledge and judgment acquired by personal contact with beings and things. In fact, *Emile* and the *Contract* testify to a richly varied cultivation of life and a long, patient, and tenacious application of the mind to arrive at a conception of spiritual truth on that basis. We may therefore conclude that his "classical" qualities are authentic. They result from a genuine effort on his part to adhere to his Greco-Latin aesthetic profession of faith. That is true even though when he carries the doctrine into the sphere of practical creative activity, his achievements may be unorthodox at the same time as they become suffused with "romantic" lyricism.

If they are thus transformed, it is because, as we have seen, his observation of the nature of man and the human condition is also largely based upon a close watching of his own soul and inner life. Of course, that was likewise the case with Montaigne, whom he greatly admired and who was the first French litterateur to probe the mysteries of the human spirit by plumbing the depths of his own. Rousseau's mode of procedure is much the same in *Emile*, where, however, he employs it rigorously enough to pass beyond the innermost recesses of the self and reach general characteristics that are common to us all and always have been. But it is largely the subjective approach that explains his peculiar view of the soul, as well as his emotional presentation of it in the two main parts of the novel. This emotional quality, typical of him, belongs to Judeo-Christian art from the Middle Ages to the nineteenth century. His "romantic" embrace of the "classical" psychological object does not necessarily preclude a realistic apprehension of human nature, at least in some aspects of it if not in all. His introspective attitude may even intensify his grasp of the theme. The reader must decide that matter for himself.

Rousseau, like his famous models, formulates the results of his psychological research, particularly in *Emile*, in the language of symbolic expression, as he himself says. Even

[403]

if he had not said so, we might have surmised that he was having recourse to myths and parables because of his professed prediliction for Plato and the Bible, which swarm with both. Yet by comparison with the ancient ones, his own are practically unknown. The investigation of them is one of the foremost aims of this study, since, as I have hinted, a collation of *Emile* with the *Contract* would be virtually impossible without it. That inquiry has shown that the Aemilian myths are, almost without exception, identical with those of the writer's sources and, like his psychology, are "romantic" and "classical," Greek and biblical at once. They represent fragments of a past more than 2,500 or rather 3,000 years old, rearranged and harmonized into a new organism designed to give outward expression to the author's intellectual purpose. The main reason we have not previously detected them or dealt with them on a large scale is that Rousseau transmutes their substance and character into his own and then handles them with the subtlety and unostentatiousness of a "classical" writer. But once we sense their existence, we discover that they make only the most reasonable demands upon the insight and sensitivity of anyone who tries to fathom them.

By way of conclusion, it might be helpful to review a few of the salient images in the collation and bring out their Socratic and Judeo-Christian qualities and ideological implications. This will provide an opportunity to gather together into a brief synthesis some of the results achieved in all three aspects of the work: the inquiry into Rousseau's Socratic and Judeo-Christian affinities in image and idea; the comparison of *Emile* and the *Contract;* and the exploration of his use of mythical forms that leads to a revelation of the aforesaid affinities and thereby renews, expands, and enhances our knowledge of his writings and especially of these two.

Apart from the Socratic and Judeo-Christian analogy of soul and city, the most impressive of all images is the biblical one of the temple that is the key to the structure of

[404]

Emile and turns into a Socratic "citadel of the soul" in the *Contract*. In spite of the origin of the image, the temple of the book is basically of Greek design. Indeed, the foregoing study shows that in form as well as content the novel is an outstanding monument of the Greek revival in French art. Yet this study also demonstrates that the mythical temple is gradually transfigured in character to conform with the biblical nature of the image, especially in the innermost chamber where the intimate, inward mystic spirit of Christianity prevails as a powerful source of poetic lyricism and immense psychological expansion. In fine, the transcendental concept of the temple structure, combining elements affiliated with both traditions, is eminently suited to convey the idea that some of the choicest features of occidental culture provide the framework of the author's art and thought.

Within this architectonic ensemble innumerable other images testify to a similar accommodation of equally varied ingredients of artistic and intellectual inspiration. The few that are not Socratic and biblical are borrowed from *Robinson Crusoe,* Plutarch, La Fontaine, and Fénelon. I shall choose examples from each of the five parts of the masterwork and indicate their historical origins and ideological associations.

In the first part, the dedication of the book to a mother, the new Geneva and city of Sophia or wisdom, whose citizens are her children, provides an initial link not only with the *Social Contract,* written in honor of the same mythical city, but also with the Socratic republic, which is mother and nurse of its citizens and is personified in the Muse, its queen. This is Socrates' "royal lie" and the first "wave" that he must overcome to establish his city. However, the Aemilian image, idealizing womanhood from the first, is, of course, also Judeo-Christian. It is followed by the myth of the swaddling clothes analogous to the social fetters that prompted the writing of the *Contract* as well as the novel. Both metaphors are comparable with the Socratic myth of

[405]

prisoners burdened with chains in an underground den and awaiting their release and ascent into the upper world through the saving power of education or legislation. Rousseau recounts the same Socratic ascent in his companion volumes. In *Emile* he paradoxically imagines the possible release of his own "prisoners" through an impossible idealization of the home and family that becomes a non-Socratic and Judeo-Christian symbol to foreshadow the perfect city of the *Contract*. The city is also anticipated in the latter treatise by corresponding reflections upon the family. Thereafter both books contain Socratic warnings against tyranny and slavery, a cipher of evil passions that threaten the natural or ideal order of things in soul or city. These admonitions are followed in each case by a concrete presentation of spiritual engagements regarded as ultimately conducive to that order. For example, in *Emile* the Socratic personification of reason in Jean-Jacques, friendly to man or human nature in Emile, is motivated by friendship to make a Socratic and biblical covenant of peace instead of property, like that of the *Contract,* for the sake of human happiness. The covenant of friendship is, as we now know, an image of the lawful social bonds envisaged by the "royal lie." Its formulation leads in *Emile* to a Socratic attack upon charlatanical physician-statesmen who go about doctoring and complicating disorders instead of calling upon the services of a true physician and renewing the constitution, as Rousseau professes to do in his two books. The austere felicity he visualizes in both is equally Socratic and Judeo-Christian and consists of the freedom of human faculties from slavish and tyrannical desires, and enjoyment of the necessities of life or, if we wish, Rousseauist "property."

As we have seen, the second part of *Emile* is divided into two sections, the first of which is the most theoretical of all and contains the substance of the entire corresponding part of the *Contract*. There, as in the latter, the author gives precedence to the discipline of the guardian will through the agency of reason in the application of law, and provides for the imposition of narrow bounds upon vagrant desires to free the sovereign faculty. The idea of disciplining the will under the guidance of reason before dealing with the ruling power itself and entrusting the moral being to the enlightened will or habit of order to make the latter into an autonomous authority is Socratic, and so is its embodiment in law. And the Rousseauist laws of necessity, negative education, and the natural bent, or rather, of necessity and freedom, reinforced by the law of opinion are all defined, in the books herein collated, in exactly the same way as they are in the *Republic*. Their object in every case is also identical, namely, the common good or unity, which Socrates tries to secure by means of his second "wave," the control of every form of property, including the family, by the highest powers with a view to avoiding dissension in the moral being and fostering common feelings. Although Rousseau subsequently handles the latter in his own way, his ideas on property hardly differ for practical purposes from the Socratic and are no less favorable to the laws and their intent.

These laws govern the educational process described in the second section of the same part of *Emile* where the Rousseauist "guardian" is trained after the manner of the Socratic, in spite of a contemporary facade. His formation consists of Greek "musical" education, including "false" myths that illustrate the law or "strain" of necessity, such as those of the Socratic husbandman, lawbreaker, and promise-breaker. The said myths have great ideological value. For example, they entail a confrontation of the Rousseauist covenant, or law of peace, with the historical one of property, a confrontation that accentuates the opposing attitudes of each toward material possessions. The author thereby contrasts what he regards as a "false" order of human life and a "true" one. Proceeding to describe the latter, he passes from the "strain" or law of necessity to that of peace and freedom (including the law of negative education and the natural bent) that fosters and cultivates

[407]

the natural constitution through "true" myths, harmony, and rhythm. The myths in question, such as nighttime games and miniature Olympics—both to a considerable degree Socratic—teach the hero to see in the dark and have no fear, and to use his mind and will in the exercise of a primitive kind of justice. Other forms of "musical" education in the Greek sense provide Socratic shadows of images of the beauty, harmony, and taste that are to characterize and safeguard the mythical city. The ultimate aim is always to ensure the same ascetic happiness promised in the beginning.

The third part of both books is mainly Socratic, although to some extent it is also Judeo-Christian. Yet in *Emile* it is dominated by the modern image of Robinson Crusoe, whose sovereignty and kingship are compared in the beginning of the *Contract* with those of Adam or of man. The image is characteristic of the writer and gives those pages of the novel a contemporary air. Nevertheless, it is used to typify the Rousseauist student king, who is the real theme therein and who remains Socratic in spite of his Robinsonian garb. For this part of the two works, dealing with the governing faculty, is linked with Socrates' third "wave," which is the theory that philosophers must be kings, meaning that reason must rule in soul or city. In both Rousseau's texts that faculty is regarded more or less Socratically as a "mean proportional" between subject desires and sovereign will, a middle power whose strength and purpose are those of the moral being. In *Emile* the author uses a sequence of similitudes to indicate that his object is indeed the cultivation of reason in the art of government or orientation, exactly as it is in the same part of the *Contract*. The myths are well contrived to exemplify concretely this phase of Emile's progress, which matches the Socratic prelude to the formation of philosopher-kings. In brief his education is that prescribed by the sage for his own student kings. The imageries in question begin with what I called the little similitude of the sun, since it prefigures the big one in the next part and serves to symbolize the dawn of reason. It is followed by what I called the parable of the conjuror Socrates and the myth of Montmorency forest, both of which are Socratic and portray the hero's need for positive government by an enlightened aristocracy of superior powers or the true kingship of Adam or of man, rather than of monarchs, if he is to find his way to civilized life. That Socratic and biblical kingship is foreshadowed in both Rousseau's books by the image of Robinson Crusoe, which is greatly expanded at this point in *Emile*. By way of preparation for the more difficult exercise of the governing power in a social setting, each book sets forth the fatal effects of wealth upon that power and upon the whole moral being, and each exemplifies the duty of the ruling authority to anticipate such effects, ensure the preservation and prosperity of the human constitution and guard the latter against abuses and dissolution. These principles are illustrated in *Emile* by a new image of kingship, that of the Socratic and Judeo-Christian carpenter who learns "to do his own business" within a social framework and to execute a "shadow of justice" by paying his debt to society with the sweat of his brow. His best faculties are thereby schooled for the practice of real justice and higher forms of sovereignty and kingship.

The fourth part of *Emile* is dedicated to the further formation of the philosopher-king. There the author shows the enormous value of lawful social bonds to combat passions and sophisms. He does so by evolving the Socratic metaphor of friendship into a vast allegory at four crucial points occurring before and after the profession of faith. Each time he virtually quotes the words of Socrates that furnish, as I have said, the leitmotiv of the book. The Socratic passage in question concludes "musical" education in the *Republic* and is by now familiar to the reader of this study. According to the sage, a youth who has received the true education of the inner being will praise the good and hate the bad "even before he is able to know the reason

.why; and when reason comes he will recognize and salute the friend with whom his education has made him long familiar." Mindful of this passage, Rousseau relies upon Emile's recognition of the voice of friendship to offset temptation at critical moments before the intervention of faith when the hero is initiated first into Plutarch's more tragic biographies, and then into harsh lessons of life conveyed through the enactment of fables inspired by La Fontaine. In both cases the acknowledged friendship of reason for human nature is conceived as effective armor against passions and errors that also haunt the writer of the *Contract* at exactly the same juncture. After the profession of faith the author has further recourse to the Socratic text when he comes to closer grips with the problems of desires and sophisms besetting the soul from within and allayed through the ministry of friendship that permits a harmonious ordering of inner life regarded as real justice. For example, in the great scene of the covenant where passion is made known to the hero in his own person, the leitmotiv recurs, reason comes and Emile definitively recognizes and salutes his familiar friend. Again later when sophist seducers make their appeal to the soul, he discomfits them by acknowledging the voice of friendship and responding to its call. Such are the four contexts wherein Rousseau alludes in *Emile* to the famous phrase of the *Republic*. This is a fact that has never before been even suggested in a published work, but which we need to know if the book is not to remain forever enigmatic.

Many ideologically invaluable myths and other literary processes are also to be found in the middle section of the fourth part, the profession of faith. Indeed, it is itself one of the greatest myths in the book and contains the real similitude of the sun or the author's concept of revelation that is supposed to consecrate the philosophy of *Emile* and the *Contract*. It is both Socratic and Judeo-Christian. Since he calls it the "song of Orpheus," I concluded that it is

[410]

meant to tame the wild beast element in man and sustain the "friendly" voice of reason that favors human nature and the human will. It coincides essentially with the civic creed of the so-called "political" treatise. But in the masterwork religious faith is a profoundly personal experience, giving reality and incentive to the expanding inner life of a "leader" and strengthening both reason and will against lawless feelings and fallacies. In the appendix it is a creed for the common people (or subject desires) and, like the brief one in the last part of *Emile,* is added at the end of the book to sanctify a mythical city and its laws in the world of men and things where, however, that city can never be seen. In fine, it may not be said that in the matter of religion the *Contract* violates the order of the novel.

In both books the creed favors the ratification of the Rousseauist Socratic and biblical covenant of peace and of freedom that is meant to liberate human beings from the tyranny and slavery of passion. In each case the sovereign ruler or philosopher-king suddenly appears in an awesome setting to bring about the "wise order" of the *Contract* by "doing his own business" and providing for the operation of lawful government. And in each case the governing faculty is reinforced by special devices that maintain the proper balance of powers within the moral person. Not the least of these, as we know, is the censor's Socratic law of true opinion concerning beauty and honor, as it is described in the *Contract.* The fact that it has already been mentioned above in various contexts underscores its immense importance. This "universal saving power of true opinion," as Socrates calls it, is alleged to guarantee the soul against dangers of every kind. Its action, hitherto discreet, now becomes almost obtrusive and is illustrated in Emile's introduction to an image of Sophia and also in his study of aesthetics, which finally prepare him for participation in social life. At that stage the novelist takes great strides in carrying out his design, indicated in the ratification of the

[411]

covenant, to intensify the bonds of friendship through love and make the taste for moral beauty an irrevocable choice. He thereby uses the law of opinion to ensure the safety of an ideal order of things and secure the soul against threats from within or without.

In *Emile* the fourth part concludes with the aforementioned Socratic and Judeo-Christian blessed vision of beauty and wisdom that is meant to enshrine the law of true opinion at a high point in the book, as keystone of the vault of the mythical temple. That vision is remote from the abstractions of esoteric philosophy and reaches its culmination in the ecstatic contemplation of the white house and its mysterious inhabitants. If, as Rousseau says, there is nothing beautiful—or honorable—but what is not, here we behold the moral beauty that "is not," except in the realm of inner experience in the case of richly endowed individuals. The piece is, of course, unmatched in the *Contract,* where such intimate personal fulfillment would be out of place in the imagery of an exteriorized city.

The entire fifth part of *Emile* is also an intense spiritual adventure, and since, like the philosophic ecstasy at the end of the fourth, it is confined to the inner resources of philosopher-kings, there is no matching part in the appendix. There the author's doctrine is clearly seen to belong to the only domain where men can be really autonomous if they so choose.

This part, containing the great myth of Sophia and honoring her, is full of other Socratic, Judeo-Christian, and Fénelonian myths that lead the reader through a maze of paradoxes to reach the ideas thus arrayed and discern therein the source and substance of the *Contract.* But without an interpretation of imaginative forms, the writer's meaning would be puzzling to say the least. For instance, having relegated the city and its freemen, together with the family and its members, to the land of lost causes in the world of space and time, he now apparently resurrects them

[412]

all, as he does in the *Contract,* and fancies the little society of the home actually materializing to typify its larger counterpart. The imagery is, as I have said, Judeo-Christian rather than Socratic. But in truth he uses it to portray the love of wisdom that consummates the education of his Socratic philosopher-king. For Sophia, like the Socratic Muse or her Judeo-Christian Solomonic and evangelical equivalent, embodies the wisdom of the ideal civil order that is the goal of the hero's life. The symbolism of her person emerges from Rousseau's treatment of her formation, which is as enigmatic as his handling of her earlier portrait was, and resounds with telltale echoes of the *Symposium.*

The symbolism of the heroine explains why the author, having said that Emile's feeling for Jean-Jacques is his one and only unfailing affection, recounts the hero's enduring love for Sophia. It also discloses why, having declared in Paris that wisdom and happiness are always "nearby," he announces paradoxically that she who promises both is very far thence, apparently referring to spiritual rather than spatial remoteness. The same literary device further reveals why, after admitting that Sophia is dead—like her unfortunate prototype and like the wise order or city of his fancy—he brings her back to life again, as he does the Spartan city of the *Contract.* In speaking of her predecessor, he clearly alludes to the Socratic Muse of Philosophy, whom he christianizes through the influence of his own persuasions combined with that of a vicar of Christ, the priestly Platonist, Fénelon. The new Rousseauist Sophia, resurrected for a skeptical age, is therefore the heir of both the Socratic and Judeo-Christian ones. The visionary apparition of the heroine, presented as the object of a courtship, affords the hero a Socratic "foretaste" of the blessed contemplation of wisdom and beauty, consisting of an equally Socratic intercommunion of all studies previously undertaken and related thereto.

The myth of Sophia, like the dream she incarnates, is

[413]

counterbalanced by a philosophical profession of faith contained in an abstract of the *Contract,* or rather, of *Political Institutions*, and encompassing the teaching of both books from the first. It leads to Emile's fruitless search through the world of matter for the Aemilian and Fénelonian city, christianized like the heroine and matching not merely the aforesaid abstract but Rousseauist wisdom herself, for the order he seeks is the only one where he might live happily with her on earth and where the two worlds might fuse into one. But in the sphere of actuality it is as mythical as she appears to be. Emile learns that the city, and probably Sophia too, exist only in the kingdom within by virtue of an inner covenant of peace pledged to ensure the moral freedom essential to felicity. He also discovers that the necessities of life, that other ingredient of austere Rousseauist happiness, belong to the domain of a very different pact — the pact of property — that allegedly favors the rich at the expense of the poor and sacrifices the weak to the strong, and the just to the unjust. Finally the governor, having proved that there is no corner in Europe where Emile may dwell with Sophia, directs him back to that corner where she abides, the human spirit where the Rousseauist city is enshrined. In case the anomalies already mentioned do not suffice to arouse our curiosity, the writer thrice refers to her in the masculine gender. Whatever else she may be for Emile, she is essentially Socratic "divine wisdom dwelling within him." She is the genius that has presided over his education from his birth and to which he is finally wedded in a mythical Socratic marriage or beatific vision that takes place in a spiritual world fashioned after the same prototype as the appendix.

The interrelationships that permit this broader interpretation of Rousseau's works and include verifiable ties with Solomon, Christ, Socrates, and the Platonic dialogues, especially the *Republic,* bring to the surface two remarkable characteristics of the way of life he teaches. Appropriately enough they are respectively associated with his laws of freedom and necessity.

The law of necessity accentuates his austerity. The very condition of the spiritual expansion he means to favor and foster is poverty. The cultivation and growth of man's noblest powers as he visualizes those processes is, in his view, possible only for persons who are content to limit themselves in material things to the mere necessities of life and are willing to forgo all else. The age of gold he promises vanishes with the amassing of gold. Happiness for him springs only from his own concept of wisdom and beauty, which positively excludes the possession of property in the modern sense of the word or in any other sense, unless it be akin to Socratic or the earliest Judeo-Christian asceticism.

Another aspect of his philosophy that looms large in this study is his extreme conservatism. The ideal order of things, born of his law of freedom, comes about through an act of the will on the part of privileged individuals who, far from thinking about reforming other people or indulging the desire for power or prestige, consider the main business of life to be the education of oneself, and the constant exercise of sovereignty and kingship in the domain of inner experience. We have seen that education thus conceived is the very theme of *Emile* and the *Contract*. It is a continuous and never ending effort at personal evolution, having nothing at all to do with revolution. That is so in spite of the disorders to which Rousseau's own startling statements, distorted by the licentious dispositions of men and colored by the follies of the time, have given rise. The conservative aspect of his thought, like his austerity, is typically Socratic as well as essentially Judeo-Christian. Both identify him as an authentic heir of the mainstreams of occidental tradition, however falsely he may interpret certain of their precepts.

In fine, to be aware of his purpose and affinities as a writer is to understand the extent of the vandalism wrought by the perpetrators of the *Emile* case, whatever their inten-

[415]

tions may have been. That the work is conceivably of a persuasion other than one's own, or of a design more or less suited to one's taste, is as irrelevant as one's private opinion of the author. But, unfortunately, provocative works of art and of thought like *Emile* and the *Contract* will always be a prey to the extravagances of the religious, moral, or political temper of which mankind is so tragically a victim.

1. "Emile," p. 849.
2. *Republic* 2.369.
3. "Emile," p. 673.

Index

Abraham, 59, 260

Absolutism, 51, 59, 93

Abstract man, 44, 57, 147

Acceptance of persons, 99, 218

Active thinking being, 63, 92, 178, 182, 235, 237, 240, 332, 359, 374, 393

Adam, 26, 51, 52, 57, 87, 168, 169, 239, 408, 409

Aemilians, 55

Aemilius, 55

Aeneas, 336, 353

Aeneid, 238, 287

Aesthetic doctrine, 15, 18, 401, 403

Aesthetics, 16, 17, 18, 31, 135-37, 276, 278, 286, 287, 288, 314, 316, 322, 326 332, 384, 387, 393, 399, 400, 411

Aesthetic taste, 287, 307. *See also* Taste

Aims of this study, 13-14, 20-21, 383, 389, 394-95, 398-99, 404

Allegory, 13, 14, 15, 17, 20, 27, 37, 47, 48, 57, 73, 155, 165, 166, 167, 198, 232, 267, 309, 310, 317, 321, 323, 333, 345, 367, 372, 373, 374, 394, 409; of the hunt, 166, 335; of the races, 243 (*see also* Olympic games); of Robinson Crusoe, 167-68, 408-409

Alps, 226, 228, 240

Amoral condition of natural man, 69 87, 396

Amusement(s), 112, 122, 135, 286, 315, 351, 386. *See also* Pleasures

Antichrist, 9, 10

Antiope, 321, 322, 336, 353

Anti-society, 24, 29, 38, 40, 41, 43, 53, 62, 69, 89, 117, 124, 125, 213, 215, 249, 346, 396

Apollo, 29, 30, 221, 229

Apostasy: Rousseau on, 250-51, 261

Apostolic epistles, 384

Appendix to *Emile*, 4, 12, 14, 15, 21, 25, 27, 31, 37, 76, 102, 170, 190, 195, 203, 211, 222, 293, 394, 411, 412, 414

Aristocracy, 160, 161-63, 174, 270, 271, 361, 362, 409

Armenian costume, 6

Art, 15, 22, 23, 25, 31, 37, 38, 41, 45, 112, 129, 134, 151, 154

Art: city or state as work of, 22, 23, 41, 178; in education of Emile, 134, 154, 167, 170-71, 339, 400-401; *Emile* as work of, 327-30; of forming men, 178, 263; and morality, 286-87; and the natural constitution, 112; and reason, 151, 156; Rousseau's use of, 14, 17, 23, 37, 38, 45, 129, 165, 210, 222, 228, 288, 327, 342, 344, 405

Assemblies of citizens, 183, 215, 266, 271, 272, 273, 274

Astronomy, 155, 165

Athens, 29, 30, 346, 385

Athlete: Emile as, 126, 128, 135, 163

Authoritarianism, 95, 283

Authority: in education of Emile, 158,

Authority *(continued)*
186, 268, 275, 355-56, 359, 375; and individual, 87, 93, 391; and lawgiver, 105, 182-83, 188-89, 409. *See also* Lawgiver; Sovereign; Sovereignty; Sovereign will

Autobiography: Rousseau's works as, 16, 19, 222-25, 280, 288, 392, 402. *See also "Confessions"*

Autodidact, 27, 376

Balance of faculties or powers, 66, 83, 87, 88, 99, 161, 170, 175, 239, 240, 262, 275, 276, 295, 398, 411

Ball between crossed fingers, 186

"Barbarians," 54, 96, 215

Beatific vision, 224, 292, 294, 351, 372, 398, 412, 414

Beauty, 148, 217, 219, 247, 341, 393, 400, 401, 408, 413, 415; absolute, 329, 339, 351; and development of inner life, 134-36, 291, 292, 327; of divine order of things, 311; moral, 325, 328; as moral influence, 246, 247, 286-87, 316, 320, 411-12; moral versus physical, 17, 246; of nature, 18, 38, 67, 133; of order, 22, 23, 29, 243, 319, 322; of Sophia or wisdom, 279, 331, 333, 350; of virtues, 233, 312-13

Beneficence, 217, 343, 356, 369

"Best for oneself and for others too," 26, 66, 75, 94

Bible: correspondances with *Emile* and *Social Contract*, 17, 19, 20, 28, 29, 43, 62, 69, 99, 101, 130, 149, 150, 180, 219, 227, 228, 231, 239, 244, 257, 266, 279, 287, 306, 313, 357, 384, 404, 405, 406, 409, 411. *See also* New Testament; Old Testament; under "Book"

Birthplace: of Emile, 262, 345, 355, 366, 368, 371; of Rousseau, 271, 289, 396

"Blocks of wood," 265, 363, 390. *See also* "Posts"

Book of Deuteronomy, 256

Book of Ecclesiastes, 228, 254, 279

Book of Ecclesiasticus, 227, 234

Book of Genesis, 256, 257, 306

Book of Job, 116

Book of Judges, 5

Book of Proverbs, 279, 336

Book of Wisdom, 279, 336

Books, 28, 122, 125, 157

Bossey, 130, 227, 253

"Broken stick": image of, 186

Caesar, 119, 182, 245, 346

Calvinism, 7, 222, 223, 224, 225, 226, 253, 267, 372, 396

Candle: image of, 127

Carpenter: as mythical image, 179-81, 184, 186, 187, 344, 356, 390, 409

Catechism, 220, 317

Catholicism, 223, 226, 230, 253, 257

Cato, 55, 209, 245, 346, 347, 367, 386

Celibacy, 230, 231, 247, 250, 258, 364

Censor, 277, 318, 399, 411

Censorship, 276, 277, 285

Charge of "padding," 28, 108-10, 173-75, 271-77, 397

Charity, 9, 116, 217, 218, 259, 260, 317, 322, 343, 345, 347, 363

Chastity, 231, 267, 284, 307, 320

Choice of life, 333, 370, 375, 391. *See also* Vision of Er

Christ, 4, 6, 10, 11, 19, 20, 22, 25, 26, 27, 28, 30, 59, 60, 69, 96, 112, 113, 138, 150, 175, 180, 189, 225, 226, 227, 229, 232, 233, 251, 254, 255, 256, 257, 259, 260, 261, 269, 288, 313, 320, 334, 347, 384, 387, 396, 413, 414

Christian tradition: in Rousseau's writings, 8, 9, 18, 22, 23, 26, 30, 39, 46, 92, 116, 119, 180, 181, 211, 218, 220, 221, 226, 227, 246, 248, 252, 259, 271, 287, 292, 321, 322, 327, 338, 345, 347, 351, 352, 363

Christianity, 9, 18, 19, 221, 231, 232, 233, 248, 253, 370, 405

Citadel, 29, 195, 282, 367, 405

Citizen: art most necessary to, 277, 285; duties of, 63, 88-89, 96, 214-15,

219, 252, 320; family role of, 201, 309, 317, 375-76; in ideal society, 63, 88-89, 96, 214-15, 219, 252, 320; and liberty, 177, 366; and "mother city" image, 48-50, 59, 352, 405; as natural man, 24, 41; and religion, 248-49, 262; ruled by own will, 183, 361

Citizenship, 9, 15, 23-24, 85, 98, 110, 113, 145, 151, 305, 309, 348, 358, 364, 395, 402

City. See Soul: equated with city-state

City-state, 10, 21, 38, 85, 109, 271, 364. See also Soul: equated with city-state

City within, 22, 113, 356, 363, 364, 366, 367, 368, 370, 375, 376, 396

Civic religion, 232, 248, 249, 251, 252, 253, 258, 260, 272, 317, 411

Civil contract, 230, 277, 331, 372, 398

Civil life, 76, 390

Civil order, 30, 40, 41, 248, 249, 266, 267, 288, 290, 294, 305, 331, 332, 352, 363, 398, 413

Civil society, 185, 358

Civil state, 24, 70, 186, 331

Classical tradition: in Rousseau's writings, 18, 128, 129, 211, 218, 228, 287, 322, 367, 384, 387, 401, 402, 403, 404

Collectivism, 15, 63, 72

Common feelings, 201, 203, 407

Common good. See Happiness

Common happiness, 61, 63, 110. See also Happiness

Common interest. See Happiness

Common pleasures and pains, 201, 203

Common sense, 146, 214, 216, 236, 319, 402. See also Reason

Common utility. See Happiness

Compass: image of, 133, 155, 157, 158, 159, 161, 163, 166, 234

Compassion, 105, 198, 199, 205, 208, 218, 224, 246, 259, 346

Condillac, Etienne Bonnot de, 39, 44

Confessions (Rousseau), 9, 12, 15, 16, 18, 19, 71, 130, 167, 173, 180, 223, 224, 250, 251, 288, 318, 334, 375

Conscience, 30, 84, 93, 184, 190, 204, 213, 214, 224, 225, 226, 228, 231, 234, 239, 245, 246, 247, 248, 251, 253, 260, 262, 263, 268, 282, 283, 288, 318, 349, 359, 360, 367, 387

Considerations upon the Government of Poland (Rousseau), 26, 42, 49, 91, 125, 180, 185, 348, 367, 389

"Constant will," 183, 215, 247, 251, 268. See also Will

Constitution of man or city, 22, 24, 48, 51, 62, 63, 65, 66, 67, 69, 83, 85, 86, 87, 88, 89, 90, 91, 92, 95, 96, 97, 103, 104, 105, 106, 109, 110, 111, 112, 113, 114, 126, 139, 140, 150, 151, 160, 169, 171, 176, 177, 178, 183, 188, 213, 215, 217, 232, 233, 248, 250, 274, 275, 276, 278, 286, 296, 307, 308, 312, 314, 322, 356, 386, 392, 396, 406, 408

Constraint, 46, 47, 107, 276, 315, 373

Contract, 59, 62, 368, 372. See also Covenant

Cosmopolitanism, 345, 397

Courage, 82, 103, 112, 130, 131, 139, 184, 187, 282, 311

Courtship, 305, 337, 413

Covenant, 60, 61, 63, 64, 66, 68, 69, 70, 93, 94, 95, 111, 120, 124, 139, 140, 150, 177, 188, 203, 213, 215, 227, 235, 237, 250, 251, 266, 267, 268, 269, 277, 279, 305, 307, 308, 313, 316, 317, 318, 323, 352, 359, 362, 364, 365, 366, 367, 368, 371, 372, 373, 374, 392, 407, 410, 411, 412; of friendship, 54, 59, 61, 65, 75, 140, 203, 215, 280, 349, 355, 366, 398, 406; of peace, 316, 406, 407, 411, 414; of promise, 59, 359, 362, 373

Creation, 154, 181, 238, 395

Creator, 38, 97, 181, 238, 239, 244, 390

Curiosity, 147, 157, 221

Death, 22, 46, 50, 84, 95, 96, 97, 128, 177, 178, 240, 241, 243, 244, 250, 251, 259, 267, 311, 312, 320, 325, 330, 339, 342, 347, 348, 350, 352, 367, 413

Deception. *See* Duplicity

Dedication: of *Emile*, 37-38, 45, 314, 377, 405; of second *Discourse*, 69, 272, 289

Delay in education. *See* "Negative education"

Delphi, 29, 30, 31, 197, 227, 229

Democracy, 160-61, 174, 189, 269, 270, 356, 361, 362

Dénouement of *Emile*, 365

Descartes, René, 187, 234, 237

Desires: as enemy within, 263-64, 279-80, 283, 349-50, 410-11; good distinguished from evil, 196, 213-14; and law of necessity, 84, 111, 415; and rulers, 139, 168-69, 269; and sovereign will, 89, 93, 94, 96, 99, 103, 149, 150, 151, 161, 170, 174, 333, 352, 359, 361, 373, 407, 408; unreasonable, 74, 83, 84, 85, 88, 100, 106, 176, 180, 185, 216, 233, 356, 360, 366, 367, 406; woman as agent of control of, 311-12

Despotism, 74, 95, 168, 174, 175, 232, 253

Detachment: from property, 366; from the world, 225, 249, 350, 371

Dialogue of Inspiration and Reason, 256-57

Dialogues (Rousseau), 16, 167, 288, 375

Dialogues of the vicar and apostles, 255-56

Dictatorship, 275, 276, 352

Dictionary of Music (Rousseau), 16, 17, 229

Diderot, Denis, 238, 260

Discourse upon the Arts and Sciences (Rousseau), 3, 6, 12, 16, 19, 28, 44, 45, 65, 154

Discourse upon Inequality (Rousseau), 3, 6, 12, 16, 19, 37, 39, 45, 52, 53, 62, 69, 72, 73, 119, 120, 124, 171, 198, 272, 334, 385

Doric influence, 30, 92, 135, 196

Drawing and painting, 133, 134

Duplicity, 95, 211, 332

Duties of man, 21, 56, 68, 82, 84, 104, 106, 107, 122, 138, 180, 204, 249, 252, 287, 294

Earning of bread, 157, 158, 173, 176, 180, 182, 355

Earthly paradise, 293, 337, 338, 372

Ecclesia, 313, 317

Ecclesiastes, 225, 255, 261

Eclogues of Virgil, 318, 327

Ecstasy, 292, 294, 314, 337, 339, 348, 374, 400, 412

Education: adapted to individual, 108; for citizenship, 15, 106, 139; and discernment of good from evil, 28, 204-5; domestic vs. public, 42-43; *Emile* and *Social Contract* as treatise on, 23-27, 81-82, 101-4, 108-9, 113, 176-77, 275, 277-78, 357, 389, 391-94; and family, 308-10; gymnastic in, 126, 128-29; and legislation, 92, 100-103, 112; literary, 206-8; on luxury, 172-73; and nature, 28, 40; "negative," 107-8, 111, 113, 125-26, 128, 197-99, 407; of philosopher-kings, 152-55, 166, 168-69, 185, 187, 203-4, 216-21, 227, 236, 337, 372, 409; "positive," 122-25, 196, 340; reason and, 105, 106, 107, 176; removed from passions, 91; *Republic* as finest treatise on, 285-86; sensorial, 71, 129-38, 408; of Socratic heroes, 20-22, 113-16, 155-56, 343; true aims of, 84, 85, 277, 400; of woman, 201, 308-9, 312-21, 376, 387; and worldly society, 280-85

Educator-legislator, 111, 115, 181, 273, 275

Elections by choice or lot, 270, 271

Emile and Sophia (sequel to *Emile*), 325

Emile case, 4-11, 415

Emotions, 195 ff., 266, 291, 327, 367, 375. *See also* Feelings; Passions

Enemies, 204, 205, 207, 211, 217, 223, 251, 263, 264, 265, 267, 349, 370

Enlightened will, 64, 65, 70, 72, 73, 85, 86, 88, 93, 95, 99, 102, 126, 268, 316, 352, 364, 373, 390, 407. *See also* Reasonable will

Environment, 55, 167, 171, 172, 200

Equality, 46, 71, 73, 74, 75, 93, 94, 110, 139, 160, 162, 172, 212, 213, 270, 286, 290, 332

Error, 46, 186-87, 209, 212, 215, 216, 236, 279, 280, 284, 410, 411

Essay upon Theatrical Imitation, 208, 296 n. 15

Essay upon the Origin of Languages, 16, 17

Essay upon wealth, 288, 335, 337, 338, 356, 375, 393, 400

Ethics, 17, 316, 400

Eucharis, 336, 353

Evangelical Christianity, 248, 249, 250, 253, 259

Evil, passim, esp. 205 ff. *See also* Errors; Passions

Executive power, 149, 150, 159, 178, 188, 275. *See also* Government; Reason

Fables: in education, 115, 123, 124, 125, 206, 210, 211, 212, 215, 216, 279, 282, 410

Faculties of man, 39, 52, 53, 56, 67, 68, 69, 71, 75, 83, 84, 88, 90, 94, 95, 99, 103, 104, 106, 110, 111, 112, 120, 125, 133, 134, 139, 140, 150, 158, 161, 162, 169, 174, 176, 180, 184, 185, 200, 212, 221, 232, 240, 247, 262, 268, 274, 275, 283, 317, 318, 333, 357, 358, 361, 366, 367, 368, 373, 390, 395, 398, 402, 406, 408, 409, 411

Fallacies. *See* Error; Sophisms

False myths, 114, 115, 117-22, 407

Family: as educational institution, 45-46; and law of the strongest, 89-90; as miniature of ideal city, 24, 45, 47, 307-10, 312, 316, 318, 319, 321, 326, 348, 375, 387, 406, 412-13; Socrates on, 45, 50, 308-9, 407; as symbol of the good life, 369-70

Father: as symbol, 49, 50, 51, 54, 58, 60, 75, 90, 97, 138, 196, 267, 282, 307, 308, 309, 310, 317, 323, 331, 353, 359, 367, 375, 376, 392

Fear, 202, 233, 282

Federation, 183, 362, 363

Feelings, 89, 107, 108, 154, 182, 196, 198, 208, 213, 246, 263, 287, 331, 337, 349, 373, 411, 413. *See also* Emotions; Passions

Felicity, 61, 82, 83, 84, 85, 139, 147, 148, 150, 163, 167, 168, 199, 202, 218, 247, 270, 287, 288, 292, 294, 311, 316, 343, 349, 356, 365, 406, 414. *See also* Happiness

Fénelon, François de Salignac de La Mothe, 38, 154, 243, 265, 321, 322, 324, 326, 329, 336, 352, 363, 364, 405, 412, 413, 414

Fidelity, 307, 308, 317, 318, 360, 365, 371, 373

Finance, 184, 324, 338, 355

First occupancy, 70, 72, 118

Force, 46, 54, 70, 273, 358, 373, 390

"Foretaste" of paradise or wisdom, 337, 339, 340, 341, 348, 350, 351, 372, 376, 398, 413

"Forget thyself," 30, 261, 269

Formey, Jean-Louis-Samuel, 16

Fortitude, 112, 128, 178. *See also* Courage

France, 7, 9, 57, 230

Freedom, 46, 51, 53, 62, 64, 70, 71, 72, 74, 84, 85, 86, 89, 91, 92, 93, 94, 95, 96, 99, 100, 105, 107, 109, 110, 119, 120, 132, 139, 140, 150, 167, 169, 173, 175, 177, 183, 185, 196, 207, 215, 236, 241, 251, 260, 289, 290, 292, 293, 331, 350, 352, 357, 358, 359, 360, 361, 363, 366, 367, 406, 411, 414, 415; and necessity as correlatives, 177, 183. *See also* Law of freedom; Law of necessity

Freudian methods, 230, 268

Friends, 21, 59, 65, 111, 113, 118, 126, 148, 157, 163, 167, 171, 173, 179, 182, 189, 204, 209, 211, 216, 217, 218, 219, 251, 259, 262, 264, 266, 267, 268, 269, 278, 282, 290, 313, 330, 346, 363

Friendship, 59, 60, 62, 63, 64, 65, 74, 86, 122, 128, 138, 139, 145, 179,

Friendship (continued)
183, 186, 198, 199, 202, 203, 211, 213, 217, 219, 246, 249, 263, 264, 266, 267, 282, 283, 290, 306, 311, 315, 337, 346, 349, 388, 396, 400, 406, 409, 410, 412

Future life, 22, 242, 243, 244, 246, 250, 317, 350

Gain, 93, 213, 289, 349, 355, 356, 365

Gainful faculties, 21, 150, 162, 174, 176, 177, 179, 180, 182

Galatea, 318, 327, 328, 329

Galilee, 181, 227, 344

General will, 85, 215, 216. See also Enlightened will; Reasonable will; Sovereign; Sovereignty; Will

Geneva, 5, 6, 10, 11, 37, 38, 41, 43, 55, 189, 214, 219, 223, 271, 272, 289, 396, 405

Genevan, 224, 243, 271, 348, 396

Geography, 115, 123, 125, 155

Geometry, 115, 123, 133, 146, 147, 154, 186, 361

God, 7, 8, 9, 22, 59, 98, 99, 130, 181, 182, 196, 208, 220, 221, 224, 226, 227, 228, 229, 235, 236, 238, 239, 242, 243, 244, 245, 247, 254, 255, 256, 259, 260, 261, 262, 288, 313, 317, 339, 345, 363, 390

Godhead, 29, 195, 221, 256, 261

Gold, 182, 206, 288, 290, 292, 293, 360, 415

Golden age, 292, 294, 350, 369, 415

Golden mediocrity, 292, 370

Good, passim. See also Wisdom

Goodness, 239, 242, 247, 292, 293, 365. See also Natural goodness

Gospel, 10, 166, 175, 231, 259, 288, 336, 384

Government (or orientation), 21, 24, 25, 30, 84, 97, 98, 104, 147, 148, 149, 150, 151, 152, 155, 158, 159, 160, 163, 168, 169, 170, 171, 172, 173, 174, 176, 177, 183, 188, 189, 190, 214, 216, 230, 249, 262, 266, 270, 275, 276, 277, 286, 293, 309, 312, 318, 352, 355, 358, 361, 364, 367,

368, 374, 386, 391, 393, 398, 408, 409, 411

Governor, 16, 22, 43, 54, 55, 56, 58, 59, 61, 67, 68, 74, 86, 97, 99, 104, 105, 107, 108, 110, 112, 115, 116, 117, 121, 122, 123, 126, 133, 139, 146, 147, 148, 149, 152, 156, 157, 158, 159, 161, 162, 164, 166, 168, 169, 170, 171, 173, 176, 178, 179, 181, 182, 183, 188, 189, 196, 198, 202, 203, 206, 207, 209, 210, 211, 216, 262, 263, 264, 266, 268, 269, 270, 271, 275, 279, 281, 283, 284, 305, 310, 332, 333, 343, 348, 350, 352, 355, 357, 359, 360, 363, 364, 366, 368, 369, 371, 372, 373, 375, 392, 414

Greco-Roman influence, 20, 175, 384, 403

Greece, 18, 185, 324

Greek culture, 19, 44

Greek education, 43, 407, 408

Greek heroes (Republic), 69, 119, 122, 131, 134, 206, 288, 368

Greek philosophers, 19, 42, 45, 138, 385, 389

Greek sculpture, 44, 286

Greek temple, 29-31, 196, 227, 305, 330, 405

Greek writers, 17, 19, 45, 207

Greeks, 183, 185, 259, 327

Guardian(s), 21, 22, 53, 59, 64, 96, 101, 103, 113, 114, 115, 125, 126, 129, 131, 135, 136, 137, 138, 139, 140, 152, 166, 176, 188, 202, 221, 233, 244, 282, 333, 355, 356, 386, 393, 400, 406, 407

Gymnastic, 114, 115, 125, 126, 128, 129, 136, 137, 163

Habit, 71, 89, 128, 265, 363, 391; of good order, 112, 128, 277, 342, 374, 375, 407

Happiness, 3, 4, 16, 18, 21, 25, 27, 28, 40, 48, 54, 57, 64, 65, 69, 71, 81, 82, 83, 84, 85, 86, 87, 92, 93, 94, 100, 103, 104, 105, 106, 110, 111, 112, 118, 122, 123, 124, 125, 138, 140, 146, 147, 148-49, 150, 153, 156,

163, 164, 165, 167, 174, 179, 184, 185, 189, 199, 200, 202, 207, 208, 209, 215, 216, 218, 223, 225, 232, 242, 247, 248, 249, 250, 262, 266, 267, 270, 278, 279, 285, 287, 288, 289, 291, 292, 293, 294, 307, 311, 312, 314, 315, 316, 319, 322, 323-24, 331, 334, 341, 348, 349, 350, 351, 352, 354, 356, 357, 360, 365, 366, 367, 368, 369, 372, 374, 388, 392, 393, 394, 406, 408, 413, 414, 415

Harmony, 115, 116, 126, 129, 133, 134, 315, 322, 327, 331, 339, 358, 368, 371, 400, 408, 410

Health, 84, 101, 103, 109, 134, 207, 245, 267, 289, 292, 356

Hearing, 134-35

Heart, 16, 17, 18, 19, 24, 26, 29, 48, 49, 50, 83, 99, 107, 123, 126, 154, 178, 197, 198, 199, 203, 205, 206, 207, 212, 219, 242, 245, 249, 254, 259, 260, 261, 262, 263, 264, 266, 267, 277, 287, 289, 306, 307, 314, 318, 322, 324, 325, 328, 329, 338, 339, 341, 346, 347, 348, 349, 353, 354, 356, 363, 367, 370, 371, 373, 374, 377, 401

Heaven, 22, 244, 391

Hell, 244

Hellespont, 128, 342

Helmsman: as symbol, 56, 57, 126, 128, 155, 157, 159, 196, 217, 234, 269, 392

Hesiod, 114, 124, 125

Hierarchy within the self, 62, 83, 85, 105, 110, 161, 232, 274; equated to government of men, 105, 110, 161, 274

History, 18, 115, 123, 124, 125, 176, 206, 211, 340, 354, 354-55, 362

Home: as symbol, 45, 46, 47, 49, 52, 319, 387, 406, 413

Homer, 114, 124, 125

Honor, 93, 104, 179, 276, 278, 279, 285, 310, 312, 319, 323, 337, 357, 411

Human beings, 26, 99, 171, 251, 255, 264, 358, 411

Human condition, 44, 83, 403

Human constitution. See Constitution of man or city

Human faculties. See Faculties of man

Human feelings. See Feelings

Human nature, 15, 27, 45, 46, 55, 60, 61, 64, 86, 87, 206, 232, 268, 293, 308, 329, 332, 336, 345, 346, 392, 396, 403, 406, 410, 411. See also Nature of man

Human rights, 251, 252, 345, 346, 347, 348, 358

Human spirit, 29, 45, 216, 283, 290, 305, 306, 360, 364, 365, 374, 403, 414

Humanism, 20, 60, 63, 65, 95, 273, 359, 396

Humanitarianism, 179, 198, 217, 251, 294, 344, 345, 346, 347, 348, 349

Humanity, 16, 83, 116, 118, 162, 198, 202, 203, 205, 218, 230, 231, 242, 294, 323, 325, 328, 344, 348

Husbandman, 75, 117, 119, 179, 180, 265, 343, 356, 407

Husbandry, 335, 356

Hymn, 229, 233, 247

IDEA of man, 44, 264

IDEA of city, 44

IDEA of harmony, 368

Imagery, 12, 13, 14, 17, 20, 22, 23, 37, 43, 50, 51, 56, 58, 59, 62, 65, 75, 102, 115, 121, 123, 124, 127, 129, 131, 136, 147, 155, 165, 174, 175, 176, 181, 190, 204, 210, 226, 227, 228, 230, 234, 238, 242, 245, 246, 253, 259, 265, 266, 268, 269, 273, 278, 282, 283, 309, 317, 320, 322, 323, 324, 327, 328, 329, 343, 344, 351, 352, 354, 357, 362, 369, 370, 375, 377, 384, 387, 390, 392, 393, 394, 396, 397, 399, 400, 404, 405, 408, 409, 411, 412, 413

"Images of virtue," 164, 187, 265, 328

Imagination, 13, 17, 18, 76, 183, 198, 227, 396

Immortality, 244, 312, 313

Impulse, 41, 68, 90, 161

Individualist desires, 64, 65, 86, 94, 99, 162

Industrial and mechanical arts, 154,

Industrial *(continued)*
170, 171, 182

Injustice, 21, 118, 122, 217, 246, 281, 365, 368, 395

Inner feeling, 234, 235, 236, 237, 245, 324

Insight, 234, 236, 293, 377, 394, 404

Instinct, 23, 41, 45, 62, 68, 87, 88, 99, 247, 263, 283, 341

Intellect, 17, 235, 331

Intelligence, 146, 235, 237, 238, 241, 324

Intercommunion of studies, 340, 341, 344, 348, 350-51

Intolerance, 88, 89, 249, 250, 251, 252, 258, 260, 317

Ionic mode, 30, 135

Isaiah, 253, 255

Italy, 175, 222, 224

Ithaca, 324, 353

Jesus, 10 n

John the Baptist, 253, 255, 260

Judeo-Christian tradition, 20, 59, 68, 116, 228, 242, 244, 251, 253, 255, 259, 291, 313, 320, 321, 325, 343, 356, 377, 384, 403, 405, 406, 408, 409, 410, 412, 413, 415

Judgment, 133, 186, 235, 236, 241, 245, 315, 393, 403

Julie, 3, 4, 12, 15, 16, 19, 28, 49, 84

Justice, 5, 21, 26, 27, 52, 56, 68, 74, 75, 91, 94, 98, 99, 100, 101, 103, 112, 117, 121, 132, 137, 139, 149, 158, 163, 165, 166, 167, 173, 176, 179, 180, 181, 182, 184, 185, 204, 205, 217, 218, 219, 230, 239, 240, 242, 244, 245, 246, 247, 259, 260, 263, 264, 265, 267, 268, 274, 281, 311, 312, 317, 335, 341, 344, 345, 347, 351, 356, 357, 358, 368, 370, 376, 388, 395, 408, 409, 410

Keystone of the vault, 113, 277, 323, 393, 398, 399, 412

Kingdom within, 72. *See also* City within

Kings, 51, 52, 54, 55, 57, 63, 147, 149, 150, 152, 153, 154, 160, 161, 163, 166, 167, 168, 169, 176, 187, 188, 201, 204, 217, 218, 221, 227, 233, 236, 244, 273, 289, 337, 351, 356, 363, 372, 376, 401, 408

Kingship, 55, 57, 147, 150, 152, 154, 168, 169, 176, 183, 269, 270, 271, 363, 393, 398, 408, 409, 415

Knowledge, 27, 146, 197, 209, 210, 215, 217, 229, 235, 236, 279, 310, 318, 333, 334, 340, 383, 389, 394, 400, 403

"Know thyself," 30, 197, 261

Lady Philosophy, 6, 8. *See also* Muse of Philosophy

La Fontaine, 18, 124, 167, 210, 211, 405, 410; "The Cricket and the Ant," 124; "The Fox and the Crow," 124, 211; "The Frog and the Ox," 211; "The Wolf and the Dog," 124

Land of chimeras, 25, 219

Law, 21, 24, 25, 30, 49, 50, 52, 53, 55, 56, 58, 59, 61, 63, 66, 72, 75, 81, 82, 90, 92, 93, 94, 97, 98, 99, 100, 101, 102, 103, 105, 106, 107, 108, 109, 110, 111, 112, 113, 117, 119, 121, 124, 125, 126, 138, 140, 148, 149, 150, 152, 155, 172, 178, 182, 183, 198, 200, 204, 205, 212, 213, 214, 215, 217, 221, 227, 230, 231, 232, 233, 235, 237, 238, 242, 245, 246, 247, 248, 249, 250, 252, 255, 258, 259, 260, 261, 262, 263, 264, 266, 267, 268, 269, 270, 272, 273, 274, 275, 276, 282, 284, 285, 286, 292, 306, 308, 311, 313, 314, 315, 316, 317, 320, 323, 341, 347, 352, 354, 355, 356, 358, 359, 360, 361, 362, 363, 364, 366, 367, 368, 370, 373, 374, 375, 386, 391, 393, 394, 397, 400, 407, 411; of education, 275, 276; of freedom, 85, 90, 97, 107, 108, 111, 112, 113, 115, 122, 139, 213, 308, 324, 398, 407, 415; of friendship, 213, 308; of love, 91, 202, 268, 307, 308, 323, 341, 373; of marriage, 268; of nature, 90, 267, 329; of necessity, 84, 85, 90, 91, 92, 97, 106, 110, 111, 112, 113, 115, 118, 119, 120, 122, 139, 146, 163, 175, 202, 213, 308, 324, 349, 350, 367, 398, 407, 415; of negative education,

107, 108, 109, 110, 111, 112, 113, 115, 125, 127, 128, 398, 407; of public opinion, 113, 276, 318, 399, 400, 411, 412; of peace, 407; of poverty, 324; of reason, 60, 98, 106, 112, 139, 169, 171, 263, 267, 307, 308, 315, 324, 331, 341, 349; of the natural bent, 108, 109, 111, 112, 213, 398, 407; of the reasonable will, 343; of religion, 235, 250, 317; of the strongest, 52, 89, 98, 205, 213; of wisdom, 337, 342

Lawbreaker, 121, 407

Lawful social bonds, 46, 203, 263, 409

Lawgiver, 103, 104, 105, 109, 139, 221

Lawlessness, 91, 98, 112, 117, 233, 283, 315, 351, 411

Legislation, 85, 91, 92, 100, 102, 107, 108, 110, 172, 199, 214, 236, 251, 276, 277, 286, 287, 367, 389, 406

Legislative power, 149, 159, 178, 183, 214, 275

Legislator, 24, 42, 49, 100, 103, 104, 105, 114, 125, 181, 201, 277, 389

Legislator-educator, 25, 49, 69, 100, 105, 217

Leitmotiv: friendship as, 59, 166, 203-4, 209, 263, 268, 283, 388, 400, 409, 410

Letters from the Country, 10

Letters from the Mount (Rousseau), 10, 11, 19, 25, 26, 38, 48, 85, 91, 214, 226, 248, 251, 252, 255, 257, 347, 391

Letter to Cristophe de Beaumont (Rousseau), 98, 230, 255, 347

Letter to d'Alembert, 42, 49, 208, 287

Levite of Ephraim (Rousseau), 5-9, 19, 32, 226, 231, 326, 327

Liberty, 47, 70, 74, 91, 92, 177, 216, 282, 365. *See also* Freedom

Lies, 114, 121-22, 124, 251, 260, 273

Literary profession of faith. *See* Aesthetic doctrine; Aesthetics

Love, 197, 201, 205, 230, 267, 268, 270, 278, 279, 280, 282, 290, 306, 308, 310, 311, 312, 313, 314, 316, 319, 323, 324, 325, 329, 331, 337, 340, 341, 342, 345, 360, 372, 396, 412; of humanity, 344, 346; of law, 284; of

learning, 335, 354; of order, 247, 319; of Sophia or wisdom, 279, 323, 334, 337, 340, 344, 345, 350, 365, 372, 388, 413

Luxury, 172, 173, 174, 175

Lydian mode, 135

Lycurgus, 50, 105, 250

Lyricism, 19, 403, 405

"Maintainers," 96, 174, 214

Majority rule, 88, 89, 215, 216, 286, 291

Malesherbes, Chrétien-Guillaume de Lamoignon de, 10, 293, 349, 375

Mammon, 4, 180

Man of understanding, 22, 73, 346, 396

Manners and customs, 112, 139, 277, 314, 361, 393, 398, 399. *See also* Law: of opinion

Marriage, 201, 230, 231, 250, 258, 266, 267, 268, 277, 281, 305, 308, 316, 323, 325, 331, 333, 352, 364, 371, 372, 373, 374, 375, 398, 414

Master of self, 103, 200, 268, 284, 293, 307, 349, 355, 359, 365, 374

Materialism, 235, 236, 237, 238, 239, 240

Mathematics, 99, 146, 151, 155, 187, 190, 236, 256, 257, 340; mean proportional, 146, 147, 150, 151, 170, 275, 408

Mentor (*Télémaque*), 265, 321, 336, 339, 353, 363, 375

Mercy, 198, 199, 204, 246, 251, 317, 345, 370

Métairie (farm), 291, 356, 369, 370

Metallurgy, 171

Metaphors, 13, 22, 23, 37, 47, 96, 338, 405, 409

Middle Ages, 31, 403

Mind, 17, 18, 23, 24, 57, 67, 107, 115, 126, 129, 132, 134, 137, 145, 153, 158, 163, 187, 212, 218, 219, 220, 236, 238, 245, 256, 261, 267, 285, 290, 291, 306, 311, 316, 318, 319, 327, 333, 337, 344, 346, 354, 370, 400, 402, 408

Minerva (*Télémaque*), 265, 281, 315,

Minerva (continued)
321, 322, 336, 339, 353, 363
"Minister of education," 268, 349
Miracles, 158, 248, 254, 255, 256, 257, 260
Moderation, 282, 333
Modesty, 282, 307
Monarchy, 51, 86, 160, 168, 169, 409
Money, 172, 180, 344
Money-making arts, 180, 184
Montaigne, Michel de, 44, 246, 403
Montmorency, 16, 60, 67, 116, 163, 166, 265, 293, 392
Moral beauty, 246, 327, 328, 329, 330, 376, 412
Moral being, 82, 85, 86, 89, 93, 97, 101, 103, 105, 111, 112, 118, 149, 152, 159, 161, 163, 167, 170, 171, 174, 197, 201, 202, 212, 213, 216, 250, 269, 270, 272, 273, 288, 294, 360, 376, 388, 392, 407, 408, 409
Moral collective body, 63, 359
Moral instinct, 245. See also Conscience
Moral law, 98, 233, 249, 318
Moral Letters (Rousseau), 121
Moral life, 53, 60, 85, 86, 92, 99, 176, 274
Moral need, 238
Moral order, 40, 53, 135, 197, 204, 246, 263, 264, 289, 295, 308, 400
Moral person, 63, 64, 65, 86, 88, 92, 93, 94, 95, 96, 97, 98, 99, 102, 104, 110, 111, 113, 149, 151, 178, 183, 189, 195, 212, 215, 218, 241, 251, 316, 360, 374, 375, 392
Moral truth, 129, 155, 156, 165, 186, 187, 225, 227, 235, 306, 358, 371, 401, 411
Moral will, 361
Morality, 53, 68, 91, 92, 117, 185, 198, 261, 323, 359, 363, 388
Morceau allégorique sur la révélation (Rousseau), 10 n
Moses, 50, 69, 105, 227, 250, 251, 253, 255, 256

Mother: as symbol, 37, 38, 39, 45, 47, 48, 49, 50, 62, 75, 137, 307, 308, 309, 314, 321, 392, 405
Muse of Philosophy, 279, 310, 314, 315, 322, 325, 326, 336, 339, 372, 377, 405, 413
Muses, 144, 339
Music, 114, 115, 122, 125, 126, 129, 135, 136, 229, 322, 339
Musical education, 133, 134, 135, 136, 157, 407, 408, 409
Mysteries, 220, 221, 278, 317, 325, 334, 335, 337, 354
Mystical body, 23, 59, 313, 317
Myth: of carpenter, 179-82; of hunter, 265, 280; of husbandman, 343, 407; of lawbreaker, 121, 131, 407; of miniature Olympics, 131, 343, 408; of nighttime games, 130-31, 408; of promise-breaker, 121-22, 407; of Sophia, 412, 413; of Sophia and peasants, 344-46; of swaddling clothes, 47, 405; of window-breaker, 120-21
Mythology, 190, 211, 408, 410, 412
Myths, 12, 18, 20, 37, 49, 62, 115, 117, 118, 120, 130, 131, 133, 159, 163, 165, 168, 169, 180, 204, 210, 244, 257, 265, 273, 313, 320, 335, 339, 340, 341, 344, 345, 365, 367, 377, 383, 385, 388, 394, 399, 404

Nationalism, 252, 341, 348, 355, 396
Natural arts, 167, 170
Natural constitution, 113, 232, 395-96, 408
Natural divine law, 249, 251, 253, 260, 262
Natural goodness, 40, 87, 107, 205
Natural history, 335, 354-55
Natural independence, 120, 363
Natural law, 98, 247, 267, 345
Natural man, 15, 19, 24, 41, 43, 44, 57, 69, 70, 163, 165, 167, 186, 219, 269, 331, 350, 392
Natural order, 84, 92, 332, 363, 406
Natural and political law, 51, 249, 262, 346, 357, 366, 371

Natural religion, 231, 249, 262, 371

Natural right, 72, 73, 93

Natural sciences, 154, 163

Natural self-interest, 94, 263

Nature, 38, 73, 74, 134, 148, 178, 185, 221, 231, 237, 238, 270, 278, 287, 307, 309, 325, 328, 329, 330, 331, 341, 365, 388; author of, 154, 244; as book of learning, 28, 335, 354; laws of, 90, 105, 215, 246, 248, 255, 263, 267, 308, 323, 359, 367; order of, 232, 284; as subject of art, 18, 286, 327

Nature of man, 15, 19, 21, 22, 23, 24, 25, 26, 27, 30, 40, 41, 43, 46, 49, 51, 52, 53, 57, 58, 60, 63, 64, 65, 68, 83, 86, 90, 98, 103, 106, 110, 114, 126, 133, 161, 179, 197, 198, 213, 216, 219, 230, 240, 241, 242, 245, 246, 332, 337, 341, 354, 355, 359, 367, 368, 401, 403

Nature of woman, 305, 306, 309, 313

Nature of things, 111, 262, 358

Necessary desires, 196, 213-14, 218

Necessity, 72, 73, 74, 75, 89, 91, 94, 95, 100, 101, 106, 107, 117, 140, 148, 162, 167, 171, 174, 177, 182, 196, 207, 214, 233, 265, 273, 292, 311, 349, 356, 360, 363, 406, 414, 415

Needs, 23, 54, 71, 72, 73, 74, 84, 90, 101, 103, 106, 118, 120, 145, 163, 165, 167, 168, 172, 174, 175, 176, 220, 312, 366, 367, 409

"Negative education," 107-8, 197

New Testament, 96, 98, 227, 229, 257, 313

Numa, 50, 55, 105, 250, 273

Obedience, 65, 86, 98, 150, 183, 203, 268, 269, 273, 308, 314, 315, 318, 332, 359, 367; and consent as correlatives, 58, 84, 188, 373; and love as correlatives, 311; and liberty as correlatives, 185

Odyssey, 353, 355

Old Testament, 5, 8, 59, 229, 257, 279, 313, 373, 384

Olympic games, 131, 132, 137, 158, 202, 206, 243, 244, 343, 408

Olympus, Mount, 200, 227

Opinion, 42, 43, 139, 173, 208, 209, 215, 233, 234, 276, 277, 278, 280, 281, 282, 286, 287, 293, 307, 308, 311, 314, 318, 393, 398, 399, 411. *See also* Law: of public opinion

Original sin, 87. *See also* Natural goodness

Orphan: Emile as, 58, 59, 119

Orpheus, 229, 239, 410

Parable: of the conjuror Socrates, 157-59, 163, 167, 187, 209, 209-10, 255, 257, 409; of the kingdom of heaven, 338; of the laborers in the vineyard, 132; of Montmorency forest, 163, 164-66, 167, 198, 204, 265, 335, 409; of the races, 131-33, 137, 343; of the sower, 117-20, 158, 172, 182, 343, 357

Parables, 17, 20, 115, 116, 126, 127, 132, 159, 210, 345, 394, 404

Parents, 58, 231, 323, 336. *See also* Family; Father; Mother

Paris, 19, 165, 277, 280, 281, 287, 291, 293, 314, 334, 413

Parthenon, 29, 31

Passions, 49, 63, 83, 88, 89, 91, 92, 96, 97, 98, 100, 104, 116, 160, 168, 175, 177, 185, 195, 196, 197, 199-200, 207, 208, 209, 210, 211, 212, 213, 214, 215, 216, 217, 220, 221, 233, 240, 241, 246, 247, 251, 262, 263, 264, 265, 269, 270, 276, 279, 280, 283, 294, 311, 314, 328, 337, 342, 346, 348, 349, 351, 363, 366, 367, 406, 409, 410, 411

Paternal authority, 51, 58, 59, 359. *See also* Father

Patience, 187, 322

Patriotism, 117, 251, 252, 309, 320, 325, 341, 345, 346, 347, 348, 349, 396

Paul (apostle), 23, 24, 132, 181, 240, 243, 247, 317, 343, 362, 373, 375

Peace, 48, 62, 202, 213, 218, 224, 225, 254, 259, 260, 264, 308, 311, 335, 357, 362, 369, 377

Pedagogy: and politics, 15, 27

Personification of reason and wisdom, 279, 280, 313, 406. See also Governor

Philosopher-kings, 56, 113, 140, 147, 152, 162, 168, 176, 190, 216, 219, 221, 280, 310, 334, 340, 363-64, 368, 372, 377, 390, 393, 408, 409, 411, 412, 413

Physicians, 65, 66, 75, 108, 109, 117, 137, 169, 180, 311, 406

Physics, 28, 163, 255, 340

Pilot, 43, 56, 65, 75, 126, 155, 156, 159, 234, 269. See also Governor; Helmsman

Pity, 74, 138, 198, 199, 200, 202, 208, 209, 210, 211, 346

Place: as key idea, 83, 90, 107, 171

Plato, 14, 18, 19, 20, 21, 27, 28, 42, 43, 55, 56, 75, 99, 102, 111, 122, 134, 152, 166, 185, 187, 200, 204, 205, 208, 210, 212, 216, 221, 230, 234, 268, 269, 279, 285, 287, 291, 292, 306, 308, 309, 310, 320, 322, 327, 334, 337, 339, 354, 355, 357, 364, 365, 367, 384, 385, 386, 387, 389, 404, 414. See also Socrates

Pleasure(s), 4, 247, 277, 285, 286, 288, 289, 291, 316, 352, 360, 399

Plutarch, 18, 137, 207, 208, 212, 213, 239, 243, 245, 279, 283, 385, 386, 405, 410

Poetry, 18, 233, 287

Poland, 42, 49, 91, 125

Politeness, 285, 316

Political economy, 48, 171, 174

Political Economy (Rousseau), 3, 22, 47, 48, 346-47

Political Institutions (Rousseau), 4, 357, 362, 414

Politico-moral laws, 99, 113

Politics, 15, 22, 23, 24, 27, 309, 351

Positive divine law, 249, 251, 253, 262

"Posts" (Socratic), 265, 363, 390, 391

Poverty, 10, 213, 288, 291, 312, 324, 326, 332, 333, 338, 415

Power, 4, 87, 110, 213, 239, 289, 290, 307, 311, 331, 356, 357, 366, 415

Prayer, 229, 230, 241, 242, 243, 244, 248

Preface of Emile and Social Contract, 25-27, 94, 354, 391

"Prelude to the chief strain," 152, 153, 157, 185, 187, 408

Primitive condition or state, 53, 62, 68, 87, 396

Prince, 53, 149, 182, 270, 271, 290, 291, 318, 324, 353, 372

Prisoners in Socratic den, 47, 69, 71, 76, 121, 129, 131, 133, 146, 153, 406

Private interests, 40, 86, 170, 205, 213, 217, 361

Profession of faith, 4, 30, 130, 152, 153, 154, 187, 220, 221, 222, 225, 228, 230, 233, 235, 280, 353, 370, 386, 409, 410

Project on Corsica (Rousseau), 364, 389

Property, 48, 62, 63, 70, 71, 72, 73, 74, 94, 95, 109, 110, 117, 118, 119, 120, 139, 162, 170, 201, 290, 332, 355, 357, 360, 365, 366, 367, 406, 407, 414, 415

Protestant(s), 223, 224, 226, 230, 253, 260

Providence, 235, 239, 243

Psychological truth, 18, 401, 402. See also Human beings; Nature of man

Pygmalion, 326-30, 375, 401

Pythagorus, 334, 354

Pythian oracle, 30, 245

Rank, 325, 332, 333. See also Hierarchy within the self: equated to government of men

Reason, 279, 281, 282, 283, 290, 311, 312, 314, 318, 322, 331, 334, 349, 359, 367, 374, 392, 393, 398, 400, 402, 407, 408, 409, 410, 411

Reasonable will, 60, 63, 65, 97, 127, 140, 281, 314, 333, 337, 343, 361, 396. See also Enlightened will

Reformation, 226, 257

Regulus, 246, 387

Religion, 131, 220, 221, 222, 224, 226, 231, 233, 235, 248, 249, 250, 252,

258, 260, 316, 317, 340, 402, 411

Representatives, 86, 184, 361

Republic, 11, 20, 21, 24, 25, 26, 30, 42, 43, 47, 52, 56, 63, 64, 65, 66, 69, 75, 98, 100, 102, 104, 108, 110, 113, 114, 115, 121, 122, 125, 128, 131, 135, 136, 137, 152, 158, 160, 164, 165, 166, 167, 170, 173, 180, 181, 184, 187, 190, 204, 205, 206, 208, 211, 213, 216, 219, 221, 222, 225, 227, 229, 247, 248, 256, 259, 265, 277, 281, 282, 289, 292, 294, 306, 309, 310, 322, 325, 327, 328, 331, 332, 333, 335, 340, 343, 344, 350, 352, 354, 362, 364 365, 368, 370, 372, 375, 376, 385, 386, 387, 388, 389, 390, 391, 393, 394, 395, 397, 398, 400, 409, 410, 414

Republic, 42, 55, 63, 99, 101, 160, 190, 271, 279, 309, 310, 316, 337, 396, 400, 405

Resurrection, 242, 330

Revelation, 130, 131, 225, 228, 229, 236, 250, 253, 254, 255, 255-56, 257, 259, 260, 387, 410

Rhythm, 114, 126, 133, 134, 316, 408

Robert the gardener, 117, 118, 184

Robinson Crusoe, 52, 147, 164, 167, 168, 169, 170, 171, 175, 176, 179, 187, 197, 405, 408, 409

Roman church, 224, 234, 253

Roman institutions, 271, 272, 397

Romans, ancient, 41, 122, 183, 207, 209, 218, 246, 266, 273-75, 276, 284, 319, 320, 347, 369

"Romance of human nature," 336, 392

Romanticism, 18, 228, 384, 403, 404

Rome, 18, 44, 55, 185, 273, 314, 320, 353, 396

"Royal lie" (Socratic), 62, 63, 138, 405, 406

Rulers, 21, 22, 51, 56, 59, 64, 69, 139, 149, 152, 154, 157, 162, 180, 182, 185, 188, 189, 218, 262, 269, 270, 271, 279, 311, 317, 331, 332, 333, 339, 356, 361, 363, 366, 372, 373, 376, 377, 411

Rural life or society, 67, 183, 364, 369, 370

"Salute to friend," 166, 204, 209, 263, 265, 266-67, 268, 283, 410. *See also* Leitmotiv

Salvation, 220, 251, 376

Samaritan woman at well, 254

Savage state, 69, 186, 331

Savoy, 224, 226

Savoyard vicar, 5, 30, 130, 220, 222, 228, 252, 280, 347, 376, 401

Scriptures, 21, 29, 228, 241, 280, 384

Sculptor or sculpture, 23, 286, 327, 328, 329

Security, 95, 177, 366, 367

Self-education, 392, 415

Self-esteem, 224, 239

Self-government, 160, 161, 162, 179, 268, 361, 391, 395

Self-indulgence, 4, 282

Self-interest, 94, 282

Self-love, 107, 196, 197, 198, 209, 235, 246, 263, 347

Self-mastery, 86, 99, 139, 284, 292

Self-rule, 189, 284, 321, 349, 355, 357, 360, 364, 368, 373

Self-sufficing, 109, 111, 182, 213

Selfishness, 196, 387

Seminarian: Rousseau as, 224, 226

Sensationalist doctrines, 129, 138

Sensations, 123, 186, 232, 236

Senses, 63, 108, 121, 125, 129, 187, 197, 235, 236, 240, 268, 283, 329, 349

Sensitive being, 236, 393

Sensitive Morality (Rousseau), 71, 318

Sensorial education, 71, 129, 138

Sermon on the Mount, 9, 56, 131, 145, 148, 205, 227, 229, 256, 288, 338

Servants, 161-62, 189-90, 290

Servius, 273, 274

Shame, 202, 282

Ship of soul or state, 57, 128, 196, 234

Shopkeeping, 148, 153, 156, 206, 358, 400

Sight, 132, 134, 316

Similitude of the sun, 96, 153, 154, 156, 220, 227, 233, 236, 244, 280, 294, 408, 410

Skepticism, 226, 253, 261, 369, 371, 413

Slavery, 46, 47, 49, 52, 53, 62, 70, 75, 89, 91, 92, 93, 95, 97, 98, 99, 100, 106, 121, 169, 175, 185, 216, 268, 355, 359, 360, 365, 367, 406, 411

Social life, 18, 41, 76, 246, 319, 411

Social man, 15, 176, 359, 392

Social order, 30, 40, 41, 46, 53, 74, 197, 204, 220, 232, 246, 248, 264, 266, 267, 271, 288, 289, 295, 377, 398, 400

Social state, 24, 186, 241, 331

Society: moral value of, 15, 368, 376

Socrates, 4, 6, 23, 25, 27, 28, 29, 30, 34 n. 27, 40, 41, 69, 75, 121, 146, 148, 175, 177, 225, 228, 241, 243, 261, 265, 282, 283, 292, 328, 353, 354, 358, 389, 392, 395, 396, 397, 399, 414; acknowledged as master by Rousseau, 19, 26, 60-61, 229, 384-87; on choice of life, 370, 391; on common happiness, 61, 63, 106, 201-2; as "conjuror," 158, 166, 187, 209; contrasted with Cato, 346-47, 386; denunciation of theater by, 19, 208; on education, 26, 39, 42, 55, 56, 84, 94, 111-12, 113-40 passim, 156-57, 187, 277, 281, 285; on enlightened will as ruler, 85-86, 102, 213-14, 216, 409; on "false" states, 355-56, 376; on family and education, 45, 50; on friendship, 59, 263, 270, 327, 346, 388, 411; on good and bad "physicians," 65-67, 406; on gymnastic as training, 128; on ignorant men, 47, 121; on immoral passions, 96, 185, 208, 229, 240, 280, 362-63; on inner conflict, 53-54, 92, 282, 362-63 (see also "on 'warfare'"); and "just man," 20, 259; on kingship, 150, 152, 153, 169, 269, 271, 289, 409; Lady Philosophy of, 6, 7, 279, 314, 315, 325, 326, 372, 377, 413; on law of the strongest, 52-53, 205; on laws, 98, 99, 101, 107, 112, 119, 245, 250; as legislator-educator, 100, 104; on

love and marriage, 200-201, 306, 308-13, 320, 333, 334-35, 352, 373; "maintainers and foster fathers" of, 96, 174, 214; on mathematics as training, 123, 256-57; on money-making arts, 54, 180-81, 184; on moral goodness, 87-88, 219-20, 246-47; on music as training, 114, 133-34, 135, 152, 315-16, 407, 408; on myths as training, 114-15, 407; on parental authority, 50, 51, 282; philosopher-kings or "heroes" of, 56, 69, 71, 73, 76, 124, 128, 131, 137, 138, 139, 168, 190, 206, 218, 264, 340, 352, 364, 368, 372, 376, 393, 401, 408-9; on reason, 107, 110, 112, 217; on religion, 221-22, 231, 233, 235, 244, 250; on the republic, 99, 160; Rousseau likened to, 10-11; "royal lie" of, 62-63, 138, 405; on sensible vs. visible, 236; on the soul as city, 21-22, 85, 103, 105, 111, 128, 150, 178, 201-2, 212, 229, 367-70, 390, 404; on sympathy, 201-2, 204; "true pilot" of, 43, 57, 65, 196, 234; on "warfare," 209, 210, 211, 240, 251, 282, 362-63 (see also "on inner conflict"); on wealth and poverty, 111, 138, 288, 289-90; on wisdom and happiness, 103, 163, 281, 339-40, 341, 343, 350-51, 367, 388

Solomon, 6, 27, 29, 169, 227, 228, 229, 254, 313, 384, 413, 414

Song, 115, 116, 126, 129, 135, 229, 315, 386

Song of Orpheus, 152, 229, 244, 259, 410

Son of man, 10, 20, 117, 118, 176, 229

Sophia. See Beauty: of Sophia or wisdom; Wisdom: Sophia as personification of

Sophisms, 216, 217, 220, 280, 282, 294, 308, 409, 410

Sophists, 229, 279, 281, 282, 410

Soul, 15, 17, 38, 39, 40, 48, 49, 68, 81, 119, 121, 176, 190, 197, 228, 234, 239, 247, 294, 312, 324, 329, 330, 331, 333, 343, 351, 358, 395, 396, 400, 401, 403, 405, 411, 412; care of body and, 66-67; effect of physical training on, 128-29, 137; effect of worldly goods on, 56, 366; enslaved by desire, 52-53, 86, 92, 180, 216, 233, 240, 282, 283, 360, 361, 410; equated with city-state, 21-23, 41, 45, 52, 57, 67, 74, 85, 92, 94, 96, 101, 102, 103, 104, 105, 110, 126, 128, 140, 149, 170, 178, 181, 185, 188, 202, 216, 229, 230, 238, 250, 267, 309, 322, 344, 362, 364, 375, 388, 390, 404, 406, 408; freedom and, 177; future life of, 242-43, 244, 370, 391; institution of natural order in, 24, 84, 92, 94, 106, 291, 406; justice and, 101, 218, 230, 368; music and, 135, 150, 229, 322; pursuit by, of truth or good, 148, 155, 156, 214-15, 240; reason or enlightened will as ruler of, 43, 53, 83, 96, 99, 114, 151, 160, 170, 174, 188, 238, 241, 245, 267, 333, 373, 374, 408; as temple of the Godhead, 29-30, 181, 261; "warfare" within, 52, 96, 97, 114, 233, 366; wedded to wisdom, 323, 325-26, 327, 328, 336, 337, 375

Sovereign, 22, 52, 64, 72, 85, 147, 149, 150, 160, 178, 183, 189, 269, 270, 272, 275, 317, 361, 366, 411

Sovereignty, 57, 63, 64, 85, 87, 93, 94, 97, 99, 104, 149, 151, 154, 178, 183, 184, 270, 272, 273, 275, 359, 360, 361, 363, 374, 408, 409, 415

Sovereign will, 63, 65, 70, 71, 73, 90, 93, 96, 151, 160, 161, 170, 177, 178, 185, 188, 203, 213, 214, 215, 218, 237, 250, 264, 339, 341, 360, 361, 374, 408

Sparta, 42, 44, 49, 55, 314, 315, 320, 395

Sparta or Spartans, 30, 41, 42, 43, 44, 46, 49, 50, 55, 84, 101, 126, 137, 314, 315, 319, 320, 349, 385, 296, 413

"Spectator," 204, 206, 207, 210, 243

Spirit (Socratic), 53, 101, 103, 111, 114, 126, 130, 135, 137, 139, 150

Spiritual ascent as theme, 39, 68, 69, 71, 129, 146, 154, 156, 180, 227, 406

Spirituality, 286, 288, 314, 332

Spiritual order, 265, 377

Statesman or statesmanship, 22, 66, 75, 169, 181, 184, 366, 406

Steersman. See Helmsman

Stoic or Stoicism, 84, 87, 92, 128, 291

Stories. See False myths; Myths; True myths

"Strain of peace and freedom," 115, 125, 135, 152, 407

"Strain of necessity," 115, 117, 125, 135, 152, 407

Strength, 84, 93, 94, 100, 104, 108, 125, 126, 128, 139, 145, 148, 149, 151, 182, 186, 267, 307, 314, 333, 349, 356, 408

Study or studies, 145, 146, 154, 156, 163, 171, 312, 340, 341, 344, 348, 351, 354, 355, 358, 400, 411

Subjects, 64, 147, 150, 151, 170, 174, 177, 183, 189, 275, 311, 316, 361, 408, 411

Subtitles in Emile, 353

Suffering, 10, 116, 198, 205, 243, 246, 287

Suitability, 278, 279, 323, 332, 339, 342, 352, 354, 355, 357, 361, 366, 372

Supreme Being, 61, 220, 235, 255, 317

Swaddling clothes, 47, 68, 405

Symbolism, 17, 48, 49, 57, 63, 66, 121, 155, 157, 165, 167, 173, 175, 233, 226, 265, 266, 268, 270, 273, 278, 290, 305, 306, 308, 310, 312, 313, 314, 315, 316, 318, 328, 332, 334, 335, 337, 342, 351, 356, 371, 374, 387, 399, 403, 409, 413

Symbols, 13, 14, 24, 37, 38, 62, 132, 154, 209, 231, 320, 259, 406

Symmetry, 145, 196, 200, 206, 212, 305

Sympathy, 74, 153, 198, 199, 201, 204, 205, 208, 209, 285, 287, 322, 347, 370, 396, 400

Symposium, 18, 173, 287, 291, 292, 306, 310-13, 319, 320, 323, 327, 331, 336, 338, 339, 340, 352, 376, 387, 413

Tableau of the "true runner," 344

Taste, 17, 18, 115, 116, 126, 133, 135, 136, 276, 277, 278, 280, 281, 285,

Taste *(continued)*
286, 287, 289, 290, 314, 316, 319, 323, 331, 337, 342, 387, 393, 399, 400, 408, 412, 416

Télémaque (Telemachus) or *Télémaque* (Fénelon), 196, 265, 321, 324, 325, 326, 328, 329, 336, 352, 353, 363, 370, 375

Temperance, 103, 112, 128, 139, 187, 282, 284, 289, 311, 312, 376

Temple: as image, 29, 30, 31, 59, 75, 116, 125, 138, 167, 181, 190, 195, 196, 223, 226, 228, 245, 250, 261, 266, 277, 279, 282, 305, 327, 344, 357, 367, 371, 372, 375, 404, 405, 412

Theater, 208-9, 287, 349

Three R's, 115, 123, 125, 315, 316

Travel, 334, 348, 352, 353, 354, 364, 369, 376, 387

Treaty, 58, 372, 374, 375

True lie, 105, 211

True myths, 114, 115, 116, 122, 126, 129, 408

True self, 196-97, 264

Truth, 57, 153, 281, 285, 294, 312, 340, 368, 371, 400

Tyranny, 49, 52, 75, 88, 89, 91, 92, 93, 94, 100, 106, 169, 170, 175, 185, 233, 249, 311, 356, 406, 411

Tyrants or tyrannical passions, 91, 124, 150, 169, 174, 214, 283, 355, 362-63, 367

Ulysses, 196, 269, 282, 324, 353, 370

Unanimous being, 88, 213, 215, 216, 323, 391

Union, 212, 213, 308, 317, 318, 323, 337, 358, 359, 372, 373

Unity, 46, 63, 92, 93, 99, 201, 218, 232, 233, 395, 407

Useful, 17, 94, 146, 147, 148, 153, 154, 155, 156, 164, 165, 179, 228, 233, 285, 308, 315, 340, 358, 359, 386, 390, 400

Utility, 94, 149, 164, 179, 202, 308

Vanity, 46, 157, 209, 229, 341

Venus, 315, 328, 329

Virgil, 238, 287, 318, 336, 387

Virtue, 48, 81, 82, 89, 100, 101, 102, 103, 107, 112, 119, 124, 128, 130, 131, 133, 139, 158, 160, 164, 173, 181, 186, 187, 198, 207, 208, 218, 219, 221, 224, 233, 241, 242, 244, 245, 246, 252, 259, 265, 267, 279, 280, 286, 292, 310, 311, 312, 313, 319, 320, 322, 333, 335, 341, 344, 349, 351, 352, 358, 363, 365, 368, 374, 376, 387, 391, 400

Vision, 13, 291, 292; of Er, 222, 244, 333, 370, 376, 377, 391

Visionary, 25, 183, 324, 326, 328-29

War, 22, 53, 62, 69, 92, 184, 204, 209, 210, 231, 233, 269, 274, 309, 320, 362

Warfare, 22, 24, 53, 62, 89, 96, 97, 114, 124, 208, 209, 210, 211, 215, 216, 251, 294, 349, 352, 363

"Waves" (Socratic): first, 29, 63, 388, 405; second, 111, 407; third, 149, 408

Wealth, 4, 93, 110, 111, 151, 162, 170, 171, 173, 174, 175, 213, 267, 274, 279, 287-93, 311, 330, 331, 332, 333, 338, 344, 356, 357, 366, 397, 409

"What is not," 324, 326, 329, 350, 358, 412

Wild beasts, 116, 138, 207, 208, 229, 240, 411

Will, 24, 26, 41, 53, 60, 93, 94, 95, 114, 128, 129, 133, 151, 155, 159, 178, 183, 189, 190, 199, 231, 235, 237, 239, 240, 242, 246, 248, 261, 264, 267, 284, 307, 315, 323, 333, 344, 352, 358, 359, 360, 361, 374, 393, 408; and desire or the passions, 89, 212, 213, 221, 241, 367; general and individual, 85-88, 182, 215, 216, 276; for the good, 91, 99, 182, 214, 216, 247; governors as servant of, 161-62; as guardian of inner man, 21, 101, 406; as law, 97, 99; and law of freedom, 85, 91, 92, 213, 398, 415; and law of necessity, 84-85, 213, 398; precedence of, over reason, 106, 132, 188; reason and, 139, 149, 150, 161, 268, 273, 282, 283, 406-7,

411; reasonable or enlightened, 60, 63, 64, 65, 83, 99, 126, 234, 238, 245, 314, 343, 373; sensorial training of, 71; and sovereignty, 85-87

Wisdom, 7, 21, 30, 65, 99, 105, 108, 112, 121, 125, 137, 180, 184, 216, 239, 242, 259, 270, 292, 305, 308, 309, 310, 311, 312, 314, 318, 319, 324, 325, 332, 333, 334, 343, 344, 357, 360, 363, 365, 368, 372, 376, 393, 412; associated with happiness, 3, 18, 27, 69, 82, 84, 85, 100, 103, 106, 123, 146, 147, 163, 179, 209, 247, 288, 291, 293, 294, 307, 316, 323, 350, 351, 352, 366, 367, 369, 372, 374, 388, 392, 394, 413, 415; as discernment of good and evil, 169, 281, 333; divine, 104, 159, 227, 230, 238, 264, 327, 336, 339, 345, 351, 367, 414; "false," 83, 84, 99; "foretaste" of 337, 339, 340, 341, 348, 350, 351, 372, 376, 398, 413; as opposed to knowledge, 27-28; search for, by human soul, 16, 57, 320, 323, 331; and Socratic symbol of hunt, 167, 335; Sophia as personification of, 6, 82, 129, 132, 159, 277, 278, 279, 280, 306, 313, 315, 322, 327, 330, 336-38, 340, 342, 348, 352, 367, 374, 375, 376, 387, 393, 405, 413, 414

Wise order of life or things, 38, 59, 268, 307, 313, 315, 316, 317, 323, 332, 387, 411, 412, 413, 415

Worldly society, 278, 284, 319

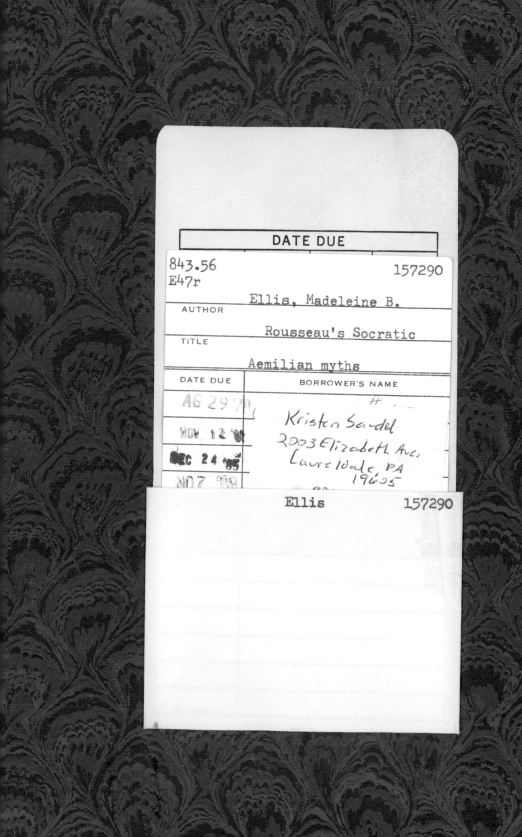